Lincoln

P9-BYH-802

"Fred Kaplan's *Lincoln* offers penetrating insights on Lincoln's ability to explain complex ideas in language accessible to a broad range of readers and listeners. . . . Kaplan is especially effective in tracing the influence on Lincoln's literary style of his lifelong course of self-education by reading English-language classics."

—James M. McPherson, *The New York Review of Books*

"Lively. . . . Kaplan does a good job of tracing the young man's reading habits, identifying favorite books, and noting their influence on the mature politician. . . . Powerful and convincing. . . . Kaplan is a biographer on a mission."

—*The Los Angeles Times*

"Compelling. . . . This revealing view of our sixteenth president focuses on his literary skills, on his deep appreciation for the classics, and on his lifelong search for the most precise and eloquent way to communicate his convictions and his ideas. . . . In this election season, Fred Kaplan's book might encourage us all to bear in mind the relationship between clear speech and clear thought."

—Francine Prose, *O, The Oprah Magazine*

"Superb. . . . This intensely researched, thoughtfully written volume is more than a biography; it's also a practical and inspiring guide for writers. . . . Quoting many of Lincoln's texts, Kaplan demonstrates how their author organized his thoughts and blended them into logical, effective, and often soaringly eloquent treatises."   —*The Seattle Times*

"There's plenty here to reveal how Lincoln learned to inspire. . . . The future president's love letters, speeches, essays, poems, and even his dirty jokes all get their due. Kaplan also looks for connections between Lincoln's reading material and his words, finding influences of Shakespeare and the Bible, among other sources."

—*The Christian Science Monitor*

"An elegant portrait of Lincoln's literary sensibility."

—Ted Widmer, *The New York Observer*

"A top choice. *Lincoln* recounts the ingredients of Lincoln's life that went into making him the man who could pen such memorable words as the Gettysburg Address and the Second Inaugural Address."

—*Detroit Free Press*

"Essential reading for any Lincoln student preparing to dip into the rich field of Lincoln's writings. . . . Just when you think every aspect of Lincoln's life and thought has been covered, someone like Kaplan sees him from yet a new perspective."   —Allen Barra, *The Baltimore Sun*

"A sophisticated take on the Lincoln revival. . . . A gifted writer himself, Kaplan even manages to get us interested in young Abe's satirical verses and the contents of the primers he devoured."

—*The Boston Globe*

"Biographer Fred Kaplan's close reading of Lincoln's personal letters and drafts brings a fresh perspective to one of the most mythologized figures in American history. He reveals that Lincoln the orator got his start as Lincoln the poet, the lover, the humorist."

—*The New York Observer*

"*Lincoln* captures, vividly, the young Illinois lawyer and politician, by turns funny and melancholy, as he tried to give meaning to the power of his words by attaining 'the power to implement them.'"

—*The Philadelphia Inquirer*

"Kaplan undertakes an unparalleled analysis of Lincoln the creative writer, digging more widely and deeply than any of his predecessors in examining Lincoln's writing. . . . *Lincoln* is an innovative offering in a crowded field and will become a staple for Lincoln enthusiasts and scholars."   —*American Heritage*

"If you ever wondered what Lincoln read, how he thought about words and ideas, or what made him into one of our country's most distinctive speechwriters, this is the book for you."   —*The Chicago Tribune*

Lincoln

Lincoln

The Biography
of a Writer

Fred Kaplan

HARPER ● PERENNIAL

NEW YORK ● LONDON ● TORONTO ● SYDNEY ● NEW DELHI ● AUCKLAND

HARPER ⬤ PERENNIAL

A hardcover edition of this book was published in 2008
by HarperCollins Publishers.

HarperCollins books may be purchased for educational, business, or sales promotional use. For information please write: Special Markets Department, HarperCollins Publishers, 10 East 53rd
Street, New York, NY 10022.

FIRST HARPER PERENNIAL EDITION PUBLISHED 2010.

Designed by Nicola Ferguson

The Library of Congress has catalogued
the hardcover edition as follows:
Kaplan, Fred.
    Lincoln : the biography of a writer / Fred Kaplan.—1st ed.
        viii, 406 p. ; 24 cm.
    Includes bibliographical references (p. [357]–362) and index.
    ISBN 978-0-06-077334-2
    1. Lincoln, Abraham, 1809–1865. 2. Lincoln,
Abraham, 1809–1865—Language. 3. Lincoln, Abraham,
1809–1865—Correspondence. 4. Lincoln, Abraham,
1809–1865—Oratory. 5. Presidents—United States—Biography.
6. Political oratory—United States—History—19th century.
7. Speeches, addresses, etc., American—History and criticism.
I. Title.
E457.2 .K357 2008
973.7092B 22   2007042330

ISBN 978-0-06-077336-6 (pbk.)

10 11 12 13 14   OV/RRD   10 9 8 7 6 5 4 3 2 1

To the memory of my father, Isaac Kaplan (1906–1987); and to Hattie M. Strelitz, the teacher who, on the Lower East Side of New York City in December 1918, awarded him a copy of *The Perfect Tribute*, an idealistic myth about the writing of the Gettysburg Address. It was given to him for "Proficiency and Excellent Class Spirit" and came into my hands a generation later. It impressed me deeply with a truth that empowers us all: the power of Lincoln's language.

Contents

Reading Lincoln's Words

For Lincoln, words mattered immensely. His increasing skill in their use during his lifetime, and his high valuation of their power, mark him as the one president who was both a national leader and a genius with language at a time when its power and integrity mattered more than it does today. His was a personality and a career forged in the crucible of language. The novelist William Dean Howells's claim about his friend Mark Twain, that he was the "Lincoln of our literature," can effectively be rephrased with the focus on our sixteenth president: Lincoln was the Twain of our politics. Since Lincoln, no president has written his own words and addressed his contemporary audience or posterity with equal and enduring effectiveness.

Lincoln was born into a national culture in which language was the most widely available key to individual growth and achievement. It dominated public discourse. No TVs, DVDs, computers, movie screens, radios, or electricity, and no sound-bites. Language mattered because it was useful for practical communication and for learning and because it could shape and direct people's feelings and thoughts in a culture in which spoken or written words had no rival. In Lincoln's case it also mattered immensely because it was the tool by which he explored and defined himself. The tool, the toolmaker, and the tool user became inseparably one. He became what his language made him. From an early age, he began his journey into self-willed literacy, then into skill, and eventually into genius as an artist with words.

Lincoln is distinguished from every other president, with the exception of Jefferson, in that we can be certain that he wrote every word to which his name is attached. Though some presidents after him wrote well, particularly Grant, Wilson, and Theodore Roosevelt, the articulation of a modern president's vision and policies has fallen to speechwriters and speech-writing committees, with the president serving, at best, as editor in chief.

Lincoln was also the last president whose character and standards in the use of language avoided the distortions and other dishonest uses of language that have done so much to undermine the credibility of national leaders. The ability and commitment to use language honestly and consistently have largely disappeared from our political discourse. Some presidents have been more talented in its use than others. Some, such as Franklin Roosevelt and John F. Kennedy, have had superior speechwriters. But the challenge of a president himself struggling to find the conjunction between the right words and honest expression, a use of language that respects intellect, truth, and sincerity, has largely been abandoned.

CHAPTER 1

"All the Books He Could Lay His Hands On"

1809–1825

At six years of age, for a few weeks in the fall of 1815, in the town of Knob Creek, Hardin County, Kentucky, the boy went to his first school, taught by a typical frontier teacher commissioned by local parents to provide children with basic skills and only sufficiently knowledgeable himself to rise modestly above that level. Teachers were in short supply on the frontier that ran along the western ridge of the Appalachians; beyond was the sparsely settled western portion of Ohio and the territories of Indiana and Illinois; southward, much of the states of Kentucky and Tennessee. Cash also was in short supply. Material possessions were minimal. By modern standards it was a starkly rudimentary life.

In this community of Protestants the supremacy of the Bible as the book of daily life encouraged acquiring basic reading skills. Simple arithmetic came next. "His father," the grown-up boy later recalled, "sent him to this school with the avowed determination of giving him a thorough education. And what do you think my father's idea of a thorough education was? It was to have me cipher through the rule of three." Beyond that, education was a luxury that neither time nor money permitted. Intellectual curiosity in a society in which it had no likely practical reward was rare, except for the occasional child who, inexplicably, without any relation to who his parents were and what the community valued, was transfixed by the power of words.

Words and ideas were inseparable in a nation in which the Bible dominated. It was given full currency as the source of the dominant belief system. It was also the great book of illustrative stories, illuminating references, and pithy maxims for everyday conduct. More than any other glue, it held the society together, regardless of differences of interpretation among Presbyterians, Baptists, and Methodists. This was a world of believers. Here and there was a deist, an agnostic, or an atheist, but even those who had grounds of disagreement with Christian theological claims generally did so within the tribal circle and expressed themselves in small deviances, such as not attending church regularly or at all. Deistic voices from afar, from the East Coast, from the Founding Fathers, even from Europe, occasionally could be heard in the Appalachian woods and beyond. The deists rationalized religion, eliminated mystery: there is a creator, a God; otherwise, human beings are on their own, dependent on reason and action. But rural American Protestants in the nineteenth century much preferred miracle, redemption, brimstone, the literal truth of the Bible, and the apocalypse to come. As six-year-old Abraham Lincoln began to learn to read, his household text was the Bible.

His parents were fundamentalist believers, regular worshippers. Without education and illiterate, Thomas Lincoln was also blind in one eye and had weak sight in the other, which may have perpetuated his illiteracy. To sign his name, he made his mark. To worship, he recited and sang memorized prayers and hymns. Since words and beliefs were inseparable, he depended on cues from others and especially on his memory, which was the agent of sacred prayer and biblical knowledge. Both literate and illiterate American Christians often memorized long stretches of the Bible. And as young boys like Abraham became literate, they developed their ability to remember. From an early age, Lincoln had a tenacious memory. By modern standards, few books were available to him. Those he could recite almost by heart.

His first teacher was his mother, who had learned to read but not write. Thin, slight, dark-haired, Nancy Hanks was born in 1783 in Virginia, the daughter of Lucy Hanks and an unidentified father. In 1806, she married Thomas Lincoln. The next year, in Hardin County, Kentucky, where they had settled, she had her first child, Sarah; on February 12, 1809, Abraham; then another son, who died in infancy. Unlike her prolific Hanks predecessors and contemporaries, she was to have no more children.

What young Abraham learned from his father had nothing to do with books. In his later testimony to the absence of family distinction, he gave short shrift to his father's contribution to his upbringing. His stocky, muscular, dark-haired, large-nosed father, about six feet and almost two hundred pounds, seemed a Caliban of the carpentry shop and the fields. Thomas Lincoln's illiteracy, though, was less remarkable to his son than what the boy took to be his father's disinterest in learning to read and his lack of ambition in general. It left him a marginal man who at an early age had fallen out of the mainstream of American upward mobility, a plodder without ambition to rise in the world. But he had not been born to that necessity. The father that the young adult Lincoln knew had been substantially formed by circumstances, though for the son the totality was subsumed into a sense of his father's character. It was not a character that he admired. And it was one that he needed later to distance himself from. Thomas Lincoln "was not a lazy man," a contemporary of Abraham's remembered, but "a piddler—always doing but doing nothing great—was happy—lived Easy—and contented. Had but few wants and Supplied these."

Both father and son knew less than modern scholars about the paternal family's history, mostly because Thomas Lincoln had been cut off from much of his past. He knew only that his great-grandfather came from Berks County, Pennsylvania, to Rockingham County, Virginia, where his grandfather, the Abraham he named his son after, had four brothers. Everything before was lost in the haze of illiteracy and family tragedy. Actually, the first American Lincoln, Samuel, had emigrated from England to Massachusetts in the seventeenth century. A next generation had been Quakers in Pennsylvania, where Samuel's grandson, Mordecai, had prospered. Mordecai's son, John, became a well-to-do farmer in Virginia. And it was one of John's sons, Abraham, who moved in the 1780s from Virginia to Kentucky with his five children, three of whom were sons, Mordecai, Joseph, and Thomas. In 1786, while planting a cornfield, Abraham was killed by Indians. As his body lay in the field, ten-year-old Thomas sat beside it. An Indian ran out of the woods toward him. Fifteen-year-old Mordecai, concealed in the cabin, aimed and shot the Indian in the chest. It was the eponymous story of Thomas's life, retold many times by a man who had a gift for narrative, got along with his neighbors, and attended church regularly.

Primogeniture gave his eldest brother the family possessions. The other sons were expected to move on. Thomas was not sent to school, even to learn arithmetic. A manual laborer as a teenager, then a carpenter, and then a farmer, he managed sustenance and little more. He made rough tables and cabinets on commission, built barns and cabins, made coffins. When he eventually acquired property, it provided mostly backbreaking work and disappointment. He had bursts of pioneer energy, resettling twice. Decent in every way, he struggled through life, gave no one any trouble, and made do. He started more strongly than he finished and, as he grew older, did only the irreducibly necessary.

In spring 1806 he had a glimpse beyond Kentucky. Hired to build a flatboat for a local merchant, he took it, loaded with goods, to New Orleans via the Ohio and Mississippi rivers. As a carpenter and day laborer, he accumulated enough cash to buy, soon after his son was born, almost 350 acres in Hardin County. He still owned some of the 200 he had purchased in 1803, on Nolin River, near Hodgenville, called Sinking Spring Farm. Then, in 1811, he bought 230 acres on Knob Creek, northeast of Hodgenville, to which he moved his family. On each farm, he built a one-room log cabin. So, too, did everyone else of his station and means, and the small commercial buildings of the local townships were identical, at most slightly larger. Thomas Lincoln's land transactions, including promissory notes and delayed sales, had title and debt complications. In the end, their actual value amounted to the equivalent of three or so years of what he could save from his earnings. It was not inestimable, given his start, but it left a narrow margin and next to no cash.

Thomas mainly seems to have taught his son by negative example. To Abraham, manual labor, especially farming, was the enemy of self-improvement. It needed to be transcended by the accumulation of capital, profit of some sort. The capital that, from the start, overwhelmingly attracted Abraham was the capital of the mind, though in his adult life he also revealed an affinity for literal capital, interest-bearing loans that made his money work while, as a lawyer, he used his mind to work for money. Poring over his first lessons, he could have had little awareness of why he was reading. Pleasure in language and pride in literacy probably compelled his engagement. But later, when he read for opportunity, he certainly had a purpose. Among other things, he did not want to suffer the economic fate of his father. And in his adult life he found little room for his father's presence.

At first, manual labor seemed likely to be his lifelong fate, though competition between the attractions of intellect and the demands of physical labor began at an early age. His mother's lessons and his own efforts to merge memory and literacy as he attempted to read the Bible were assisted by lessons in spelling and arithmetic at his first school. In 1816, Caleb Hazel, a family friend living next to the Lincoln farm, became Abraham's second schoolmaster. Lincoln's first formal lessons in literacy came from Thomas Dilworth's *New Guide to the English Tongue*, popularly known as *Dilworth's Speller*, a widely reprinted textbook first published in London in 1740. The boy may have seen from the title page that his copy had been published in Philadelphia in 1747, but he would not have known that the printer was Benjamin Franklin, who had also "made the woodprints" illustrating the selections from Aesop's fables. Whatever the edition he had in hand, it apparently became a family possession, providing him with his introduction, other than the Bible, to the power of the written word.

If he puzzled, as is likely, over Dilworth's lessons in spelling and grammar, he quickly mastered the former, his sharp ear picking up the phonetic basis of English spelling and its variants, his voice soon capable of imitation and mimicry, his acumen sufficient to make him an excellent speller. A few years later, in 1818, when he attended his third school, "we had Spelling Matches frequently," a schoolmate recalled, "Abe always ahead of all the classes he Ever was in." Grammar came more slowly, probably because of the gap between Dilworth's rules and the colloquial grammar of everyone around Abraham. The textbook's examples of correct grammar would have seemed like the speech of aliens from another world. Like every British and American textbook in the eighteenth and nineteenth centuries, this *New Guide to the English Tongue* also taught Protestant theology and moral behavior, its substance inseparable from its pedagogy. The purpose of literacy was to advance the teaching of religious, moral, and civic values. For innumerable Dilworths, the only literature of value was wisdom literature: the synthesis of language, imagination, and literary devices that taught one how to live as a good and theologically correct Christian. The mission of such books was to introduce children, step by step, level by level, to Christian moral perfection.

With his parents, Abraham attended the Little Mount Separate Baptist Church, near Knob Creek. Each Separatist Baptist congregation determined church policy by democratic vote. Preachers preached. Calvinist dogma was asserted. The cast of mood and expectation about this life and the next were formed. Life was depicted as a battleground between good and evil impulses, and human destiny was in God's hands. Indeed, since Adam's fall had sealed human fate in this world forever, earth was a vale of tears where men had to earn their bread by the sweat of their brows and women bring forth children in pain. There was also the expectation of rebirth for the saved and a strong sense of communal solidarity, the conviction that believers shared a moral foundation, a spiritual communion, and a social connectedness that made them an engaged community. One was never alone if one had a church. Lincoln's parents and their church believed that only adults should be baptized into membership in the congregation. The boy would come to that when he was of an age to feel God's presence and make an informed decision.

In the meantime, *Dilworth's Speller* was a help and a challenge, a formative book whose message, like his parents' religion, influenced him selectively. Some of the language and its lessons entered deeply into him. They became touchstones of his temperament and memory, not because they formed him but because they were there as guideposts in his formative years. Dilworth gave him permission to be different from his father and to transcend the limits of his frontier community. "It is a commendable thing," he read, "for a boy to apply his mind to the study of letters; they will be always useful to him; they will procure him the favor and love of good men, which those that are wise value more than riches and pleasure." Dilworth gave the highest value to reading as a repository of social and emotional utility, words of wisdom and words for advancement. Even if the pen was not mightier than the axe, at least it was a desirable alternative. There were trees to be cut, lumber to be stacked, firewood to be split, fields to be cleared. In a world in which physical labor predominated, a boy's strength was measured and noticed from the start. Strong and tall for his age, he was required to do his share. His parents and community assumed that this would be his lifelong work. Dilworth helped him to see himself differently.

If to modern ears, jaded with centuries of self-help maxims, Dilworth's words seem unexceptional, they spoke resonantly to many nineteenth-century Americans, reinforcing the values of their Christian homes and of Protestant due diligence. Since children needed to have no doubt about man's position on earth, Dilworth taught that "by the Fall of Adam from that glorious and happy state, wherein he was created, the Divine image in [man's] Mind is quite changed and altered, and he, who was created but a little inferior to the Angels above, is now made but little superior to the Angels below." The phrase stayed strongly enough in Lincoln's consciousness to emerge eventually as an expression of post-Calvinist appeal to "the better angels of our nature."

It was also a short distance from Dilworth's expression of the common wisdom about obedience to Lincoln's adult view. "Obedience compre-hendith the whole duty of man," he read in Dilworth's *New Guide to the English Tongue*, "both towards God, his neighbor, and himself; we should therefore let it be engraven on our hearts, that we may be useful in the common-wealth, and loyal to our magistrates." Lincoln was continually to give highest priority to his duty to the law, as embodied in the Con-stitution, and to the preservation of the commonwealth. Obedience to the magistrates became the guiding pole of his public life. More or less, he walked in the paths of such communal piety always, except in regard to Christian theology, though even there Dilworth's language remained part of him. During the last half-dozen years of his life, when the pres-sures of war and his obligation to rally the nation in terms that it under-stood pushed hard, he drew heavily upon the Judeo-Christian language that had dominated his childhood.

As the repository of the values of a widely shared common culture, Dilworth played both a germinating and a reinforcing role. Lincoln's pri-vate life and his public image merged as an exemplification of the maxim that "Personal merit is all a man can call his own. Whoever strictly ad-heres to honesty and truth, and leads a regular and virtuous life, is more truly noble than a debauched abandoned profligate, were he descended from the most illustrious family." "Honest Abe" emerged as a fulfillment of this widely held ideal. Better an honest than a clever politician. And Lincoln's life soon became an embodiment of an economic ideal that Dil-worth neatly expressed: "Trade is so noble a master that it is willing to entertain all mankind in its service; and has such a variety of employ-ments adapted to every capacity, that all, but the lazy, may support at least, if not enrich themselves." In search of vocation, Lincoln sampled a variety of employments. In the main, he became a lawyer-businessman, a frugal lender rather than a borrower, who believed that free labor was man's supreme self-definition and that all capital resulted from the sweat of the physical and mental brow. Dilworth urged boys to take the busy ants as their model, "For in their mouths we see them carry home / A stock for winter, which they know must come."

He also provided the boy with his introduction to written stories other than those in the Bible. The twelve stories in the *Guide* came from Aesop's fables, each exemplifying the advice and guidance of the previous lessons in reading and values. He quietly absorbed the wisdom of fables that concluded that "He that will not help himself, shall have help from nobody," "Make no friendship with an ill-natured man," "Honesty is the best policy," "Let envy alone and it will punish itself," "One good turn deserves another," "Evil be to them that evil think," and "A bird in hand is worth two in the bush." Such commonplaces seemed profound wisdom simply expressed. Aesop became an enduring favorite. As soon as Abraham himself began telling stories, these fables, and then the fable-like stories he invented to amuse and persuade others, became self-defining.

He also read, probably aloud, the small number of poems in Dilworth, sounding out the verses as a strange but beautiful use of language. Though the Calvinistic frame of mind judged much poetry frivolous, the poetry the boy encountered now was as pedagogic as Dilworth's prose maxims. It too focused on developing Christian character, and it seems likely that Dilworth either created or borrowed many of the selections from unidentified sources. One dealt with "Ambition," a topic that soon preoccupied Lincoln, on which he was to quote other, more famous authors later in his life, and to write and speak about publicly. The note of the adult Lincoln's concern is struck:

> Dazzled with hope, we cannot see the cheat
> Of aiming with impatience to be great.
> When wild ambition in the heart we find,
> Farwell content, and quiet of the mind:
> For glittering clouds, we leave the solid shore,
> And wanted happiness returns no more.

Another poem, "Heavenly Love," emphasizing forgiveness and reconciliation, summarized a less deterministic view of the drama of Christian salvation than that of his parents' church:

Christ's arms do still stand open to receive
All weary prodigals, that sin do leave;
For them he left his father's blessed abode;
Made son of man, to make man son of God:
To cure their wounds, he life's elixir bled,
And dy'd a death to raise them from the dead.

While none of the Jesus-centered theology of his childhood world remained central to his adult life, the power of poetic language, some of it secular, some religious, stayed with him.

Soon he was writing his own verses. His temperament responded to the emotional force of poetry. Meter and rhyme appealed to him. At first he wrote brief squibs, not all of his own creation. Later he tried his hand regularly as a poet, especially in times of sadness. Indeed, one of Dilworth's poems was his first introduction to a poetic subject and tone that suited his developing personality. It became the hallmark of his temperament. Later he would memorize poems of loss and bereavement, such as Thomas Gray's "Elegy Written in a Country Church-Yard" and Oliver Wendell Holmes's "The Last Leaf," the heightened sense of the transience of all things attracting him deeply and helping him cope with loss. Elegiac stoicism became the weight that he carried; it sculpted the stoop of his shoulders and it darkened the cast of his face. His eyes, later observers remarked, were filled with sadness even early in his life. Though events eventually made the emphasis permanent, Dilworth's "Life Is Short and Miserable" gave him one of his first poetic gateways into melancholic self-discovery:

Ah! Few and full of sorrow are the days
Of miserable man: his life decays
Like that frail flower, which with the sun's uprise
Her bud unfolds, and in the evening dies:
He like an empty shadow glides away
And all his life is but a winter's day.

* * *

Knob Creek provided his earliest impressions of daily life, his first memories of any specific place. Nothing distinguished the farm, with its hogs and four horses, from many other low-yield properties. Some of the land was still being cleared; all of it needed constant maintenance. It was rocky, difficult to work, and barely profitable. There were the usual animal and agricultural smells, the daily labor, the seasonal conditions——mild autumns, early springs, humid summers, winter cold, a single fireplace for heating and cooking. Hunting provided meat, with butchering and death a household commonplace. Huge flocks of birds, especially pigeons, filled the sky in Audubon's avian paradise. Boys chased and shot them for sport and food. Water had to be carried from a distance. Sarah and Abraham were kept busy with suitable chores. It was, though, far from an isolated existence. There were neighbors. Hodgenville, where they bought supplies, was ten miles distant. The well-traveled Cumberland Road between Louisville and Nashville ran directly by the property. Travelers going southwest and returning were in sight and hearing.

News of national events came by voice to people who did not subscribe to newspapers, even if they could read. Travelers brought news that Congress had declared war against Great Britain in 1812, that the war was going badly between 1812 and 1814, and that the nation had good reason to crow in January 1815 when Andrew Jackson's army defeated the British at New Orleans. Some soldiers, returning home, "came by Lincolns house," a contemporary remembered, "and he fed and Cared for them." Word of the victory may have gotten to Hardin County before it got to Washington, probably arriving in time for Abraham's sixth birthday. That America had gained nothing tangible by the war, not even a formal end to Britain's impressing American sailors, hardly mattered to Western enthusiasts and to the Democratic-Republican Party: the war was an affirmation of nationalism, a reassertion of American independence, and a spur to further western expansion. It became the basis of Jackson's popularity. At six years of age, Abraham may have cheered the general and the victory.

The impression slavery made on him as a child can be guessed at in the light of his parents' disapproval and his later comment on his abhorrence of the institution. "I cannot remember when I did not think so, and feel," he wrote. Slavery was widespread in Kentucky, though much less so in the hardscrabble north-central part of the state than in the lush areas to the east and south. For well-to-do Kentuckians, especially in emerging cities such as Louisville, house slaves were commonplace, and slaves labored in central Kentucky tobacco fields. In counties such as Hardin, where people made modest livings from the reluctant land, slaves were of marginal utility. As cash purchases, they were beyond the means of small farmers, who had reason to feel threatened by slavery. There were, though, slaves in Hardin County, probably many more than the estimate of fifty by a contemporary and maybe as many, according to a recent biographer, as a thousand in a population of less than three thousand. Unlike mainstream Baptist churches, the Lincolns' Separate Baptist Church abjured slavery. Most Kentuckians did not.

Thomas Lincoln's economic viability had been shaky from the start, including his land purchases. Title in Kentucky was complicated by the established practice of each property owner's setting out his own boundaries. Consequently, clear title was often difficult or impossible to establish. The farm Lincoln had purchased at Mill Creek in 1803 was insecure because of an erroneous recording of the survey. In 1811, when he attempted to sell his Sinking Spring farm at Nolin Creek, a legal tangle ensued. Getting his money back was difficult. In the meantime, his ownership at Knob Creek was compromised, mainly because a Philadelphia family claimed a huge tract that included his farm. In 1816 he received an eviction notice. Rather than contest the Philadelphia family's claim to Knob Creek, he decided to leave Kentucky. He wanted to go where government-owned land was for sale and where solid procedures were in place to guarantee clear title. In the tradition of his family, he again went west, this time northwest to Indiana.

In fall of 1816, Thomas sold his farm for about three hundred dollars worth of whiskey, a portable and salable commodity, probably the best offer he could get. He built a flat boat at the mouth of Knob Creek, loaded the whiskey, his tools, and some of the family possessions, and pushed off by himself onto the Rolling Fork River, his passageway to the Ohio River and then to Indiana, the same route that had started him on his way to New Orleans ten years earlier. When the boat turned over, he lost much of the whiskey and most of his tools. With the wet remnants, he and the flatboat made it to Indiana. Seventeen miles northwest of the river, in Perry County, at a small stream called Pigeon Creek, he marked out with logs and brush piles a homestead of 160 acres, for sale at $2 an acre, later reduced to the 80 for which he could afford to pay. He then trekked 300 miles back to Kentucky. In December, he traveled the same route again, this time with his wife, their two children, their clothing, two feather beds, a small number of household items, including kitchen implements and a spinning wheel, and two horses, perhaps pulling a rudimentary homemade wagon. The trip may have had its excitement for the children, but nothing could have prepared them for the change. Despite the fact that it became a state on December 11, 1816, Indiana was a wilderness.

Thomas's decision to leave comparatively civilized Kentucky for primitive Indiana guaranteed that the Lincoln family would have more difficult than fair days ahead. Late fall and early winter were unpropitious times to make such a move. If clearing land and farm work were hard in Kentucky, they were backbreaking in Indiana: the land was tangled with intractable undergrowth and thick stands of trees, "an unbroken forest," as Lincoln recalled. In the freezing first winter, very little could be done except to erect "a little two face Camp open in the front" in which the family huddled for warmth. Log and brush fires provided the only heat. Food was in short supply, provided mainly by the game that Thomas Lincoln shot, particularly deer and wild turkey. Idealistic about animals and squeamish about killing them, Abraham contributed to the food supply by shooting a turkey. "He has never since pulled a trigger on any larger game," he told his campaign biographer in 1860. The axe was the daily weapon of choice. By his seventh birthday that February, tall, lithe, and muscular for his age, he could swing it effectively. Father and son spent hours chopping trees and clearing land through snowy weather.

The Lincolns spent the next year establishing themselves in a one-room cabin, clearing six acres, and registering the land. Soon they had long-term visitors, Nancy Lincoln's aunt and uncle, Elizabeth and Thomas Sparrow, who also had been ejected from their Hardin County farm and who brought with them eighteen-year-old Dennis Hanks, Elizabeth's nephew and Nancy Lincoln's first cousin. They all crowded into the temporary structure, a testimony to frontier hospitality and the sacredness of family. They also soon shared disaster, a depth of misery for which not even Dilworth's gloomy meditations could have prepared Abraham. Elizabeth Sparrow became sick in September. So did her husband. The illness was a form of poisoning spread by cows that had grazed on the snakeroot plant when dry weather made better grazing sparse. It was widely known as "milk sickness" because it was connected with drinking milk, though its basic chemistry and origin were then unknown. Late summer was its season. It signaled its presence with trembling in poisoned cows. Then, with seeming randomness, its human victims became fevered, chilled, nauseated, and comatose. Within a week, most were dead. The Sparrows died in late September 1818.

At the end of the month, Nancy Lincoln became ill. "There was no physician near than 35 miles," Dennis Hanks remembered. "She knew she was going to die & Called up the Children to her dying side and told them to be good & kind to their father—to one another and to the world." Day and night the family lived in the presence of her suffering. On October 5 she died. Thomas Lincoln made a coffin for his wife, perhaps assisted by his son. They put the coffin on a sled and pulled it to a grave site on a little hill a short distance from the cabin, burying her next to her aunt and uncle. An elder of the Little Pigeon Baptist Church intoned the burial service. "Man like an empty shadow glides away / And all his life is but a winter's day."

For himself and his children, Thomas Lincoln needed a replacement. One year after her death, with the harvest in, he returned to Kentucky, to familiar Elizabethtown, the seat of Hardin County, where he proposed marriage to his wife's childhood friend, the sister of the man with whom he had gone to New Orleans and the child of a well-known local family. Sally Bush Johnston had become a widow in 1816, a welcome end of a marriage to a man who had wasted her modest inheritance and provided poorly for his family. A formidable woman, good-looking and energetic, she probably breathed a sigh of relief at the death of her husband, whose ragged estate, which left her only debts, she declined to administrate. It seems likely that Thomas, who knew of Sally Johnston's widowhood before he left Kentucky, had gone to Elizabethtown with her in mind, and probably had told Sarah and Abraham of his intentions. He may have been attracted to Sally before his own marriage. He had seen her numbers of times thereafter and admired her. After some discussion and consultation, she agreed to marry him, provided that he pay the small debts her husband had saddled her with. A Methodist minister performed the rite in early December 1819. Sally was thirty-one years old, Thomas ten years older. "Thomas Lincoln and Mrs Lincoln never had any Children, accident & nature stopping things short," Dennis Hanks later remarked, though both were well within child-bearing age. Thomas was now the father and sole support of three more children, the price of the marriage, and the husband of a literate and competent wife. They journeyed by wagon, loaded with Sally's possessions, the same route that Thomas Lincoln had traveled twice before.

The eleven-year-old boy, who deeply, silently missed his mother, was at times chatty, assertive, and social; at other times withdrawn, moody, and silent. He also had an alert interest in the world, an attraction to verbal performance and jokes, an inquiring interest in the complexities of adult life. He asked questions, sometimes persistently. He read and reread as much as time and his few books allowed. Except for his sister and an occasional playmate, he was often alone. He began to find it comfortable to alternate between solitude and talkative sociability. He could, though, switch quickly from one to the other, and when Sarah Bush Lincoln arrived at Pigeon Creek, she brought with her three children who would become playmates, a predilection for order and cleanliness, and also a small but marvelous library. The new regime flared into excitement when she took from her luggage the *Arabian Nights*, Daniel Defoe's *Robinson Crusoe*, Noah Webster's *Speller*, Lindley Murray's *The English Reader*, and William Scott's *Lessons in Elocution*.

The autodidact was about to become immersed in new reading experiences. Previously limited to the Bible and *Dilworth's Speller*, he now also got editions of Aesop's fables and John Bunyan's seventeenth-century Puritan allegory, *Pilgrim's Progress*. It may be that the latter had been bought or bartered for him by his father, who, the story goes, saw it at a neighbor's house and thought his book-loving son might like it. Maybe both were brought by the new Mrs. Lincoln. The addition of more fables to the twelve from Dilworth increased Abraham's store of animal stories, which he could refashion to fit the language and the circumstances of family, neighbors, and friends. In his rural world, Aesop had point and pungency, especially with alterations that reflected the realism of daily life, gave humor and effect to animals standing in for people, and reflected the coarser language of the Indiana frontier. A storyteller by instinct, Abraham began to entertain his family and others with tales that drew on these fables. "He was always full of his Stories," his cousin John Hanks recollected.

Pilgrim's Progress was received much like the Bible, a book providing moral guidance through what it said and how it said it, the language as important as the substance. Its sonorous, intricate sentences embodied the power of words to transcend the ordinary, to raise the moment and the message to the impressiveness of larger truths. It exposed Abraham to elevated writing, the weaving together of sound, rhythm, and imagistic language for special occasions, for heightened moments that emphasized the extraordinary. And *Pilgrim's Progress* achieved these effects while telling a story. The young Lincoln would have felt engaged by the riveting narration of Everyman's travels through earthly difficulties in search of moral perfection and heavenly salvation, and the Puritan tradition of allegory was sufficiently alive in his Baptist world for him to have felt at home with its abstractions. He seems not to have taken to heart the underlying theology. But the story of a young man struggling on his journey toward a higher life could readily be adapted to his own secular version, particularly how to find a path out of the limitations of his father's world. *Pilgrim's Progress* could be read as a story about upward mobility.

With eight people crowded into the one-room cabin, it had to be a challenge to find space and light, as well as time, for reading, more difficult in the short winter days than in the summer. He "would go out in the woods & gather hickory bark—bring it home & Keep a light by it and read by it—when no lamp was to be had—grease lamp—handle to it which Stuck in the crack of the wall," John Hanks remembered. Abraham, his stepbrother John D. Johnston, and his cousin Dennis slept in the loft. Sarah Lincoln, her two stepsisters Elizabeth and Matilda Johnston, and Thomas and Sally Lincoln slept in the ground-level single room. Dennis and John Johnston, who were not readers and went to bed early, the norm in rural society, learned to sleep with a light burning close to them. "As Company would Come to our house," his stepmother recalled, "Abe was a silent listener—wouldn't speak—would sometimes take a book and retire aloft—go to the stable or fields or woods" in the good weather and read. The classic image of the solitary boy reading by the fireplace in a log cabin would rarely have been the reality.

But he read whenever and wherever he could. "Abe was not Energetic Except in one thing," his newly arrived half-sister Matilda remarked, "he was active & persistant in learning—read Everything he Could." He "devoured all the books he could get or lay hands on; he was a Constant and voracious reader," John Hanks noticed. "When he went out to work any where he would Carry his books and would always read while resting," a friend recalled. He had a regular round of chores, which included taking corn for grinding to the grist mill a few miles off, which he did on horseback. If, over the next four years, his father became impatient with his obsession, it was not because he disapproved of his reading but because he needed him for field work. A boy with a passion for reading often isn't there or disappears quickly into solitude. By age eleven, Abraham had a mental life that he could not share with his father. Sally, though, endeared herself to her stepson, particularly by helping him envision himself as a literate boy with a promising future at a time when he had little other support for not becoming what his father was. He "didn't like physical labor—was diligent for Knowledge," she later observed, "wished to Know and if pain & Labor would get it he was sure to get it. He was the best boy I ever saw. He read all the books he could lay his hands on." Thomas Lincoln's limitation was that he could not envision for his son a future different from his own past. The books gradually become an impediment to their relationship.

The young reader immediately established a familiarity with *Robinson Crusoe*, a tale that riveted him: the frontier world identified with the shipwrecked Crusoe's struggle against isolation and adversity. It was a seminal story for dissenting outsiders, separated from the mainstream of American and English polite culture, who saw in Crusoe's survival the triumph of their fundamentalist religion and their code of self-sufficiency. Crusoe helped himself in order to be helped by God; so did they. Crusoe defeated primitive savages and found subsistence in a primitive world; so did they. It was a culturally confirming story about the superiority of the Protestant worldview and work ethic. Like *Pilgrim's Progress*, *Robinson Crusoe* was read as a didactic book with a moral purpose, asserting eternal providence and justifying the ways of God to man.

For Lincoln it was also an absorbing adventure story. As with his other books, he undoubtedly read it numbers of times, perhaps aloud to others in the household, both for the pleasure of the reading performance and for the deeper memorization of the story. He read "all he could get & learned the most of it by heart quickly & well & alwys remembered it." Much of his reading stayed vividly in his mind, often word for word. A variant of a comment by Crusoe resurfaced years later in one of Lincoln's two most famous compositions: "I ought to leave them," Defoe's hero says, "to the justice of God, who is the Governor of Nations, and knows how, by national punishments to make a just retribution for the national offenses and to bring public judgments upon those who offend him in a public manner by such ways as best please him." When a nation commits offenses, God will make a "just retribution" in His inscrutable way. Lincoln was to write in his second inaugural address, "If we shall suppose that American Slavery is one of those offences . . ."

His reading for a short time had its fantastic side, more so than his life. Whether or not Sally Johnston had actually brought with her a copy of *Arabian Nights* or he got it at the house of a friend, as was claimed, he had it in hand within a few years of his stepmother's arrival. It was one of his few sustained engagements with fantasy. He sometimes read the stories aloud, Dennis Hanks later recalled, especially "Sinbad the Sailor" and "Aladdin's Lamp," and may have responded to Dennis's protest, if the latter's recollection is accurate, that they were nothing but a pack of lies, with the quip that they were "mighty fine lies." Exotic tales from a distant culture, they had nothing of the moralistic about them. Unlike his other reading, they did not teach lessons. They were exercises for the imagination, holidays from everyday life. Pigeon Creek Baptists did not sanction that kind of escapist activity. Sunday was a holiday because it was a holy day, and fiction had to have a didactic purpose. Even then it was still suspect, a product of the fancy, in itself a dangerous faculty.

Lincoln absorbed this culture's values and modified them to suit his temperament. To be of value, literature had to be serious, except when it was funny or whimsical. Effective humor, both in writing and speech, he was later to believe, had the virtue of being cathartic, an antidote to the weighty world, not an escape but a restorative. Later, the theater, including popular drama, was to have some of the same value for him. The *Arabian Nights* of his boyhood provided brief pleasure, and then he moved on, never to be a fan of fiction of any sort, including the dominant literary genre of his age, the novel. It is possible that he did read a small number of novels, and he was familiar with the names of many of his famous novelistic contemporaries, particularly Charles Dickens and Harriet Beecher Stowe. Late in life, while on a legal case in Chicago in 1857, he enjoyed a widely popular dramatization based on a character in Dickens's *Dombey and Son*. But he had no direct experience of his contemporary Victorian novelists. The Baptist imprint and his temperament moved his imagination into different genres. He did, however, have a strong interest in narrative, not in fantasy or realistic fiction but in narratives of fact, especially biographies and histories, and in poetry, where he found his favorite authors and his deepest touchstones.

Shy and frequently withdrawn, especially in the presence of girls, a typical pattern for young boys, he was also at some moments articulate and outgoing, an eager playmate, a teller of jokes and tales, a player of performance roles, such as standing on a log to give a sermon to his siblings in imitation of a preacher, showing off his cleverness and his speaking ability. His sister had been his main playmate for years; they were deeply fond of each other. His cousin Dennis seems to have been present without being there in any meaningful sense, and his new siblings represented chatter and activity but not intimacy. At the same time, they and their parents lived in the closest quarters, slept together, so to speak, observed one another. It was not the practice, though, to confide, other than superficially. And for a boy like Abraham, noted for being different, which expressed itself mainly by his constant reading, the conditions encouraged shyness and withdrawal, though not ignorance, about sexual matters. Life on the farm and in the crowded cabin undoubtedly made him aware of the facts of life. But it was also, at least verbally and in its Christian standards, a puritanical world. Prudence and propriety, no matter how coarse daily life, were values that demanded respect.

In the winter of 1820/1821 he attended Andrew Crawford's school. *Dilworth's Speller* was Crawford's major text. Arithmetic was emphasized. The short school year, confined to the fallow late fall and winter, was additionally shortened for some children by the exigencies of their individual households. As a lesson in social etiquette, Crawford had each child leave the room, return in the guise of a stranger, and introduce himself formally to each of his classmates. Despite this training, Lincoln, for his entire life, remained noticeably awkward entering a room for a social occasion, never confident that he would say the right thing, especially to women.

The next winter he walked four miles each way to James Swaney's schoolhouse on a neighbor's farm. In 1824/1825 he went to a school run by Azel Dorsey for six months. His closest friend and schoolmate Nathaniel Grigsby, whose brother Aaron was soon to marry Sarah Lincoln, recalled that the six foot, two inch young man, wiry and thin at about 160 pounds, was "Studious," deeply immersed in his books. And "if he Ever got a new Story—new book or new fact or idea he never forgot it." He was also distinctive in his temperance, his dislike of quarreling, his democratic disposition, and his abhorrence of cruelty to animals. He particularly disapproved when his schoolmates caught and "put fire" on the backs of turtles. He accepted that some animals were necessarily beasts of burden; others had to be killed for food and clothing. But he detested gratuitous cruelty. It became one of his first subjects as a writer, and Grigsby recalled that at Crawford's school Lincoln wrote "short sentences against cruelty to animals," probably using Dilworth's maxims as his model.

Stimulated by his reading, he had begun to write brief essays on topics that interested him. With his changing moods, his tone was sometimes serious, sometimes comic. He wrote an essay on the evils of intemperance, a topic he was to take up later in life, though perhaps also partly about intemperate speech and actions, which Dilworth warned schoolchildren against. He was also "full of fun—wit—humor." Squibs and funny rhymes appealed to him. He "wrote a piece of humorous Rhyme on his friend Josiah Crawford that made all the neighbors, Crawford included, burst their sides with laughter." Dennis Hanks observed that "at this Early age he was more humorous than in after life." And his stepmother thought of him not as sad but contemplative. He seemed to think much, and quietly, and at length.

Precocious, eager to learn and to be heard, a private personality who already had a stage persona, he began to think about serious issues and connect them to his speaking and writing performances. When the mood took him he would declaim, without the slightest urging, often on a makeshift stand or pulpit, about higher things, whether for humorous effect or for serious persuasion. He practiced "elements of Gesture" and read an essay on the principles and rules of elocution in William Scott's *Lessons in Elocution*. In argument, he was sometimes satiric, even scathing. Facts attracted him, the special pride of the self-taught in the knowledge attained by their own efforts. Some of the young man's pronouncements were about political issues and leaders. He had strongly developed opinions. Local news came quickly by word of mouth. Statewide and national news came slowly, mostly but not entirely orally, disseminated by cracker-barrel conversation, some of which occurred on visits to neighbors, trips for supplies, and chance meetings on country roads. Since the Lincoln household did not take a newspaper, whatever came to hand was often weeks out of date. The tall, gangly youngster began to appear at sessions of the local justice of the peace, aware that he could learn something there about people, speech, and argument. And the law and its dispensation interested him.

He also memorized some of Henry Clay's speeches and "often for amusement for his play fellows—neighbors and friends made quite good stump speeches when between the ages of 15 and 20," John Hanks recalled. In the contentious presidential contest of 1824, John Quincy Adams, supported by Henry Clay, defeated Andrew Jackson in an election decided by the House of Representatives. The controversial, argumentative, and domineering Jackson, who became president in 1828, commanded the national scene. Those who favored Jackson were against a national banking system, high protective tariffs, and a government-financed national infrastructure. Henry Clay became Lincoln's hero, against the grain of his working-class origin and probably in opposition to his father's views. In contrast to Jackson, Clay seemed an embodiment of the cultured citizen whom the young autodidact would like to become, an articulate master of language, reason, and logic.

Now, in the early 1820s, reading biography for the first time, he became fascinated by Benjamin Franklin's autobiography and Mason L. Weems's *Life of Washington*. Narrative biography was the dominant source of American history on the frontier, and the twelve-year-old boy occasionally read *Life of Washington* to the family, having borrowed it from Josiah Crawford, Sr., his schoolmate's father. Franklin and Washington became his heroes. Both helped mold him into the advocate of upward mobility he was in the process of becoming. Franklin's Horatio Alger story gave value to his own ambition: the printer, inventor, writer, and diplomat was the most capable and articulate representative of an America that embraced commerce and social improvement. Like Franklin, he, too, could rise in the world; ambition and hard work would win out. Washington's deification as the father of his country provided a model of bipartisan patriotism, the gentleman-soldier whose temperament stressed rational prudence, the unifying progenitor whose presence he could invoke for emotional sustenance and political guidance.

In addition to great lives to inspire him, he also needed to learn the facts of American history. There was little available to him, partly because he lived on the western frontier and also because American historiography was in the process of its early formation. The United States had been in existence for forty-five years when, in 1821, William Grimshaw, an American who had written a history of England, published a *History of the United States from Their First Settlement as Colonies to the Cession of Florida in Eighteen Hundred and Twenty-One*. It quickly became the most widely read history of the republic. Grimshaw's version of American history begins with reflections "On Improvements in Astronomy, Navigation, and Geography" from the ancient days to the seventeenth century, which made possible Columbus and the voyages of discovery. One third of the book's three hundred pages are devoted to these voyages, to the early settlements, and to the eighteenth-century conflicts for possession between France and Britain, a sensible allocation for a nation of readers whose political progenitors were only one generation behind and who desired to learn their earlier lineage. By the mid-1820s a copy was in

Lincoln's hands. It was the perfect book for an autodidact who had read little to nothing about American or any other history and who would not have been disappointed if Grimshaw had begun with ancient Greece and Rome.

An economical stylist, Grimshaw wrote well and interestingly, with a flair for dramatic accounts of crucial events. He chose words carefully, composing balanced sentences of the sort that his young reader would have admired. His pen portraits of the main historical personages have both biographical specificity and stylistic neatness. Writing for a popular audience, he emphasized wars, battles, defeats, victories, and the role of great leaders in determining events. The forging of a nation is his theme. On the whole, discord is minimized, common purpose valorized. Politics, economics, and social conditions hardly have a presence. But as he read, Lincoln had to sense that there was more to this history than facts and stories. It had an underlying worldview and an ideological emphasis. In its tone and values, Grimshaw wrote Whig history, a view of America as not only a national entity but a nation with a destiny that required applying Enlightenment values and humanitarian principles to the national condition. American history was and would be a steady march forward, with progress and improvement in every area of life.

Nevertheless, Grimshaw reminded readers, the United States had been founded on two primal sins that held the nation back. The first was the appropriation of the land from its native inhabitants. On this subject he treads lightly. Neither the British nor the Dutch, he writes, "had a just claim upon the property of the native possessors." By extension, the French, the British, and their heirs did not have a just claim on the rest of the continent. Throughout, he depicts sympathetically the plight of the deceived and dispossessed Native Americans, the inhumanity of whose treatment he deplores. Though they are savages, they are still human beings. He rejoices in those rare instances in which "no violence was committed on the unoffending natives." But the land, he implies, now unquestionably belongs to white Americans by right of the superiority that made the conquest possible. And the conquest was still in process in the 1820s, to continue for another fifty years. Like Grimshaw and most Americans, Lincoln accepted the basic premises of the dispossession. There was no going back. It was now simply a question of how to treat the Indian tribes. If at all possible, humane treatment was called for. But the land could not and would not be returned.

Slavery, the other primal sin, Grimshaw believed an embodiment of human greed, incompatible with the humanitarian values of the nation best represented in the claim of universal equality in the Declaration of Independence. "What a climax of human cupidity and turpitude," he wrote, when the Dutch first brought slaves to Virginia, which by 1820 had resulted in a population of more than a million and a half black slaves, mainly in the southern states. "Since the middle of the last century," Lincoln read, "expanded minds have been, with slow gradations, promoting the decrease of slavery in North America," which would eventually remove "the fetters, which are no less alarming to the master, than galling to the slave." One day American Negroes would join other "free people of color" in Sierra Leone. Like Thomas Jefferson, whom he refers to as his model, Grimshaw believed that slavery would be abolished without bloodshed. Compromise, compensation, and moral principle would make that possible over time. Hence radical abolitionism was unnecessary. Religious antislavery views, such as those of Lincoln's parents, would bear practical fruit. Enlightened Americans, with their country's best long-term interest at heart, would prevail by consensus, not armed struggle. At this fountain of hope, the young Lincoln drank.

If he needed any further solidification of his own detestation of slavery, he had it in another book that he now read closely, James Riley's *An Authentic Narrative of the Loss of the American Brig "Commerce"* . . . *with an Account of the Sufferings of the Surviving Officers and Crew Who Were Enslaved by the Wandering Arabs, on the African Desert.* It was a harrowing and dramatic true story that gave vivid specificity and a white man's voice to the horror of what it meant to be a slave. Published in 1817 and frequently reprinted, it appealed to American curiosity about the Arab world and exotic Africa. Its account of suffering, slavery, and freedom attained against formidable obstacles had its attraction both as an adventure story and as an embodiment of American ingenuity, courage, and talent. It is narrated in the first person by a man of high moral character who never forsakes his humanistic loyalty to his crew. He regularly sees the guiding hand of providence in his survival and wants nothing more than to be reunited with his family, who will suffer destitution without him. In Riley, American readers saw, as if looking into a mirror, their own virtues.

Like Henry Clay and William Grimshaw, Riley advocated gradual emancipation of American slaves. But only in the final climactic paragraph does the author make his point directly:

My proud-spirited and free countrymen still hold a million and a half, nearly, of the human species, in the most cruel bonds of slavery, many of whom are kept at hard labour and smarting under the savage lash . . . besides the miseries of hunger, thirst, imprisonment, cold, nakedness, and even tortures. . . . I myself have witnessed such scenes in different parts of my own country, and the bare recollection now chills my blood with horror. . . . I have now learned to look with compassion on my enslaved and oppressed fellow-creatures; I will exert all my remaining faculties in endeavours to redeem the enslaved, and to shiver in pieces the rod of oppression. . . . I am far from being of opinion that they should all be emancipated immediately, and at once. I am aware that such a measure would not only prove ruinous to great numbers of my fellow-citizens, who are at present slave holders, and to whom this species of property descended as an inheritance; but that it would also turn loose . . . a race of men incapable of exercising the necessary occupations of civilized life, in such a manner as to ensure to themselves an honest and comfortable subsistence; yet it is my earnest desire that such a plan should be devised . . . as will gradually, but not less effectually, wither and extirpate the accursed tree of slavery, that has been suffered to take such deep root . . . [and] put it out of the power of either the bond or the released slaves, or their posterity, ever to endanger our present or future domestic peace or political tranquility.

At home and at school, with rudimentary writing materials, sometimes a chalkboard instead of paper, Lincoln had topics to write about—temperance, slavery, cruelty to animals, Washington, Franklin, American history. Like other autodidacts and young authors, he began to keep a notebook, at first "writing rude verses of his own . . . in his coppy Books also working out Mathematical problems. . . ." The compositions for his schoolmasters took as their model some of the prose pieces he was reading in the two anthologies his stepmother had brought from Kentucky. Lindley Murray's *The English Reader: or, Pieces in Prose and Poetry* was mainly prose, with an introductory essay on "The Principles of Good Reading." William Scott's *Lessons in Elocution, Or, a Selection of Pieces, in Prose and Verse, for the Improvement of Youth in Reading and Speaking*, despite its misleading title, was a substantial anthology of literary gems, a veritable treasure-house of literature, with a large and representative selection from some of the now obscure and many of the still most famous poets of English literature.

Beginning in 1821, Lincoln became an avid reader of poetry, and by 1825, at the age of sixteen, stellar poems by Thomas Gray, Alexander Pope, and John Milton became his regular sustenance. Thirty tightly printed pages of selections from Shakespeare's histories and tragedies revealed to him a world of literary brilliance and an insight into human character the existence of which he had previously been aware of only vaguely. And why could he himself not write poetry? Verse and rhyme came easily to him. With models from Scott's anthology in his memory, particularly Gray's "Elegy Written in a Country Church-Yard," he continued to try his hand at it. The young man was at the beginning of an extraordinary education.

CHAPTER 2

Shakespeare

1825–1834

As he cleared land, split logs into fence rails, helped butcher pigs for meat, plowed fields, and reaped corn, Lincoln began to be noticed as that very big kid who seemed exceptionally smart and had an unusual liking for reading. He had an inquisitive mind about how things worked in the natural world, puzzled about cause and effect, about physical properties, mechanical relationships, tools, and leverage. Franklin's experiments with lightning were part of his reading experience. The world around him riveted his attention, especially the elements of nature, the changing appearances of forest, soil, and sky. And he was attracted to animals: cats and dogs, for whom he felt a special tenderness; farm animals, whose labor and blood helped make crops grow and satisfied stomachs; people, whether they migrated on, seeking better places, or disappeared entirely, as his mother had. Everyday sights and memories rooted him to earthly realities.

He had little mind for transcendence, let alone permanence. The lessons of his textbooks, Aesop's fables, Washington's and Franklin's achievements, James Riley's escape from slavery, and Grimshaw's account of American history deepened his connection to the rooted quotidian. Reason, logic, and experience seemed the best guides. "He did not seem to think that to be of much value which could not be proven or rather demonstrated," a friend, Joseph Gillespie, recalled. Skeptical and logically assertive, any faith he had had in the literal truth of biblical claims slipped away. His mother had been a pious believer. His father and stepmother embraced their Baptist Calvinism. Touched by the dark side of that pervasive vision, the young man absorbed the mood but not the practice or theology. He returned from church with enthusiasm for imitating the preacher's style, not affirming his claims. "He would . . . say to the boys & girls that he could repeat the Sermon—got on Stumps—logs—fences and do it well and accurately . . . he was calm—logical & clear alwys." And he enjoyed the performance. "Abe would take down the bible, read a verse—give out a hymn . . . he would preach & we would do the Crying," Matilda Johnston remembered. Theology became a subject for rational dispute. "He was a great talker on the scriptures and read it a great deal" but "never made any profession," Nat Grigsby recalled. Years later Lincoln remembered that he had heard an old man testify "that when he did good he felt good, when he did bad he felt bad. That . . . is my religion—deeds done in the body."

Language mattered because he needed it to work through what seemed to him real, to separate fact from falsehood. It mattered even more because he began to feel that only through writing and speech could he understand the world. He needed language as the tool by which knowledge was acquired and communicated. Also, he took satisfaction in how language worked and in the pleasure of words and rhythms. Learning gave him an intellectual high. And it had the potential to define him positively to other people. On the one hand, he did not care much what others thought of him. On the other, reading the lives of famous men, he decided that he wanted to make his mark in some grand way, including the path of service. "He said that he would be Presdt of the US. . . . Said it jokingly—yet with a Smack of deep Earnestness in his Eye & tone," Elizabeth Crawford recalled. "He Evidently had an idea—a feeling in 1828 that he was bound to be a great man—No doubt that in his boyish days he dreamed it would be so. Abe was ambitious—sought to outstrip and override others." He would be someone important and recognized, like

George Washington. Or perhaps he would be a great poet, like Shakespeare. And the models from whom he could learn to be a master of language and intellect were at hand.

Around 1825 he began immersing himself in Lindley Murray's *The English Reader* and William Scott's *Lessons in Elocution, Or, a Selection of Pieces, in Prose and Verse*, absorbing the ideas and language that great literature provides. It was his introduction to a world of sophisticated authors, the British literary canon as it was understood by the late eighteenth century. These anthologies may occasionally have been leafed through in the five years since Sarah Lincoln brought them to the Lincoln household. Now they became her stepson's formative books. Such anthologies were widely available to those who had an interest in literature beyond basic literacy and who were not restricted by the Baptist pietistic temperament. Sarah Lincoln valued education more than piety. Lincoln "was better read then than the world knows or is likely to Know Exactly," Caroline Gentry, his friend Allen Gentry's wife, later recalled. "He often & often Commented or talked to me about what he read—seemed to read it out of the book as he went along—did so to others—he was the learned boy among us unlearned folks."

Unlike *Dilworth's Speller*, Scott's and Murray's anthologies assumed that the basics of literacy had been mastered and that, since their young readers had already been inculcated in Christian virtue, much of the moral pedagogy could be implicit. Both equate, as William Scott does on his title page, "READING and SPEAKING." Scott placed emphasis on reading aloud, a practice that Lincoln had already adopted. From the start, reading seemed to him an aspect of oral performance, the words enunciated in the theater of his own head or aloud to himself or to family and schoolmates. Public recitation as a teaching device emphasized the connection. The repetition that Lincoln believed facilitated comprehension also promoted memorization. "Abe could Easily learn & long remember and when he did learn anything he learned it well and thoroughly," his stepmother recalled. "What he thus learned he stowed away in his memory . . . repeated over & over again & again till it was . . . fixed firmly & permanently. . . ." He developed an anthology of the mind, independent of whether he had the actual book in hand. "My mind is like a piece of steel," he later remarked, "very hard to scratch anything on it and almost impossible after you get it there to rub it out."

Each anthology begins with lessons in elocution, from which it is a short step to oratory. The selections are organized to provide models of different kinds of discourse, "Narrative Pieces," "Didactic Pieces," "Descriptive Pieces," "Pathetic Pieces," "Eloquence of the Pulpit," "Eloquence of the Senate," "Eloquence of the Bar," and "Dramatic Pieces," under which are "Dialogues," and "Speeches and Soliloquies." It seems almost certain that Lincoln repeatedly read both volumes from cover to cover. He had few other books to choose from, and those did not have similar range and quality. These anthologies, created in the spirit of Anglican tolerance and respect for literary history, transformed him.

Part of the transformation adhered in the incremental advance on Dilworth's moral agenda. Like the *Speller*, both readers articulated the mainstream Protestant program highlighted on Murray's title page: to "inculcate SOME OF THE MOST IMPORTANT PRINCIPLES OF PIETY AND VIRTUE," particularly diligence in work and the acquisition of knowledge. The axiomatic words of wisdom and moral guidance had their impact, and Lincoln later reworked occasional phrases into original and stylish effectiveness. "We should cherish sentiments of charity towards all men" became "with malice toward none with charity for all." The affirmation that men are "near allied / To angels on thy better side" added another version of the conventional Christian view of human nature that contributed to "the better angels of our nature."

For the first time, he found combinations of language and meaning that provided support for the emergence of his own ideas on what were to be the major concerns of his adult life. Lord Mansfield's words to Parliament in 1770, "True liberty . . . can only exist when justice is equally administered to all," and the eighteenth-century poet William Cowper's "Indignant sentiments on . . . slavery" and race prejudice, decrying slavery in the British Empire and, by implication, in the United States, had to rivet an inquiring mind to the issues of his immediate world. Slavery, Cowper writes, is "most to be deplor'd, / As human nature's broadest, foulest blot" in which "The nat'ral bond / of brotherhood is sever'd" by one who "finds his fellow guilty of a skin / Not colour'd like his own." Lincoln's reading of Demosthenes' speech to the Athenians, exhorting them to perform heroically like the men of the previous generation, became the anchor of Lincoln's emphasis on the difficulty of living up to the achievements of the heroes of the American Revolutionary period. And what did Lincoln make of Scott's inclusion seriatim of Publius Scipio's speech to the Roman army and Hannibal's speech to the Carthaginian army as they are about to do battle, each spurring his soldiers on with the high rhetoric of noble purpose and the blessing of the gods? When each side believes God is on its side, how are we are to ascertain whose side God is on? This was a question Lincoln returned to in a more perilous time for himself and his country.

The anthologies provided the intellectual groundwork on which to advance his cautious and reasoning temperament: Hugh Blair on moral philosophy, David Hume on history, Edward Gibbon on the Roman Empire, Samuel Johnson on Joseph Addison's style, Laurence Sterne on benevolence, and Alexander Pope on the "Great Chain of Being." He found in these readings antidotes to Protestant emotionalism, which valued religious enthusiasm more than Enlightenment rationalism. "Do you count it no merit, no service to mankind, to deliver them from the frauds and fetters of priestcraft, from the deliriums of fanaticism, and from the terrors and follies of superstition?" The answer John Locke provides in this dialogue with John Bayle is that "the root of these evils . . . was false religion." True religion values reason and evidence rather than irrational enthusiasm. Lincoln was now in touch with the temperament of the European Enlightenment. "We ought to distrust our passions, even when they appear the most reasonable," one of Scott's authors declares. And these were writers who gave high value to intellect, to language and reason as a process of discovering and understanding the world, including human nature. Most of them denied the supernatural, within or outside Scripture. Reason, logic, and evidence were the guides to truth.

Lincoln had no argument with Pope's evocation in "The Universal Prayer" of the "Father of All! In every age, / In ev'ry clime ador'd, / By saint, by savage, and by sage, / Jehovah, Jove, or Lord!" There was a universal God of order, reason, and equity. God in the abstract was not in doubt. Miracle and transcendence were. And though the strands of Enlightenment thought had room for variety and divergence, from Johnson's Anglicanism to Hume's rationalistic naturalism, the prevailing synthesis, which Lincoln absorbed, emphasized a combination of Christian ethics, classical style, and natural law. It assumed that the power that made the universe had placed in it certain "self-evident truths." There could be disagreement about some of the truths and about which to emphasize, but not about their existence. Like numbers of the writers he read, his skeptical mind never lost faith that justice eventually would triumph, that human nature was in essence good, and that the human community was progressing toward a better future.

The Enlightenment, which in general affirmed optimism, "for a cheerful countenance betokens a good heart," also contained a streak of melancholy. The mood turns, the mask changes. All-absorbing melancholy becomes temporarily the dominant theme. For a youth given to dark moods, Thomas Gray's "Hymn to Adversity" would have struck home, even if its high-flown intensity overtopped even Lincoln's worse moments: "And Melancholy, silent maid, / With leaden eye, that loves the ground. . . . With screaming Horror's funeral cry, / Despair, and fell Disease, and ghastly Poverty. / Thy form benign, Oh, Goddess! wear." Reading a poem on the death of an infant in which the dead child speaks, Lincoln heard the lament of a world with high rates of childhood mortality. It contributed to a vision of life he found compelling, and he may have thought of his infant brother who had died in 1812: "To the dark and silent tomb, / Soon I hastened from the womb. . . . / All our gaity is vain, / All our laughter is but pain."

Gray's most anthologized poem, "Elegy Written in a Country Church-Yard," became one of the formative poems of Lincoln's sense of himself and his position in life. As with many of the poems he read during these years, he memorized it. Having discovered it at an age early enough to be deeply impressed, he was also old enough to feel how closely connected were its themes to his concerns about himself and what he might become. The "Elegy" memorializes the failure of talent and ambition to overcome obscure birth in a society with little social mobility. It is a stoic affirmation of the likely fate of the lowborn. Lincoln saw in the country boy's obscure station and gloomy temperament a mirror image of himself; his own and his family's history was also one of "homely joys and destiny obscure." And even if Elizabeth Crawford took seriously his ambition to be president, he had at best a small chance of writing a life story for himself that would transcend "the short and simple annals of the poor," the fate of "a youth to fortune and to fame unknown." He may have feared that the fate of the "rustic moralist," whom "melancholy" had marked "for her own," prophesied his own likely end.

And at some moments and moods the "Elegy" had to have been a haunting warning about where his ambition might lead, what its likely end might be. "The paths of glory lead but to the grave" is a finely expressed universal truism that made its mark on him. Ambition is dangerous, all accomplishment temporary. At the same time, he believed that America provided an important variant on the universal birthright. He had no desire to avoid "the madding crowd's ignoble strife" and he strongly desired to escape the constraints of country poverty. British class rigidity underlay Gray's sense of human limitation. America offered more. While Lincoln embraced as his own the melancholy of the "Elegy, " he did not share, as a young man, its dark stoicism. Like his young country, he had an alternative vision of class mobility and the opportunity for people to rise in the world. He was in the rising mode, but how to do so was very much in question.

The poetry from his Indiana years expressed his satiric rather than his melancholic side, and Elizabeth Crawford recalled that "Abe wrote a good Composition—wrote prose and poetry." He regularly wrote essays, which he showed to Nat Grigsby. "He has often shown and read to me his first Composition he prized it highly—it was full of witt . . . informed me that he was about fourteen years old when he wrote it," a friend of a few years later recalled. Poetry was much in his thoughts, as reader and writer. "The Poetry of Abe was good—witty—&c as said by all who read it," Grigsby remembered. Quick to be sharp-tongued in speech and in writing, he found that satiric bite came easily to him. The squibs he entered into the notebook he kept between 1824 and 1826 expressed the usual self-satisfied adolescent cleverness, part of the smart-alecky school-boy inheritance from generation to generation. "Abraham Lincoln is my name / And with my pen I wrote the same / I wrote in both hast and speed / and left it here for fools to read" conveys the tone and adolescent cuteness. By 1828, the nineteen-year-old "was the best penman in the Neighborhood," a friend, Joseph Richardson, later observed, by which he meant that he had a facility with written language. Richardson, who thought Lincoln "exceedingly studious," recalled an example that Lincoln had written in Richardson's notebook that was more resonant than the earlier squibs, though equally unoriginal: "Good boys who to their books apply; will all be great Men by and by." Lincoln took the maxim seriously.

The standards for effective writing that he learned, particularly clarity and wit, were avowed explicitly in some of the essays in Murray and Scott. Johnson's "Character of Addison as a Writer" and Thomas Fitzosborne's "On Grace in Writing" argued for a combination of naturalness and wit. Few of the selections in either anthology could appeal to Lincoln's comic and satiric side. But Pope's "Humorous Complaint to Dr. Arbuthnot, of the Impertinence of Scribblers" and William Cowper's "Facetious History of John Gilpin" had to have riveted his attention. Pope's satiric couplets provided an example of the power of wit that would have impressed a young man eager to transcend the commonplace. The fast-paced, comic, down-to-earth narrative of Cowper's "John Gilpin," with its runaway horse and evocation of a small community's activities, with a chase scene and wryly comic ending, belonged to a genre that had popular appeal and seemed familiar to a frontier society. Lincoln made use of its three-three metrical pattern and some of its narrative features in a poem he wrote years later, "The Bear Hunt."

A painful family situation provoked him into satiric expression. In 1826 his sister Sarah married Aaron Grigsby, the son of a neighboring family. Noted for her amiability, Sarah was widely liked and praised. When she died in childbirth in January 1828, her death revived Abraham's pain at the loss of his mother. The family believed that Sarah might have been saved had a doctor been called immediately. Grieving and angry, he accused Aaron Grigsby of culpability. The resulting bitterness, "a Kind of quarrel," became exacerbated in April 1829 when none of the Lincolns were invited to the wedding party that Josiah Crawford orchestrated for the marriage of two of Aaron's brothers, Reuben and Charles. The record is unclear as to whether Lincoln connived to have each brother brought to the bedroom intended for the other as a hostile joke or whether the mix-up occurred for other reasons. The incident became the subject of ridicule in the Pigeon Creek community. Lincoln intensified the Grigsby family's humiliation by writing a verse account of the incident, sarcastically titled "The Chronicles of Reuben." Some contemporaries claimed to recall occasional stanzas. It may have been part prose and part verse. "The Satire was good—sharp—cutting," Nat Grigsby later remarked, "and showed the Genius of the boy: it hurt us. . . ." The neighbors "burst their sides with laughter," Dennis Hanks remembered.

Years later, Elizabeth Crawford, blushing, recalled some of the lines and insisted on communicating them through an intermediary. "The Poem is Smutty and I can't tell it to you—will tell it to my daughter in law: she will tell her husband and he shall send it to you." The humor of the poem was profane and obscene, a semi-doggerel version of the barn-yard anecdotes that became a staple of Lincoln's storytelling. From the start, he was attracted to off-color jokes. Earthy, naturalistic, and frank, he told stories and used language considered appropriate only for male ears. His comic depiction of what happens when two people of the same sex are bedded has a heterodox clarity that reveals his familiarity with bodily realities and a subversive edge that provides a touch of titillation.

John Romaine recalled one verse: "Reuben & Charles have married 2 girls / But Billy has married a boy . . . Billy and natty agree very well / Mamma is pleased with the match. / The Egg is laid but won't hatch." And Billy, another Grigsby son, is told by the woman who has rejected his marriage proposal, "you Cursed ball head / My Suitor you never Can be / besides your low Croch proclaims you a botch / and that never Can anser for me."

Sterility, impotence, and physical inadequacy, subjects rarely discussed in the Victorian parlor, were suitable but scandalous ploys in the kind of rough satire that Lincoln wrote, and jokes about such subjects were part of the usual repartee of male frontier life. There was nothing pure, let alone refined, about the young writer. He took great pleasure in the literary low road. It suited the time, the situation, and the audience. As part of its appeal, the "Chronicles" flouted decorum in the tradition of Carnival, when license is granted to speak and act transgressively. Mock marriages were a staple of the discourse, and Lincoln apparently enjoyed the widely expressed frontier humor about same-sex relationships.

If his own sexuality made him anxious, there is no sign of that. Approaching twenty years of age, he was shy with women and consumed with work, study, and ambition. Courting and marriage were beyond his pocketbook and his intention. Though attracted to pretty women, he had a keen sense of the impracticality of a studious young man, with no means of support, marrying. In Scott, he read "Adam and Eve's Morning Hymn" and "Evening in Paradise Described," from Milton's *Paradise Lost*, idyllic presentations of marital bliss before the fall. Marriage could also, he noticed, be hell. Its comically subversive depiction in "Chronicles of Reuben" segued into the three courtship relationships he was to have in the next fifteen years, embodying Romantic angst, semi-comic hesitation, and debilitating anxiety.

Drawing on frontier humor, on the tall tale as a characteristic Western genre, with a touch of Aesop's fables and mock biblical chronicle, and on satiric wit honed by his reading of poems such as "John Gilpin," the young writer vented his anger at the Grigsbys through verse. At the same time, he reveled in the pleasure of literary creation. It was revenge with the pen, and it was a satisfying exhibition of his talent to a community to whom low verse and doggerel rhyme would have seemed the height of literary wit. His poem was anonymously distributed, and its authorship immediately identified. He may have enjoyed the praise of his readers and the act of writing it enough to have written a few more such satires, as some of his contemporaries recollected. But "this was . . . the first production that I know of that made us feel that Abe was truly & realy *some*. This called the attention of the People to Abe intellectually," Richardson remarked. "The production was witty & showed talent—it marked the boy—as a man." There was now no doubt that they had a prodigy among them, and one with a talent for the literary low road, for common speech and down-to-earth language, for obscenity and comic frankness, as well as for intellectual intensity and Enlightenment rationality.

Lincoln identified with both melancholy and laughter. Lyric poets such as Gray provided touchstones for mood and self-definition. The satiric voice spoke through Pope and Cowper. Issues of concern were given language by the Enlightenment writers. But the writer he most fully absorbed was Shakespeare. The selections in Scott's anthology he savored in his mouth and heart, and he committed many to memory. Though some years later he had an edition of Shakespeare, between 1825 and 1830 he had only what Scott provided. Consequently, he knew little to nothing about the plays themselves other than what these selections conveyed, probably an advantage to someone who read slowly and repeatedly, gifted at getting the most quality out of the least quantity. Here was a master of language, of the human situation, and of human nature to learn from. Later, when he took the opportunity to become a regular theatergoer in Washington, rarely missing a Shakespeare production, he readily confessed that he preferred his own readings in the theater of his mind to those of professional actors. What Shakespeare's lines sounded like, and the best way to recite them, became settled in his mind from his first exposure.

Scott's fifteen Shakespeare dialogues and soliloquies from eight plays were uniquely fitted to Lincoln's concerns. Some of them taught the pitfalls of ambition-driven pride. On that subject, about which Lincoln became thoughtfully ambivalent, Cardinal Wolsey in *Henry VIII* speaks eloquently: "I charge thee, fling away ambition . . . Farewell, a long farewell to all my greatness!" The cardinal warns against ambition because "the paths of glory lead but to the grave" but also because high ambition often distorts values and endangers the well-being of society. How much ambition is appropriate and to what end was a riveting topic for an introspective, ambitious young man eager to rise in the world. Shakespeare assured him that overweening ambition leads to an inevitable fall. The cardinal's is from the king's grace. Compliant in a system in which the king can do no wrong, he inevitably blames himself, not the king. All Scott's selections on the subject, which include King Henry's soliloquy from *Henry IV, Part I*, "Uneasy lies the head that wears a crown," and King Richard's soliloquy before his final battle in *Richard III*, extended into dramatic example what Lincoln had absorbed in his earlier textbooks: that ambition is a two-edged sword. It could be used in Christian humility, serving virtue and the larger good, or it could assert the egomania of the narcissistic self, a manifestation of the sin of self-glorification. And he could not have missed the point of Hotspur's bombastic, boastful, incendiary speech in *Henry IV* in support of conspiratorial rebellion and honor as self-glorification. That could have been many a Southern voice in the 1850s and 1860s.

Falstaff's "Soliloquy on Honor," an embodiment of another of Lincoln's preoccupations, contributed a witty exposure of the uses and misuses of honor as a rationale for action. The portly knight, who concludes that honor cannot preserve what he most values, his physical life, represents an aspect of human nature that Lincoln came to understand well. Later he made reference to and joked about his own lack of physical courage. In contrast, Henry V's exhortations at Agincourt and Othello's "Apology for his Marriage" offered examples of the Renaissance view of honor as virtue, requiring bravery, truthfulness, and self-sacrifice. By family and culture, and now by self-education, Lincoln was developing an image of

himself as honorable. He had taken George Washington as his most revered American historical model. Scott's selection from Joseph Addison's *Tragedy of Cato*, Washington's favorite play, added a Roman hero,
a widely admired eighteenth-century exemplification of civic virtue, to
Lincoln's pantheon. "Sempronius's Speech for War" and "Lucius's Speech
for Peace," from Addison's play, made their impression. Years later, Lincoln echoed, as he proposed to "bind up the nation's wounds . . . for his
widow and his orphan," Lucius's plea for peace—"Already have our quarrels fill'd the world / With widows and with orphans."

Hamlet the character and *Hamlet* the play became a permanent part of
his consciousness. Scott provided him with three of *Hamlet*'s most tren-
chant soliloquies. One expressed what became Lincoln's view of how
lines should be read and a play acted. Hamlet advises the "players" to
"O'erstep not the modesty of nature," and states his criteria for effective public performance: balance, temperance, and restraint, even in the
expression of passion, and a naturalistic performance style, holding "the
mirror up to nature." Lincoln set similar standards for his own speeches.
Some of them, like his second inaugural address, were to be Shakespearean soliloquies of a sort. In an age when histrionic performance was the
norm, his development of a naturalistic style occurred under the influence of Scott's and Murray's Shakespeare selections.

Hamlet's other two soliloquies in Scott did Lincoln great service: "To
be or not to be" and Claudius on the murder of his brother, "Oh! My offence is rank; it smells to heaven." In two personal crises, Ann Rutledge's
death and his courtship of Mary Todd, suicide had verbal presence for
Lincoln in Hamlet's lines. And, during his presidency, Claudius's soliloquy came frequently to mind, in reference to his own "offences," at least
in moments in which he thought it possible the war might not be worth
so much Southern and Northern blood. Was the war not also a form of
self-murder, brother against brother, which, as a Southerner by birth,
Lincoln could especially feel? "What if this cursed hand / Were thicker
than itself with brother's blood— /Is there not rain enough . . . ?" Like
Claudius, he hoped that, despite the bloodshed, "All may be well."

To conclude his selections, Scott provided pithy examples from his preferred models—particularly Shakespeare, Pope, Johnson, Blair, Demosthenes, and Montaigne—of how to use language economically and effectively. They stress eighteenth-century rhetorical devices such as antitheses, enumeration, interrogation, and climax, which became elements in Lincoln's style. But his schooling in the relationship between language and human nature went much beyond such rhetorical devices. And though he never became an eloquent speaker mechanically, he did become a self-taught intellectual who could speak well and write brilliantly. Two of the poetic maxims from Pope that Scott includes, "True ease in writing comes from art, not chance" and "Two principles in human nature reign, / Self-love to urge, and reason to restrain," express the fundamentals of Lincoln's art and mind. Indeed, Scott included as his premier example of "the Principle Emotions and Passions" Hamlet's soliloquy, "What a piece of work is man! How noble in reason. . . ." No matter how powerful the appeal of bombast, moodiness, and melancholy, Lincoln found in his Enlightenment models and in Shakespeare the affirmation of his tested but sustained faith in man's reasoning faculty as his highest and in reason's power to advance good works.

The people whom he observed and who observed him in his first sixteen years provided, years later, a fragmentary record of the type of person he had seemed to them. Clever, perceptive, observant; stubborn, witty, studious; moody, withdrawn, restless, ambitious; and always reading— came to their memories. He was rustic in dress and etiquette but not in intellect and analysis. As a boy and young man, his eagerness and ability to be at ease with people dominated, and often overcame, his shyness. He liked to talk about issues and ideas, about reading and knowledge. He told stories, many of them colloquial and funny, some obscene, to make a point and persuade. Quotations from his favorite writers, especially the Bible, Aesop, and Shakespeare, were always at hand, useful in the interplay between what he learned about human nature from his reading and what he learned from observation and direct experience. There may have been verbal flights of fancy, but his acculturating tendency was toward the laconic. Precision, brevity, and plain speech became his characteristic style. Local Indiana speech had special colloquial power. The young man grasped and embraced that. It emphasized the demotic language that eventually, as the nineteenth century progressed, became the literary language of America, the gradual burgeoning of a consensus that a practical people could create a literature that took its linguistic values from the distinctive features of American speech.

By late summer 1826, he had taken his elongated seventeen-year-old frame beyond Pigeon Creek to Rockport, on the Ohio River, where he became part of the larger world of commerce. With his cousin Dennis and his stepbrother-in-law Squire Hall, he left the Lincoln family farm, intending to cut wood to sell to steamboats on the river, to be paid either in cash or merchandise. His labor was not needed at home between planting and harvesting. He got work poling a ferry across the Anderson River at its entrance to the Ohio for six dollars a month, lodging with the proprietor. In his spare time, using his skills as the son of a carpenter, he built a rowboat and created a small business transferring passengers between the riverboats and the shore. Two men he rowed to a steamer each tossed him a silver half-dollar. That he could earn so much in so little time startled him. When two brothers brought him before the local justice of the peace, claiming he had infringed their exclusive right to ferry passengers, he was even more startled. Since he had not carried people across but only to a boat already on the river, the suit was dismissed.

Two years later, he embraced an opportunity to extend his experience from Rockport to New Orleans, the city of commerce and Carnival, the port of entry and exit for thousands of settlements in the Mississippi and Ohio river valleys. Goods and people traveled mostly by river. The journey equaled the longest he was ever to take, a trip to an exotic land where French was widely spoken and into the heart of the slave states. It was his most intense, extended exposure to an institution that had a real but only peripheral presence in the part of Kentucky where he had been born.

Employed by a neighbor, James Gentry, a trader and store owner whose business was mostly by barter, to transport goods to New Orleans, he knew the large Gentry family well. The Gentrys' eldest son, Matthew, a former schoolmate, had struck terror into all their hearts. Without warning, he became violent and attempted to kill his parents. His permanent madness became a touchstone for Lincoln of the unpredictability of human nature at its extremes. The power of reason had its dark side, its demented inversion. After almost twenty years of brooding about what he had witnessed, Lincoln described Matthew Gentry's madness in a poem that resembles Wordsworth in tone, diction, and balladic meter, and even in the coincidence of the name of the boy: "Poor Matthew! Once of genius bright,— / A fortune-favored child— / Now locked for aye, in mental night, / A haggard mad-man wild." To Lincoln, he was "an object more of dread, / Than ought the grave contains." Matthew's madness set up a mirror into which Lincoln gazed, looking for signs of his own potential collapse.

With another of Gentry's sons, Allen, he prepared (and probably helped build) a flatboat about sixty feet long and twenty wide. Loaded with cargo, it departed from Rockport in December 1828. Lincoln and Gentry were entrusted to sell goods, primarily corn, oats, beans, and cured meats, and return with cash and/or supplies. The 2,400-mile round trip took almost three months. It was a hefty responsibility, testifying to the early onset of adulthood on the frontier and the high regard James Gentry had for the maturity of the two young men. The physical demands of the boat kept them constantly at work, except for turns sleeping. Along the Mississippi, they traded at plantations eager to barter Gentry's provisions for cotton, tobacco, and sugar, which could readily be sold in New Orleans. The flatboat was a floating small-scale nineteenth-century grocery store. In Louisiana, below Baton Rouge, "seven negroes" attacked them "with intent to kill and rob them," Lincoln wrote in a brief autobiography in 1860. "They were hurt some in the melee, but succeeded in driving the negroes from the boat, and then 'cut cable' 'weighed anchor' and left." Gentry's wife recalled that "Abe fought the

Negroes—got them off the boat—pretended to have guns—had none—the Negroes had hickory Clubs—my husband said 'Lincoln get the guns and Shoot—the Negroes took alarm and left." The incident left an impression strong enough for Lincoln to highlight it in 1860 in a document, with otherwise little such detail, composed when feelings about black-white relations were divisively raw and his every word on the subject closely scrutinized. The thieves, apparently, were slaves, not free blacks.

After selling the remainder of the cargo in New Orleans, they had time to observe the colorful urban scene bright in a warm southern winter so different from the winter they had left behind. There were hundreds of tall sailing ships; a marketplace with a variety of goods larger, more colorful, and more exotic than they had ever seen; people of various social classes dressed in fashions entirely new to them; raunchy, sensual street life and entertainments; black faces everywhere in numbers larger than they had ever experienced; and the slave market. "We stood and watched the slaves sold in New Orleans," Gentry is reported to have said, "and Abraham was very angry." The evidence for his anger at the slave market is thin: the report is thirdhand and was made after his death. Whatever he felt, most likely his presence at the slave market brought to mind the depiction of slavery in James Riley's *Narrative*.

A year later, the almost twenty-one-year-old Lincoln made one of the determinative trips of his life, his last substantial act of fealty to his family. Thomas Lincoln had decided to migrate again. John Hanks, a first cousin of Nancy Hanks, had moved to Illinois, which had become in 1818 the twenty-first state of the union. Describing an agricultural paradise, his glowing letters prompted Dennis Hanks, now married to Lincoln's stepsister Elizabeth and the father of five children, to make an exploratory visit. Eager for what Illinois offered, Dennis decided to join John Hanks in Decatur, a small town on the Sangamon River in south-central Illinois. Squire Hall, the husband of Lincoln's stepsister Matilda, shared their enthusiasm. With her two daughters, two sons-in-law, and six grandchildren about to emigrate, Sarah Lincoln persuaded her husband to join the exodus. The move had little economic justification. Thomas Lincoln's farm and carpentry had flourished: the sale of his eighty acres, a bumper crop of corn, more than five hundred pigs and other animals, and the sale or barter of all their non-transportable possessions provided animals and vehicles for the wagon trip and about five hundred dollars in cash. It was the most wealth fifty-four-year-old Thomas had ever had.

Bidding farewell to friends they had made during thirteen years, the family, in wagons pulled by oxen and horses, left Pigeon Creek, Indiana, in early March 1830. After staying with Hanks family relatives at a town called Paradise, they arrived in Decatur, in Macon County, Illinois, on the north bank of the narrow, shallow Sangamon River, about the middle of the month. Clearing ten acres about ten miles northwest of town, they established legal title and planted corn. Soon the extended family built a cabin, barn, and smokehouse for Thomas Lincoln. The same was done for the Dennis Hanks and the John Hanks families. To earn cash, Abraham cleared fields for neighbors, splitting thousands of rails to make fences. In the fall "all hands were greatly afflicted with augue and fever, to which they had not been used, and by which they were greatly discouraged." During a winter of extraordinarily heavy snow, they discussed moving back to Indiana.

Capable as he was, Lincoln rebelled at the notion that manual labor was his destiny. In Pigeon Creek he had gotten a copy of the 1824 edition of *The Revised Laws of Indiana*, containing also the federal and state constitutions, the Declaration of Independence, a brief history of Indiana, and assorted other documents, probably from a neighbor who recalled that "he was apt to be talking about what he had read and would Sometimes quote nice pieces of Prose & Poetry." The law had a special appeal to him as a commentary on human nature and a set of rules with the appearance of rational application. But he had no credentials other than disparate reading, a thoughtful character, and common sense. In the summer he made a political speech, advocating that the Sangamon River be made navigable with public funds, an anti-Jacksonian position. "I turned down a box or Keg," John Hanks recalled, "and Abe made his Speech. The other man was a Candidate—Abe wasn't. Abe beat him to death. . . . The man after the Speech was through took Abe aside and asked him where he had learned So much. . . . Abe Explained, Stating his manner & method of reading and what he had read: the man Encouraged Lincoln to persevere." Literate, articulate, physically distinctive, he had a noticeable presence. And his youth was not a liability in a society in which men took on responsibilities early and died young.

Still, the only way to earn money was with his hands and back. And though he never made a reference to the timing or motivation for leaving his father's household, it seems likely that he had for some time been contemplating separation. Now, twenty-one years old, having assisted with the move to Illinois and with no local opportunities for self-improvement, he left his family home. Not a dramatic break, it had the appearance of another work jaunt. A loudmouthed, restless, and entrepreneurial merchant from Springfield, Denton Offutt, came to Decatur to ask John Hanks, who had a reputation from his Kentucky days as a flatboat man, to establish a boat enterprise for him, transporting his goods to New Orleans. Hanks "went & saw Abe & Jno Johnson . . . introduced Offutt to them," Hanks recalled. "We made an Engagement with Offutt . . . to make the trip to N Orleans," with Offutt accompanying them. Since the March thaw made land travel difficult, "Abe & I Came down the Sangamon River in a Canoe in March 1831." Flowing westerly, the river could be navigated only by canoe or rowboat from Decatur to Springfield. Beyond, as it turned from west to northwest, were a number of towns eager for the river to be made navigable for commercial transportation. At one of them, New Salem, it had been dammed and a sawmill opened by a tavern keeper, James Rutledge, who had founded the village in 1829. Farther along, at Beardstown, the Sangamon joined the Illinois River, which flowed into the Mississippi. With mostly impassable dirt roads in a pre-railroad decade, how to make the river navigable to Beardstown preoccupied public discourse in south-central Illinois.

Offutt envisioned that there was money to be made if he could procure a boat and crew to transport his goods to more reliable waters. When the boat he had intended to buy proved unavailable, his new employees agreed to build him a flatboat at a convenient place seven miles northwest of Springfield, near New Salem. They were to be paid twelve dollars a month each for their work. Lincoln, who had experience building such boats, was eager. The immediate challenge was to cut timber at the mouth of a creek, float the logs to the river, have the lumber cut, score it, and build and stock the boat. With his boots, coat, and hat off, his pants rolled up to his knees, his shirt wet with sweat, combing his lank black hair "with his fingers as he pounded away on the boat," Lincoln told jokes as they worked, so Dennis Hanks remembered. He also did the camp cooking at a "shantee-shed" they built. At the end of April 1831, the boat was ready. As the four men pushed and pulled it past New Salem, it stuck on the mill dam. When it began taking on water, townspeople gathered to watch the tense spectacle. Lincoln organized the removal of the cargo, transferring it to a borrowed boat. After working through the night, they rolled the remaining barrels to the prow, tipping the boat downward over the edge of the dam. When they bored a small hole for the water to pour out, the boat lifted and then slid down into free water.

Having seen more of New Salem than they had intended, they navigated the thirty miles to Beardstown on the shallow river. "We Kept our victuals & in fact Slept down in the boat—at one End—went down by a Kind of ladder through a scuttle hole," John Hanks remembered. "We used planks as Sails—& Cloth—Sometimes." At Beardstown, "people Came out & laughed at us." On the wider, deeper Illinois, they sailed, rowed, and drifted into the Mississippi. Soon they passed Alton and St. Louis. By late May, Lincoln, who stayed for a full month, was in New Orleans for the second and last time. Hanks, who had turned back at St. Louis, later reported that "there it was we Saw Negroes Chained—maltreated—whipt & scourged. Lincoln Saw it—his heart bled . . . was thoughtful & abstracted—I Can say Knowingly that it was on this trip

that he formed his opinions of Slavery." Hanks cannot have been reporting as an eyewitness. Anyway, Lincoln, who spent June 1831 in the Cres-
cent City, already viewed slavery as unjust. He could not have been anything but pained by the degradation of the public slave market.

Apparently, he had no thought of staying in New Orleans or seeking his
fortune eastward or westward. Even St. Louis, a city that would have provided western familiarity and urban opportunity, did not tempt him. His
reading and intellectual curiosity had exposed him to the attractions and
opportunities of a sophisticated world. With some money in his pocket
and no family obligations, he could have gone anyplace, but he was, so to
speak, a local man; he had no desire to be a sophisticate or a cosmopo-
lite or to see the world. The reading at the core of his self-education had,
however, provided hints of direction. And he now had a personal style, a
manner of expressing himself. His literacy distinguished him noticeably.
Being able to write was a skill of use when illiterate friends and neighbors
needed letters written or documents copied. But, in mid-summer 1831,
he had few friends nearby, and no neighbors or family, unless he chose to
live with or near his parents in Cole County.

Unsurprisingly, he soon established himself in an alternate version of
the Pigeon Creek community, as if he felt his Western identity crucial
to being comfortable with himself and the world. In July 1831, at the
urging of Denton Offutt, he went back to New Salem, which he had seen
mostly from a flatboat for one day, to manage, at a salary of fifteen dollars a month, a retail grocery store that Offutt was opening. Like most
such stores, it would be an all-purpose emporium, stocking everything
that might sell, including whiskey. It was a noticeable cut above what he
had done before. A carpenter-farmer's son, he now became a clerk, an
occupation that required literacy and arithmetical capability. By itself, it
did not bring either a change in social status or wealth, but it brought him
into the mercantile world, into an occupation commensurate with the
values and principles of his Whig mentality. And it placed him in town

life, in a service and commercial economy, rather than in the country. He was never again to earn his living by manual labor, and thereafter he rubbed shoulders daily with neighbors, a life considerably more social than what he had been used to.

At Offutt's store he got to know the twenty-five families of New Salem and the nearby farming families the village served. Hand-wrestling was a popular sport. Forced by a challenge into combat with local toughs from nearby Clary's Grove, he held his own with their leader in a heavily wagered wrestling match. That he was a capable young man with an interest in ideas, politics, people, and getting ahead was widely noticed. His reputation as a storyteller quickly came into place. In the August local and congressional election, he voted for the first time, serving as a clerk of the election board when the regular clerk became ill and it became known that he could write. He began accepting requests to take letters at dictation, creating sales agreements and receipts, and signing as witness to deeds. New acquaintances provided a social and intellectual circle. William Greene, three years his junior, assisting him at the grocery where they both slept on the floor, became a lifelong friend. Three of the town's influential senior citizens took an interest in him: Mentor Graham, the schoolmaster; James Rutledge, who soon sold his mill to Offutt and moved his family to the countryside nearby; and Bowling Green, an amiable, educated, rotund justice of the peace who took a paternal interest in Lincoln, allowing him to speak up at court sessions. Rutledge had founded a debating club at which Lincoln became a regular participant. Most of the topics were political, and he had definite views.

Having approached insolvency once too often, Offutt's enterprises failed in March 1832. At the same time, New Salem celebrated the arrival of a steamboat from Beardstown, the first successful attempt to bring a large boat upriver, an entrepreneurial gamble by a businessman who shared the widely held view that the town had a great future if goods could be transported by river to the Mississippi Valley market. Lincoln and others broke ice and cleared snags, navigating the steamboat through the narrow river obstacles. The celebration proved premature. Without widening, straightening, and dredging, the Sangamon was not reliably viable for steamboats. The sponsor of the enterprise, one of whose notes Lincoln had endorsed, declared bankruptcy. Despite a judgment against him, Lincoln was not penalized for nonpayment. It was clear, though, that only extensive, costly improvements could make the river navigable. Private capital would not do it.

That same month, Lincoln, who needed no arm twisting, put his name in as a candidate for the state legislature from Sangamon County in the election scheduled for August 1833. Candidates did not run as party designees or even with party identification. Each of the thirteen candidates for the four positions in effect nominated himself. Lincoln's platform combined entrepreneurial values and bombastic patriotism. It had local application to south-central Illinois. And it had national resonance. But in addition to the relevant issues at hand, he needed something equally important—a style, a voice, a way of expressing himself, in print and before audiences, that would establish his distinction, that would be characteristically and effectively a representation of who he was and how he wanted his audience to know him. He could imitate various styles of speech, from didactic sermons to overheated political oratory; he had read great speeches from the classical world and the British Parliament; he had a good feel and a natural propensity for the colloquial voice and the plainness of American diction; and, most of all, he admired clarity of presentation, the application of reason and logic to the challenge of persuasion. All the elements for a distinctive style were coming into place. In his first public statement, which the *Sangamo Journal* published in mid-March 1832 under the title "Communication to the People of Sangamo County," he made a tentative step in that direction.

Lincoln's argument for his candidacy was detailed, precise, and cohesive. Emotional exhortation suited neither his temperament nor his models of public address. He argued at length his case for internal improvements. If pitched at too intellectual a level for the average voter, it was only slightly so; and his sponsors and supporters had Whig, not Jeffersonian, proclivities. "I believe the improvement of the Sangamo river, to be vastly important and highly desirable to the people of this county," he wrote, "and if elected, any measure in the legislature having this for its object, which may appear judicious, will meet my approbation, and shall receive my support." He also argued against exorbitant interest rates, for appropriations for "a moderate education" for everyone so that all citizens may "be able to read the histories of his own and other countries, by which he may duly appreciate the value of our free institutions," and "that we must not too readily tamper with existing laws, for it is probable" (though not always certain, he implies) that "the framers of those laws were wiser than myself." This was an early statement of his characteristic conservatism in regard to precedent and the wisdom of the framers.

If there is a degree of ponderousness in his style, it expressed the strain of a self-taught man to appear qualified for the office he sought. Enlightenment standards of good writing and logical discourse influenced his sentence structure and his diction. And in the shorthand of argument, he also revealed his conservative respect for the "wisdom of mankind," for the value of the lessons that widespread human experience has taught. "Time and experience have verified to a demonstration, the public utility of internal improvements. That the poorest and most thinly populated countries would be greatly benefited. . . ." The final paragraph declares his awareness that in public discourse the rational argument benefits from a touch of the existentially personal.

> But, Fellow-Citizens, I shall conclude. Considering the great degree of modesty which should always attend youth, it is probable I have already been more presuming than becomes me. . . . Every man is said to have his peculiar ambition. Whether it be true or not, I can say for one that I have no other so great as that of being truly esteemed of my fellow men, by rendering myself worthy of their esteem. How far I shall succeed in gratifying this ambition, is yet to be developed. I am young and unknown to many of you. I was born and have ever remained in the most humble walks of life. I have no wealthy or popular relations to recommend me. My case is thrown exclusively upon the independent voters of

this county, and if elected they will have conferred a favor upon me, for which I shall be unremitting in my labors to compensate. But if the good people in their wisdom shall see fit to keep me in the background, I have been too familiar with disappointments to be very much chagrined.

A man who writes like this does so purposefully. He has a strategy. He wants to combine a lucid public prose with an intellectual analysis of issues. And though the analysis requires levels of logic and reason associated with the educated, its effectiveness requires the presence of enough colloquial and common diction to give it the feel of accessibility and to convey the writer's respect for the larger audience. The person behind the argument, the voice embodying the identity that the reader locates as the person whose words he is reading, represents himself as a humble fellow citizen, an unpretentious neighbor whose rational leadership will contribute to the greater good of the community. Slightly stiff in its approach, and a little uneasy in the creation of what is a work in progress, it is unmistakably a strategic, artfully designed statement. Its author is a man who has read Shakespeare, Gray, Addison, Cicero, Lord Mansfield, and Lord Chesterton. He knows enough to have benefited from his mentors without flaunting his credentials as a literate man. The final emphasis provides both prescient self-revelation and touching, self-defensive confession. His ambition was indeed immense, though its motive at least partly pure. And he could have hardly been younger and more unknown. He had no influential sponsors, though his friends in the New Salem establishment were behind him. And if he was "too familiar with disappointments to be very much chagrined" if he lost, he and everyone with any knowledge of human nature knew that he would be deeply disappointed.

A spare, ascetic young man who dressed badly and ate modestly, used to sleeping on floors and counters, whose New Salem friends were generous in small but meaningful ways, Lincoln needed little to support himself. But he needed something. The August election was three months off.

When, in early April 1831, the Sac warrior Black Hawk crossed into Illinois, it was a timely event for Lincoln. His friends and neighbors, none of whom had military experience either, soon elected him, to his surprise and pleasure, captain of their newly formed volunteer militia company. Unlike most, he could read and write and fill out forms, and he stood taller on the ground and in the saddle than anyone else. Like his comrades, he had a stake in Illinois as a white state, a place in which the claims of American citizens to ownership were indisputable. They had purchased the land with sweat and blood, and they would shed blood to keep it.

Such settlers, many from the Scots-Irish and English dissenting world, had brought with them their own scars and tribal memories. They had been formed and sustained by the particularities of their language, by their Anglo-American agricultural tradition, and by the rough-hewn republicanism of the early years of the United States. The Bible was their common referent. So, too, were the Declaration of Independence and the Constitution. George Washington was the Jehovah-like father of them all. Thomas Jefferson and Andrew Jackson provided principles and temperament. Politically, most were what was then known as "Democrats," the party of the working people, especially farmers and immigrants; it had originally been known as the Democratic-Republican Party. A smaller number were about to be Whigs, a new party that espoused the principles of Alexander Hamilton and the Federalists, with a strong emphasis on centralization, economic development, and upward mobility. Jackson's main rival, the Kentuckian Henry Clay, spoke eloquently for them. Whigs tended to be merchants, businessmen, professionals, more dependent than Democrats on cash, banks, and trade. Each party, of course, had its significant share of those who fit the profile of the other. In national politics, the Democrats dominated, especially in the frontier states. Both parties had little to no sympathy for inconvenient Native Americans.

Little blood, in fact, was shed in an Indian war that had in it more panic, racial hostility, incompetence, and disorganization than actual threat to the white settlers and their supremacy. The incursion was a rearguard effort by an impoverished tribe of Northern Plains Indians to return to sacred ground, unwilling to accede to thirty years of treaties whose terms they had accepted under duress or misunderstanding. Under Chief Black Hawk, about four hundred warriors, accompanied by fifteen hundred old men, boys, women, and children, crossed the Mississippi into the tribe's former homeland in northwestern Illinois and southwestern Wisconsin. They wanted to raise corn and worship their ancestral gods at sacred sites in the Rock River Valley, which, years earlier, they had been persuaded to leave. Dispossessed, they always remembered their former possessions, a lost paradise of ancestral familiarity. When pursued and attacked, the Sacs were willing to kill in self-defense. Mostly, they stole horses and provisions in a three-month-long attempt to evade the pursuing Illinois militia and the smaller regular army, whose leaders bungled a conflict that called for a political solution. From early on, outnumbered, aware that he could not achieve his aim, Black Hawk desired to negotiate. Renegade groups from other Indian tribes exacerbated tension by small theft and occasional murder. Quick to envision dispossession by murderous savages, the settlers favored relocation at a minimum, extermination if necessary.

A small catastrophe, initiated by Maj. Isaiah Stillman's militia in mid-May 1831, prolonged an unnecessary war. It also brought Lincoln, for whom it had been a good war, into the presence of bloody corpses. Eager for glory, Stillman's poorly trained Indian-hating soldiers, having learned that the Sacs were moving in the direction of the main encampment, "rushed on them—got frightened—Scared—and got badly whipt." Later in the day, twenty-three-year-old captain Abraham Lincoln, in command of a company of volunteers, found twelve "scalped and mangled" white bodies strewn in disarray on what the day before had been a battlefield. "Heads cut off—heart taken out—& disfigured in Every way," a comrade in arms, Royal Clary, recalled. There were also twenty-five wounded men. Lincoln's response to these mangled corpses is unknown. He had no particular interest in or sympathy for Native Americans. One had killed his grandfather and orphaned his father.

At a time when he needed occupation, with his one career opportunity on hold until the August election, he found employment in the military attractive. When his captaincy expired at the end of the six-week enlistment of the Thirty-first Militia Regiment, he enlisted twice more, as a private in other companies. At first he spent much of his time drilling, sufficiently commanding to be able to control an untrained, rowdy, heavy-drinking company drawn from Sangamon County's 350 volunteers. "He was acquainted with nearly every body," his friend George Harrison recalled. His physical size, strength, and patience distinguished him. Like many of the volunteers, he found army life companionable, despite discomfort and inadequate provision. He had no family responsibilities or farm duties to return to. "We passed our evenings by jumping, playing checkers, chess, swimming our horses, which was a favorite sport when near Rock-river . . . and telling tales, stories &c. &c," Harrison remembered. Lincoln made the acquaintance of men who were to become friends, particularly the Springfield lawyer John Todd Stuart and the Quincy lawyer Orville Browning. He may occasionally have been in the presence of two army officers whose careers later intersected with his own, Zachary Taylor and Albert Sidney Johnston, and of an army colonel, the son of Alexander Hamilton, whose views on national economic policy had already become Lincoln's via Henry Clay.

In late May 1832, his company of New Salem neighbors was mustered out, having continuously marched up and down both sides of the Rock River and adjacent northwestern Illinois in search of the elusive enemy. Lincoln wrote out the muster roll, with explanatory remarks, certifying that it was "a true Statement," then enlisted in a company of mounted volunteers, providing his own arms and horse. In mid-June, this company was also mustered out. He reenlisted for another thirty days in a company that did messenger and scouting service. It came close to battle when it reinforced a unit that had just fought a skirmish northwest of Dixons Ferry. But the small Sac party under Black Hawk retreated and soon disappeared. "The only part we could then act," George Harrison recalled, "was to seek the lost men, and with hatchets and hands to bury them. We buried the white men." The regular army refused to allow the nonprofessional militia to pursue the Indians farther. Colonel Taylor wrote to General Atkinson that "the more I see of the militia the less confidence I have of their effecting any thing of importance." During the summer, helped by Indian allies, the army destroyed Black Hawk's people. Some died fighting. Many were hunted and killed by Sioux, Winnebago, and Menominee Indians. Some drowned fleeing across the Wisconsin and the Mississippi rivers. In September, escorted by a young army officer, Lt. Jefferson Davis, Black Hawk was taken to prison in St. Louis.

Having collected about $175 in service pay, Lincoln canoed down the Illinois River and then walked through sand ridges to New Salem. In the August 1832 election, he placed eighth in a field of thirteen, the first four of whom were elected. He then purchased a share in one of the two grocery stores in New Salem. Within six months, it went bankrupt. Having purchased his share with a promissory note, he was now broke, unemployed, and in debt for a formidable amount of money: $1,100. It remained an irksome obligation for more than ten years, though he was not pressed hard to repay it, let alone threatened with legal action. When the grocery store expired in mid-1833, he did odd jobs, boarding at the home of his friend John Rowan Herndon, from whom he had bought his interest in the failed store, and then with Mentor Graham.

In May 1833, New Salem friends came to his rescue, providing him with a minor patronage job that a vocal supporter of Henry Clay normally would not have gotten. Party lines were still fluid, though, and the position of New Salem postmaster was "too insignificant, to make his politics an objection," the pay of fifty dollars a year so low that competition was nonexistent. At the same time, he developed a more substantial source of income. The county surveyor, who had more work than he could handle, suggested that Lincoln study surveying and become his assistant. With a borrowed textbook and a small field manual, he mastered the subject. A gift for mathematics and a spatial imagination served him well. By the end of the year, he was tracking the countryside, mapping sites, creating serviceable plats, and making more money than he had ever made before. The autodidact now had enough to pay his ongoing expenses. Soon he was so busy surveying that he subcontracted the post-mastership to a friend. His surveying excursions made him a familiar face to those whose votes he had it in mind to ask for.

To no one's surprise, he decided to run in the August 1834 legislative election. Perhaps he could do better this time. When he came in second in a field of thirteen, only fourteen votes behind the absolute leader, he was eligible to take his seat on December 1 at the state capital in Vandalia, one of fifty-five House members entrusted to do the important business of the rapidly growing state. Identifying himself as a member of the new Whig Party, which, supported by dissatisfied Democratic-Republicans, had emerged out of the remains of the Federalist Party, he had a party affiliation and an agenda. He also had unorthodox intellectual and religious ideas, a fact that was well known in New Salem and slightly troublesome. And he had a passion for reading, which he now directed toward the borrowed law books he was determined to master. He had begun to think, prompted by ambition and friendly encouragement, that perhaps he could make the law his profession. The available legal text-books required diligent study more in the nature of the grindstone than of the intellect or imagination. But for that he had other authors at hand. He spent much time reading a volume of Shakespeare, which he carried with him. And two writers new to his experience, Burns and Byron, began to help shape his vision of character, human nature, and society.

CHAPTER 3

Burns, Byron, and Love Letters
1834–1837

As Lincoln settled into his life and duties as a twenty-five-year-old freshman legislator, he needed to attend to both his vocational and personal education. Politics was a far from dependable career. His legislative salary, added to what he continued to earn as a surveyor and his pittance as postmaster, paid his basic bills. But his debt from the failed grocery business weighed heavily on his mind, a vast sum that would somehow have to be paid from an income that had no margin. When, in February 1835, the debt resulted in the attachment of his horse, saddle, and surveying instruments, a friend's kindness restored to him these tools of his livelihood. His New Salem supporters, particularly its senior citizens, respected and liked him enough to want to keep him afloat. There was an extra edge of self-interest among those who stood to benefit from his political career, particularly Springfield boosters eager to have the state capital moved to their city.

Dressed in a new suit he had borrowed money to buy, Lincoln made the two-day stagecoach journey to Vandalia in south-central Illinois for the session that started on December 1, 1834. In the next two and a half months, he survived handsomely his baptismal session. His skills as a speaker, a negotiator, and especially as a writer gave him immediate presence. That he was good with numbers and precise with arithmetic was an asset, the fulfillment of his father's vision of what education was all about. Appointed to the Committee on Public Accounts and Expenditures, he soon proved he had a competence with language, both spoken and written. This made him from the start a clear and welcome voice for the Whig platform advocating appropriations for public works, a government bank, and a school fund, for all of which he had campaigned. His comparatively sophisticated literacy resulted in his committee colleagues turning to him to draft reports. In a world of poor spellers and writers, his skill earned him respect and prominence.

These same skills could help him address his vocational problem—how to earn a living doing work that would fulfill his ambition to rise in the world and advance the satisfaction that he got from political service. He liked speaking. He liked writing. He was a passionate reader. The law seemed the answer. His fellow warrior in the Black Hawk War, John Todd Stuart, now a friend and political colleague practicing law in Springfield, encouraged him. Also a Kentuckian and two years older than Lincoln, Stuart was a college graduate from a well-connected, socially sophisticated Lexington family. New Salem and Springfield were close enough for Lincoln to walk to Stuart's office to borrow legal textbooks—the autodidact at work again, attempting to master the basics of contract law, pleadings, and legal process, and to provide a textbook and casebook foundation for the amateur appearances he had made before justices of the peace in Indiana and now in New Salem, where he was the protégé of Bowling Green. Legal study did not prove easy. He was never to attain the knowledge of basic theory possessed by most graduates of law schools, and he was not to have the equivalent of an apprenticeship or clerkship. Stuart assumed that Lincoln could learn well enough on his own: when there was some presumption of readiness, he would advance.

His friend William Greene, his co-clerk at Offutt's store, recalled that "he generally mastered a book quickly. . . studying & reading." But when, in 1834, he attacked Stuart's law volumes, he found his progress "laborious, and tedious." It seemed the professional equivalent of splitting fence rails. It had to be done, but there was no happiness in doing it. The subject matter appealed exclusively to logic and memory. The borrowed volumes of Blackstone, Chitty, Greenleaf, Storey, and Kent had little in common with the books that had made reading his greatest pleasure. Stuart, the closest observer of Lincoln's legal education, remarked that he "was a schollar from 1835—rather a hard student to 1845." "Work, work, work, is the main thing," Lincoln commented years later. It took him much of ten years to learn the legal rudiments, partly because at the start he relied entirely on books, and because his better-educated law partners allowed him to rely on his obvious assets, his personality, intellect, and rhetorical skills. He never fully mastered the principles of legal research, organization, and application, and he tended to rely on intuition rather than preparation. His colleagues often compensated for his professional flaws.

At the same time, he worked at legislating, politicking, and surveying. He held the post office job until it was discontinued, in May 1836. When he ran for reelection to the legislature that summer, he received the most votes among seventeen candidates. In March his name had been recorded at the Sangamon County Court as a person "of good moral character," with Stuart and others testifying on his behalf. In September 1836 he was approved to practice law in all the courts of the state, and a few weeks later he swore the relevant oaths. The two Supreme Court justices who admitted him to the bar asked no questions. "He was not required to pass any examination. . . . The only requirement for the granting of a license . . . was a certificate procured from the court of some county certifying to the applicant's good moral character."

That he had risen from déclassé clerk to legislator and lawyer in less than five years was an impressive achievement. But it did not speak to his mind or heart. He now began to read two Romantic literary voices that addressed his deepest needs. His passion for Shakespeare, whom "he nearly knew . . . by heart," continued. But during the ten years between his arrival in New Salem and his marriage in 1842, "Burns and Byron [became] his favorite books." "Lincoln read Shakespeare Byron and Burns all extensively while he lived at Salem," William Greene remembered, but "I should say that Burns was his favourite."

The anthologies that provided Lincoln's initial education had brought their readers through the eighteenth century and the mind-set of Enlightenment rationalism. That mind-set sought a balance between chaos and order, melancholy and cheerfulness, self-interest and communal well-being. It promoted restraint and harmony, a balance of interests and powers within the individual and society. From early on, Lincoln identified with the Enlightenment emphasis on rational self-control. A reader of Gibbon on Roman history, Charles Rollin on Middle Eastern and Greek history, and William Grimshaw on the American story, he had begun to envision the American republic as the culminating achievement of the Enlightenment, the fulfillment toward which all political history had tended. In the course of history, the written word, he believed, had become an increasingly significant force in the advancement of humanity, culminating in the Declaration of Independence, in the Constitution, and in the canonical literary achievements from the Bible to Shakespeare to Pope. Lincoln's "Conversation very often was about Books—such as Shakespear & other histories and Tale Books of all Discription in them Day," recalled a New Salem neighbor with whom he sometimes boarded. His own position in life had risen on this tide of literacy, his progress inseparable from his command of language.

From about 1832, Robert Burns became a kindred spirit, Lincoln's daily companion. He was to remain a lifelong passion. Burns's poetry was widely available in Illinois by the 1830s. Single-volume editions had been published in Philadelphia and New York in 1788, with multiple-volume editions beginning in 1801. The large Scots-Irish population cherished Burns's poems of love and sentiment, many of which had been set to music. His folkloristic, storytelling poems, especially those of character and ideas, appealed to Lincoln. With Jack Kelso, a New Salem friend with whom he briefly boarded, "an Educated as well as a well read

Man—deeply & thoroughly read in Burns & Shakespeare," he discussed the Scots poet's humanistic genius, especially his comic and satiric sharpness, his identification with the common man, his skepticism about religion and theology, and his affirmation of personal and political liberty. In early 1865, unable to attend a celebration honoring the 106th anniversary of the poet's birth, Lincoln expressed himself eloquently about how much Burns had meant to him. "I can not frame a toast to Burns. I can say nothing worthy of his generous heart and transcending genius. Thinking of what he has said, I can not say anything which seems worth saying."

Burns's language also appealed to him. With a gift for mimicry and articulation, Lincoln recited the Scots dialect in an imitative lilt that embodied its distinctiveness. He delighted in both its economy and exotic expressiveness. It was not strange to his ear: he had heard the burr and the vocabulary in the speech of Scots-Irish immigrants in Indiana and Illinois. Apparently the Illinois world had enough of the Scots dialect in its ears for Lincoln to quote Burns's description of the devil, "For prey, a' holes an' corners tryin," in a letter in the *Sangamo Journal* in 1837, on the assumption that it would be understood. And dialect speech appealed to him. Giving value to common speech affirmed the primacy of the common man. At the same time it affirmed a communal bond, a way for people to unite as a group. His was the voice of the people, and the Scots found in Burns their national poet. Overall, the Romantic movement highlighted the language of ordinary people as the language of poetry, a linguistic affirmation of the democratic values with which Lincoln identified. Poets such as Coleridge, Wordsworth, Keats, and Shelley had little to no presence in Lincoln's frontier world. Whether he ever read any words of theirs is open to question. But Burns was there from the beginning.

The Scots poet's emphasis on common speech inhered in his message, combining political idealism with humanistic realism. Lincoln identified with Burns's patriotism, his love of Scotland and the Scots people, especially their long-standing struggle for independence. Like Americans, the Scots had fought against English domination. And Lincoln found correlatives in his own life for Burns's emphasis on the inherent value if not the moral superiority of the common man, whose poverty did not prevent him from being equal to a king. In Burns's poetry, political legitimacy and moral authority arise from the consent of the governed, and those in power are not superior as human beings to the humblest dweller in a cottage, the Scots equivalent of the log cabin. Among Lincoln's favorites were "Tam O'Shanter," "The Cotter's Saturday Night," "Holy Willie's Prayer," "Willie's Wife," and "Epistle to a Young Friend." A New Salem contemporary remembered that when Lincoln "got possession of a Copy of Burns," he "repeated with great Glee 'Sic a wife as willy had I wudna Gie a button for her.'" He most likely read every poem in the volume he had in hand, including "For A' That and A' That," with its emphasis on "honest poverty," "the man of independent mind," and the worldwide democratic brotherhood, and "Here's a Health to Them That's Awa," with its toast, closely tracking Lincoln's personal and political ideology, to the connection between literacy, free speech, and liberty:

> *May liberty meet wi' success!*
> *May prudence protect her frae evil!*
> *May tyrants and tyranny tine in the mist,*
> *And wander their way to the devil!*

> *Here's freedom to him that wad read,*
> *Here's freedom to them that wad write!*
> *There's nane ever fear'd that the truth should be heard,*
> *But they wham the truth wad indite.*

The Scots poet's political rhetoric stirred Lincoln because it cohered with his own belief in literacy, upward mobility, respect for the common man, and democratic governance, and because it affirmed the connection between language and moral vision.

Lincoln's was not a moral vision that embraced social decorum. In Burns, he found an affirmation of his own indifference to it. Since worth

had nothing to do with decorum, why make a fuss about dress and manners? He was indifferent to his own appearance with a consistency that
might have seemed purposeful if it had not been evident that it was un-
selfconsciously genuine. In Burns's poetry, Lincoln found "honest poverty" affirmed. His own rise from rags to respectability had its parallel
in Burns's life. The Scots poet's particular expression of Romantic hostility to materialism met a kindred sympathy in Lincoln. He would have
identified with the values of "The Cotter's Saturday Night" and appreciated Burns's declaration "a honest man's the noblest work of God," that
"luxury's contagion" is a great danger to the nation, and that liberty needs
to be protected anew by the "patriot, and the patriot-bard" who will "in
bright succession raise, her ornament and guard." Lincoln was to weave
this line of thought and language into his first substantial essay, his 1838
address to the Springfield Lyceum.

In his storytelling mode, he reveled, as did Burns, in the pleasures of
the short quip and the funny narrative. He "was passionately fond of humorous jokes & stories. . . . He had no superior in Story telling," William
Greene recalled. "No man could tell a story as well as he could," Joseph
Gillespie told John Rowan Herndon. "He never missed the nib of an anecdote. He always maintained stoutly that the best stories originated with
Country boys & in the rural districts. . . . He could convey his ideas on
any subject through the form of a simple story or homely illustration with
better effect than any man I knew." Laughter was corrective and didactic.
If Aesop's fables gave him his earliest lesson in brief narrative as the embodiment of moral analogy, Burns's "Tam O'Shanter," which he recited
aloud repeatedly, provided a sophisticated example of how narrative, satiric deflation, and moral vision could be combined to give instruction
and pleasure. Such Burns poems provided lessons in timing and pace.
They helped make Lincoln a master storyteller.

The indecorous aspect of Burns's storytelling that fit most aptly into
Lincoln's oral culture was the realistic earthiness of its language. The
speech of ordinary people had as part of its natural expressiveness the
pithy coarseness of vulgarity, from the slightly off-color to the obscene.

Burns's comic genius was fertilized by selective vulgarity, a crucial element in the interplay between the realistic and the idealistic. The best and deepest humor was, Lincoln understood, humanistic: The most effective storytelling for a wide audience riveted attention by appealing to common language and daily experience. It was also linguistically transgressive, drawing on the language of excretion and sexual explicitness, an immersion in the profane, the mixed and often dark nature of life. He was intensely aware of existence as a voyage through misery. He had not been and never would be a cheerful man. "There was a strong tinge of sadness in Mr Lincolns composition," Gillespie observed. "He was not naturally disposed to look on the bright side of the picture. He felt very strongly that there was more of discomfort than real happiness in human existence under the most favorable circumstances." His humor, his stories, and his profanity were never in the service of joy. Some of it took the form of ribald stories, though always with a point, a partly repressed discharge of tension that embodied anger and proceeded from a vision of life's limitations. His was the narrative of cathartic release. It provided a counterbalance, even an antidote, to depression. And these humorous versions of his anger compelled the attention of his frontier grocery store and woodstove community.

Many of his stories were what the Victorians called "smutty." Since he and his contemporaries rarely broke the taboo against writing them down, only a few fragments and inferences survive. He frequently told the story of how an Englishman kept a picture of George Washington in a privy, since it had the effect of making "an Englishman S-h-t. . . ." "In the morning after My Marriage," Christopher C. Brown told William Herndon, "Lincoln met me and Said—'Brown why is a woman like a barrel—' C.C.B. could not answer. Well Said Lincoln—You have to raise the hoops before you put the head in.'" His friend and colleague Henry Whitney recalled that Lincoln was "once prosecuting a man . . . for seduction & one S. H. Busey an adverse witness tried to create the impression that he was a great ladies man. Lincoln went for him in his speech thus, 'there is Busey—he pretends to be a great heart smasher—does wonderful things with the girls—but I'll venture that he never entered his flesh but once and that is when he fell down & stuck his finger in his—'; right out in open Court." In the year before his election to the presidency, "Lincoln . . . had been telling his yarns. . . . A farmer Said—Lincoln why do you not write out your stories and put them in a book.' Lincoln drew himself up—fixed his face, as if a thousand dead carcusses—and a million of privies were Shooting all their Stench into his nostrils, and Said 'Such a book would Stink like a thousand privies.'" Whitney commented, "I can't think he gloated over filth however. I think that . . . he had great ideality and also a view of grossness which displaced the ideality."

More genteel than Lincoln, Whitney struggled to explain the president's "filth," and to be sparing with his examples. "The great majority of [his] stories were very nasty indeed. I remember many of them but they do us no good." Apparently they did Lincoln good. They helped him politically and professionally. And rather than displacing his "ideality," they expressed an element of his personality and experience inseparable from his moral idealism. Like Mark Twain, he had a genius for pithy narrative, and a sense that his stories and obscenities expressed something crucial about the underlying flaws in the universe and the inexplicable darkness of the human situation. And often the darkness found its best expression in humor.

The ironic and ribald humor of Burns's "Tam O'Shanter," the comic but dangerous misadventures of heavy drinking and sexual temptation, provided a model for Lincoln's storytelling. Tam's drunken encounter with the devil and his minions, from whom he and his horse barely escape, exemplifies much of what appealed to Lincoln about Burns: earthy language, frankness about the body and its expressions, comic exaggeration about a serious subject, and a pedagogy that accepted human frailty without condoning its excesses. In his drunkenness, Tam mistakes haglike witches in "cutty sarks" (shirtlike garments so short that they expose the witches' partial nudity) for beautiful women. When at last he and his horse, Maggie, flee, "the witches follow: "Ah, Tam! ah, Tam! Thou'll get thy fairin'! [reward] / In hell they'll roast thee like a herrin'!" Tam and Maggie escape, though at the cost of Maggie's tail: a witch "caught her by the rump, / And left poor Maggie scarce a stump." Like Burns, Lincoln had a fondness for exemplary "tails" that synthesized the high and the low, the moral and the profane.

As his daily companions, Burns's anticlerical, anti-Puritanical, and anti-theological poems gave him a touchstone for his attempts to think through his own beliefs. He took delight in Burns's satiric exposure of the misuse of religious belief. His "mind was skeptical," William Greene recollected, "and hence his deep humanity & skeptical tinge of mind made him love Burns." And he particularly appreciated the satirical bite with which Burns captured the self-serving mind-set of the Calvinist who conveniently believes that he has been chosen for salvation and, with gleeful cruelty, calls on God to chastise his enemies. James Matheny remembered Lincoln often quoting Burns "with great pleasure," particularly "Holy Willie's Prayer." "That it was L religion," Matheny said, meaning that it expressed Lincoln's hostility to the fundamentalism dominating nineteenth-century American Protestantism. His Christian-influenced deism defined itself in opposition to a mind-set and theology he detested. Holy Willie is not holy at all. He believes that the Lord is on his side, by which he means that God is always automatically against his enemies. His own sins, which are many and which he readily confesses, he hypocritically absorbs into his condemnation of others. He has the absolving advantage of having been chosen for special grace. He belongs to a chosen people, God's favorites. And he has a list of enemies (ipso facto therefore enemies of God) whom he cites by name and requires God to punish:

> Lord, in the day of vengeance try him [his enemy];
> Lord, visit them wha did employ him [his enemy's supporters],
> And pass not in thy mercy by them,
>   Nor hear their pray'r:
> But, for thy people's sake, destroy them,
>   And dinna spare. . . .
>
> But, Lord, remember me and mine
> Wi' mercies temp'ral and divine. . . .

It was a line of reasoning that Lincoln heard from both sides in the long lead into and through the Civil War. Burns had prepared him for it and had suggested ways in which to make use of and sometimes counter the claim of religious exceptionalism. As a young man, Lincoln did not believe that God was on anybody's side. Though he occasionally referred to God in public discourse, his inclination was to do as Burns did, emphasizing the misuse of religion rather than anything positive it contributed to social well-being. He saw no good being done by the religion characterized by Holy Willie's frame of mind. It was, he concluded, a self-serving better-than-thou creed, relying on claims of transcendence that had no basis in reality. In Lincoln's view, a moral creator and first cause had emotional and rational plausibility. But it seemed to him an absurd contradiction that God had given human beings reason and forbade them to apply it to matters pertaining to God. "He held opinions . . . utterly at variance with what are usually taught in the Churches," observed Jessie Fell, who began a long friendship with Lincoln in 1834. His emphasis was on "'the Fatherhood of God, and the Brotherhood of Man.' He fully believed in a Superintending and overruling Providence, that guides and controls the operations of the world; but Maintained that Law and Order, and not their violation or suspension; are the appointed means by which this providence is exercised."

Deeply versed in the Bible, he rejected the literal truth of supernatural claims. As a boy, he had drunk deeply at the Puritan fountain, whose dark waters had the flavor of stoicism. The biblical tone and language always remained part of him, available for reference and citation. But if there were a God, Lincoln had come to believe, He neither interfered in the processes of nature nor interceded in the affairs of men. Apparently, at times, Lincoln doubted whether any deity existed at all, though that doubt gradually resolved itself in the 1830s into a belief in a creator who remained outside nature, a deism of the sort that the eighteenth-century rationalists and anti-sectarians had evolved. It had been the belief system of most of the vaguely Christian Founding Fathers. Lincoln continued to be a non-churchgoer and not, in any meaningful sense, a Christian at all. A rationalist and a skeptic, he did not, and was never to, believe in the divinity of Jesus, the atonement, the resurrection, or the immortality of the soul.

Between 1832 and 1836, he read widely in the literature of religious skepticism, applying the standards of reason and realism to Christian religious claims. In Thomas Paine's *Common Sense* and Constantin Volney's *The Ruins; or, A Survey of the Revolutions of Empires*, he found convincing arguments against the intercession of God in human affairs. Apparently he also read Voltaire. Eager to put pen to paper, "he employed his intellectual faculties in writing a dissertation against the doctrine of the divinity of the scriptures," a well-informed local newspaper later reported. Testimony varies as to whether it was an essay or a pamphlet-length argument. Samuel Hill and some of Lincoln's other friends, thinking it imprudent for a rising politician to publish such views, convinced him to destroy, or forced the destruction of, the manuscript.

In Springfield, where Lincoln had begun to spend time and to which he soon moved, John Todd Stuart had ample opportunity to hear the young lawyer on the subject. "He was an avowed and open Infidel— Sometimes bordered on atheism . . . always denied that Jesus was the son of God as understood and maintained by the Christian world." So did one of his closest friends, James Matheny, who knew that Lincoln "was an infidel," by which he meant not a Christian. He had "heard Lincoln call Christ a bastard. . . . Lincoln attacked the Bible & New Testament on two grounds—1st From the inherent or apparent contradiction under its lids & 2ndly from grounds of Reason—sometimes he ridiculed the Bible . . . never heard that Lincoln changed his views. . . . Sometimes Lincoln bordered on absolute Atheism; he went far that way & often shocked me." As president, he was to have no objection to the rhetoric of Christianity as a vehicle to assist in the nation's redemption, and he encouraged all churches to rally to the Union. But his own views required that the God of his invocation be, at His most limited, a formal reference, and, at His most engaged, a mysterious and distant deity.

* * *

When Lincoln met nineteen-year-old Ann Rutledge, soon after arriving in New Salem in summer 1832, he was in the process of developing his passion for the poetry of Byron. William Greene observed that Lincoln read Byron "all extensively while he lived at Salem." Some of what he read suited the passion of first love. Much of it expressed and gave intensity to the full range of his interests and anxieties. Ann's younger brother Robert "frequently heard him repeat pieces of prose & poetry, his practice was, when He wished to indelibly fix anything he was reading or studying on his mind, to write it down, have known him to write whole pages of books he was reading." He kept a notebook that contained his favorite passages, and it is likely that Ann heard him read selections from Byron and other poets at her father's tavern, where Lincoln boarded briefly, and then at the Rutledge farm at Sand Ridge, seven miles from New Salem, which he visited frequently during his surveying forays, starting early in 1834.

When, in August 1835, Ann Rutledge died, Lincoln's despair had Byronic resonance. Greene recalled that "friends after this sudden death of one whom his soul & heart dearly lovd were Compelled to keep watch and ward over Mr Lincoln, he being from the sudden shock somewhat temporarily deranged. We watched during storms—fogs—damp gloomy weather Mr Lincoln for fear of an accident. He said 'I can never be reconcile[d] to have the snow—rains & storms to beat on her grave.'" Those who provided similar accounts of his grief, among them John Hill, James Short, Lynn McNulty Greene, Benjamin Irwin, and John Jones, had no reason to be dishonest in their recollections. Unless a large number of contemporary observers lied, it is reasonable to conclude that Lincoln was deeply in love. Three additional witnesses are especially credible. Ann's brother remembered that "The effect upon Mr Lincoln's mind was terrible; he became plunged in despair, and many of his friends feared that reason would desert her throne." Henry McHenry recalled, "As to the condition of Lincoln's Mind after the death of Miss R. . . . he seemed quite *changed*, he seemed *Retired*, & loved *Solitude*, he seemed wrapped in *profound thoughts*, *indifferent*, to transpiring Events, had but Little to say, but would . . . wander off in the woods by him self, away from the association of even those he most esteemed, this gloom seemed to deepen for some time, so as to give anxiety to his friends in regard to his Mind." Elizabeth Abell, with whom Lincoln occasionally boarded, told William Herndon, "He was staying with us at the time of her death it was a great shock to him and I never seen a man mourn for a companion more than he did for her he made a remark . . . he could not bare the idea of its raining on her Grave that was the time the community said he was crazy he was not crazy but he was very disponding a long time." Isaac Cogdal reported that Lincoln, in 1859, had said that it was true that he "ran off the track" after the death of Ann Rutledge. That would have been confirmation of what was already known to his New Salem contemporaries rather than an unlikely confession by a reticent man. In 1862, three years before his death, the Menard County *Axis* printed an article that included a description much like Greene's of Lincoln's despair.

For a man noted for emotional restraint, his intense misery at Ann's death has some of the resonance of a sensibility immersed in Byron's poetry. Lincoln's favorites were "The Devil's Drive, "The Destruction of Sennacherib," "Darkness," *Childe Harold's Pilgrimage*, *The Bride of Abydos*, *Lara*, *The Corsair*, *Mazeppa*, and *Don Juan*. And those reported to be his favorites had to be the tip of the iceberg: editions containing these also would have had the lyric poems of *Hours of Idleness*, *Occasional Pieces*, *Hebrew Melodies*, *Domestic Pieces*, and probably *Satires*, including *The Vision of Judgement*. Numbers of multivolume editions, published in England and America, had been widely disseminated, even to the western frontier, since Byron's death in 1824. The single-volume edition published in New York in 1832, edited by the Byron enthusiast Fitz-Greene Halleck, whose humorous poems also became favorites of Lincoln's and whose "beautiful lines on Burns" he praised in 1860, could have been in New Salem by autumn 1832. Joshua Speed, whom Lincoln met in 1837 and who told Herndon that "I do not think he had ever read much of Byron previous to my acquaintance with him," was wrong by about five years. But Speed also had no doubt that Lincoln "was a great admirer of some of Byrons poetry—Childe Harolde the Bride of Abydos Mazeppa & some of his fugitive pieces. . . . Lincoln loved The Bride of Abydos—Devils drive." He even had the makings of a literary critic. Byron had added to *Childe Harold's Pilgrimage*, at a date later than its first publication, an additional story within the story. "Piece Put in was Inez—Spanish maid—Lincoln [said?] it was a mistake," Speed recalled.

Without belief in an afterlife and with a fatalistic sensibility, Lincoln's familiarity with Byron would have provided him appropriate language with which to articulate his grief. It's likely that he carried lines from Byron in his mind as he struggled with the shock of Ann's death, and that they helped to give expression to his deepest responses. Byron's "On the Death of a Young Lady," one of the first poems in the 1832 edition, contains language that Lincoln may have revisited as he mourned at Ann's grave site:

> *Within this narrow cell reclines her clay,*
> *That clay, where once such animation beam'd;*
> *The King of Terrors seized her as his prey,*
> *Not worth nor beauty have her life redeem'd.*

> *Oh! Could that King of Terrors pity feel,*
> *Or Heaven reverse the dread decree of fate,*
> *Not here the mourner would his grief reveal,*
> *Not here the muse her virtues would relate.*

Since his arrival in New Salem and his election to the legislature, the world had become, for Lincoln, a more congenial place. That Ann returned his feelings in a way that might overcome obstacles provided an additional counterweight to his previous bereavements and struggles. And even if, in whatever analysis he was capable of, his struggles did not have singularity, they gained depth from his deep-seated attraction to sadness and solitude. He had numbers of antidotes: humorous storytelling, cathartic profanities, books and authors he loved to read, and his determined but not always satisfying effort to master the law. Between 1833 and 1835, Ann had made life seem more happily bearable. Her death upset the delicate balance. His contemporaries testified to how dark Lincoln's mind was in August 1835 and through the remainder of the year. That aspect of Byron's poetry that expressed loss and pessimism—the death of love and lover, tropes of suicide, solitude, and the grave, the impossibility of life after death and of reunion with loved ones—suited Lincoln's temperament.

The melancholic poet of bereavement, though, had more to offer than Romantic angst. Lincoln found the Byron who focused attention on cultural and political issues, particularly slavery, revolution, and democracy, an ideological soul mate. These were matters Lincoln had a deep interest in. And they engaged personal and cultural concerns simultaneously. Gray's depiction of the conflict between ambition and limitation in "Elegy Written in a Country Church-Yard" reverberated anew in Byron's "The Adieu." The poet's inflection of the theme of loss paralleled Lincoln's concern about the price to be paid for fame and its potential for good and evil. The poem offered a correlative for Lincoln's feelings at the time of Ann's death and his long-standing ambivalence about his ambition:

> All, all is dark, and cheerless now!
>   No smile of love's deceit
> Can warm my veins with wonted glow,
>   Can bid life's pulses beat:
> Not e'en the hope of future fame
> Can wake my faint, exhausted frame
>   Or crown with fancied wreaths my head.
> Mine is a short inglorious race—
> To humble in the dust my face,
>   And mingle with the dead. . . .
> But me she beckons from the earth,
> My name obscure, unmark'd my birth,
>   My life a short and vulgar dream:

Lost in the dull, ignoble crowd,
My hopes recline within a shroud,
My fate is Lethe's stream.

In 1860, still preoccupied with the theme, Lincoln echoed Byron and quoted Gray in reference to his "obscure" origins to one of his first biographers. And he publicly recited, on at least one occasion, his favorite lines from *Childe Harold's Pilgrimage*. A colleague recalled that "in my office in 1854," when he was reentering public life, "he picked up Byron and read [aloud] . . . as impressively as it ever was read in the world." The passage was Byron's description of the ambition that drives "Conquerers and Kings, / Founders of sects and systems, to whom add / Sophists, Bards, Statesmen." It extends through four stanzas, emphasizing the agitated and isolated life of such a leader:

He who ascends to mountain-tops, shall find
The loftiest peaks most wrapt in clouds and snow;
He who surpasses or subdues mankind,
Must look down on the hate of those below.
Though high above the sun of glory glow,
And far beneath the earth and ocean spread,
Round him are ice rocks, and loudly blow
Contending tempests on his naked head,
And thus reward the toils which to those summits led.

Even he who leads in the name of liberation from oppression, Byron warns, cannot readily control his own impulse to command. And the ideals that inspire the overthrow of thrones and the establishment of republics have not the strength to maintain themselves against human nature's attraction to materialism, dependency, and corruption:

There is the moral of all human tales;
'Tis but the same rehearsal of the past,

First freedom, and then Glory—when that fails,
Wealth, vice, corruption—barbarism at last . . .

The exception that Byron cites was already dear to Lincoln's heart. Byron's laudatory evocation in *Childe Harold's Pilgrimage* of George Washington, "The Cincinnatus of the West," provided Lincoln with another touchstone text for his hero worship. It gave him language and a model for his own peroration of Washington in 1838. Byron's Washington is the poet's exception to the maxim that power corrupts. It provided resonant lines for the maturing Lincoln, who, like Byron, valorized the American Revolution as a rebellion against traditional tyrannies and emphasized national self-determination:

Can tyrants but by tyrants conquer'd be,
And Freedom find no champion and no child
Such as Columbia saw arise when she
Sprung forth a Pallas, arm'd and undefiled?
Or must such minds be nourish'd in the wild,
Deep in the unpruned forest, 'midst the roar
Of cataracts, where nursing Nature smiled
On infant Washington? Has earth no more
Such seeds within her breast, or Europe no such shore?

Having himself come from the "unpruned forest," Lincoln also might have given some credence—as did a widespread nineteenth-century American rhetoric—to the myth that the American wilderness produced nobler people than the monarchical governments of "the old world."

When Lincoln spoke to the Young Men's Lyceum of Springfield in January 1838, his first memorable speech, now best read as an essay on its subtitle, "The Perpetuation of Our Political Institutions," he had in mind not the European need, as Byron saw it, to have a Washington of its own, but America's to preserve what Washington and his contemporaries had achieved. It seemed to Lincoln—and to others, especially in the Whig

Party—that the commitment to liberty that the Revolution and the Constitution had embodied was eroding. The republic, in danger, had become susceptible to demagogues, mobs, and militarists. Andrew Jackson and his ilk, driven by the tendency to transform national acclaim into dictatorial rule, were potential tyrants who might undo what Washington had achieved. Byron had expressed the threat in universal terms. Lincoln worried that America, having had its Washington, was now in danger of developing its Caesar or Napoleon.

In a combination of eloquently simple and elaborately rhetorical prose, anticipating his mature style, Lincoln argued that America was in danger of losing what those of the Revolutionary age had shed their blood to attain. The way to keep it was to revere the law and the Constitution—let that "become the *political religion* of the nation"—and to be beware of demagogic leaders. Otherwise the "temple of liberty" will fall. "Reason, cold, calculating, unimpassioned reason . . . moulded into *general intelligence, sound* morality, and, in particular, *a reverence for the constitution and laws*" must take the place of the revolutionary passion of the age of the Founders. "If destruction be our lot, we must ourselves be its author and finisher." Byron's words were his poetic subtext: "First Freedom, and then Glory—when that fails." In the struggle that Lincoln saw in progress in the late 1830s, affirming Washington and what he stood for—reason, prudence, calmness, and dedication to liberty—would provide a guideline and a secure future for the nation. "That we improved to the last; that we remained free to the last; that, during his long sleep, we permitted no hostile foot to pass over or desecrate his resting place; shall be that which to learn the last trump shall awaken our WASHINGTON."

As it was for Weems and Byron, the idealization of Washington was for Lincoln thematically empowering. It was also rhetorically awkward. If Byron is the better writer, Lincoln's fall into the occasional strained sentences of his 1838 essay is a lapse in a learning process that later would bring such flourishes under the control of a tighter, more natural style. And Byron as poet was never to be a model for Lincoln, at least in the few poems of his that survive. The Lyceum address gave him the opportunity to hone his thoughts on the state of the nation. The audience was small, the occasion obscure, and the speaker irrelevant to the national debate. But Lincoln gives no sense that he thinks himself or his ideas peripheral, let alone irrelevant. The language positions itself in the first-person voice of authorial self-confidence: he speaks from himself, for himself, with the voice of someone whose literary style creates the impression that he has earned the right to speak. What he says is credible because he has thought deeply, carefully, impartially, and with noble intentions; because he believes he has something important to contribute to the national discussion; and because his argument is based on a combination of evidence, reason, and analysis.

If the themes and political values are Byronic, the message is not. Byron argued for the primacy of passion in political life, especially love of liberty and hatred of tyranny. Lincoln argued for the rational expression and prudent application of the law. Context partly made the difference. Byron preached revolutionary change in Europe; Lincoln preached reinvigoration of a revolution in America that had already occurred. And Lincoln, in regard to this aspect of Byron, can be readily identified with the statement of another nineteenth-century English writer, Thomas Carlyle: "Close thy Byron, Open thy Goethe." Carlyle advised mature wisdom, not Romantic passion. Lincoln had only a modest measure of Romantic passion in him from the start, and much of it was channeled into darker currents, into melancholy and loss as a frame of mind. He expressed it in his behavior after Ann Rutledge's death. And he was to have at least two more opportunities to express himself on the subject of Romantic love. By the mid-1840s, that aspect of Byron was behind him. Perhaps his friend Joshua Speed meant exactly that when he remarked that Lincoln "Forsook Byron—never Shakespear—& Burns." What bound him to Byron was his identification with the poet's Romantic republicanism. To that Byron, he retained a lifelong loyalty.

Byron's lyric power and narrative flair Lincoln also found compelling. He "took from my library once," his friend Henry Whitney remembered, "a copy of 'Byron' & read with much feeling several pages commencing with 'There was a sound of revelry by night,'" Byron's evocation of the prelude to the Battle of Waterloo in *Childe Harold's Pilgrimage*. In the account of Childe Harold's travels to Spain, Germany, Switzerland, Italy, and Greece, Lincoln had a narrative of the traditional grand tour, as close as he ever got to actual travel in Europe. Four of his cherished Byron poems idealized high adventure by larger-than-life-characters. And Byron's mock epic *Don Juan*, whose comic episodes provide an antiheroic realism and erotic frankness about human nature, became one of his favorites.

But lyric beauty, narrative pace, descriptive vividness, and comic realism—important as they were to Lincoln's attraction to Byron—were supporting elements. The most widely read poet championing freedom from national oppression, Byron gave expression to Lincoln's developing political and philosophical beliefs. It was with Byron's political republicanism that Lincoln identified, and Byron's eloquent evocation of those republics that had failed had to have impressed him. Byron's warning that "religion—freedom—vengeance—what you will, / A word's enough to raise mankind to kill" surely registered in Lincoln's concerns. "I have a love for freedom too," the main character of *The Bride of Abydos* proclaims. In *Lara*, "slavery half forgets her feudal chain." The poem's hero frees "the soil-bound slaves, / Who dig no land for tyrants but their graves!" The itinerary of *Childe Harold's Pilgrimage* led Lincoln through a Europe whose past and present had special meaning for Americans concerned about the fate of the American republic. In Spain, Byron dramatizes the nationalistic struggle against Napoleonic invasion and oppression. In Venice, Florence, and Rome, he valorizes centuries of republican self-rule and laments the fall of ancient city-states into decadence and tyranny. And his depiction of the current state of Greece under Turkish tyranny highlights its fall from ancient republican glory. In *Don Juan*, Byron championed the struggle to liberate Greece, where he died. What would be the American fate? Lincoln wondered. Would it go the way of the republics of the past? What were the best tools and strategies to prevent that from happening?

* * *

Starting in the mid-1830s, matters of the heart tested another aspect of Lincoln's command of language. In October 1833, Mary S. Owens, the sister of Lincoln's friend Mrs. Elizabeth Abell, visited from her family home in Green County, Kentucky, where her prosperous father ran a private school he had founded. She stayed four weeks. The Owens family valued literacy, literature, and achievement. Tall, full-figured, with dark hair and bright blue eyes, Mary was a dedicated reader and spirited conversationalist who made a striking impression on Lincoln. Her sister thought something might develop between them and, eager for their happiness, gave whatever push she could to bring them together. When Mary left, Lincoln had gotten the possibility of a love relationship between them into his heart and mind. Apparently he let it be known that if she returned to Illinois, he would marry her, though whether it was a comment he intended to be confidential or a boast or joke in bad taste is unclear. Nothing had been said between them. The penniless, profession-less Lincoln had not explicitly been courting her, and Mary, who probably heard of the remark from her sister, was put off by its presumption.

Three years later, in November 1836, she returned to New Salem, at her sister's invitation, this time for an open-ended visit. She was two months beyond her twenty-eighth birthday, an age that made marriage unlikely. Still, she gave no indication that she was eager for a husband. Lincoln welcomed Mary's return. That he had been deeply in love with Ann may have made the prospect of loving again compelling. His colleague Henry Whitney remarked about a later period in Lincoln's life that he had "heard him say over & over again about sexual contact: 'It is the harp of a thousand strings.'" Friendly observers noticed over the years his alertness to attractive women. And his own singularity had its attractiveness: his face was expressively homely, interesting rather than handsome, alternating between quiet intensity and lively alertness; his long body made him appear vulnerably unbalanced, a man who both could take care of himself and needed to be cared for. In the years since Mary's

previous visit, he had moved up in the world. His election to the legislature had given him prominence and income, though of a minor sort. His
preparation for the bar had given him professional prospects. At the same
time, he had deep insecurities, especially about his appearance, his place
in the world, and his ability to support a family. And Mary was noticeably
different from Ann; she was the cultured, mannered, and well-educated
daughter of a superior Kentucky family. "My education was thoroughly
english," she later told William Herndon. Witty and outspoken, she had
a mind of her own.

Encouraged by Elizabeth Abell, who shared the local conviction that
he was destined to rise in the world, Lincoln made assumptions about his
prospects. Hoping to secure her sister's proximity and retain Lincoln's,
Elizabeth had encouraged him to think himself a suitor. Playing match-
maker, she "proposed to me, that on her return [from a visit to Kentucky]
she would bring [her sister] . . . with her, upon condition that I would
engage to become her brother-in-law." He was eager; Mary less so. Determined not to marry the wrong man, she would put him to the test,
which meant that she would give him the opportunity to reveal himself
in regard to the things that mattered to her. As a Southerner, she particularly valued courtly manners, the outer garment of the values of a
gentleman. She also required that a suitor be sensitive to the feelings of
women, kind to animals, and have an interest in culture. In the latter
two areas, Lincoln met her standards. In regard to manners, he did not.
In numbers of instances, he showed himself "deficient in the nicer and
more delicate attentions, which she felt to be due from the man whom
she had pictured as an ideal husband." In an incident that troubled her,
he did not give a helping hand to a lady struggling to carry a young child
uphill. Her criticism led to argument and then coldness. They struggled
over their differences: she was mannered and educated; he was awkward
and an autodidact; she had wealth and family position; he was poor, from
an obscure home.

From the start, he found it useful to work out in writing the process
of courting her and understanding himself. Of the entire correspondence

only three letters survive, all written by Lincoln. It is only his voice we hear. A month after her second visit began, he went to Vandalia for the legislative session. On arrival, he felt depressed and physically sick. Apparently he had left New Salem thinking that he and Mary had a special relationship and expecting separation to be softened by regular correspondence. Having written immediately before departing or soon after arriving, he had not gotten a reply. Should he now write another letter, he asked himself, and in what style and tone? How much of his feelings should he reveal? Should he assume an intimacy that she might think unwarranted or an amiable friendliness that she might find more acceptable? And could he manage not to come off looking like a self-pitying and vulnerable whiner? After a week of waiting for a response to his earlier letter, he decided to take the plunge.

As usual, he devised a writing strategy to meet the situation. He began with the personal: a frank, dignified, but still beseeching request for her attention. Without concealing his disappointment and anger at what he felt to be a slight, he admitted his vulnerability, at the same time appealing to her sympathy and asserting that he was manly enough not to be discouraged. And he did it laconically, in a simple, direct style:

> I have been sick ever since my arrival here, or I should have written sooner. It is but little difference, however, as I have verry little even yet to write. And more, the longer I can avoid the mortification of looking in the Post office for your letter and not finding it, the better. You see I am mad about that *old letter* yet. I dont like verry well to risk you again. I'll try you once more anyhow.

For most of the letter's remaining five hundred words, he leaves it at that: in this instance, the most effective way to express personal feeling is neither to exaggerate nor to extend but to write about other things. The obvious matters at hand are political. He has reason to think that Mary, her family, and their New Salem circle will be interested. He tells her that little progress has been made in building the new statehouse, that the chances for the proposed division to create the new county desired by New Salem are poor, that efforts are in progress to pass a loan bill for internal improvements, that politicking will decide who will be the next United States senator, and that the likelihood that Springfield will become the state capital has improved.

Cleverly, he ends the letter in a neat circularity, returning to the subject with which he had started—his desire to create some remedy for himself, his situation, and his relationship with her. Gracefully but obviously, with a glide that almost startles, he segues within the final paragraph from political matters back to himself, as if now the best way to effect his personal agenda is to make it seem a natural attachment to more impersonal matters:

> The opposition men have no candidate of their own [for senator], and consequently they smile as complacently at the angry snarls of the contending Van Buren candidates and their respective friends, as the christian does at Satan's rage. You recollect I mentioned in the outset of this letter that I had been unwell. That is the fact, though I believe I am about well now; but that, with other things I can not account for, have conspired and have gotten my spirits so low, that I feel that I would rather be any place in the world than here. I really can not endure the thought of staying here ten weeks. Write back as soon as you get this, and if possible say something that will please me, for really I have not [been] pleased since I left you. This letter is so dry and [stupid] that I am ashamed to send it, but with my pres[ent feel]ings I can not do any better.

Delicately direct, it is a touchingly plaintive love letter. It expresses unambiguous feelings with emotional nuance and epistolary cleverness. The writer of course is neither Byron nor Burns. Romantic expostulation would not suit his mood, his talents, or the situation. But lonely and in love, he recognizes the need to express his feelings without ornamental language or extended emphasis upon the language of the heart, in a style that embodies who he is. Here sincerity and simplicity are their own best literary effects, a representation of the process language enacts as the writer searches for the best words and their most effective arrangement.

Between December 1836 and August 1837, Lincoln and Mary attempted to define their feelings to themselves and to each other. By May 1837, she had concluded that Lincoln could not meet her standards for a husband, though he did not know this, and Lincoln, believing he had proposed to her, directly or indirectly, or at least made known his intention to do so, had strong doubts about whether he actually wanted her to accept. For him, the process had elements of perplexing irresolution, and it is of course his voice that we hear in his two additional letters to her, one dated May 7, the other August 16. The problem of finding the best way to address her he incorporates into the May 7 letter, a self-aware writer making the subject of the difficulty of writing and his standards as a writer part of his text. "I have commenced two letters to send you before this," he writes, "both of which displeased me before I got half done, and so I tore them up. The first I thought wasn't serious enough, and the second was on the other extreme. I shall send this, turn out as it may."

Actually, since he found this third draft satisfactory, the phrase "turn out as it may" is more rhetorical than a statement of true intent, and it turned out well because he had found an effective opening paragraph and also because he immediately returned to the theme of his letter from Vandalia. He did so in prose that has the best qualities of that letter without its indirectness. The moment is intense, the stage of the discovery process and the relationship dramatic. In the second paragraph he describes his lonely Springfield existence, his absence of company, especially female, and his awareness of his lack of social manners: "I am quite as lonesome here as [I] ever was anywhere in my life. I have been spoken to by but one woman since I've been here, and should not have been by her, if she could have avoided it." The second paragraph takes as its assumption that Mary might marry him. If she did, he warns her, his poverty would eventually make her regret her choice. There is "a great deal of flourishing about in carriages here, which it would be your doom to see without shareing in it. You would have to be poor without the means of hiding your poverty."

> Whatever woman may cast her lot with mine, should any ever do so, it is my intention to do all in my power to make her happy and contented; and there is nothing I can imagine, that would make me more unhappy than to fail in the effort. I know I should be much happier with you than the way I am, provided I saw no signs of discontent in you. What you have said to me may have been in jest, or I may have misunderstood it. If so, then let it be forgotten; if otherwise, I much wish you would think seriously before you decide. For my part I have already decided. . . . My opinion is that you had better not do it. You have not been accustomed to hardship, and it may be more severe than you now imagine. . . . I am willing to abide your decision.

Even if Mary still had an open mind on the matter, his words would have closed it. That seems to have been his intention: the language and tone are deliberate. Either way, he gains something. If she accepts his proposal notwithstanding his having enumerated the reasons why she should not and his being on record as having so advised her, she cannot blame him thereafter. If she declines, it is the letter that will have made her refusal a certainty. Either he is unaware that she would have refused him even if he had never written this letter or is unwilling to take the chance that she will accept him. Whatever her response, emotionally and strategically he is a winner, and he concludes with an insensitive, ambiguously slighting remark: "You must write me a good long letter after you get this. You have nothing else to do, and though it might not seem interesting to you, after you had written it, it would be a good deal of company to me."

In his last letter, in mid-August 1837, his laborious rationale is that he loves her too much to make her unhappy in a marriage to him: she would have to lower her material expectations. "You must know that I cannot see you, or think of you, with entire indifference," he proclaims, a statement so far short of Byronic passion that it suggests a desire to evade rather than persuade. His rationale for pursuing the possibility that she has spurned him without knowledge of his true feelings (no matter how tepidly expressed) is that he wants

> in all cases to do right, and most particularly so, in all cases with women . . . and if I *knew* it would be doing right, as I rather suspect it would, to let you alone, I would do it. And for the purpose of making the matter as plain as possible, I now say, that you can now drop the subject, dismiss your thoughts (if you ever had any) from me forever, and leave this letter unanswered, without calling forth one accusing murmer from me. And . . . if it will add any thing to your comfort or peace of mind, to do so, it is my sincere wish that you should. Do not understand by this, that I wish to cut your acquaintance. I mean no such thing. What I do wish is, that our further acquaintance shall depend upon yourself.

Still, if she wished to marry him, for whatever the reason—if "you feel yourself in any degree bound to me"—he was "anxious to bind [her] faster, if I can be convinced it will, in any considerable degree, add to your happiness." They both knew that it would not. "If it suits you best not to answer this—farewell—a long life and a merry one attend you. But if you conclude to write back, speak as plainly as I do." In a sense, he had spoken all too plainly or not plainly enough. The words are clear. But the gap between the direct language and the complicated strategy makes the letter chillingly calculated. Its purpose is to court a refusal or allow an acceptance on terms entirely in his favor. Most readers would conclude that the author preferred a refusal. Language and strategy work brilliantly together.

Neither the passionate Byron nor the lyric Burns express themselves in Lincoln's peculiar love letters. As a suitor, he is insecure and indecisive. His heart certainly does not sing, and sexual passion is held in check by temperance, insecurity, and his fear of making a lifelong mistake. Mary's voice comes to us only though the agency of Lincoln's words, as if his letters are stanzas in a dramatic monologue in which the writer and the speaker are of course the same, and the writer is not consciously writing in a poetic genre. But the letters together, and the coda that he wrote to a friend, provide his version of the story of the relationship. For hers, we have to read between the lines. The key issue for Lincoln is character, as it is in most dramatic monologues, and the relationship between language and ends. And it is his character that is at stake.

The coda, a semi-comic attempt to come to terms with his inadequacies, came in a letter to a new friend, Eliza Browning, the wife of Orville Browning, his political colleague in Vandalia, one of numbers of married women whose company Lincoln found congenial. It is a letter that he had no external reason to write, and in many senses it is a letter to himself, an attempt to create a narrative that would fictionalize into a palatable emotional truth the unpleasant actual account of his performance with Mary. The joke of the letter, written on April 1, 1838, is that Lincoln himself is the butt of the ironic twist that the letter recounts. He is the target of his own satire, though the slightly humorous tone is overwhelmed by the stark awfulness of how the story is framed and what self-revelations the writer provides. His account to Mrs. Browning of the plotline does not differ from what the three letters provide. But a second level of the story, an interpretative account of motivation, is now added, with elements not hinted at in the letters or the comments of contemporary observers. The coda is Lincoln's self-serving, partly self-deflating, semi-fictional account of the affair, the facts transformed into a more useful retelling of the story, an instance in which a master storyteller invents a narrative superior, for his purposes, to what reality provided. It is a partly self-exculpatory lie. It is also self-consciously literary, a Shakespearean comic drama of exaggeration in regard to Mary's appearance and Lincoln's dialectic between honor and language, values and words.

He was eager, he accurately tells Mrs. Browning, to take up Elizabeth Abell's suggestion that he resume courting Mary. But his narrative takes a quick turn into a cruel distortion that reveals what a strict factual account could not:

In a few days we had an interview. . . . She did not look as my imagination had pictured her. I knew she was over-size, but she now appeared a fair match for Falstaff; I knew she was called an 'old maid' . . . but now, when I beheld her, I could not for my life avoid thinking of my mother; and this, not from withered features, for her skin was too full of fat, to permit its contracting in to wrinkles; but from her want of teeth, weather-beaten appearance in general, and from a kind of notion that ran in my head, that *nothing* could have commenced at the size of infancy, and reached her present bulk in less than thirtyfive or forty years; and, in short, I was not at all pleased with her. . . . I now spent my time between planning how I might get along through life after my contemplated change of circumstances should have taken place; and how I might procrastinate the evil day for a time, which I really dreaded as much— perhaps more, than an Irishman does the halter.

After a long hesitation, he fulfills what he believes is his commitment to propose. With an ironic turn worthy of a satiric short story, the lady refuses him. Immensely relieved, he is also disbelieving. He will not let himself off the hook so easily. Perhaps she only refused him out of modesty. He repeats the offer, then "again and again," until he is finally "forced to give up." She really does not want to marry him. Happily, he is "out clear . . . no violation of word, honor, or conscience," which, with his early reference to Falstaff, suggests that Falstaff's definition of honor is the counterpoint soliloquy that he has been attempting to distinguish himself from. Yet he is also "mortified almost beyond endurance," for two reasons: he realizes that perhaps he actually did love her "a little"; and, more tellingly, because his vanity is "deeply wounded by the reflection, that I had so long been too stupid to discover her intentions, and at the same time never doubting that I understood them perfectly; and also, that she whom I had taught myself to believe no body else would have, had actually rejected me with all my fancied greatness." The April fool's joke is that "I most emphatically, in this instance, made a fool of myself. I have now come to the conclusion never again to think of marrying; and for this reason; I can never be satisfied with any one who would be block-head enough to have me."

Ambivalent about marrying anyone; lonely and erotically compelled; clumsy and unsophisticated in his courtship; confused about how to apply his conventional and traditional code of honor in regard to "breach of promise" and even a higher standard, "breach of intention to promise"; and then shocked to his deepest core of self-regard by his proposal, which it cost him so much to make, having been declined, Lincoln had good reason to rewrite and fictionalize what had actually happened, especially in regard to his own feelings and motivations. It was Lincoln in the process of learning to use language to help himself, to make better, more useful sense out of who he was and what he had done. The purpose of the imaginative narrative, the alternative world, was to make more satisfying sense of reality. It was also a feint in the direction of self-understanding. And it was cathartic to be the butt of the joke if one were also the teller of the story. That Lincoln, over a year after Mary's departure from Illinois, had the narrative enough on his mind to tell a new version of it to an unknowing friend, who assumed that it was indeed an April fool's joke, suggests that he had been deeply hurt by what occurred and that he had come to some conclusion about the lesson to be learned. Ironically, the improved story and its lesson provided only temporary service. Four years later his conclusion "never again to think of marrying" went for naught, and the lady, also with a weight issue, aggravated by shortness of stature, *was* "block-head enough" to have him.

Even while depressed in Vandalia and sorting out his relationship with Mary Owens, he had his hands full as a leader of the statewide Whig Party, brokering majorities in legislatures dominated by the other party. After much arm-twisting, most Whigs and some Democrats concluded that it was sound to float bonds for infrastructure improvements, particularly canals, roads, and railroads. Though the tax base was small, they expected that investments in transportation would expand commerce sufficiently and increase tax revenue enough to repay the borrowed money; and to process large loans, the state needed a financial system, especially a state bank. Lincoln also spent political chits horse-trading to have predominantly Whig Springfield designated the state capital. The votes of the nine Sangamon County legislators, with Lincoln as their spokesman, were made available for barter, including reluctant consent to separate outlying sections of their huge county into three new counties. Lincoln, naturally, wrote the bill. Springfield lobbyists expended money freely. After an indecisive popular referendum, legislation was enacted that put the decision about relocating the capital into the hands of the legislators. At one point Lincoln feared "that he had traded off everything he could dispose of, and still had not got strength enough to locate the seat of government in Springfield. 'And yet . . . I cant go home without passing that bill. My folks expect that of me, and that I can't do—and I am finished forever.'" Lincoln and his friends changed tactics, enticing legislators to support a bill to change the capital by not specifying a city.

The Springfield enthusiasts triumphed, subject to a two-year transition period, in March 1837. The city burst into celebration at this guarantee of prosperity. In the summer, there was a self-congratulatory oratorical orgy, in which Lincoln participated, with dozens of toasts to Illinois, "'destined to be fairest and tallest among the sisters of this great Republic,'" to the legislators, the "'Long Nine of Old Sangamon—well done good and faithful servants . . . to the people of Illinois, to Internal Improvements, to everybody and everything, and particularly to our absent friends . . . who stood by us in our time of need.'"

The pork barrel politics of infrastructure improvement, the complication of setting up a state-sponsored banking system, and the intracity competition for the advantage of being designated the new capital were enmeshed in a shifting but intertwined network of political trades. On the first two matters, the initial success of Lincoln and the Whigs came home to haunt them. The improvements and the bank expansion, whatever their merit, exceeded the fiscal capability of the state. That a tax base to support such expenditures would come into existence through economic growth was based on a rosy scenario, and reality, in the form of a worldwide economic depression in late 1837, soon made such assumptions hollow. British and European investment dried up. Illinois verged on bankruptcy, and the public backlash largely blamed the Whigs. By the late 1830s, a weakened Whig Party, which had aspired to majority status, found itself likely to be permanently in the minority in Illinois.

In April 1837, six weeks after its selection as the state capital, the former New Salem clerk, postmaster, and surveyor became a Springfield resident. With a population of about two thousand, the city was on the verge of becoming the center of statewide as well as county government. Lincoln seems to have felt no regret in leaving the town he had lived in for five years, a move made comfortable partly because he already had friends in both places and because proximity made traffic easy between them. He came to Springfield with an impressive credential: his legislative efforts had contributed heavily to the city's new identity and had earned him credit in the capital's legal and business community. Because he was a prominent state legislator, his residence there could only bind him closer to Springfield interests.

Professionally, the move was a predictable necessity. New Salem had too little legal business to support a lawyer; the county courts were in Springfield; the state judicial apparatus was soon to be consolidated there; and a prominent Springfield attorney, John Todd Stuart, had offered to take him into his office. Apparently, Stuart had decided that Lincoln would fit into the larger Whig scheme for success in politics and business. With another year to serve in his second term and the expectation that he would run again, Lincoln had reason to locate himself at the new center of Illinois political life. He would be among friends who valued him highly. Together, he expected, they could and would do great things for their state and even for the country. With his eyes on the 1840 election, he fervently hoped there would be a Whig president.

In the meantime, there was work to do, including an unusual case. It provided a promising combination of legal and political business, which turned out to be a volatile mixture. Within weeks of moving to Springfield, he took on a client, a widow, Mrs. Joseph Anderson, who claimed that she and her son had been defrauded of their rightful inheritance: ten acres of land two miles from town, now occupied by Gen. James Adams, the attorney of the widow's husband. A founding member of the Springfield legal community, the fifty-four-year-old Adams, who had attained high rank in the Winnebago and Black Hawk wars, had been probate justice of the peace since 1823. A popular Democrat, he was his party's candidate for county probate judge in a special election scheduled for August. His opponent, Dr. Anson G. Henry, with whom Lincoln had begun a friendship, was noted for his abrasiveness, "a fiery fighter with a capacity for making two bitter enemies for each warm friend." Having been appointed a commissioner to supervise building the new statehouse, Dr. Henry had become the target of vitriolic Democratic criticism. Party partisanship, held in check during the state capital campaign, erupted into hard-hitting editorials and letters in the Democratic *Illinois Republican* and the Whig *Sangamo Journal*, the latter edited by Lincoln's friend Simeon Francis, who provided Lincoln open access to its pages. By early spring, both papers were printing accusations and challenges. Lincoln and his political friends wanted to minimize the chance that Adams rather than Henry would be elected county probate judge.

To the satisfaction of most Whigs, Lincoln published six letters signed "Sampson's Ghost," the first of which appeared on June 17, 1837. They made two distinct but overlapping accusations. Exercising his imagination and with literary ghosts vaguely in mind, including the ghost of Hamlet's father, Lincoln invented the restless, accusatory ghost of a former owner of the property on which James Adams resided. The ghost cannot rest until justice is done, the criminal exposed, and the property restored to its rightful owner. A literary device, the ghost makes his accusations by insinuation, asking a series of questions that cast aspersions on Adams's character, among them that he was a Tory at heart, that he had committed treasonous acts against his country in the War of 1812, and that he had come into possession of the property through devious means. The claim that Sampson's Ghost haunts the Adams residence, compelled by a desire for justice to repeat his tale of horrible misdeeds, segues in the sixth letter into an additional charge, an afterthought to Sampson's Ghost but soon paramount to the author behind the invention: the ghost now has specific knowledge that James Adams had fraudulently obtained title to a ten-acre plot once owned by Joseph Anderson. Those alert to Springfield political life would have known that on June 22 Lincoln and Stuart instituted a suit against Adams on real charges that paralleled the ghost's fictional allegations. Lincoln's second "Sampson's Ghost" letter was published on June 24, the sixth on July 29.

Lincoln's template for the creation of Sampson's Ghost was the Anderson case, which he took on a contingency basis for political reasons. It turned out, though, to be a weak literary device, a vehicle of satirical attack too obviously self-serving, sophistical, and whining in its insinuations to be sympathetic, let alone convincing. "I have only sought to promote inquiry," the ghost concludes duplicitously: "All I ASK—all I WISH is that TRUTH SHOULD PREVAIL. And before I am charged as a slanderer, I wish all the evidence in the case be fairly freely and fully examined." In responding to the six Sampson's Ghost letters, Adams handled himself well, given the circumstances. An experienced lawyer, he repeatedly challenged his accuser to provide evidence. Each time Lincoln responded with more charges. His strategy was to attack Adams's character. For that, evidence was irrelevant.

On August 5 he laid out his case in a "Handbill: The Case of the Heirs of Joseph Anderson *vs* James Adams." Lincoln's language is cool and matter-of-fact; also, at and just beneath the surface, it is strained by evasions, assumptions, and rhetorical devices, revealing that in essence the documents are political, not legal. Lincoln's strategy was to provide a narrative of the chain of events and the evidence that resulted in the conclusion he had reached. The focus was exclusively on "Joseph Anderson *vs* James Adams." Sampson's Ghost had gone back to his grave. The firm of Lincoln and Stuart, he told his readers, had agreed to take on the case at the request of the heirs only if they could find some legal ground on which to contest it. Naturally, he did not mention what most readers would have known: that since Lincoln and Stuart were high-level Whig politicians, such a suit would be in their political interest.

In his initial investigation, Lincoln wrote, he had discovered that a succession of deeds, the oldest about ten years old, had all been recorded on June 18, 1836. "This I thought a suspicious circumstance." He does not mention that it was not illegal and probably not unusual. "And I was thereby induced to examine the deeds very closely, with a view to the discovery of a defect by which to overturn the title, being almost convinced then it was founded in fraud." Eager to find fraud, he found it in a discrepancy between the record book and deed. At Lincoln's request, the recorder of deeds, Benjamin Talbott, obtained the original from Adams. The discrepancy, though, turned out to be an "error of the Recorder." Talbott, so Lincoln narrates, then brought the deed to his office and placed it in his hands. When Lincoln opened it, "another paper fell out . . . an assignment of a Circuit Court judgment in favor of Joseph Anderson against one Joseph Miller," which included a statement dated May 1827 in which Anderson assigned "all my right, title, and interest *to the said judgment*, to John Adams which is in consideration of a debt I owe." The date, Lincoln claimed, appeared altered, the writing new, the paper old. It must be a forgery, he concluded. It proved that Adams possessed land that properly belonged to the Anderson heirs. Lincoln then made a copy of the document in his own hand. Talbott then returned the deed to Adams. But whether or not he returned the assignment document Lincoln does not say. "At least one half" of the eight people to whom Lincoln claimed he showed it "will swear that IT WAS IN GENERAL ADAMS' HANDWRITING!" But in order for Lincoln to have had solicited opinions about the handwriting, he needed to have kept the original. He apparently returned the alleged forgery only after he had taken the time to show it to eight people, four of whom would not say it was in Adams's handwriting. And how could the recorder have examined the deed in detail at his own office, before bringing it to Lincoln, but not discovered the loosely interleaved document? It is a bizarre narrative; perhaps, like Sampson's Ghost, a fiction.

What Lincoln did not state in his "Handbill" was that those he consulted about the handwriting were Whig partisans and that the recorder, the only witness to Lincoln's discovery of the allegedly fraudulent document, acted improperly in not returning the deed directly to its owner. Was Talbott also a Whig and friendly to Lincoln? And Lincoln, usually a stickler for logic, did not pursue the possibility that the assignment may have been a clumsily written copy of a document the original of which would give no cause for suspicion. Recently, Lincoln complained, Adams had asserted "that no such assignment as the one copied by me ever existed" (Lincoln's copy of what he had in hand is not extant; Adams filed what he claimed to be the original, which differs from Lincoln's copy, on July 5, 1837). If it did exist, "it was forged between Talbott and the lawyers, and slipped into his papers for the purpose of injuring him." He must speak out, Lincoln concluded, because "silence might be construed into a confession" that Adams's charges are true.

Whatever the truth, Adams, whose victory in the election settled one aspect of the affair, soon published a point-by-point rebuttal of Lincoln's account, which Lincoln responded to in early September and then again in mid-October. Neither man had hard evidence. But Adams's account has as much if not more plausibility than Lincoln's. In both his replies, Lincoln strained to defend his accusations and to counter Adams's counterattack, particularly the claim that Lincoln's witnesses were prejudiced. "The General asks for proof of disinterested witnesses. Who does he consider disinterested?" Would honorable men "deliberately perjure themselves, without any motive whatever, except to injure a man's election?" Some readers must have rolled their eyes at this rhetorical question, and been further amused (or bored) by Lincoln's pettifogging tweaking of the available facts in which possible inaccuracy is elevated into perjury and in which an irrelevant discrepancy, attributed to a cover-up, is defined as tellingly important. Having described himself as "almost convinced" that the title had been founded in fraud, Lincoln was "*now . . . quite convinced*" by his own further analysis, which he had been forced to make public. Otherwise it would appear that he had withdrawn his charge, since it was widely known that Adams had proposed that *"If you'll quit I will."* But "we ask no such charity at his hands," Lincoln responded, and in fact it is Adams who in the meantime "is prowling about, and, as Burns says of the devil, *'For prey, a' holes and corners tryin,'*" and who is also asking everyone he meets *"if he ever heard Lincoln say he was a deist."* And the *Republican*, Lincoln complained, has the nerve to say that "public opinion has decided in favor of Gen. Adams."

Having undertaken the case to score political points, Lincoln may have convinced himself that Adams had obtained the land by fraud. If the desire to obtain justice for the widow had been his major motivation, it could have been pursued in court, without public accusations and literary inventions. But he knew that an accusation of criminality had the potential to damage Adams's chances in the August election. And as a partisan Whig, a rising star of the Springfield Whig establishment, in legal partnership with a leading Whig politician, he would have calculated the political effect of the charge that Adams had defrauded a helpless widow. Did Lincoln manufacture evidence or use evidence that others may have manufactured to serve mutual ends? Or was the copy of the "assignment of judgment" that he found suspicious created by Adams or someone in Adams's interest in order to discourage Lincoln's case? Or was it a clumsy attempt to bring to Lincoln's attention that a valid assignment did exist, even if the date had been inaccurately copied? And even if there were errors and fabrications, how could he be sure that Adams's right to the property wasn't valid anyway, as long as the relevant legal documents supported his ownership?

In the Sampson's Ghost letters, Lincoln engaged in slander. He also collaborated in what may have seemed to him and his friends a pious fraud, the claim that a document existed that implicated Adams in criminality. Adams was a political enemy, and he was far from a saint; he had been accused of fraud in the possession of property once before, though Lincoln did not know that then, and the political atmosphere of the time had a high tolerance for slander and skullduggery, especially the raising of outrageous charges for the purpose of eliciting a denial that would in

itself damage the accused. At the start, all Lincoln provided was his fic-
tionalized innuendo about the legitimacy of Adams's ownership of what
had once been Joseph Anderson's property. Perhaps by early June he had
concluded that Adams had committed forgery and defrauded Anderson's
heirs. If he had, would it not have been desirable for his political purposes to segue much earlier in the sequence of letters from Sampson's
Ghost's accusations to the Anderson accusation? That he did not provide
in his September 6 "reply to James Adams" a chain of dates stating exactly
when the allegedly forged document had fallen out of the book and into
his hands suggests that he was aware that the facts were not in his favor. If
so, it made sense to wait until two days before the election, when it was,
in effect, too late.

Apparently, the "Sampson's Ghost" letters alienated rather than attracted voters. The public had no reason to believe such undocumented
charges against a well-liked public figure. For all Lincoln's skill with language and his literary talent, the effort backfired. The language and the
devices of the "Sampson's Ghost" letters are shrill and stilted. They have
none of the personal or the rhetorical depth of the letters to Mary Owens
or of his address to the Springfield Young Men's Lyceum, which were
being created more or less concurrently. The evidentiary argument of
the two replies to Adams is thin, the tone aggressively self-defensive. In
the end, Lincoln's skills were in the service of a poor strategy, and the
call for justice was too deeply enmeshed in politics to be anything but
corrupted by self-interest. The cause contaminated the language.

CHAPTER 4

"How Miserably Things Seem to Be Arranged"

1837–1842

The fledgling lawyer who, in April 1837, arrived in Springfield on horseback with all his possessions in his saddlebags and walked into a general store to inquire about what "furniture for a single bedstead would cost" had already put distance between himself and provincial simplicity. He was neither country bumpkin nor rural innocent, and he did not adhere to any of the cultural myths about the superiority of country to city life or the moral inferiority of corrupt city ways to pastoral purity presented in literature from the Roman satirists to nineteenth-century Romanticism. Its particular American version, created by the Jeffersonian tradition, valorized independent farmers and small-town life. The Lincoln who moved to Springfield embraced the city as a dynamic reality. And in the Dick Whittington–Benjamin Franklin tradition, he had come to the city, at twenty-seven, to make his fortune.

Lincoln was an experienced and clever legislator; he had a grasp of local and national issues; he had done his best to prepare himself for the law; for his time and situation, he had read widely; and he had talent as a writer and speaker. He had come to Springfield to take up a junior partnership at a distinguished law firm whose head, John Todd Stuart, had narrowly lost as the Whig congressional candidate in 1836 and who, in 1838, was to be elected in a close contest with another Springfield lawyer, the short, pugnacious, and flagrantly ambitious state's attorney and aspiring Democratic politician Stephen Douglas. Lincoln had rough edges, which hardly seemed a liability. They could sometimes even be an advantage in his trade. What he did lack was money, his income essentially only his legislative salary, about ninety dollars a year. Fortunately, he had the temperament and habit of minimizing expenses. The furniture would cost seventeen dollars, Joshua Speed, part owner of the store, told him. "It is probably cheap enough," Lincoln responded, "but I . . . have not the money to pay. But if you will credit me until Christmas, and my experiment here as a lawyer is a success, I will pay you then. If I fail in that I will probably never be able to pay you at all."

An enthusiastic Whig, Speed knew who Lincoln was: he had heard him give a well-received stump speech the year before; he knew about his legislative career and his work on behalf of making Springfield the capital; and he had reason to anticipate benefit from his presence. When Lincoln expressed discomfort at the prospect of being further in debt, Speed offered an alternative, a commonplace arrangement in nineteenth-century America, especially in the west. "I have a very large room, and a very large double-bed in it; which you are perfectly welcome to share with me if you choose." Lincoln went upstairs, put his saddlebags down on the floor, "came down again, and with a face beaming with pleasure and smiles exclaimed, 'Well Speed I'm moved.'"

Years later Speed recalled that Lincoln was "almost without friends, and with no property except the saddle-bags," implying that he took him in without knowing him and that his success thereafter was the more astounding because he had arrived in Springfield friendless. In fact, Lincoln had been elected twice by the voters of the county. He had many friends and supporters. Speed now became one of them. Like Lincoln, he belonged to the large community of Kentucky-born settlers in central Illinois. Five years younger, he was a slim, handsome man of middle height who dressed and carried himself with casual elegance. A college graduate, the son of nurturing parents who owned a plantation outside Lexington, he had come to Illinois in 1835 determined to succeed in business. With money to invest, he bought an interest in a prominent general store. Like Lincoln, he loved reading. They soon discovered they had Byron in common, and Speed thereafter always believed that he had introduced Lincoln to Byron. Speed, as an intelligent amateur, and Lincoln, as a burgeoning professional, found current affairs fascinating. Soon their growing intimacy made conversations on personal matters a shared pleasure. It was Lincoln's only close exposure to an upper-class contemporary.

As bachelors, they both had an eye for attractive women. It is likely that Lincoln had some sexual experiences during his travels as a surveyor, perhaps also with a prostitute in Beardstown, a town he visited regularly in 1835–1836 to help promote its canal. In Springfield, Speed had "a pretty woman," a prostitute with whom he had semi-exclusive or exclusive privileges. When Lincoln expressed an interest, Speed sent him to see the girl with a note, so Speed told William Herndon. When they were naked, Lincoln remembered to ask the price. It was two dollars more than he had. "I'll trust you, Mr Lincoln, for $2." He mulled it over. "I do not wish to go on credit—I'm poor & don't know where my next dollar will come from and I cannot afford to Cheat you." He got dressed "and offered the girl the $3.00, which she would not take, saying—Mr Lincoln—You are the most Conscientious man I ever saw." Speed "asked no questions and so the matter rested a day or so." He then got an account of what had occurred from the girl. As close as the friendship was, on this matter silence did the speaking.

On others, Lincoln was expressive enough. His poverty, which went hand in glove with his frugality, became a leitmotif, mostly because he suffered under the mental burden of the debt incurred from the bankruptcy in New Salem. He still owed that money. It was a badge of honor and a claim of rustic integrity, a projection to him and others that he was a man who knew how to watch his pennies, primarily because his wants were such that he needed only a limited number. If he was poor, it was not because he spent unwisely, and he would never borrow himself into poverty again, partly because he feared indebtedness, mostly because, given his simple needs, a modest income would keep him solvent. Lincoln, though, was not a poor man when he arrived in Springfield, only short of cash for capital expenditures. Within a year, with his legislative salary and his earnings, he was saving money; small sums, but the start of an accumulation of capital.

And the law began to provide legal fees, averaging ten to fifteen dollars a case in a general practice, mostly debt collection, bankruptcies, and suits for recovery in business and property disputes, civil actions in which Stuart and Lincoln represented the plaintiff or the defendant, before either a justice of the peace or the circuit court or the Illinois Supreme Court in Springfield, or in one of the courts of the other Eighth Circuit counties to which Lincoln and Stuart regularly traveled. The junior associate was sought after for inspections, analyses, and arbitrations, activities in which his unpretentious manner and logical mind were valued. The firm had no share in the business generated by the state's indebtedness. Apparently, Lincoln made no effort to leverage his legislative position to get such business. After deducting the cost of office and travel expenses, the partners divided fees equally. Though not the best-regarded law firm in town, it was a close second to that of Stephen T. Logan, another stellar Whig lawyer-politician whom Lincoln admired. Stuart provided the gravitas and the expertise, Lincoln the down-home, common-folk touch that made him effective with clients and juries. Gradually, he found his voice and his confidence. The ability to think and write coherently that marked his success as a legislator began to characterize his performance in the law.

Though Lincoln had the usual daydream of lawyer-politicians about higher office, he was still serving an apprenticeship, though in its latter stages. He was in the process of developing an expressive public voice, capable of modulating between genres that encouraged informality, such as campaign speeches, and those that required formal presentation, such as bills, legislative speeches, and addresses to public audiences, such as his Springfield Lyceum address. Though they were delivered as speeches, they were in effect carefully crafted essays. From the start, he was uncomfortable speaking spontaneously. Even his campaign speeches were crafted by drafts and memory into a text visible to his inner eye, with parts that he could shift and adapt for the occasion. When he spoke without a text, he usually spoke from memory, creating the illusion of spontaneity. The invention of the moment—often a riposte or witticism or joke—had its occasional place, and he became adept at creating introductions and transitions that gave the set material local flavor. For formal occasions, he wrote out his words, often with the essay model in mind. His predilection always was to write before he spoke.

From the start, his stylistic model served him well: plain speech— the direct sentence, the building of rhythm and emphasis through selective syntactical repetition, with climax as the moment of maximum sense rather than of the highest oratory. He studied composition, continuing his analysis of model essays and speeches from the ancients to the moderns that his first anthologies had provided. Washington's sensible succinctness and Jefferson's eloquent simplicity were recent additions to the canon. His senior contemporaries, Daniel Webster and Henry Clay, at their best produced memorable oratory. But the most effective writing and speech, Lincoln concluded, eschewed preaching for calm persuasion, a demonstration not of superior oratorical powers but of succinct expression in the service of truth. It had an element in it of talk, of one person speaking to another with no distinction of class. And he could admire and learn from the best models whether or not he was friendly to their ideology or their careers. "So far as I now remember of his study for composition it was to make short sentences & a compact style," Speed recalled. "Illustrative of this—he was a great admirer of the style of John C Calhoun—I remember reading to him one of Mr Calhouns speeches in reply to Mr Clay in the Senate—in which Mr. Clay had quoted precedent. . . . Mr. Calhoun replied 'that to legislate upon precedent is but to make the error of yesterday the law of today.' Lincoln thought that was a great truth greatly uttered. . . . [Lincoln's] familiar conversations were like his speeches & letters."

Running for reelection in 1836, he announced his platform in a letter, as was the practice, to the editor of the *Sangamo Journal*. It was an example of his campaign style at its most colloquial. "In your paper of last Saturday, I saw a communication . . . in which the candidates who are announced in the Journal, are called up to 'show their hands.' Agreed. Here's mine! I go for all sharing the privileges of the government, who assist in bearing its burdens," by which he meant the suffrage for every white person who pays taxes or bears arms, including women. "If elected, I shall consider the whole people of Sangamon my constituents, as well those that oppose, as those that support me. While acting as their representative, I shall be governed by their will." And he and his fellow Whigs had a proposal about how to pay for public improvements without borrowing money. "Whether elected or not, I go for distributing the proceeds of the sales of public lands to the several states, to enable our state, in common with others, to dig canals and construct railroads, without borrowing money and paying interest on it," a scheme that the federal government was to find unattractive. He ended his brief announcement with a humorously phrased statement of whom he would vote for in the presidential ballot if he were "alive on the first Monday in November."

The presidency was an office that he had daydreamed about since childhood. He knew, though, that the road even to modestly higher position than state legislator was blocked by the obstructing presence of established Whig politicians in Springfield and around the state, all ambitious for higher office, especially congressional and senatorial seats. Ambition and advancement, he saw, would best be served by the most effective application of his talents in the state legislature, where he could write and speak about the issues at hand with whatever degree of formality and technical detail the situation required. On the campaign trail, he had the opportunity to mix serious issues with humorous anecdotes. The electorate responded best, he had observed, to colloquial first-person informality; to the experience of direct engagement with a campaigner who spoke their language; and to the image of the calm, sensible man of the people that he effortlessly projected.

They also liked his sharp tongue, as long as it did not seem premeditated. His talent for satirical deflation often broke through the kinder surface. An opponent's flaws could be fair game. He had a keen eye for personal vulnerabilities, which he could connect to political values and positions. He did exactly that in the speech Speed had heard in 1836. A complacent Whig turned Democrat who had recently built the most expensive house in Springfield, topped with a lightning rod, apparently the only one in town, responded to Lincoln's well-received speech that "this young man would have to be taken down." He then did so, Speed recalled, "in a style . . . able and fair," while "in his whole manner [he] asserted & claimed superiority." Lincoln responded: "The gentleman has alluded to my being a young man—I am older in years than I am in the tricks and trades of politicians—I desire to live—and I desire place and distinction as a politician—but I would rather die now than like the gentleman live to see the day that I would have to erect a lightning rod to protect a guilty Conscience from an offended God."

Lincoln indeed was adept at "the tricks and trades of politicians." What better device to disarm the charge of ambition than by admitting it in simple and direct language, and by cleansing it of the implication of egomaniacal selfishness by placing the emphasis on "distinction," with the inference that it is something earned, not stolen, an award for merit rather than chicanery. He was not in the game, he emphasized, to win for himself but to serve others, by contributing to the betterment of mankind. With his verbal quickness, he persuasively conveyed that ambition coupled with noble purpose can be transfigured into a device that transcends trickery. Such effective language cannot be anything but a vehicle of truth. Thus, what he does not have is "a guilty Conscience."

Lincoln's satirical thrust exhibited a genius for locating the effectively telling detail and for the calmness of verbal expression that projects cool ruthlessness. In campaign debate, his usual command of tone—

his calm rationality and his emphasis on analysis of issues rather than personalities—worked well with only occasional resort to the knife of Horatian satire. But "when thoroughly roused and provoked he was capable of terrible passion and invective," a friend recalled. "His '*skinning*' of one of his political opponents" was long remembered "as awfully severe." From an early age, his family had noted his biting tongue, his attraction to irony and sarcasm. When campaigning for the Whig presidential candidate in 1836, his anti–Van Buren invective was so strong that "a girl might be born and become a mother before the Van Buren men will forget Mr. Lincoln," who "was frequently interrupted by loud bursts of applause from a generous people," in the words of the pro-Lincoln *Sangamo Journal*. By the late 1830s, he had learned to make his satiric barbs less aggressive, to soften them into deflation rather than destruction, emphasizing ideas and persuasion rather than invective.

Since preparing bills, resolutions, and petitions drew on a skill that many of his colleagues did not possess, he was called on in the legislature for more than his fair share of drafting. And even when the bill at issue had multiple sponsors and signatures, it often was in Lincoln's handwriting, as if he had been delegated to come up with a carefully worded, coherent text. The January 1837 "Report and Resolutions of the Committee on Finance" was entirely in his handwriting. Its sharpness of diction and phrasing, its marshalling of evidence, the logical structure of its argument, and especially its combination of subtlety and clarity, also make it unmistakably his. The difference between it and the awkwardly written January 1840 "Report on the Condition of the State Bank," which he signed but had no hand in composing, is striking. In occasional instances his skills were so valued that a colleague persuaded him to act as ghostwriter, as in a bill that William Brown introduced in January 1836 to "Establish a State Road from Peoria to Pekin." There was, of course, no literacy standard for public office; some elected officials wrote so badly as to make it impossible for them to produce a serviceably written text of anything, and the more democratic the ethos, the lower the level of writing skills.

In a speech to the legislature early in 1837, Lincoln added his voice to the defense of the newly created state bank against accusations that it was corrupt and elitist. The Democrats had called for a special commission to examine the bank's conduct, insinuating that there had been criminality. Lincoln responded that since there was no evidence of any misconduct and no legal authority to conduct an investigation, the taxpayer should be spared the expense. "Mr. Chairman, this movement is exclusively the work of politicians; a set of men who have interests aside from the interests of the people, and who, to say the most of them, are, taken as a mass, at least one long step removed from honest men. I say this with the greater freedom because, being a politician myself, none can regard it as personal." The simple statement, effective in word choice, syntax, and tone, makes it clear that Lincoln valued the category enough to accept that he belonged to it. Consequently, he could not be accused of painting with a broad brush and without personal exposure those who did not live up to the highest standards of public life, such as the legislators who had proposed the investigation. Cases might occur, he admitted, "when an examination might be proper." But this was not one. And even if it were, he will explain why he still would be opposed.

Characteristically, he now raised the specific issue into a moral principle. In the hurly-burly of politics, he granted, self-serving arrangements can be tolerated. But when an attempt to resolve a local issue overrides a basic principle of Republican government, then the issue needs to be placed in the larger perspective. Change of any sort, he proclaimed, must occur within the framework of the law and constitution. The point that he was to stress in his address to the Springfield Lyceum one year later was already part of his thought and disposition: the secular religion of the country is adherence to the law, based on the conviction that right will triumph through persuasion and the ballot box. Later in 1837, when a prominent Illinois abolitionist was lynched, Lincoln had a much more vividly dramatic point of reference for the argument he had made in the state bank speech: the framework of the law must be respected in all cases. Jefferson's claim that "the tree of liberty must be refreshed from time to time with the blood of patriots and tyrants" made him uneasy, especially when it had become so difficult to define patriotism in a divided country in which half the nation embraced slavery as a positive good. "I am opposed," he told his colleagues, "to encouraging that lawless and mobocratic spirit, whether in relation to the bank or any thing else, which is already abroad in the land; and is spreading with rapid and fearful impetuosity, to the ultimate over throw of every institution, or even moral principle, in which persons and property have hitherto found security." To be true to itself, moral principle required lawful enactment.

Three months later, moral principle resulted in his being one of two signers and probably sole author of a protest against four resolutions that the legislature passed on the topic of slavery. His colleagues overwhelmingly agreed with memorials from five northern and southern states proclaiming that the national government was constitutionally prohibited from interfering with "the rights of property in other States" and that while Congress had jurisdiction over slavery in the District of Columbia, the exercise of its power "would be a manifest breach of good faith" unless it had the consent of the District's citizens. Those who claimed otherwise, the resolutions announced, especially the abolition societies, were an abomination, a source of discord and illegality.

Anti-abolitionism was strong in Illinois. Abolitionists were perceived as rabble-rousers sticking their noses into other people's business and anomic instigators determined to elevate a moral cause over the unifying imperative of constitutional law. Antislavery sentiment had been barely successful in shaping the 1818 Illinois state constitution that made slavery illegal at the cost of disenfranchising free blacks and strict regulation of "black settlement and employment." Southern and central Illinois, settled largely from Kentucky, with Missouri on its western border, maintained a cultural, historical, and ethnographic tolerance for slavery. The constituency for antislavery agitation was minimal; for antislavery proclamation it was larger but not extensive. Much of the Illinois working class in 1837 thought the controversy a distraction or a nuisance, unconnected to the problem of earning a living and creating a culture. Some could be reached by an appeal to personal moral standards. Many more, though, deplored the threat that antislavery agitation posed to civil discourse and lawful order.

The substantive distance between Lincoln's 1837 protest against the Illinois slavery resolutions and the Emancipation Proclamation almost twenty-five years later is considerable, but the moral difference is modest. In 1837, Lincoln agreed with most of his contemporaries: abolitionism is counterproductive, and the Congress of the United States "has no power, under the constitution, to interfere with the institution of slavery." On the first matter, Lincoln had no doubt in 1837 that "the promulgation of abolition doctrine tends rather to increase than to abate [slavery's] evils." But he also felt certain "that the institution of slavery is founded on both injustice and bad policy." And Lincoln's protest emphasized more strongly than the legislature's resolutions that Congress does have the authority to abolish slavery in the District of Columbia "but that that power ought not to be exercised unless at the request of the people of said District." Since the Constitution did not prohibit emancipation by majority vote, he implies that democracy can trump property rights, and lurking in the phrase is the suggestion of monetary compensation to slaveholders. Lincoln is no great distance from his later advocacy of gradual, compensated emancipation to be achieved through public enlightenment and the democratic process. "The difference between these opinions," Lincoln and his cosigner wrote, "and those contained in the said resolutions [submitted to the Illinois legislature], is their reason for entering this protest."

There is another difference—the language of the legislative resolutions *tends* toward slackness, baldness, legalese, and boilerplate: unthinking and unmodulated political thickness. Lincoln's phrasing, particularly in the key statement about "injustice and bad policy," is more exact in its wording and syntactically sharper. Its linguistic tensions—especially the crucial use of "but" after the semicolon in the phrase "They believe that the Congress of the United States . . . has the power under the constitution to abolish slavery in the District of Columbia; but that that power ought not to be exercised unless at the request of the people"—give the central moral claim much of its force. His command of language is measured to the intellectual complexity of the issue, to the balance of heart and head, of moral vision and legal constraints. The legislative resolution excoriates "abolition societies." Lincoln's protest uses language that recognizes that there are two sides to the scale, and that the balance needs to be thoughtfully calibrated in terms both of policy and morality. For example, he believes "that the institution of slavery is founded on both injustice and bad policy; but that the promulgation of abolition doctrine *tends* rather to increase than to abate its evils."

Between 1836 and 1842, he was also distinguishing himself in another aspect of his literary expressiveness, exemplified in his only two substantial essays during that period other than his address to the Springfield Young Men's Lyceum: his December 1839 "Speech on the Sub-Treasury" and his February 1842 "Temperance Address." Neither was a legislative speech. The legislature was not a forum conducive to extended discourse on subjects with moral and philosophical content. Those were sponsored mostly by educational and ideological organizations, such as the Lyceum and the Washington Temperance Society and, to a lesser extent, by the two political parties.

In November 1839, after a verbal flare-up in Speed's store between Stephen Douglas, supported by his Democratic colleagues, and Lincoln and the local Whigs, Douglas challenged his opponents to an immediate public debate. They had a second go-round in December. Lincoln had begun months before to play a major role in the Whig effort to contest state offices and elevate Gen. William Henry Harrison to the presidency and John Tyler, an ex-Democrat and former senator from Virginia, to the vice-presidency. On the day after Christmas, following a week of alternating Whig and Democratic speeches on the subject of the Van Buren administration's proposed substitute for the defunct National Bank, Lincoln concluded the pro-Bank argument before a small audience. It was a bravura presentation, a carefully composed political essay on a technical subject whose underlying argument focused on human nature and the lessons of experience.

Douglas's pro-sub-treasury speech preceded Lincoln's. A master of argumentative rhetoric, the dynamic Douglas had a gift for making inaccurate claims seem authoritatively factual and a genius for energizing the already persuaded. With more bravura than intellect, lightly touched by rational standards and moral philosophy, he found practical accommodation more compelling than moral persuasion. With the 1840 national political campaign well under way, Douglas set out the Van Buren platform vigorously, particularly on the issue of a sub-treasury versus a national bank, a continuation of the almost forty-year-long battle between the paper-based centralized monetary policy and banking system originated by Alexander Hamilton and the hard-money decentralized anti-Bank policy of Thomas Jefferson and Andrew Jackson. Centralized banks were pernicious, so the Democrats argued: they encouraged borrowing, which resulted in debt and produced inflation, which eventually led to deflation and then depression, such as the painfully remembered depression of 1819. When banks foreclose, they take autonomy away from the individual and the local community, placing it in the hands of the wealthy elite.

Point by point, with logical precision and a better regard for the facts, Lincoln rebutted Douglas. His counterargument was straightforward, an analytic description of the recent history and current state of budgetary policy, particularly the mechanisms for the collection and retention of tax money, the point of which was to demonstrate that the "sub-treasury" proposed by the Democratic administration would be wasteful of public money and subject to political corruption. It would take money out of circulation by requiring taxes to be paid in hard money (specie, usually silver or gold coins); it would not allow tax-raised funds to be invested in interest-bearing vehicles; and the revenue would remain in the hands of individual tax collectors, customs officials, and political agents, subject to misuse and peculation.

In his counterargument, Lincoln attends respectfully to what he does not agree with, summarizing Douglas's position without misrepresentation or trivialization, challenging Douglas's claims of fact only after he has laid the ground that enables his audience to believe he has earned that right. His argument takes additional force from the precision of his language and from his implied claim of absolute intellectual honesty. He makes lucid a subject prone to jargon and opacity by his cogent claim that economic policy develops out of a larger vision: it is the marketplace enactment of values and ideology. A national bank, Lincoln believes, serves the interest of democratic values by increasing the potential for economic growth. It provides the monetary instruments that benefit trade and manufacturing. It sets the table for those of energy and ambition to accumulate capital and rise in the world. By decreasing the money supply, the sub-treasury, he believes, will restrict growth and limit opportunity. A restricted economy would favor those who already have rather than those who aspire to get. It will help the favored few rather than the democratic many.

To set the personal stage and draw his audience's sympathetic attention, Lincoln began his carefully written and polished text with an imaginative twist on the conventional opening, expressing the orator's humility and awareness of the obstacles he must overcome:

> It is particularly embarrassing to me to attempt a continuance of the discussion, on this evening. . . . It is so, because on each of those [preceding] evenings, there was a much fuller attendance than now, without any reason for its being so, except the greater *interest* the community feel in the *Speakers* who addressed them *then*, than they do in *him* who is to do so *now*. I am, indeed, apprehensive, that the few who have attended, have done so, more to spare me of mortification, than in the hope of being interested in any thing I may be able to say. This circumstance casts a damp upon my spirits, which I am sure I shall be unable to overcome during the evening. But enough of preface.

With a strong sense of essay structure, Lincoln divided his into three parts: the merits of the proposed sub-treasury compared to a national bank; a substantive refutation of Douglas's claims of fact and the agency of his arguments; and a conclusion that casts in hortatory terms the immensity of the stakes at issue, the Whig charge that if Van Buren were to win, the country might lose its liberty. The sub-treasury address introduced for the first time the flexible pattern he was to draw on thereafter: a simple opening, often in the first person, with some reference to the difficulty of the task and the inadequacy of the speaker; a review of the what, how, and why of the occasion; an analytic presentation of the relevant facts and arguments; a synthesis of the underlying rationale for feeling, thought, and action; a story or anecdotal example, often humorous, for illustrative and humanizing purposes; and then a hortatory, rhetorical conclusion.

Strikingly, his undergirding argument against the sub-treasury appealed more to human experience, human nature, and values than to facts or rational analysis. His philosophic frame, the core of his public policy, appears at three decisive points, as if to say that after all the evidentiary argument is made, ultimate recourse must be to widely shared wisdom. "The experience of the past" proved that a centralized and regulated National Bank is a more secure place for public money than a dispersed, unregulated sub-treasury.

> And here, inasmuch as I rely chiefly upon experience to establish it, let me ask, how is it that we know any thing—that any event will occur, that any combination of circumstances will produce a certain result—except by the analogies of past experience? What has once happened, will invariably happen again, when the same circumstances which combined to produce it, shall again combine in the same way. We all feel that we know that a blast of wind would extinguish the flame of the candle that stands by me. How do we know it? We have never seen this flame thus extinguished. We know it, because we have seen through all our lives, that a blast of wind extinguishes the flame of a candle whenever it is thrown fully upon it. Again, we all feel to *know* that we have to die. How? We have never died yet. We know it, because we know, or at least think we know, that of all the beings, just like ourselves, who have been

coming into the world for six thousand years, not one is now living who
was here two hundred years ago.

It is a simple yet sophisticated argument, elegantly expressed, in which
Lincoln positions himself within the tradition that claims all knowledge comes from experience. Its language suggests that he has read the
eighteenth-century Scottish philosopher David Hume on the subject.

Two years later, he composed an essay even more literary and philosophical than his Sub-Treasury address. It was a presentation without
an overt political message or context, not a call to the ballot box but
a meditation on aspects of human nature and the human condition,
especially in regard to instruments of change and the connection between moral reformation and political freedom. The topic at hand was
"temperance," about which he had written a schoolboy essay; its larger
subject, the search for liberty, our potential to liberate ourselves from
those aspects of human nature that prevent the triumph of reason and
moral vision. The essay on temperance is Lincoln's least-appreciated
composition, written with the literary skill and philosophical perspective that were to make him our most distinctively expressive and morally decisive president.

The Springfield branch of the Washington Temperance Society had
invited him to deliver its annual address to celebrate the 110th birthday
of its namesake. As always for Lincoln, the ultimate model for civic emu-
lation was George Washington, and both the namesake and the cause had
their sacred power. "Washington is the mightiest name of earth—*long
since* mightiest in the cause of civil liberty; *still* mightiest in moral reformation," so Lincoln told an audience whose reverence for Washington was so great it rose to a hagiographical belief in his absolute good-
ness. The connection between moral and civic reform was to be Lincoln's
theme. And the Washington worship was sincere, though strategic also,
and an ironic anticipation of the fetishistic worship, after his death, of an
idealized Lincoln. "On that name, an eulogy is expected. It cannot be. To
add brightness to the sun, or glory to the name of Washington, is alike

impossible. Let none attempt it. In solemn awe we pronounce the name, and in its naked deathless splendor, leave it shining on."

Rather than preaching reform to alcoholics from the pulpit of the virtuous, the Washingtonians enlisted ex-alcoholics to deliver the message. In the 1830s, with a Christian evangelical fervor sweeping the country, part of the Second Great Awakening, a national temperance movement sprang up in reaction to an America awash in whiskey—as comfort, drug, and medicine of first and last resort, the national drink for celebratory occasions, an opiate particularly of the urban and rural poor, widely purveyed with minimal regulation and little social stigma. The intensity of the reaction, spearheaded by religious crusading societies, waving flags, banners, hammers, and axes, with rallies, bands, parades, and the coercive rhetoric of sin-and-damnation Protestant revivalism, testified to how deeply a part of American life whiskey had become. "When all such of us, as have now reached the years of maturity," Lincoln writes, "first opened our eyes upon the stage of existence, we found intoxicating liquor, recognized by every body, used by every body, and repudiated by nobody. It commonly entered into the first draught of the infant, and the last draught of the dying man." Lincoln's sentences embody the temperance message: complementing and contrasting words in balance; repetition as the building block of variety; the personal and the universal use of pronouns in a sympathetic bonding.

The Washington Society's advocacy of reformation both by example, on the premise that an ex-alcoholic's words carry the force of successful experience, and by enlightened persuasion, assuming that a "drop of honey catches more flies than a gallon of gall," as Lincoln put it, appealed to him. A nondrinker himself, he had no moral objection to alcoholic consumption, and those "of us who have never fallen victims, have been spared more from the absence of appetite, than from any mental or moral superiority over those who have." Though as a host he did not provide alcohol to others, from childhood on he was often in the company of convivial drinking. On that level, he made no protest. He did, though, object to alcoholism, a destructive nationwide phenomenon that took a heavy social and economic toll. But he agreed with the Washingtonians that it was counterproductive to demonize those who sold and consumed liquor. The path to reform needed to take the road of example, persuasion based on a realistic assessment of human nature, the effective use of moral influence, and an appeal to the desire of people to control their choices and thus be free in the highest sense.

Throughout, Lincoln's text resonates with a four-level story: the literal narrative about alcoholism, stressing the superiority of the Washingtonian approach; a critical gloss, through a web of biblical allusions, of the evangelical emphasis on sin and redemption, which Lincoln rejected; the traditional eighteenth-century model of the temperate life that he had absorbed from his earliest reading in Scott's and Murray's canonical anthologies; and the vision of an ideal national American community in which rational discourse, sweet persuasion, and moral influence characterize the civility of public discourse and in which "there shall be neither a slave nor a drunkard."

The literal narrative analytically compares the superiority of the new approach to that of the traditional agents of reform. "The *preacher*, it is said, advocates temperance because he is a fanatic, and desires a union of Church and State; *the lawyer*, from his pride and vanity of hearing himself speak; and the *hired agent*, for his salary." But the reformed drunkard appears as the exemplary model. "Nor can his sincerity in any way be doubted; or his sympathy for those he would persuade to imitate his example, be denied." The argument continues in Lincoln's characteristic style—a prose so lucid to read it is like looking a hundred feet through clear water. The paragraphs have a tight-knit unity, held together by a seamless appeal to the role of human nature, as Lincoln sees it, in all matters of persuasion. Human nature can never be changed. It has, though, many facets and is subject to the influence of internal and external forces:

> To have expected [the drunkard and the liquor dealer] not to meet denunciation with denunciation, crimination with crimination, and anathema

with anathema, was to expect a reversal of human nature, which is God's decree, and never can be reversed. When the conduct of men is designed to be influenced, *persuasion*, kind, unassuming persuasion, should ever be adopted. It is an old and true maxim, that a "drop of honey catches more flies than a gallon of gall." So with men. If you would win a man to your cause, *first* convince him that you are his sincere friend. Therein is a drop of honey that catches his heart, which, say what he will, is the great high road to his reason, and which, once gained, you will find but little trouble in convincing his judgment of the justice of your cause, if indeed that cause really be a just one. On the contrary, assume to dictate to his judgment, or to command his action, or to mark him as one to be despised, and he will retreat within himself, close all the avenues to his head and heart; and tho' your cause be naked truth itself, transformed to the heaviest lance, harder than steel, and sharper than steel can be made, and tho' you throw it with more than Herculean force and precision, you shall no more be able to pierce him, than to penetrate the hard shell of a tortoise with a rye straw.

Both a realistic and an idealistic view of the degree to which people are accessible to rational persuasion, this assessment of human nature underlies Lincoln's approach to the discussion of public issues. "Such is man, and so *must* he be understood by those who would lead him, even to his own best interest." The true leader rejects extremes, understands and respects human nature, and leads by sweet persuasion. He is temperate, and true temperance is a combination of wisdom, respect, and rationality. You will be persuasive, he adds as a qualifier, "if your cause is just," though events were to teach him that whether or not a cause is just is often defined by the vantage point of the perceiver and that there are some differences of view that amiability, persuasion, and reason will not reconcile.

The unhappy results of intemperance, Lincoln argued, were all too evident, and the larger reach of the illness extended much beyond alcoholism. The harmonizing balance that temperance represents is valuable

in all aspects of life, public as well as personal. "Temperance, by fortifying the mind and body," Lincoln had read in Murray's anthology, "leads to
happiness; intemperance, by enervating them, ends generally in misery."
Lincoln's Shakespeare had provided him with dramatic examples of intemperance, from the two Richards to Macbeth and Hamlet, the excess amplified by misjudgment, ambition, arrogance, and irrationality; and Burns
and Byron had provided lyric and narrative representations of the Romantic attraction to intemperance from the drunkenness of "Tam O'Shanter"
to the Byronic hero intoxicated with personal autonomy and revolutionary change. "The demon of intemperance ever seems to have delighted in
sucking the blood of genius and of generosity."

The literal temperance revolution, Lincoln observed, does not require bloody struggle. Its battle is fought on the field of moral reform.
But the settled views that human nature have found congenial over time
do not readily give way. "The universal *sense* of mankind, on any subject,
is an argument, or at least an *influence*, not easily overcome." For example, "the success of the argument in favor of the existence of an overruling Providence, mainly depends upon that sense; and men ought not,
in justice, to be denounced for yielding to it, in any case, or for giving it
up slowly, *especially*, where they are backed by interest, fixed habits, or
burning appetites." As with all revolutions, he reminded his audience,
there will be a price to be paid to bring it to a happy result. Even our
"political revolution of '76," of which "we are all justly proud," exacted a
heavy cost, and it is the challenge of distinguishing between various kinds
of revolutions and the different prices they exact, especially weighed in
the balance of what they achieve, that inevitably came to the mind of Lincoln the politician, aware of the American past and apprehensive about
its future. When sweeping change is required because a long-suffering
people will no longer bear the ills of oppression or a long-festering divisive wound will not be healed and can no longer be tolerated, then temperance may no longer offer relief, let alone resolution.

That happened in 1776, Lincoln emphasized. That revolution "has
given us a degree of political freedom, far exceeding that of any other

of the nations of the earth" and demonstrated "the capability of man to govern himself." But it should not be forgotten that "with all these glorious results, past, present, and to come, it had its evils too. It breathed forth famine, swam in blood and rode on fire; and long, long after, the orphan's cry, and the widow's wail, continued to break the sad silence that ensued. These were the price, the inevitable price, paid for the blessings it bought." But temperance as a moral value, as a frame of mind, and as a governing policy can avert such horrors. "And when the victory shall be complete—when there shall be neither a slave nor a drunkard on the earth—how proud the title of that *Land*, which may truly claim to be the birth-place and the cradle of both those revolutions. . . . How nobly distinguished that People, who shall have planted, and nurtured to maturity, both the political and moral freedom of their species." In conjunction with the phrase "neither a slave nor drunkard," it is clear that the word "species" includes slaves. By 1842, Lincoln had made his views clear: he deplored slavery; he believed its existence detrimental to the American polity; and he desired the completion of the revolution that would bring liberty to all, though he hoped it would come through a reformation that would avoid "the orphan's cry, and the widow's wail."

Though the Whigs won nationally in 1840, they were defeated in Illinois. Lincoln's own margin of victory was considerably less than ever before, partly a testimony to the dominance of the Democratic Party in the state and a harbinger of what were to be his poor chances for statewide electoral success as a Whig. None of his speeches from the 1840 campaign survives. His hundreds of talks in the brawling, sloganeering campaign began and remained spoken rather than written, except for occasional summaries in newspapers, which reveal that, despite his slotting in memorized chunks of argument on issues such as the National Bank, the main emphasis for both sides was on harsh, no-holds-barred attack and defense. Lincoln poured his talent as a satiric deflator with a gift for sharp-tongued sarcasm into this leave-no-survivors campaign: Van

Buren epitomized decadent anti-American evil; General Harrison was a paragon of patriotism and wisdom, a reincarnation of Washington. After twelve years of being out in the cold, Lincoln and the Whigs married ideology and anger into a paranoid, last-defender of Liberty, anti–Democratic Party rhetoric, a superior example of which Lincoln had provided in the peroration of his Sub-Treasury speech.

At the same time, mostly on the fly, with John Todd Stuart either away in Washington or campaigning himself, Lincoln conducted much of the day-to-day business of the law firm, the profits from which were still split equally. Though he had little formal social life, he was rarely alone, except when reading at night, though Joshua Speed was nearby for conversation. Privacy was neither a virtue nor practical in the small spaces in which Springfield people lived and worked. Mainly it was available outdoors and, for Lincoln, also in the interior space of his self-communing, the inner world concealed by a reserved face that seemed to oscillate between unreadable and joyless. The comment that his was a sad face and that he was a sad man became a later leitmotif, and he himself acknowledged that when he wasn't enlivened by public performance or personal conversation his face rested, as if life had gone out of it. "There was more difference between Lincoln dull & Lincoln animated, in facial expressions, than I ever saw *in any other human being*," a journalist later remarked. How often Lincoln's lack of facial animation was merely a face at rest and how often a reflection of depression cannot be determined, though clearly periods of engagement with ideas and politics alternated with periods of emotional withdrawal.

Since his arrival in Springfield, his feeling of social isolation, which he had confided to Mary Owens in 1837, had been sustained both by circumstance and his difficulty in making friends beyond those with whom he lived and worked. Speed had become his reliable companion, making isolation less onerous. Lincoln still slept in a shared room above Speed's store, and there is no information about what he paid Speed, if anything. He took his meals mostly at the home of his friend William Butler, who helped him financially in small ways and whose wife did his laundry. He had no end of lawyerly and political people for conversation, argument, and debate at his musty downtown office, at the nearby courts and legislature, and in front of the fireplace at the rear of Speed's grocery store. The atmosphere was rough-and-tumble masculine, an appropriate place for slang, country humor, and vulgar stories.

Just as Speed facilitated other sorts of access for Lincoln, he now played a role in his entry into the Edwards-Todd circle, the upper crust of Springfield society in which parlor-speaking gentlefolk of both sexes held teacups and exchanged social pleasantries. His legislative colleague, Ninian W. Edwards, a lawyer and Whig politician, the son of the former Illinois territorial governor, and Edwards's wife Elizabeth Todd, one of four daughters of a Lexington family of privilege, welcomed him. Her father was Robert Smith Todd, a socially prominent Lexington banker, lawyer, and Whig politician. As a Kentuckian of good breeding, Speed was a welcome guest at the Edwardses' home. He introduced Lincoln, who, without birth, education, or society manners, was nevertheless an up-and-coming Whig legislator and the legal partner of a Todd relative, John Todd Stuart. Lincoln began to attend teas and parties at the spacious Edwards home.

Late in 1839, Elizabeth Todd Edwards introduced him to twenty-one-year-old Mary Todd, who had just begun an extended visit to her sister, just as Mary Owens had been on an extended visit to hers. Both ladies had desired a change in venue, Mary Todd to escape a contentious family environment, especially a difficult stepmother, and to prospect for advantages of the sort her sister had. The well-to-do families of unmarried young women had a vested interest in arrangements that would increase courtship opportunities. Two years older than her sister, Elizabeth had married at sixteen, probably eager to escape a father preoccupied by a new family and dominated by his second wife, who had liberated herself from her husband's children by sending them at an early age to boarding school. Later, Mary was to describe her childhood as "desolate," the boarding school as her actual home. In Springfield, she had excellent contacts and a friendly forum, including three distinguished first cousins, all from Kentucky: John Todd Stuart, Lincoln's partner; Stephen Trigg Logan, the capital's most respected lawyer and a circuit court judge who was to be Lincoln's next partner; and John J. Hardin, the son of a United States senator from Kentucky, a successful lawyer and legislator, who was rising quickly in Whig politics. Stuart, Hardin, and Edwards, all college graduates, were about Lincoln's age; Logan ten years older.

Mary Todd literally and metaphorically danced into the center of this circle, an eminently eligible young lady, though an unlikely prospective wife for the badly dressed, socially guileless, and temperamentally asocial Lincoln. Short, large-boned and -bosomed, she was light enough on her feet to dance gracefully and stylish enough to dress well. Mary was a lively conversationalist who had been educated at a finishing school, and her verbal wit had a sarcastic edge—repartee, usually about social matters and people, rather than insight. With men whose esteem she desired, she was playful. With underlings, she varied between indulgent and nasty. In a temper tantrum, she was prone to throw the first thing at hand. Angry and conflicted about her father, whose second marriage she blamed for her comparative poverty, she was eager to be loved and obeyed. Imperious, quick-tempered, and spoiled, she oscillated mercurially between self-esteem and insecurity. She was nothing if not animated, "a bright, lively, plump little woman—a good talker, & capable of making herself quite attractive to young gentlemen." An excellent mimic, her French was said to be perfect, and she adored parties. She commanded attention in social conversation, was playful in repartee and effusive in monologue. Her narcissism had glitter, a sparkle that went a long way in Springfield social life.

Having grown up in a political family, she also loved political talk. Like her father and family, she worshipped their Lexington neighbor Henry Clay. To be the wife of a powerful political figure, a senator or president, she considered the next best thing to being one. Expert in the gossipy side of politics and "a violent little Whig," she was flirtatious and egomaniacal, a romantic sentimentalist with a volatile temper. At the same time, she was lonely and eager to have some sort of success. She had a musical education, especially dancing and the opera, which she adored. Her education had also provided her with a literary background, wide reading in the English literary canon from Shakespeare to Sir Walter Scott. She loved "poetry, which she was forever reciting." As a letter writer, she handled language effectively, with skill and expressiveness, with exact diction and a fine sense of sentence structure and rhythm.

Lincoln's interest and Mary's flirtatiousness were encouraged by the Edwardses, who considered the "rising" Lincoln unlikely but not impossible, part of a group of four or five men who hovered about Mary. That winter and spring he was intensely busy as a legislator and lawyer. Serving as an elector in the Whig effort to elect Harrison, between April and November 1840 "he was gone from Springfield well over half the time," campaigning and appearing at various circuit courts. Mary visited relatives in Missouri the entire summer. If there were letters exchanged between them, they were probably not the product of a presumption of intimacy by either. Perhaps the excitement of their common political passion kept each vivid in the other's mind. Most likely they saw one another at social and political occasions in early fall 1840. They were rarely together and probably never alone in each other's company.

Later that autumn, Lincoln went through an emotionally wrenching experience: he believed he was in love with Mary Todd, and then he believed that he no longer was. No evidence exists that he had proposed to her. Mary flirted with various men. No one in their circle had any awareness of a commitment between them. Apparently, though, both were aware that a proposal was a possibility. Soon after the Whig victory in November, Lincoln no longer felt himself in love with her, which he seems to have believed he had given her reason to assume he was. Rather than allow a misrepresentation to stand, he told her so, or words to that effect. Apparently, he told her twice, soon after the election and then again at the end of November. The episodes embarrassed and pained him. Mary apparently responded that he was acting dishonorably. To complicate matters, she may have believed, as did Speed and Elizabeth Edwards, that Lincoln's head had been turned by Matilda Edwards, the eighteen-year-old daughter of a Whig politician and state senator from Alton, who was also visiting and probably shared the guest bedroom with Mary. Amid emotional turmoil, Lincoln withdrew from the relationship with Mary Todd.

In December and January 1841 he immersed himself in legislative activity, except for some interspersed days, even weeks, when he was too depressed to work and disgusted enough with himself to frighten his friends, who thought he might harm himself, just as his New Salem friends thought him suicidal after the death of Ann Rutledge. Speed recalled that Lincoln expressed despair because he had "done nothing to make any human being remember that he had lived," perhaps a displaced expression of unhappiness about his failure to live up to his high standards of character and, if more than that, a measure of how huge was his political ambition since he had by most standards already achieved considerable success, given his age. The "Poem on Suicide" that Speed believed Lincoln wrote in the spring or summer of 1840, published in the *Sangamo Journal* soon after it was written, may actually have been composed in early 1841. The claim that such a poem once existed is creditable, though indeed if Lincoln wrote it, it is likely evidence that he had no intention of killing himself. "The paths of glory lead but to the grave" and other lines from his memorized poetic anthology spoke to his despair at the situation he had created: a woman had accused him of dishonorably spurning her; he hadn't the slightest chance of attaining the affection of another; and in a second relationship with the first woman, he had again shown himself feckless to her and to himself, ambivalent, indecisive, and unworthy—attributes especially damaging to a man who prided himself on his honesty and manly virtue.

All the self-tormenting demons of depressive melancholy that were deep in his consciousness, the languages of Gothic and Romantic despair from Gray's churchyard to Byron's "Darkness," had to be part of his brooding self-flagellation. He had indeed been reading Byron that autumn, and he never was long absent from his favorite authors. Shakespeare's *Hamlet* was an available corollary. Lincoln's two confrontational conversations with Mary Todd seemed, in Speed's account of Lincoln contradicting his words by kissing her consolingly, to resemble Hamlet's oscillation between indecisiveness and precipitate action. By late January 1841, various versions of what had happened between Todd and Lincoln were circulating in Springfield, including that he had fallen out of love with her and in love with Matilda. Gossipy voices disparaged him. Various accounts of who had rejected whom circulated. Apparently, friends let Lincoln know that they thought he had acted badly.

On January 1, 1841, his misery, in retrospect associated with that date, had plunged him into what he recognized as a nervous breakdown, or at least the start of a breakdown. In the next week or so he acted with uncharacteristic irritability in the legislature. By mid-January, he could no longer attend sessions. Deeply depressed, he put himself under the care of his friend Dr. Anson Henry. Different reports state varying degrees of despair. "He was very sad and melancholly, but being subject to these spells. nothing serious apprehended." Or, he was "so much affected as to talk incoherently, and to be delirious to the extent of not knowing what he was doing." Another close observer told her sister that "Mr Lincoln was wearing his life away in an agony of remorse." But, he said, "It would just kill me to marry Mary Todd."

By the end of the third week of January he was back at work, the always thin man noticeably emaciated but functional again. He was better but not well, though he was well enough to describe his condition and to contemplate an alternative life in a tersely effective and characteristically well-written letter to his law partner in Washington: "I am now the most miserable man living. If what I feel were equally distributed to the whole human family, there would not be one cheerful face on the earth. Whether I shall ever be better I cannot tell; I awfully forebode I shall not. To remain as I am is impossible; I must die or be better, it appears to me. The matter you speak of on my account," a government patronage job in Oregon, "you may attend to as you say, unless you shall hear of my condition forbidding it." He was not offered the job, and he was in the process of recovering. By February 1, he prefaced a business letter to Stuart, "You see by this, that I am neither dead nor quite crazy yet."

Over a year later, in March 1842, in a letter to Speed, he referred to "that fatal first of Jany. '41," as if something decisive had happened on that day. Perhaps it had nothing directly to do with Mary, who was away from Springfield. Since Lincoln's withdrawal, she had continued her usual social activities, and whatever the degree to which it was a performance, a friendly observer noted in January that "Miss Todd is flourishing largely. She has a great many Beaus." Lincoln, though, "is in rather a bad way." It was the day on which Speed sold his interest in the grocery store, having decided sometime before, because of his father's death and his obligation to his Louisville family, to return to Kentucky. Lincoln, though, had to have known of Speed's plans. The sale could not have come as a total shock. Probably Lincoln's reference to the "fatal" first of January was in response to Speed's happy news that his marriage in Kentucky was a superlative success. His point to Speed was that he had had very little happiness since his breakdown until the arrival of Speed's letter. Indeed, he would have been "entirely happy" since the arrival of the good news except "for the never-absent idea, that there is *one* still unhappy whom I have contributed to make so. That still kills my soul. I can not but reproach myself, for even wishing to be happy while she is otherwise." With misleading syntactical awkwardness, he placed "since then . . . I should have been entirely happy" immediately after "the fatal first of Jany. '41," though "since then" refers to the time of his receipt of Speed's recent letter.

By spring 1841, he was considerably better. While he worried about Mary's frame of mind, he kept his distance. But in June he began a series of epistolary exchanges with Speed in which Speed's courtship and marriage experiences, and Lincoln's own effort to work out the peculiarities of his personality in regard to making a marital commitment, led to what he had never believed he wanted or could readily survive—his marriage to Mary Todd in November 1842.

Two of Lincoln's letters during this period are distinctively different from those about courtship and marital commitment: both depend on the author's skills as a storyteller. The first, written in June 1841, exists mainly for the pleasure the writer takes in penning a narrative and the anticipation of the pleasure that Speed will have in reading it. It relates an incident that Lincoln found fascinating and published in April 1846 in a revised version, "The Trailor Murder Case, Remarkable Case of Arrest for Murder." The June 1841 letter is written to the moment, the events that compose its plot narrated with a sense of spontaneous presentness that gives it pace and vividness. Lincoln begins, "We have had the highest state of excitement here for a week past that our community has ever witnessed; and, although the public feeling is now somewhat allayed, the curious affair which aroused it, is verry far from being, even yet, cleared of mystery. It would take a quire of paper to give you anything like a full account of it." In the expanded version, published in the Quincy *Whig* almost five year later, he retold the story in a more formal, deliberate style. He begins, "In the year 1841, there resided, at different points in the State of Illinois, three brothers by the name of Trailor. Their Christian names were . . ." The earlier version is a vivid, fast-paced account for Speed's eyes; the revised account, for the readers of the Quincy *Whig*, is a formalized third-person narrative, drawing on some of the language and devices of literary narrative.

In both versions the plot is the same. Two brothers, one of whom lives a hundred miles from Springfield, are accused by a third brother, who lives in Springfield, of having murdered for his money a mentally damaged man who resided with the most distant brother. The alleged murder took place on a trip to Springfield. It is widely believed that the brothers had disposed of the body in a pond in the woods near Springfield before returning home. A dragnet of the area does not produce the body, but circumstantial evidence suggests there has been a murder, though some of the brothers' actions imply either that they are not culpable or that they are engaging in a cover-up. The key witness against the accused is the Springfield brother who claims he saw what led up to the murder and then the body itself. At the last moment, the two accused men are saved from conviction by the appearance of a doctor from the deceased's hometown, who claims to general disbelief that the dead man is indeed alive, which is soon proved by his appearance in Springfield. Deranged and incoherent, he can throw no light on where he has been or what happened. The other principals refuse to talk.

Lincoln's account in the 1841 letter reveals his delight in capturing the details that enrich the characters and situation. He concludes:

> Thus stands this curious affair now. When the doctor's story was first made public, it was amusing to scan and contemplate the countenances, and hear the remarks of those who had been actively engaged in the search for the dead body. Some looked quizical, some melancholly, and some furiously angry. Porter, who had been very active, swore he always knew the man was not dead, and that *he* had not stirred an inch to hunt for him; Langford, who had taken the lead in cuting down Hickoxes mill dam, and wanted to hang Hickox for objecting, looked most awfully wobegone; he seemed the *"wictim of hunrequited haffection"* as represented in the comic almanic [*sic*] we used to laugh over; and Hart, the little drayman that hauled Molly home once, said it was too *damned* bad, to have so much trouble, and no hanging after all.

It is the human interest that fascinates Lincoln, who uses descriptively pithy, colloquial language to capture the distinctiveness of his characters and the complexities of human nature. The narrative exists not to illustrate a point or persuade an audience but to evoke the details of life in order to make an indirect comment on life itself.

In the 1846 literary version, Lincoln told the story with a deliberate pace that provides a more detailed, logically structured, expository account. Aware that he has now raised the professional storyteller's pen, he also recognizes that he is a storyteller of facts, not an inventor or a creator of fictions. But the genre requires that he arrange the facts to make the story effective as a coherent narrative. And because a mystery that is unresolved arises out of the known facts, the account is open-ended or at least lacks fully satisfactory resolution, which no nineteenth-century novelist need settle for but that Lincoln must. "Thus ended this strange affair," he writes, "and while it is readily conceived that a writer of novels could bring a story to a more perfect climax, it may well be doubted, whether a stranger affair ever really occurred." Without plot materials to serve as a climax, he makes a virtue of this necessity. In the letter version, though, he finds his climax in the amusing catalogue of the reactions of the participants and the telling humor of "it was too *damned* bad, to have so much trouble, and no hanging after all."

In the revised version, Lincoln makes excellent use of what he has to work with. Though he excels as a spontaneous storyteller, he does well enough as a self-conscious writer. Indeed, the "Mark Twain of our politics" had the potential to be a variant of the Mark Twain of our literature. The facts of both accounts, especially those in the letter, have the feel of a novelist's notebook entry for a fiction that engages one or more of the possibilities for the "curious speculation" Lincoln refers to in the conclusion of the published version. That version dryly concludes:

> It is not the object of the writer of this, to enter into the many curious speculations that might be indulged upon the facts of this narrative; yet he can scarcely forbear a remark upon what would, almost certainly have been the fate of William and Archibald, had Fisher not been found alive. It seems he had wandered away in mental derangement, and, had he died in this condition, and his body been found in the vicinity, it is difficult to conceive what could have saved the Trailors from the consequence of having murdered him. Or, if he had died, and his body never found, the case against them, would have been quite as bad, for, although it is a principle of law that a conviction for murder shall not be had, unless the body of the deceased be discovered, it is to be remembered, that Henry testified he saw Fisher's dead body.

It is not the conclusion of a storyteller who writes fiction, and it is characteristic of Lincoln's predilection to conceive of story as illustration rather than as an independent creation valued for its version of an alternative world.

In a letter to Mary Speed, Joshua's half-sister, written soon after returning from a visit to the Speed plantation in 1841, Lincoln provided a memorable example of his effective use of illustrative storytelling. A paragraph-long description, it is as sharply etched a passage of meaningful descriptive writing as Lincoln ever composed, created both for the sake of those to whom it was addressed and for the writer's need to use language to clarify his feelings. For the first time since his 1832 New Orleans voyage, he had again visited a slave state, traveling in July 1841 with Speed to Lexington and back via St. Louis, part of the journey by steamboat. At the Speed plantation, the family provided a restorative embrace and restful comfort. The holiday was a great success, marred only by a painful toothache. Speed introduced Lincoln to his fiancée-to-be, Fanny Henning, whom Lincoln thought "one of the sweetest girls in the world," with only one flaw: she has "a tendency to melancholly. This, let it be observed," he remarked, partly as self-diagnosis, "is a misfortune not a fault." His detestation of slavery did not undermine the decorum he required of himself as a guest. Still, three weeks on a plantation serviced by slaves required him to observe an inequity that insulted his existential being, debasing the value he attached to a document that stated that "all men are created equal."

A month later, in Springfield, he attempted to come to terms with the experience. The existential exercise took the form of a narrative, a story embedded within a chatty letter, an account in the form of a digression that became the fullest, most sustained, and dominant section of the letter, more than half its length:

> We got on board the Steam Boat Lebanon, in the locks of the Canal about 12. o'clock. M. of the day we left, and reached St. Louis the next monday at 8 P.M. Nothing of interest happened during the passage, except the vexatious delays occasioned by the sand bars be thought interesting. By the way, a fine example was presented on board the boat for contemplating the effect of *condition* upon human happiness. A gentleman had purchased twelve negroes in different parts of Kentucky and was taking them to a farm in the South. They were chained six and six together.

A small iron clevis was around the left wrist of each, and this fastened to the main chain by a shorter one at a convenient distance from, the others; so that the negroes were strung together precisely like so many fish upon a trot-line. In this condition they were being separated forever from the scenes of their childhood, their friends, their fathers and mothers, and brothers and sisters, and many of them, from their wives and children, and going into perpetual slavery where the lash of the master is proverbially more ruthless and unrelenting than any other where; and yet amid all these distressing circumstances, as we would think them, they were the most cheerful and apparently happy creatures on board. One, whose offence for which he had been sold was an over-fondness for his wife, played the fiddle almost continually; and the others danced, sung, cracked jokes, and played various games with cards from day to day. How true it is that "God tempers the wind to the shorn lamb," or in other words, that He renders the worst of human conditions tolerable, while He permits the best, to be nothing better than tolerable.

The storyteller's lead that "nothing of interest happened" alerts the reader that something of interest that *did* happen is about to be presented. "By the way" signals that what follows is neither digressive nor casual. Lincoln's fascination with human nature and its adaptability to changing circumstances provides the cover umbrella for a description that highlights two irreducible givens: the misery that slavery devises for black human beings whose intimate communities are regularly destroyed, and human beings adapt to the worst of conditions by finding ways of making them tolerable in order to survive. To Lincoln, for whom cheerfulness was at best a momentary evasion of the tragic view of life, the seemingly cheerful slave and the melancholy freeman are in that respect not far apart, though they approach the mean of the human condition from opposite extremes. His own misery resulted from his awareness that his gloomy temperament mirrored the unalterable cosmic disarrangement; it was both objective and existential, the basis of his tragic view of the universal human situation. But, he believed, slavery was not built into the cosmic fabric; human beings had created the institution, and what they had done could be undone. Lincoln's description of the slaves, chained "like so many fish upon a trot-line," creates a linguistic dissonance between the cool descriptive tone, the precision of language, the refusal to indulge in hyperbole, and the focused emotional evocation of broken homes and perpetual separation. By contrast, the cool philosophic framework adds heated intensity to Lincoln's depiction of the reality of slave life, and the broader observation firmly implicates everyone: Lincoln, the Speed family, the South, the North, the nation.

Lincoln's six 1842 courtship and marriage letters to Speed exemplify his skill in the practice of the self-exploratory letter. Private letters, they were privileged exchanges on a confessional subject. They are Lincoln's most intimate documents extant. In a few instances, he wrote two versions of the same letter: a frank one for Speed alone and a decoy for Speed to share with his uninitiated fiancée. As with his letters to Mary Owens, we have only Lincoln's side of the correspondence. The letters consequently read like stanzas or sections of a dramatic monologue in which a single speaker grapples with a consequential issue or situation. In the process of addressing his words to a second party, he discovers something important about himself. In doing so he reveals his character to the reader. And the letters have an additional dimension: they embody the Damon and Pythias literary archetype, Lincoln's and Speed's extension of the classical motif of two deeply bonded male friends who identify so closely with one another that each shares the other's problems. The emotional well-being of one cannot be separated from that of the other. In the legend, Damon pledges his life for his friend. In the end, both are saved. In these letters, Lincoln and Speed are surrogates for each other in a relationship that had developed since 1839 as a mutual rescue fantasy. Each struggled to save the other, though the terms that defined salvation shifted over time.

Between November 1840 and January 1841, Speed had tried to save

Lincoln from what both thought a likely disaster. As confidant and advisor, Speed had helped him recover after his self-torturing performance and breakdown. By spring Lincoln apparently had recovered, at least to the extent of seeming to be his old self. In a letter to a friend, Mary Todd, referring to one of Lincoln's favorite plays, *Richard II*, which they may have read parts of together, expressed her hope that "Richard should be himself again." At their last meeting, she had "released" him from any obligation he believed he had incurred, apparently with the proviso that she had not changed her thoughts about him. If he desired, they could resume their relationship. In the summer of 1841 and thereafter, Speed's situation with Fanny Hemming paralleled what Lincoln's had been with Mary Todd, though with an important difference. Speed had without any ambivalence proposed and Fanny had consented to marry him, probably during Lincoln's Lexington visit. Speed now needed his friend's assistance, and the issue was similar to what had been at issue for Lincoln: Did he love Fanny to the degree that he should in order to proceed confidently and happily with the engagement? Lincoln was pledged by brotherly obligation to be Speed's confidant and guide, to play Damon to his Pythias.

By early 1842, with his wedding scheduled for mid-February, Speed apparently was in a panic of self-doubt and commitment anxiety. Unlike Lincoln, he had no need to think about whether he could support a wife and family. But the notion of whether he would prove worthy preoccupied him. Sexually experienced, he questioned whether he loved Fanny sufficiently to make her the sole focus of his erotic life, a marital obligation widely observed in principle but less so in fact, especially in the culture of wealthy Southern slaveholders. Could he make such a commitment, and if he made it, what price would he pay? And even if the price were worth paying, had he steady enough nerves to consummate the bargain? Lincoln, probably his only confidant, knew better than anyone those aspects of Speed that were at play and would determine the outcome. They now positioned themselves for a second performance on the same theme, though with the roles reversed.

Before Speed left for Lexington in January 1842, Lincoln wrote his first guide-letter, for his own sake as well as Speed's. "Feeling, as you know I do, the deepest solicitude for the success of the enterprize you are engaged in," he laid out point by point, with his usual mix of analytic argument and personal experience, formal authority and emotional sincerity, why he felt so much concern; and in the subtext he revealed that his own experience as a self-doubting suitor controlled his analysis of Speed's personality and predicament. In describing Speed, he described himself, not because he was misrepresenting Speed but because their similarities were the basis of their friendship. The letter was not to be mailed but given to Speed at his departure, to be read later and be available thereafter. "I think it reasonable that you will feel verry badly some time between this and the final consummation of your purpose, it is intended that you shall read this just at such a time." If he were "to say it orrally, before we part, most likely you would forget it at the very time when it might do you some good," evoking his own counterproductive performance with Mary after having gotten Speed's excellent advice. He thinks this because it is what he would have been experiencing if he had been in Speed's situation and what he had experienced, in a more fragmentary pattern, with Mary Todd. Lincoln had no doubt that the written word was superior to the spoken: a text provided the advantage of stable portability and unalterable futurity. The power of language is increased immeasurably when married to the miracle of writing, which was to be the theme of his 1859 essay on discoveries and inventions.

Like himself, Speed is *naturally of a nervous temperament*," and it is that general cause, as well as three local reasons, Lincoln points out, why he will suffer until the marriage is consummated. The first of the local reasons draws on a widespread nineteenth-century conviction that bad weather lowers the spirits of those with "defective nerves." In that regard, the six winter weeks until the wedding were likely to be unpropitious. The second reason is *"the absence of all business and conversation of friends,"* which would divert his mind and "give it occasional rest from that *intensity* of thought, which will some times wear the sweetest idea thread-bare and turn it to the bitterness of death," which Lincoln hopes his surrogate presence by letter will do something to alleviate. His legislative and legal obligations have prevented him from accompanying Speed in person. Letters, then, will have to carry his voice. The third reason is the rapid *"approach of that crisis on which all your thoughts and feelings concentrate."*

But it is Speed's general "nervous debility" which is the dominant guarantor of his misery, by which Lincoln means Speed's sensitivity, his regard for the feelings of others, his fright at the notion that others will also have to pay if he makes a mistake, his deep existential desire to do the right thing consistent with his feelings, and his apprehensive questioning of his own sincerity. In Speed's case, Lincoln believes that he can demonstrate that his friend's concern that he "does not love her" as he should is unfounded. "What nonsense!——How came you to court her? Was it because you thought she desired it; and that you had given her reason to expect it," as had been his case with Mary Todd, though the comparison is there only between the lines. Not so. And "did you court her for her wealth?" Again, between the lines, Lincoln alludes to the widespread comment in Springfield that if he were to marry Mary Todd he would marry up. "Why, you knew she had none." Indeed, Speed should admit that he proposed to Fanny because he loved her. "Say candidly, were not those heavenly *black eyes*, the whole basis of your early *reasoning* on the subject?" The knowledge that love itself was the determining motive should allay all apprehension. Still, "I shall be so anxious about you, that I want you to write me every mail."

Though he does not say so explicitly, the logic of Lincoln's argument is that he broke off his relationship with Mary Todd because he did not love her. He replied to a woeful January 25 letter from Speed that "you well know that I do not feel my own sorrows much more keenly than I do yours." Indeed, Speed's deep worries about Fanny's recent illness and her health in general, including his vision of being at her deathbed, were proof of his love for her. That should "forever banish those horid doubts," for a measure of love is the degree to which the anticipation of the death of those we love is both horrible and natural. "The death scenes of those we love, are surely painful enough; but these we are prepared to, and expect to see. They happen to all, and all know they must happen. Painful as they are, they are not an unlooked-for-sorrow." We can measure the extent of how deeply we love by the painful vividness with which we regularly anticipate the death that will bring that expected sorrow.

With the wedding fast approaching, Lincoln received another letter from Speed to which he responded with the hope that all would have gone well by the time Speed had Lincoln's letter in hand. "You know my desire to befriend you is everlasting—that I will never cease, while I know how to do anything." Even if he still felt despondent after the wedding, "should excessive pleasure still be accompanied with a painful counterpart," he would soon feel better. "I am now fully convinced, that you love her as ardently as you are capable of loving." On February 25, Lincoln read the letter Speed had written him on the morning after his marriage, announcing that "Miss Fanny and you 'are no more twain, but one flesh. . . . I feel som[e]what jealous of both of you now," he responded; "you will be so exclusively concerned for one another." Speed would not return with his bride to live in Springfield. "I regret to learn that," Lincoln confessed. "I shall be verry lonesome without you." The Damon-Pythias relationship was over. And the lesson was clear to anyone of a realistic and philosophic temperament. "How miserably things seem to be arranged in this world. If we have no friends, we have no pleasure; and if we have them, we are sure to lose them, and be doubly pained by the loss."

A month later, Lincoln again wrote to Speed, indirectly acknowledging that he had resumed the possibility that he, too, might find a wife and a marital friend. The news that Speed was *"far happier"* in his marriage than he had *"ever expected to be"* provided, Lincoln announced, his first fully happy moment since his January 1841 nervous breakdown. If Speed's courtship had not turned out so well and if Lincoln had not been so deeply complicit in the process, it seems unlikely that he would have resumed his relationship with Mary Todd. She was still in Springfield, still uncommitted, without a proposal. By summer 1842, they were occasionally together again, in meetings maneuvered by mutual friends. Lincoln was needy, wary, but vulnerable. In principle, domestic comfort and stability seemed compellingly attractive.

On September 8, 1842, Mary's good friend Julia Jayne, probably with Mary's assistance, sportingly added a letter to a series published in the *Sangamo Journal* that had begun as general criticism of Democratic policies and had continued as humorous satire of the Illinois state auditor. A well-known Springfield Democrat, James Shields had the unenviable job of enforcing the state government's unpopular decision to refuse acceptance of the Illinois State Bank's paper notes for payment of taxes. With the bank collapsing into imminent receivership and its currency devalued, the state had found itself compelled to accept payment only in gold or silver. Four years before, a series of letters had been published in the *Journal*, probably written by its editor, Lincoln's friend Simeon Francis, under the rubric "From the Lost Townships." The letters humorously criticized the legislature's redistricting of counties for partisan advantage. Francis revived the "Lost Townships" rubric when he published (and probably wrote) a letter on August 19 under that heading, signed "Rebecca," attacking Democratic policies in general. It was followed by a similarly headed and signed letter dated August 27 and published on September 2, this one by Lincoln, attacking Democratic monetary policy; then by a third letter, probably again by Francis, and then by a fourth, on September 8, this last composed by Julia Jayne, to which Mary may have contributed; and, finally, by some satirical verses written by Mary.

Lincoln's contribution to this series shows him writing in the satiric mode, with humorous irony, much of it gentle, at a level that reveals his talent for the colloquial and idiomatic voice, his gift as an impersonator of voices, and his attraction to narrative about the tension between human nature and political values. It is a witty performance, a considerable advance on his early satiric verses, the "Chronicles of Reuben." Like Francis, he drew on the widely popular comic genre that highlights a single character presenting a short monologue in dialect, usually with a satiric target. The humor arises from the oddness of the language or personality of the speaker, or from some ironic gap between the speaker's words and the implied reality, or from the cleverness with which the target is satirized. All these elements are present in Lincoln's satire. Characteristically, he is not the inventive agent. Francis's initial letter had established the first-person voice of the fictional monologist: Rebecca, the wife of a farmer named Jeff. It had also introduced the general topic of the state's fragile finances. At Lincoln's point of entry into the sequence, external events encouraged a more focused satiric target. In the week between Francis's and Lincoln's letters, Shields had announced that the state would not accept the bank's notes as payment for taxes.

The comic Rebecca is assertive, earthy, and witty, with a gift for gab and dialogue, deft at quoting other voices and providing supposed transcriptions of her snappy dialogue with her husband and others. A country lady, she specializes in common sense. At her most aggressive, she is both sharply deflationary and barnyard coarse, more like Chaucer's Wife of Bath than Dickens's Esther Summerson. Lincoln's skill with narrative and dialect, his creation of character voice, and his feel for country people give the presentation literary credibility. At the same time, the political satire sparkles with the clear intellectual sharpness of ideological delineation. "Tyler appointed him?" Jeff asks about Shields. Rebecca's paragraph-long response epitomizes much of the literary quality throughout. At the climactic moment, aspects of the author's own voice supersede Rebecca's language. The dominant use of dialect is toned down, and Lincoln moves from impersonal political satire to personalized parody, drawing on the widespread view that Shields was excessively vain about his physical attractions, a representative of the puffed-up elite rather than a populist Democrat. Rebecca concludes, in Lincoln's ironic reversal, that Shields must be a Whig:

"Yes (if you must chaw it over) Tyler appointed him, or if it wasn't him it was old granny Harrison, and that's all one. I tell you, aunt Becca, there's no mistake about his being a Whig—why his very looks show it—every thing about him shows it—if I was deaf and blind I could tell him by the smell. I seed him when I was down in Springfield last winter. They had sort of a gatherin there one night, among the grandees, they called a fair. All the galls about town was there, and all the handsome widows, and married women, finickin about, trying to look like galls, tied as tight in the middle, and puffed out at both ends like bundles of fodder that hadn't been stacked yet, but wanted stackin pretty bad. And then they had tables all round the house kivered over with baby caps, and pin-cushions, and ten thousand such little nicknacks, tryin to sell 'em to the fellows that were bowin and scrapin, and kungeerin about 'em. They wouldn't let no democrats in, for fear they'd disgust the ladies, or scare the little galls, or dirty the floor. I looked in at the window, and there was this same fellow Shields floatin about on the air, without heft or earthly substance, just like a lock of cat-fur where cats had been fightin. . . . He was paying his money to this one and that one, and tother one, and sufferin great loss because it wasn't silver instead of State paper; and the sweet distress he seemed to be in,—his very features, in the exstatic agony of his soul, spoke audibly and distinctly—'Dear girls, *it is distressing* , but I cannot marry you all. Too well I know how much you suffer; but do, *do* remember, it is not my fault that I am *so* handsome and *so* interesting.'"

Appalled at the ungentlemanly insertion of a personal attack into a political discussion, Shields demanded that Francis reveal the name of the author of the letter. He soon did, with Lincoln's consent. Shields had reason to feel insulted. The belittling sexual imagery was unmistakable. He had been at a party at which the women "wanted stackin pretty bad." He had been in an "exstatic agony"; he had vainly commiserated that he knew how much the women suffered because he could not marry them all; and then, with "a most exquisite contortion of his face . . . seized hold of one of their hands and squeezed, and held on to it about a quarter of an hour." If Shields thought the earlier satire at least not dishonoring, this demeaning personal attack was intolerable. Lincoln had used words to insult Shield in a way that was beyond the possibility of words to avenge, even if Shields had been adept enough with language to harness it for a counterattack.

Another Rebecca letter appeared on September 9, this one also by Julia Jayne. It coarsely continued the attack on Shields. On September 16, Mary's verses were published, a series of rhymed couplets, the satiric fulcrum of which is that Shields and Rebecca have married. Lincoln's admission of authorship after the August 27 letter tacitly assumed responsibility for the September 9 letter and the satirical verses. When Shields challenged him to a duel, Lincoln accepted. As the men were about to fire on each other on a dueling ground in Missouri, the duel was averted by the determined intervention of two of the seconds, particularly Lincoln's Whig colleague John Hardin. If either of the men had been killed, the survivor would have had to deal with criminal charges. Lincoln was deeply relieved.

Mary, who intruded herself into the Shields matter, may have done so both as an aggressive Whig and as a woman interested in deepening her association with Lincoln. The episode helped bring them together again, the sort of mutually exciting political activity that had provided the context for the start of their courtship during the 1840 presidential campaign. His participation in a duel, which she could have construed as being at least partly in defense of her, had to have been exciting as well as worrisome, the kind of event that creates erotic ripples. Two weeks after it was canceled, Lincoln importuned Speed to answer the question "'Are you now, in *feeling* as well as *judgement*, glad you are married as you are?' From any body but me, this would be an impudent question not to be tolerated; but I know you will pardon it in me. Please answer it quickly as I feel impatient to know."

Speed's answer may have helped to solidify his commitment, but his need to ask Speed at all suggests that the kind of commitment he desired was at least partly absent. He was not "entirely satisfied that his *heart* was going with his hand," Speed tactfully recalled. "If I had not been married & happy—far more happy than I ever expected to be—He would not have married." If Lincoln was "impatient" to have Speed's answer because a process from which he could less and less extract himself was transpiring, the end result had some of the inevitability that Lincoln associated with the events of life in general. James Matheny recalled that Lincoln came to him one evening in 1842 and said, "'Jim—I shall have to marry that girl.'" Apparently he felt that he had unintentionally or with divided mind again given Mary the impression that he intended to propose. Had there been some sexual activity? Had he actually proposed? Lincoln could not have been unaware that some people encouraged the marriage because they thought it would be an advantageous partnership, the good sense of which may have influenced his decision. John Todd Stuart believed "that the marriage of Lincoln to Miss Todd was a policy Match all around."

As late as the beginning of October 1842, he had made no commitment, let alone precise marriage plans. Still, on the evening of November 4, Lincoln and Mary Todd were married in the parlor of the Edwardses' home. The hosts learned of the plan that morning, apparently because Mary did not trust them not to intercede or at least counsel delay. The small party of witnesses was notified early that afternoon; the best man, Jim Matheny, at noon. Lincoln's father and stepmother had no idea their son was to be married until after the event. None of his Hanks relatives was invited. Julia Jayne served as bridesmaid. Her brother recalled that "only meager preparation could be made on so—short notice." As the evening of the wedding came on, Matheny thought that "Lincoln looked and acted as if he was going to the Slaughter." Rev. Charles Dresser, an Episcopal minister, performed the ceremony, with Judge William C. Brown of the Sixth Circuit Court standing directly behind him. Lincoln placed the ring on his bride's finger and pronounced the prescribed formula, "'with this ring I thee endow with all my goods and chattels, lands and tenements.'" Judge Brown, Matheny recalled, "who had never witnessed Such a proceeding, was Struck with its utter absurdity and spoke out So everybody could hear . . . 'Lord Jesus Christ, God Almighty, Lincoln, the Statute fixes all that.'" Reverend Dresser "broke down under it—an almost irresistible desire to laugh out, checked his proceeding for a minute or so—but finally recovered and pronounced them Husband and Wife."

Lincoln's love for Ann Rutledge had expressed and even expanded his capability for Romantic absorption and intensity. His relationship with Mary Owens had deflated it. In marrying Mary Todd, he embraced, hesitantly, domestic regularity and family—the relegation of Byron to text rather than to life. "Close thy Byron, open thy Goethe!" in Carlyle's words, was the superseding strategy, and whatever the erotic component of his courtship, it had, during its two tumultuous years, been undermined by his hesitancy, his skepticism, and his concern that he could not carry it through successfully. At the same time, as he struggled in his personal life to impose his commitment to reason, prudence, and order on unruly emotions, he began to see that his wife-to-be was not reasonable, prudent, or orderly. His immersion in Byron's poetry had its resonant passages in Ann Rutledge's death. But the cynical Byron of *Don Juan* III.8 is more appropriate to his marriage and embodies Lincoln's sensitivity to his father's advice that if one has made a bad bargain, one should "*hug* it the tighter." Byron previewed what was to be the pattern of the Lincoln-Todd marriage in a poem that, by the late 1830s, was one of Lincoln's favorites:

> There's doubtless something in domestic doings
>   Which forms, in fact, true love's antithesis;
> Romances paint at full length people's wooings,
>   But only give a bust of marriages:
> For no one cares for matrimonial cooings,
>   There's nothing wrong in a connubial kiss:
> Think you, if Laura had been Petrarch's wife,
> He would have written sonnets all his life?

Life with Mary Todd was sometimes to be like Don Juan's hell, the domestic haggling of what to the Romantic mind is "true love's antithesis." After 1842, even more than was necessary, Lincoln arranged his work schedule and professional travels on the court circuit to escape "domestic doings." He increasingly made a marginal necessity into a pleasurable absence. And even his relationship with the four sons he and Mary were to have—whom he loved dearly, eager to be a better (and certainly more supportive) father than his had been—needed to be factored into his formula for domestic peace. His most important strategies were to be patience, forbearance, and distance.

CHAPTER 5

"Were I President"
1842–1849

Though he never pretended to like the detail work, under the direction of his new partner, Stephen T. Logan, whose law firm he joined in spring 1841, Lincoln started to get an education in the necessity of thorough and exact preparation. His association with Logan, a former circuit court judge and arguably the most highly regarded lawyer in Springfield, with an extensive Illinois Supreme Court practice, increased Lincoln's professional credibility. A short thin man with a "wrinkled, wizened face" and a "shrill, sharp, and unpleasant" voice, Logan was brilliant in his no-nonsense briefs and oral arguments. He expected his junior partner's main contribution to be his down-home articulateness and common touch. Logan appeared to be all business; Lincoln gave the appearance of being un-businesslike. Logan tested the mettle of jurors; Lincoln made them feel comfortable.

During the two years of their partnership, Lincoln's management style, typified by his habit of carrying important papers in his hat, became less slovenly, though always light-years from Logan's administrative generalship. Lincoln's attraction to the spontaneous and the pragmatic kept him at a disadvantage in preparation and heavily reliant on the power of his language to influence juries. Unlike Logan, who enjoyed the intellectual gymnastics of legal theory, Lincoln revealed little intellectual curiosity about the law itself. Solvency required a high caseload, repetitive paperwork, and regular court appearances. Perched on a rented horse that always appeared small, Lincoln traveled throughout the Eighth Circuit counties, usually for three months in the fall and three in the spring, occasionally away from home each entire sequence. He carried his Shakespeare, and sometimes Burns and Byron, in his saddlebags. If he read Shakespeare's sonnet 30, "When to the sessions of sweet silent thought, I summon up remembrance of things past," he would have recognized the poet's use of legal and judicial imagery and the language of English common law.

If Lincoln had any complaint about Logan, it was that his generalship required more discipline and exerted more pressure than he wanted to submit to, without sufficiently benefiting his pocketbook. Lincoln got a minor share of the firm's income, apparently one third, though its large practice still resulted in his income being greater than ever before. That permitted him to save, slowly decreasing his outstanding indebtedness and allowing him to purchase a half-interest in a downtown building. He now had a wife to support, first at the Globe Hotel, then in a rented house, and then in the four-year-old one-story residence at Jackson and Eighth streets that he bought for $750 in May 1844 from the minister who had married him. When Logan decided to bring his son into the firm, the partners knew that even Lincoln's one third would be untenable.

Deciding to set up for himself, the thirty-five-year-old Lincoln invited Kentucky-born, college-educated William Herndon, nine years his junior, whom he had first met in 1832 and who was now clerking for Logan, to become his partner in a new firm. Lincoln knew Herndon's father, Archer, a vocal proslavery partisan, and his uncle, a river pilot whom he had assisted in attempting to prove the Sangamon navigable. An avaricious reader of history, literature, and political theory, William Herndon had at college become an enthusiastic left-wing Whig who favored immediate abolition. Archer Herndon forced his son to leave school on the ground that he would not contribute to the education of "a damned abolitionist pup." Widely known as "Billy," Herndon returned to Springfield and worked part-time for Speed, often sleeping in the same room with Speed and Lincoln. He participated in the debating sessions around the grocery store stove and at the Springfield Young Men's Lyceum. Energetic, dark-haired, good-looking, and of average height, he was ambitious and capable, with strong ideas of his own and immense reverence for the tall, grave, avuncular older man who had honored him with this invitation. They opened their office in an unpretentious room above the post office, across the hall from the United States District Clerk's office, with a small number of the standard legal books and some odds and ends of furniture. They would share fees equally, with Herndon primarily handling the office work. Lincoln soon discovered that his partner's management skills were not much better than his own. Like an affectionate older brother, valuing trust more than utility, he persisted in his belief that they would make a good team. It proved a loyal and enduring partnership.

An old leather office couch became Lincoln's favorite place to read, his feet extending far out, propped on chairs above a floor that seemed always dirty. Stretched out on the couch, he spent many workdays reading newspapers and books, handling legal papers, walking to the courthouses or the legislature, scheming about politics, apparently neither happy nor unhappy, a difficult man to read, who loved jokes and stories, usually to make a point, but who otherwise was so self-contained that he seemed secretive, especially to his chatty colleagues and friends. If he had complaints, he kept them brief and subdued. If he was angry, he read or walked it off. If he was disappointed, he had reserves of stoicism with which to discharge it, a frame of mind that found solace in the notion that all things pass, including human life. If he had views, as he did on most things, he did not go out of his way to express them except on political matters, and even there he had begun the habit of holding things close to his chest. With a few intimate friends, such as Jim Matheny, he would sometimes unbutton, and at home the pleasures and the problems of his marriage maintained a conciliatory balance. He discovered quickly that Mary's temper needed to be smoothed or avoided, and these may indeed have been the happiest years of his marriage. His circuit court travels helped keep him out of the firing line.

"Nothing new here," he had written a week after the wedding, "except my marrying, which to me, is matter of profound wonder." It was not a marriage that he had willed into existence. Three days short of nine months after the wedding ceremony, in August 1843, Robert Todd Lincoln was born; almost three years later, a second son; four years later, a third; a fourth and last in 1853. For at least ten years they were a sexually active couple, and also political partners of a sort. Mary had a deep stake in her husband's career. Some of her problems as a wife and mother, especially tantrums that sent her husband into flight and her children into evasion, may have resulted from her realization that the melancholy man she had married might never reach the high political office she had from childhood expected a husband of hers would occupy. Married to a taciturn unsentimental man who was often away, she struggled, sometimes at the edge of hysteria, with household chores that she had not been born or educated to handle. Mary's father, visiting Springfield and observing their domestic circumstances, gave her an allowance of $120 a year, primarily to pay for a servant, the largesse of a well-to-do slaveholder embarrassed by his daughter's drudgery.

Lincoln had brought his Illinois legislative career to an end in March 1841. Eight years of service had exhausted his energy and optimism; his last two legislative sessions were variants of Whig hell. Little to nothing went right. By narrow majorities, the Democrats ruled both the Illinois Assembly and the Senate. Ideological Democrats and practical Whigs needed to devise ways to save the state from financial ruin. Having been a leading voice for borrowing and expansion, Lincoln fought numbers of rearguard defensive actions, most of them unsuccessful. In a widely mocked incident, he exited from a window of the statehouse in a bungled attempt to deprive the house of a quorum and prevent a vote adverse to the state bank on the specie-redemption issue. The Whigs and the state bank lost credibility. Lincoln, the floor leader, was caricatured with legs so long that he didn't have to jump at all. He writhed under graphic derision. A Douglas-led court-packing bill enlarged the state supreme court, placing that, too, in Democratic hands. Lincoln's attempt to award some of the state printing business to Simeon Francis failed. Fighting roughly in rough politics, he was mostly on the losing side. In his 1838 reelection campaign, his vote total dropped noticeably, and, with a slim Democratic majority in both houses, Whigs had no committee chairs. Once again he narrowly lost the contest for Speaker of the House.

When he walked out of the statehouse for the last time as a legislator, his political career was on hold, his personal affairs dismal. He was slowly recovering from a nervous breakdown. He did not want to go back to the legislature. The next year, Whig newspapers created the rumor that he would be a candidate for governor. Probably in consultation with friends and with Mary, he made it clear that he would not run: at best he would be a Whig sacrificial lamb. The United States Senate was out of the question, especially because that seat went to the party with a legislative majority rather than according to the vote of the people. The House of Representatives was another matter. His own county, Sangamon, was the most heavily populated Whig county in the eleven-county Seventh Congressional District. "Now if you should hear any one say that Lincoln don't want to go to Congress, I wish you as a personal friend of mine," he wrote to a Whig activist in February 1843, "would tell him you have reason to believe he is mistaken. The truth is, I would like to go very much. Still, circumstances may happen which may prevent my being a candidate."

With Lincoln taking a forceful role, the Whig Party in Illinois had recently reorganized its nominating process, against much opposition. Previously, individuals had announced their candidacies to state and local electoral officials. As many as did so appeared on the ballot. Parties consequently had no official lists, let alone designated nominees. Each candidate was identified by party association but not by party endorsement. When, led by Douglas, the Democrats created a convention-nominating system, endorsing a single candidate for each office, they gave themselves a distinct advantage. The Whigs now imitated their successful rivals. In a

"Campaign Circular" coauthored with two other Whigs, Lincoln summarized the party's platform: the tariff as the main source of national revenue, the establishment of a National Bank, and a scheme for Illinois to benefit from the sale of government land. His guiding pen dominated the tight structure and expressive language of the circular, noticeably in its description and defense of the newly adopted "Convention System." With the Bible and Aesop as his literary referents, he stressed the importance of party unity in language that he was to use again in 1856. "That 'union is strength,'" the local politician wrote in early March 1843, "is a truth that has been known, illustrated and declared, in various ways and forms in all ages of the world. That great fabulist and philosopher, Aesop, illustrated it by his fable of the bundle of sticks; and he whose wisdom surpasses that of all philosophers, has declared that 'a house divided against itself cannot stand.'" Ironically, Lincoln lost out in the first test of the new system he had helped devise. As he had anticipated, "circumstances" arose that prevented his nomination. "We had a meeting of the whigs of the county," he wrote to Speed in March 1843, "to appoint delegates to a district convention." After seven ballots, "Baker beat me & got the delegation instructed to go for him."

It was a painful defeat, partly because of the irony that the self-educated son of an illiterate man had been damaged by the charge that he was the candidate of the snooty Edwards-Todd circle. To a limited extent, he was. His wife and her family eagerly anticipated his rise in the world, which they had always regarded as his and their destiny. To discover that otherwise friendly Whig voters felt alienated because of his marriage and believed his egalitarian values and personality suborned by an association with the Springfield elite deeply distressed Lincoln. It was also a wake-up call about his vulnerability in a society in which voters gave weight to church association and Christian identification. Politics and religion overlapped considerably. Even the comparatively tolerant Episcopalians of the Edwards-Todd circle had reservations about Lincoln's Christianity. So, too, did middle- and working-class Presbyterians. The more severe Protestant sects rejected any candidate whose religious views did not tightly adhere to their own.

Lincoln found himself in the position of being out of favor with every sectarian group. Not belonging to a congregation, he did not have the support of a church, and his absence from weekly Christian fellowship was noticed. Even more damaging, he was known by some and rumored by others to be an "infidel"—a non-Christian. A close reader of his 1842 "Temperance Address" would have noticed that he positioned himself in relation to Christians as if he were not one of them. "Surely no Christian" will object to joining a "reformed drunkard's society," he wrote. "If they believe, as they profess, that Omnipotence condescended to take on himself the form of sinful man, and, as such, to die an ignominious death for their sakes, surely they will not refuse submission." He chose not to write, "If *we* believe . . . ."

Despite the charge of elitism and his questionable Christian credentials, he barely lost to Baker, whom he liked and respected. At the district convention, notwithstanding the endorsement of his own county, Baker lost to another prominent Whig, John J. Hardin, who had helped avert Lincoln's duel with Shields. Friendly with one another, and laborers in the same political vineyard, these three ambitious young men, all residents of the Seventh Congressional District, confronted the unyielding fact that there was only one national office available for which a Whig candidate would be competitive. All three were talented speakers and campaigners; they had served in the Black Hawk War; they were successful lawyers; and Hardin had a formal law school education. At the convention, they and their fellow Whigs searched for a way to keep the three satisfied and the party united. Baker, they decided, would get the next nomination after Hardin; Lincoln, the one thereafter. Convinced that each had pledged his word to this arrangement, Lincoln campaigned vigorously for Hardin, who won the congressional seat. Two years later Hardin acceded to Baker's candidacy, which was also successful.

When, early in 1846, Hardin began to maneuver to get the Whig congressional nomination for a second time, Lincoln was outraged. "To yield to Hardin under present circumstances, seems to me as nothing else than yielding to one who would gladly sacrifice me altogether. This,

I would rather not submit to. That Hardin is talented, energetic, usually generous and magnanimous," he did not deny. "My only argument is that 'turn about is fair play.' This he [Hardin], practically at least, denies." Lincoln pushed back against Hardin's initiatives, including spreading the rumor that Hardin preferred to run for governor. "If I am not," Lincoln wrote to Hardin in February 1846, "(in services done the party, and in capacity to serve in future) near enough your equal, when added to the fact of your having had a turn, to entitle me to the nomination, I scorn it on any and all other grounds." Not spreading opportunity and widening allegiances, he argued, would prevent the Whigs ever gaining the majority status they deserved. In mid-February, Hardin withdrew.

With the nomination in hand, Lincoln faced a tough campaign. His major opponent, sixty-one-year-old Peter Cartwright, the Democratic nominee, was especially formidable. Evangelical Christianity personified, he was a Southern-born charismatic preacher who breathed hell-and-brimstone fire. He opposed the tariff, favored excluding the issue of slavery from politics, and championed western expansion, especially the annexation of Texas and California. Slavery indeed played no role in the campaign, and apparently little was said by either candidate about the war with Mexico that began in spring 1846, partly because so much was murky about what had actually happened on the Texas-Mexico border. When, later, the facts became known, Lincoln became a vocal critic of the popular conflict. If he had opposed the war prior to the election, he almost certainly would have lost to Cartwright, as he nervously anticipated he might do anyway when Cartwright hit him in one of his most vulnerable places, his alienation from Christianity.

In July 1846, Lincoln learned that Cartwright was "whispering the charge of infidelity against me." He needed to respond immediately. With the election scheduled for August 3, he wrote an open letter "To the Voters of the Seventh Congressional District." It appeared in the newspapers four days before the election, a two-paragraph statement of his attitude toward Christianity and the role of religion in American society, an attempt to assure voters that he was safe on this issue, though he was in fact not safe in the literal sense in which many voters would have framed it. The charge against him, he wrote, is that he is "an open scoffer at Christianity." The essence of the charge, which he preferred not to respond to directly, was that he was a nonbeliever, a more telling accusation since it involved not transient words but actual beliefs. "That I am not a member of any Christian Church, is true; but I have never denied the truth of the Scriptures; and I have never spoken with intentional disrespect of religion in general, or of any denomination of Christians in particular. It is true," he continued, that he had "in early life" believed that human beings do not determine their own actions and he had privately "tried to maintain this position in argument. The habit of arguing thus however, I have, entirely left off for more than five years." That was the entire truth on the subject.

Effective as the rhetoric and language were, it was not the entire truth. Lincoln carefully chose his words so that he could be simultaneously truthful and evasively ameliorative. The language of the central assertion, that he had "never denied the truth of the Scriptures," he left conveniently undefined. In the sense in which most of his readers would have taken the phrase, he had indeed denied the literal truth of the Bible frequently in private conversation and in small group discussions. He also avoided asserting that he believed in the literal truth of the Bible, which would have immediately resolved the matter and discharged the issue. That the Bible as wisdom literature contained truths about the human condition and provided moral guidance he did indeed believe. His claim that five years before he had left off "the habit of arguing" that human beings were biologically determined creatures neatly evaded the question of what his current belief actually was. He did not assert that he had changed his view, only that he no longer engaged in arguments in favor of the doctrine of necessity. Whether or not he still privately believed the doctrine, he did not address. It was a sensible approach for a man ambitious to hold public office in a society that required its officeholders to attest to their Christian allegiance.

The mixture of evasiveness, confession, personal history, and ambiguous assertion in the first paragraph led to a clever shifting of the ground in the second. The world *intentional* in his claim that he had "never spoken with intentional disrespect of religion in general, or of any denomination of Christians in particular," provided weak protection, as the recollections of some of his contemporaries demonstrate. "When [he] first Came to Springfield in 1837," James Matheny recalled, Lincoln, "when all were idle and nothing to do, would talk about Religion—pick up the Bible— read a passage—and then Comment on it—show its falsity—and its follies on the grounds of *Reason*—would then show its own self made & self uttered Contradictions and would in the End—finally ridicule it and as it were Scoff at it." In 1837, Lincoln's argument had been with a miracle-based Christianity that claimed the intercession of divinity in human affairs and required a suspension of rational standards. By the mid-1840s, the terms of his argument had changed from analytic rejection of Christian theology to relative evasion. And for the sake of his life as a public man, he now needed to shift Cartwright's charge of infidelity to what seemed the more serviceable ground of human relations, particularly the respect due to the beliefs and the conscience of each individual. "I do not think," he concludes, that

> I could myself, be brought to support a man for office, whom I knew to be an open enemy of, and scoffer at, religion. Leaving the higher matter of eternal consequences, between him and his Maker, I still do not think that any man has the right thus to insult the feelings, and injure the morals, of the community in which he may live. If, then, I was guilty of such conduct, I should blame no man who should condemn me for it; but I do blame those, whoever they may be, who falsely put such a charge in circulation against me.

In fact, Cartwright's charge of "infidelity" was accurate, a truth that Lincoln could not afford to admit openly. But the charge itself, he made clear, has no place in the public forum. If indeed, he granted, he had *publicly* shown disrespect for the religious beliefs of others, he would not deserve to be elected. "No man has the right to insult the feelings, and injure the morals of the community in which he may live." But religious belief and public discourse have no desirable, let alone necessary, connection. What is required is public respect for the sanctity of individual religious belief, whatever one's own position on any particular religious claim. The public forum is a place for the discussion of public issues, and, he believed, religious faith is a private matter. Drawing on his command of language in a situation in which he needed to be wily as well as convincing, he elevated a campaign charge into a larger statement about the proper relationship between religious belief and public discourse in American political life.

Lincoln's fear that the charges of elitism and infidelity might defeat him in the 1846 election was reasonable, based on electoral realities. In the end, though, the Whig proclivities of the Seventh Congressional District provided him with a substantial margin, especially since the core Democratic vote wavered in its support of Cartwright. Lincoln soon succeeded his two Whig predecessors as the only Whig congressman from Democratic Illinois. It was not an entirely happy distinction, which he discovered even before he began his term. "Being elected to Congress," he wrote to Speed, "though I am very grateful to our friends, for having done it, has not pleased me as much as I expected." He was not a man who readily took to pleasure. The Calvinist heritage had made its imprint. And his delayed accession to the public office to which he had aspired diminished the pleasure he might have felt in at last getting his chance to serve beyond Illinois.

Stretched out in his office or at home in the evenings, he found that reading his favorite authors provided pleasure that little else did. It allowed for withdrawal and immersion simultaneously. Shakespeare, Burns, and Byron continued to dominate his literary attention. But he also, gradually and slowly, since he still tended to memorize many poems, expanded his reading experience. Oliver Wendell Holmes's lugubrious lyric celebration of transience, "The Last Leaf," became a great favorite, which he frequently recited from memory. He soon read all Holmes's poetry, both melancholy and humorous, the two habitual and dynamic poles of Lincoln's personality. He loved "gloomy" poetry, John Todd Stuart recalled, and, sometime after 1846, he "carried Poe around on the Circuit—read and loved the Raven—repeated it over & over." "Nevermore" was, for Lincoln, not a literary affectation but a philosophic and emotional self-definition. Comic and satiric narratives, whether in poetry or prose, appealed to him, many by authors whose names never subsequently entered the literary canon but whose reputations were high in Lincoln's lifetime. Newspapers and magazines; books on philosophy, psychology, history, and current affairs; and both new literature and the literary classics were available in Springfield. "His favorite way of reading when at home was lying down on the floor," a second cousin living with the Lincolns at the time recalled. "When not engaged in reading law Books he would read literarry works, and was very fond of reading Poetry and often when he would be or appear to be in deep Study—Commence and repeat aloud Some piece that he had taken a fancy to and Committed to Memory," such as William Knox's "Mortality," which he memorized and quoted frequently, "and the burrial of Sir Tom Moore [by Charles Wolfe]." But he also "told laughable Jokes and Stories when he thought we was looking gloomy."

What he also did in 1846 was try his hand as a writer of literature, attempting to use language as a vehicle of self-exploration and pleasurable expression in a way distinctly different from the writing that he had done as a political man addressing public issues. He had written poetry before, though little to none of it survives, and he had written prose essays, particularly as a schoolboy in Indiana. His compelling interest in language as the instrumental vehicle for civilization and culture had always found its best examples in the canonical wisdom literature he had absorbed in his childhood reading. From early on, he had embraced language as the necessary condition both for public and personal discourse. He had established himself both as a consumer of other people's language and as a creator of language, the usual symbiotic connection between the reader as writer and the writer as reader. And language, for Lincoln, remained, as always, instrumental in more than the practical sense. His facility with it gave him pleasure.

Early in 1846 he revised into a formal narrative his June 1841 epistolary account of the Trailor brothers' alleged crime. Despite its anonymous publication, first in Andrew Johnston's Quincy *Whig* in April and then in the *Sangamo Journal*, his friends had no doubt that he was the author, which he had no reason to conceal. There was a long-established convention of anonymous publication in newspapers, which in this case Lincoln adhered to, partly because of his uncertainty about presenting himself to the public in a new role, the oral storyteller now writing for publication. Many of his *Sangamo Journal* readers would have recognized his characteristic intellectual and stylistic imprint in "Remarkable Case of Arrest for Murder": the tightness of the prose, the precision of word choice, the effective handling of pace and climax, the vivid use of selective detail, the reportorial presentation of fact like a lawyer building a case, the logical force of the mind controlling the materials.

Writing poetry had its riveting attractions, especially in 1846, when he wrote his most sustained extant poems. In late October and early November 1844, campaigning for Henry Clay, he had visited the area of his childhood home in Indiana. "Seeing it and its objects and inhabitants aroused feelings in me which were certainly poetry," he wrote to Andrew Johnston, "though whether my expression of those feelings is poetry is quite another question." In Spencer County, Indiana, he gave a speech so close to the site of the family farm "where my mother and only sister were buried" that it's inconceivable he did not visit their graves. Childhood friends whom he had not seen for over fourteen years shook his hand, among them David Turnham, who had lent him books, and Nat Grigsby, his schoolmate whose brother had married his sister Sarah. Lincoln was deeply stirred. In the same letter to Johnston he fulfilled his promise to send a copy of a poem he admired, "Mortality," the name of whose author neither Johnston nor Lincoln knew because it had been published anonymously. "Feeling a little poetic this evening, I have concluded to redeem my promise." When Johnston intimated that Lincoln might be its author, the latter made clear how much he aspired to write such excellent verses. "I would give all I am worth, and go in debt, to be able to write so fine a piece as I think that is."

He had indeed been writing a poem of his own. "By the way, how would you like to see a piece of poetry of my own making?" he asked Johnston in late February 1846. "I have a piece that is almost done, but I find a deal of trouble to finish it." How long had he been at work on this poem? How many other evenings had he been "feeling . . . poetic?" How often had the feeling been part of a reading occasion and how often of a writing occasion, as it clearly was in late February 1846? The occasional poet who had trouble finishing this autobiographical poem most likely had trouble finishing others as well. "Let names be suppressed by all means," he wrote to Johnston. "I have not sufficient hope of the verses attracting any favorable notice to tempt me to risk being ridiculed for having written them."

When he set pen to paper to give what seemed to him suitable expression to the thoughts and feelings stirred by his Indiana visit, the two alternative modes of his personality—the melancholy and the humorous—provided literary guidelines. His skill with meter, rhyme, and word choice were considerable. Poetic coherence as structure was another matter. With this he struggled. It's unclear whether or not he had initially conceived the poem as a four-canto account of his visit to his childhood home or whether the four-canto idea arose only after he had written a substantial number of stanzas and then decided to divide them. He seems to confess, tentatively, to the latter. But only three entities are extant; the fourth may not have been created or, as leftover material, so to speak, may have been lost. The Romantic melancholic tradition in English poetry from Gray to Wordsworth provides the tone and the lyric parameters of "My childhood home I see again" and "But here's an object more of dread." The comic narratives of rural life from "John Gilpin" to Robert Burns inform the situation, the pace, and the humor of "The Bear Hunt," and though there is no direct record of Lincoln having read Chaucer, his evocation of the excitement of a rural chase scene has much in common with Chaucer's account of the flight of the fox in "The Nun's Priest's Tale."

The three poems are unmistakably autobiographical. "My Childhood Home" addresses the conventional themes of mutability and memory in which images from the past provide both pain and pleasure:

> My childhood's home I see again,
>   And sadden with the view;
> And still, as memory crowds my brain,
>   There's pleasure in it too.
>
> O Memory! Thou midway world
>   'Twixt earth and paradise,
> Where things decayed and loved ones lost
>   In dreamy shadows rise. . . .

"Memory will hallow all / We've known, but know no more," he continues, a phrase that prefigures his use of *hallow* on another elegiac occasion, his 1863 oration at Gettysburg.

The emphasis in "My Childhood Home" on the power of childhood impressions to shape the life of the adult and on memory as a faculty mediating between past and present suggests that Lincoln by the mid-1840s may have read Wordsworth or his imitators or eighteenth-century predecessors:

> Near twenty years have passed away
>   Since here I bid farewell
> To woods and fields, and scenes of play,
>   And playmates loved so well.

In the aesthetic space between autobiographical accuracy and poetic creation, Lincoln feels enough the poet to substitute the mellifluous "near twenty years" for the flatter "fourteen years ago." And in his skillful cre-

ation of each stanza as a quatrain, as is the case for all three poems published in 1846, the rhyme scheme and metrical pattern show his familiarity with the widely used poetic techniques of the writers he admired.

The brief time he spent in Spencer County was enough to a devo-
tee of the mutability tradition to cast his reunion with childhood friends
into his own version of "Elegy Written in a Country Church-Yard," his
visit to the grave sites of loved ones dramatized in the language of late-
eighteenth- and early-nineteenth-century elegiac poetry:

> *The friends I left that parting day,*
>   *How changed, as time has sped!*
> *Young childhood grown, strong manhood gray,*
>   *And half of all are dead.*

> *I hear the loved survivors tell*
>   *How nought from death could save,*
> *Till every sound appears a knell,*
>   *And every spot a grave,*

> *I range the fields with pensive tread,*
>   *And pace the hollow rooms,*
> *And feel (companion of the dead)*
>   *I'm living in the tombs.*

Though the canonical influences are obvious, there is no gainsaying
the element of skill, sincere feeling, and poetic authenticity in "My childhood home" and "But here's an object more of dread." The latter describes a formative experience in Lincoln's childhood, the madness of
Matthew Gentry. The incident became a focus for his concern about his
own stability and about the mystery of mental illness. "I am neither dead
nor quite crazy yet," he had assured John Todd Stuart in February 1841,
though he had come close to one or the other or both. The precious gift
of "reason" might be as inexplicably taken away as given, and the sight of

a human being without what Lincoln considered his humanizing essence, his mental faculties, struck fear into those who understood that everyone had the potential for such dehumanization. His use of Matthew Gentry's first name makes unavoidable in this poem in particular the parallel with Wordsworth, who uses the name Matthew for the friend he addresses in numbers of poems, such as "The Tables Turned" and "Expostulation and Reply"; and Lincoln's rhyme scheme, metrical pattern, and simple diction resemble Wordsworth's in some of the latter's lyrical ballads. Whoever his predecessors, the poem is very much Lincoln's in its awed preoccupation with the horror of madness:

> But here's an object more of dread
>   Than ought the grave contains—
> A human form with reason fled,
>   What wretched life remains.
>
> Poor Matthew! Once of genius bright,
>   A fortune-favored child—
> Now locked for aye, in mental night,
>   A haggard mad-man wild.
>
> Poor Matthew! I have ne'er forgot,
>   When first, with maddened will,
> Yourself you maimed, your father fought,
>   And mother strove to kill;
>
> When terror spread, and neighbors ran,
>   Your dange'rous strength to bind;
> And soon, a howling crazy man,
>   Your limbs were fast confined.

As if it were himself being bound, Lincoln empathetically describes the fearful transformation of a rational man into a maniac "by pangs that killed thy mind." The wailing "mournful song" of the enchained mad man haunted him thereafter:

> I've heard it oft, as if I dreamed,
>   Far distant, sweet, and lone—
> The funeral dirge, it ever seemed
>   Of reason dead and gone.

Lincoln discovered in 1844 that the raving madman still lived, "lingering in this wretched condition," as he described him to Johnston. But the lunatic whose sight had struck terror into him in his childhood was now a quiescent shell of a human being, unaware of his aberrant condition, an object of pity rather than fear. In a final stanza, added in his revision from manuscript to published poem, Lincoln provided his version of the question asked by Christian theodicies: How can there be justice in a world in which a madman like Matthew lives into old age while others who have been blest with sanity die young? How, in the face of contrary evidence, can we assert eternal providence and justify the ways of God to man? Unlike Milton, Pope, and Tennyson, the first two of whom he had read by the 1840s, Lincoln apostrophizes death, not God, as the agency:

> O death! Thou awe-inspiring prince,
>   That keepst the world in fear;
> Why dost thou tear more blest ones hence,
>   And leave him ling'ring here?

The emphasis on the power of death to keep people in fear and the absence of any reference to a countervailing power attests to Lincoln's view of the randomness of the world and the difficulty of seeing in human affairs the hand or mind of a caring God. It is a theme characteristic of Lincoln's philosophy and theology, though he was to take only a few opportunities, such as his second inaugural address, to reveal it in public discourse. Death asserts itself as the agent of control. Deity is absent at best, irrelevant at worst. None of the answers that he had heard to the question of how to justify the ways of a God who permits the good to die young and allows human life to have in it so much misery seemed satisfactory. If they had, his response to Gentry's madness would have been different.

As a writer of poetry, Lincoln is undisguisedly sincere, even in his satiric delight in the foibles of human nature. It may have been part of his ambition in attempting a four-canto poem about his childhood to include a humorous section to contrast with the melancholic solemnity of "My childhood home" and "But here's an object more of dread." After all, he did have a keen appreciation of the role of laughter in his Indiana childhood. The poem he did write, "The Bear Hunt," was probably conceived as an independent poem. It is an evocation of daily life, a narrative of action and humor. The pursuit and destruction of the bear is dramatized as a celebratory event, not a break in nature's harmony but an affirmation of man's primacy. Have you ever seen a bear hunt? Lincoln asks somewhat awkwardly in the first stanza. If you haven't, "then hast thou lived in vain." The second stanza provides the autobiographical setting:

> When first my father settled here,
> 'Twas then the frontier line:
> The panther's scream, filled night with fear
> And bears preyed on the swine.

The energy of the bear hunt dominates the next fourteen quatrains:

> But wo for Bruin's short lived fun,
> When rose the squealing cry;
> Now man and horse, with dog and gun,
> For vengeance, at him fly.

>   . . . .

> The tall fleet cur, with deep-mouthed voice,
> Now speeds him, as the wind;

While half grown pup, and short-legged fice,
  Are yelping far behind.

And fresh recruits are dropping in
  To join the merry corps:
With yelp and yell,—a mingled din—
  The woods are in a roar.

The bear sniffs the breeze, bounding into the woods, pursued by men and dogs. The point of view at first is that of the bear, then the men, then the dogs, though all absorbed into the quick-paced narrative overview. Ambushed, the mortally wounded bear is brought to bay:

And furious now, the dogs he tears,
  And crushes in his ire.
Wheels right and left, and upward rears,
  With eyes of burning fire.

But leaden death is at his heart,
  Vain all the strength he plies.
And spouting blood from every part,
  He reels, and sinks, and dies.

In the end, Lincoln transforms his poem into an animal fable about human nature, a form whose attraction had its origin in his childhood reading of Aesop. The object of its satire is human conceit, self-delusion, and aggressiveness:

And now a dinsome clamor rose,
  'Bout who should have his skin;
Who first draws blood, each hunter knows,
  This prize must always win.
But who did this, and how to trace

> *What's true from what's a lie,*
> *Like lawyers, in a murder case*
> *They stoutly argufy.*
>
> *Aforesaid fice, of blustering mood,*
> *Behind, and quite forgot,*
> *Just now emerging from the wood,*
> *Arrives upon the spot.*
>
> *With grinning teeth, and up-turned hair—*
> *Brim full of spunk and wrath,*
> *He growls, and seizes on dead bear,*
> *And shakes for life and death.*
>
> *And swells as of his skin would tear,*
> *And growls and shakes again;*
> *And swears, as plain as dog can swear,*
> *That he has won the skin.*
>
> *Conceited whelp! We laugh at thee—*
> *Nor mind, that not a few*
> *Of pompous, two-legged dogs there be,*
> *Conceited quite as you.*

The ironic humor of the conclusion results not from the absence of a satisfactory completion of the hunt but from the contentious argument between the hunters, both human and animal, about whom the dead bear belongs to, arguing like lawyers disputing the facts of a case. Its disposition is determined by a feisty blustering dog (the description suggests Lincoln's view of Stephen Douglas), who has taken no part in the actual kill, triumphantly asserting that possession is nine-tenths of the law.

Despite their obvious limitations, the three poems of 1846 are "certainly poetry." Johnston's publication of them may have been enough to allay any doubt Lincoln had on that score. Still, their existence was not the prelude to any extended attempt thereafter to express himself in verse. As far as we know, no one in his circle commented on them, and the few bits of poetry that he wrote after 1846 are not as ambitious. That he did not define himself as a poet either then or later speaks to other issues. It was not an expression of a lessening of his confidence in language as the necessary vehicle of private and public discourse. His belief in the importance of the written word, if anything, increased. His life as lawyer and politician, busy as it sometimes was, did not preclude writing whatever he chose to write. It may be that he did not have enough confidence in his talent to continue to write poems, though he remained an avid reader of poetry. And certainly his vision of his vocation and talent drew him to prose. In fact, the command of literary models and of language that enabled him to write these credible poems in 1846 were inseparable from his command of language as a prose writer. And the feel for poetic language, for the right word in the right place, the alternation between everyday diction and the colloquial on the one hand and heightened diction and metrical rhythms on the other, for the pithy language that reveals human nature and the elevated language that evokes human ideals, this synthesis of prose and poetry—this precision about distinguishing between "the lightning-bug and the lightning," to use Mark Twain's phase—had increasingly become his strength as a writer.

In late 1847, Lincoln left for Washington, D.C. It was not easy to distinguish himself in a Congress preoccupied with a war with Mexico that had suddenly become controversial and in which sat well-known national figures, including the eighty-one-year-old ex-president John Quincy Adams, the last major public figure extant from the Revolutionary generation. Lincoln apparently still felt ambivalent about being a congressman at all. "In this troublesome world, we are never quite satisfied," he soon wrote his wife, who, with their sons, spent part of these two years in

Washington and part in Kentucky with her Lexington family. In December 1846, the Illinois legislature overwhelmingly elected Stephen Douglas, who had served two terms in Congress, to the United States Senate. He became one of forty-two senators, a colleague of Daniel Webster, John Calhoun, and Thomas Hart Benton. The Democratic majority appointed the freshman senator chairman of the Committee on Territories, a launching pad for national prominence. Lincoln, in contrast, became one of more than two hundred members in a House of Representatives in which the Whigs had a four-vote advantage. He was assigned to two obscure committees: the Post Office and War Department expenditures. The White House was also in the other party's control.

With the nation at war, Edward Baker in December 1846 organized and led the Fourth Illinois Volunteers into battle. John Hardin, whose reluctant withdrawal of his candidacy had smoothed Lincoln's way to the nomination, became colonel of the First Illinois Regiment, to be killed at the Battle of Buena Vista in February 1847. Lincoln wrote the laudatory resolution and chaired a memorial meeting in Springfield. Baker and Hardin, about the same age as their Whig colleague, had heard the call of the bugle. Lincoln, though, gave no indication that he aspired to military glory, and on the home front political distinction also seemed unlikely for the lone Whig Congressman from Illinois. Having pledged not to run for a second term, he was a lame duck even before the start of his first, though he explained that he had made the "declaration . . . more from a wish to deal fairly with others, to keep peace among our friends, and to keep the district from going to the enemy, than for any cause personal to myself; so that, if it should so happen that nobody else wishes to be elected, I could not refuse the people the right of sending me again." At best, it was a minimalist career barely in the ascendant.

His passage to Washington was through the state of his birth, particularly his wife's home city, Lexington, where he had the opportunity to hear the living American statesman he most admired, seventy-year-old Henry Clay, campaigning to become the Whig presidential nominee for the fourth time. Lincoln's admiration for Clay, the most continuously dominant American political figure of Lincoln's lifetime, had almost no bounds. His imposing presence had occupied Lincoln's consciousness since his childhood, a major force in his rejection of the Jackson worship of his contemporaries. A border-state liberal who advocated moderation, compromise, reverence for the union, and equality before the law, Clay personified the best of the Whig Party, an embodiment of the ideological reasons for the party's existence. Politically, though, Clay carried the burden of not having delivered the presidency to his party in three elections. Listening to Clay's eloquent speech in mid-November 1847 on the two most important subjects of the day, slavery and the Mexican War, Lincoln had to have been anxious about his party's chances under Clay again. Like many Whigs, Lincoln worried that they would once more follow Clay to defeat. He would need to be convinced that they would not do better with Gen. Zachary Taylor, fresh from his Mexican War laurels. Lincoln, who in 1840 had placed an increased chance of victory above loyalty to Clay, was soon to realize, if he did not already suspect, the strength of anti-Clay sentiment in the party and the widespread conviction that it needed a fresh horse to carry it to triumph. His patricidal anguish was now to have a less anguished second act.

Clay's political and philosophical claims, though, had always been those of "the lone star from Illinois." On the two main issues of the campaign, Lincoln would not hesitate to support him. As always, but increasingly as sectional differences became dominant, Clay believed slavery destructively divisive, a threat to the union, and inwardly cancerous, destroying the republic's moral foundations. The best solution was to expatriate enslaved blacks to a colony established for them in Africa. To that he gave public voice as president of the American Colonization Society. The second best was gradual emancipation and absorption into the American mainstream, though the obstacles seemed insurmountable. On the issue of the Mexican War, Lincoln began to believe, as did Clay, that it was a war of unjustifiable aggression. Clay's attack on the Polk administration's war policy in November 1847 helped solidify Lincoln's views.

The Kentuckian's stylized oratory was grounded in a precision of diction and a combination of the personal and the imperial. It occasionally verged on the pompous, rarely touching the colloquial and the anecdotal. Its strength resulted from its combination of clarity and formality, the impression that it addressed a high occasion and a formal body, usually the House or the Senate. It relied more on rolling cadences and rhetorical structures than on logical argument and factual evidence. It rarely lacked the force of authoritative assertion. Unlike Lincoln, Clay valued eloquence more than rational analysis, his style devised for the public forum, created to impress by his charismatic presence and his contribution to a dramatic oratorical occasion. It was especially effective because it expressed the high-strutting verbal self-confidence of Clay's personality, an essential element in the performance. Even when ostensibly persuading, Clay commanded. A prince of the republic, he led by the attraction of his superiority, the magnetic inseparability of his presence and words.

Unlike Lincoln, Clay had a genius for semi-spontaneous speech, captivating large audiences on serious subjects with at most a handful of notes, combining verbal talent, mental agility, command of the language, and a powerful memory. His style was literate without being literary. His model was Cicero, not Shakespeare or the King James Bible. Lincoln preferred to have a text from which to read; words mattered to him as a writer. Clay rarely had a written text, his speeches surviving through newspaper reports and stenographic accounts. With a voice that reached the most distant ears of large audiences, he had the actor's ability to rivet and retain attention by speech alone. Lincoln's reedy tenor took on timber and force as he spoke, but it had no distinction of performance. The words mattered more than the manner, and he never had the luxury of star appeal.

Elderly, in weak health, certain that he was better qualified for the presidency than any other living American, Clay spoke in Lexington with an eloquence that confirmed Lincoln's high regard for "Prince Hal." As he listened, it's likely that he compared Clay's language to his own and noticed the skills that made Clay the most acclaimed orator of his day. Some features of Lincoln's own use of language did have their presence in Clay, particularly the latter's insistence on the precise word and the well-constructed paragraph. And Clay's denunciation of slavery in November 1837 had unmistakable parallels to Lincoln's later phrasing of his thoughts on the subject, though Clay's predictive evocation of "shocking scenes of rapine and carnage" has a touch of the incendiary and the hyperbolic that seems distant from Lincoln's temperament, and his words lack humanizing empathy.

> I have ever regarded slavery as a great evil, a wrong, for the present, I fear, an irremediable wrong to its unfortunate victims. I should rejoice if not a single slave breathed the air or was within the limits of our country. But here they are, to be dealt with as well as we can, with a due consideration of all circumstances affecting the security, safety and happiness of all races. Every State has the supreme, uncontrolled and exclusive power to decide for itself whether slavery shall cease or continue within its limits, without any exterior intervention from any quarter. In States, where the slaves outnumber the whites, as is the case with several, the blacks could not be emancipated and invested with all the rights of freemen, without becoming the governing race in those States. Collisions and conflicts, between the two races, would be inevitable, and, after shocking scenes of rapine and carnage, the extinction or expulsion of the blacks would certainly take place.

At best, Clay casts the subjective in personal and egocentric terms, as if the universe revolved around the importance of his views. If the union were to be dissolved, he was to tell Congress in 1850, it would be accompanied by an "exterminating" war. And, he concluded, "I implore, as the best blessing which heaven can bestow upon me on earth, that if the direful and sad event of the dissolution of the Union shall happen, I may not survive to behold the sad and heartrending spectacle." Still, Clay, who never appealed to "the better angels of our nature" or cast his arguments in the context of a philosophical view of the human condition, had something to teach Lincoln about the effective use of language.

When he arrived in Washington in early December 1847, Lincoln had already written a preliminary draft of an essay on the tariff, perhaps intending it to be the subject of his maiden congressional speech. Given his habit of writing and his preference for a text, he may have composed preliminary drafts on other topics also, though it would have made tactical sense for him to make himself even better prepared on a subject about which he was already knowledgeable and had spoken on many times before, and also to avoid immediately expressing himself on the controversial subjects of the day: the war and slavery. The tariff was a safe, tried-and-true Whig subject.

"Fragments of a Tariff Discussion," a substantial but unfinished draft of his views, begins with an outline of the essay as a whole, an example of Lincoln the writer at work, creating the skeletal frame of his argument. He starts with the thesis issue: "whether the protective policy shall be finally abandoned, is now the question," and then outlines each step of his argument:

Discussion and experience already had; and question now in greater dispute than ever.

Has there not been some great error in the mode of discussion?

Propose a single issue of fact, namely—"From 1816 to the present, have protected articles cost us more, of labour, during the *higher*, than during the *lower* duties upon them?"

Introduce the evidence.

Analyze this issue, and try to show that it embraces the *true* and the whole question of the protective policy.

Intended as a test of *experience*.

The *period* selected is fair; because it is a period of peace—a period sufficiently long to furnish a fair average under all other causes operating on prices—a period in which various modifications of higher and lower duties have occurred.

Protected articles, only are embraced. Show that *these only* belong to the question.

The *labour* price only is embraced. Show this to be correct.

This rare instance in which we can look into the Lincoln workshop exemplifies the type of outline he most likely created, at least mentally, for all his major writings. It reveals a writer with a strong sense of the relationship between experience and theory, between the human situation and public policy. The emphasis is on the pragmatic and the analytic. He neatly summarizes the Whig argument in favor of the protective tariff: by protecting American industry, it protects the American worker and the economy as a whole; an environment in which domestic industry flourishes can provide the full employment and fair wages necessary to create a domestic marketplace; the wages that labor receives in a full-employment economy create the consumer demand necessary to sustain the marketplace; that to reason and act correctly on this subject, we must look not merely to *buying* cheap, nor yet to buying cheap *and* selling dear, but also to having full employment, so that we may have the largest possible amount of something to sell; and full employment can be secured only by an ample, steady, and certain marketplace in which to sell the products of labor. Under current circumstances, he argues, a protective tariff is the government's necessary tool for sustaining a healthy domestic economy. Reliance on the international marketplace and on products manufactured more cheaply abroad will lead to a decrease in American wealth and fewer jobs or at least fewer well-paying jobs at home. "Verry soon" the American "discovers, that to *buy*, even at the cheaper rate" of foreign goods manufactured by low-paid labor, "requires something to buy with, and some how or other, he is falling short in that particular."

The draft also contains a segment revealing the economic first principle underlying his view on the tariff and on economic theory in general: that all human wealth arises from labor.

In the early days of the world, the Almighty said to the first of our race "In the sweat of thy face shalt thou eat bread"; and since then, if we except the *light* and the *air* of heaven, no good thing has been, or can be enjoyed by us, without having first cost labour. And, inasmuch as most good things are produced by labour, it follows that all such things of right belong to those whose labour has produced them. But it has so happened in all ages of the world, that *some* have laboured, and *others* have, without labour, enjoyed a large proportion of the fruits. This is wrong, and should not continue. To secure to each labourer the whole product of his labour, or as nearly as possible, is a most worthy object of any good government. But then the question arises, how can a government best, effect this? In our own country, in its present condition, will the protective principle *advance* or *retard* this object?

It was hardly, in these terms, a safe subject for a freshman congressman, and this may have been the reason why he chose not to speak on the tariff during his two years as a congressman. The framework in which Lincoln gave the highest valuation to labor implied that those who were enjoying the fruits of slave labor were depriving the slaves of what they were entitled to, the fruits of their own labor. And it also suggested that in those instances in which political and economic power was used to deprive free laborers of fair value for their labor, the source of all value, it was being stolen from the rightful owners, the laborers who created the wealth. It is a labor theory of value that implies that both slavery and free-labor exploitation are an expropriation of services, either through bondage or economic tyranny. He does not take up the question of how to distinguish between the wealth that current labor produces and the wealth accumulated in the form of assets from past labor, at least partly because the topic at hand did not require him to do so. And he had no practical or ideological reason to pursue the question. Like Clay, he believed that slaveholders deserved compensation for the loss of their property; the American taxpayer should, over time, pay for emancipation. And the notion that it would be logical to advocate, if he were to be true to his theory of value, the expropriation of other kinds of accumulated wealth was not part of his consciousness or of the national discussion of the rights of labor. His emphasis is on fair treatment for those who labor now. And one of the reasons we have government, he argued, is to secure, through wise legislation, "to each labourer the whole product of his labour, or as nearly as possible."

It is impossible to know to what extent Lincoln had expressed this labor theory of value in his speeches during political campaigns in the 1840s. None of those speeches survive. "Fragments of a Tariff Discussion" suggests a writer working out his thoughts rather than putting down what he had articulated in any substantial way before. Throughout, the emphasis is on following a train of thought as logically as possible. The tight sentences emphasize clarity and balance. Repetition of key words for contrast and emphasis, preciseness of diction, lucidity of phrasing, colloquial sentence rhythms, quotation or allusion to familiar and resonating sources such as the Bible, the slight elevation into formality and a more literary style to raise the tone—all these characteristics of his later compositions are present. Each sentence as a unit has the tautness, the balance, and the expressiveness characteristic of his writing at its polished best. His usual synthesis of intellectual and stylistic control is evident. That the draft is a work in progress is most obviously visible in a few of the excessively long paragraphs and in the discontinuity of the overall structure.

Whatever the wisdom of his decision about his maiden speech, he might have better served his political career by introducing himself to the Congress with a speech on the tariff than by what he actually did, which was to embroil himself in the most volatile issue of the day. In late December 1847 he put on the Speaker's table, without formally introducing them, a series of resolutions questioning the legitimacy of the Mexican War. In the form of seven inquiries, the resolutions requested that Congress ask President Polk to provide evidence in support of the claims contained in his message of May 11, 1846, requesting a declaration of war because Mexican forces had invaded American territory. Had they in fact invaded American territory? And since, in Lincoln's view, they had not, was not the war a predetermined pretext for a policy of American expansion rather than a response to an actual violation of American sovereignty?

Lincoln had barely been in town three weeks. He had not participated in debate, let alone risen to speak at length. The war itself was for all intents and purposes over, a triumphant American victory. At issue as public policy were an exit strategy and a peace treaty. Indeed, the enthusiasm that had initially carried many Whigs into political and military support of Polk's policy had diminished, though many still considered the war just, the spoils God-given to a superior race. For some, opposition was moral: the war an unjust aggression for territorial advantage. Perhaps Lincoln could not get out of his mind Clay's stirring denunciatory words. For others, the inevitable appropriation of Mexican territory seemed likely to extend and strengthen slavery. And for still others, territorial expansion threatened the integrity of their vision of the unitary republic true to its founding principles. Many of the pro-expansion Whigs who had agreed with the aims of the war now realized that their continued support had strengthened the Polk administration. But outright opposition had political danger, especially for a Whig congressman from a predominantly Democratic pro-war Illinois. With a presidential election less than two years off, the Whigs needed a viable policy and candidate. Any national Whig leader who opposed the war or who was not at least immunized against the accusation had little chance to be elected president. "There is a good deal of diversity among the whigs here," Lincoln wrote to an Illinois correspondent on New Year's Day 1848, "as to who shall be their candidate for the Presidency; but I think it will result in favor of Genl. Taylor," the hero of the Battle of Buena Vista, a nonpolitical slaveholding Southerner who could harmonize the party and attract Southern and Northern votes.

Congress tabled Lincoln's resolutions, which they "neither debated nor adopted." Polk, who may have had no knowledge of their existence, did not respond, and such accusatory interrogatories from a freshman congressman probably offended some on both sides of the aisle. Early in January, the Whig majority overwhelmingly supported a resolution, authored by a well-known Massachusetts Whig, stating that the war had been initiated illegally by the president. To the war hawks of both parties, the congressional Whigs' opposition seemed almost treasonous. In Illinois and elsewhere, many Whigs and most Democrats derided Lincoln's "spot resolutions" as legalistic semi-comic hairsplitting about an irrelevancy. William Herndon worried that Lincoln had committed a devastating political blunder. Criticizing the motivation for a war, already a two-year-old fait accompli, whose battlefield victories had elicited nationwide paroxysms of self-congratulation and which was likely to make the Southwest and California American territory, seemed to many a questionable political tactic. Along with other issues, it made Clay's nomination impossible and Taylor's almost a certainty. The American Colonization Society's president could not hold the South on the slavery issue; Taylor could. He could also hold the Northern Whig States and, as a military hero, attract pro-war Whigs and Democrats.

There was no advantage to Lincoln's attempting to force the submission of the resolutions to the full House and thus saddling his political prospects in Illinois with their heavy weight. To the extent that he was thinking strategically, he apparently believed that by exposing Polk's self-promoting war policy he was damaging the Democrats and advancing the Whig cause, though it was widely understood that Polk would not be the Democratic candidate in 1848. He was also either consciously or intuitively laying the ground for the two substantial speeches he was to give to Congress: in January 1848, in defense of his resolutions, and in July 1848, supporting Zachary Taylor for president, both of which had as much to do with moral and constitutional issues as with politics. If circumstances had allowed his resolutions to come to a vote, these speeches might have made him a national figure.

Both meticulously composed compositions had less than the effect he hoped for. In his January 1848 speech, his viselike logic on the question of where exactly the armed conflict had begun and his ad hominem attack on Polk directed attention away from his otherwise compelling subjects: the limits of executive power; the moral obligation to promote a coherence between language and fact; and the "most sacred right" of a minority to revolutionize, "not to go by *old* lines, or *old* laws; but to break up both, and make new ones." The intellectual content of his July speech on the presidential question got lost in the larger din that had created the occasion: the campaign of 1848. Both speeches reveal that, as always, Lincoln was incapable of separating principle from politics, philosophical values from electoral competition. That made him that rarest of public figures, one for whom language mattered so much that he felt compelled to use it honestly even when linguistic deceit was the order of the day.

Executive power came, he believed, not only from the Constitution but also from the degree to which the president used language with transparent honesty. "Let him answer" the questions posed by the interrogatories, "fully, fairly, and candidly. Let him answer with *facts*, and not with arguments. Let him remember he sits where Washington sat . . . let him attempt no evasion—no equivocation." Polk had persuaded the people and Congress to support a war with Mexico by lies of commission and omission. And Lincoln's obligation, he told Congress, was to parse Polk's sentences to expose his misuse of language in support of claims that were either not factual or could not be determined to be fact. The dominant image and frame of reference that Lincoln drew on for his linguistic analysis of the boundary dispute is appropriately spatial, and the issue of the occupancy of space—an image with great force in eighteenth- and nineteenth-century America, and one relevant to Lincoln's experience from childhood on—dominates the speech. In the history of his family and the experience of the nation, the question of how to delineate boundaries and of who owned what had had overwhelming importance. His uncle Mordecai had been killed delineating boundaries and protecting what he considered his land from Native Americans with a different definition of possession. The corpses Lincoln had observed in the Black Hawk War had been testimony to the blood shed for territorial possession. Every acre that Thomas Lincoln farmed had previously belonged to Indian nations. Every fence that the rail-splitting youth had raised to delineate one farm from another had been an authentication of his society's commitment to the belief that a combination of physical possession and property law provided the guarantee of sure title.

President Polk, Lincoln concluded, had used language dishonestly, creating a breach between the facts and the reality. Polk claimed that the Rio Grande had been the border settled by treaty. That was not the case, Lincoln showed with detailed reference to the treaties at issue. Polk claimed that American settlers occupied the land between the Nueces River and the Rio Grande. That was not the case in any large numbers. Polk claimed that Americans exercised "jurisdiction" *between* the two rivers. But he did not define *jurisdiction* in regard to how much of the land between the rivers Americans actually controlled. Lincoln knew a man, a property holder in Springfield, Illinois, "not very unlike myself, who exercises jurisdiction over a piece of land between the Wabash and the Mississippi; and yet so far is this from being *all* there is between those rivers, that it is just one hundred and fiftytwo feet long by fifty feet wide." And his neighbor directly between Lincoln's land and the Mississippi would certainly object to giving up his piece of property because another claimed "jurisdiction" and had consequently annexed it. What the president will not either directly admit or deny is that he "sent the army into the midst of a settlement of Mexican people, who had never submitted, by consent or by force, to the authority of Texas or of the United States, and that *there* and *thereby*, the first blood of the war was shed." The president's refusal to admit or deny this "could not have occurred but by design," and the use of language to manipulate public opinion and congressional decision-making undermines executive authority. In extreme cases, it calls for congressional or judicial nullification.

Lincoln's argument is at its most powerful and dangerous when, realizing that he himself cannot evade its logic, he distinguishes between a war between nations, such as the United States and Mexico, and the right of a group of people who already live within a nation to take up arms against the government that controls that nation. At issue again is space—

territory and boundaries—but in the latter instance, the issue is inseparable from the desire of those taking up arms to govern themselves, either
as the new government of the contested territory or as a separate nation
in a space of its own. It is the sacred right to revolutionize. "Any people
anywhere, being inclined and having the power, have the *right* to rise up,
and shake off the existing government, and form a new one that suits
them better." That was the case with the Republic of Texas. But it was not
the case with the American invasion of Mexican territory, which led to
a war between nations rather than a revolution, despite the obfuscating
language and lies used to create the pretext. "This is a most valuable,—
a most sacred right—a right, which we hope and believe, is to liberate
the world." But the right must be exercised by those who already live in
that space, not by external invaders. "Nor is this right confined to cases in
which the whole people of an existing government may choose to exercise it. Any portion of such people that *can*, *may* revolutionize . . . putting
down a *minority*, intermingled with, or near about them, who may oppose
their movement. Such minority, was precisely the case, of the tories of our
own revolution. It is a quality of revolutions not to go by *old* lines, or *old*
laws; but to break up both, and make new ones."

Indeed, revolutions are dangerous, he granted, and the outcome
cannot be guaranteed. But the revolution of 1776 that served as his model
encouraged his faith that an honest use of language in a nation dedicated to
the dominance of the people would prevent wars of aggression or at least
correct them. He cannot and never will, he states, oppose the "sacred
right" that brought the American republic into existence, though he was
later to argue that by constitutional contract Americans had foresworn
further revolutionizing. The philosophical implications of foregoing that
right he would later subordinate to practical issues and ideological loyalties. He would also have an object lesson in the hard fact that when one
such "right" comes into irresolvable conflict with another, only force of
arms will determine which triumphs. With a heavy rhetorical flourish
that denied Polk the purposefulness of his strategy, assuming that remorse rather than self-congratulation should be the rewards of territorial

expansion, Lincoln concluded that it was possible that the president may have believed his own lies, "a bewildered, confounded, and miserably perplexed man. God grant he may be able to show, there is not something about his conscience, more painful than all his mental perplexity."

In July 1848, Lincoln made the same charge with a lighter touch in a speech with a different strategy, one that allowed him to be less formal, more conversational, and more structurally casual. His main strategic object was to defend and glorify the Whig candidate, Zachary Taylor, and to devalue the Democratic candidate, an ersatz general and professional politician, Lewis Cass of Michigan. The colloquial informality of a campaign speech was appropriate, and Lincoln moved his language and argument through its appropriate paces, with humor and satiric depreciation rather than iron logic. The record makes clear the difference between the leadership qualities of the two candidates: Taylor is a true war hero, Cass a trumped-up politician who has eaten at the public trough, having mastered "the art of being paid for what one eats, instead of having to pay for it." He will feed his supporters "bounteously,—if—if there is any left after he shall have helped himself." His nomination exemplifies the Democrats' attempt again to ride the coattails of Andrew Jackson. "Like a horde of hungry ticks," they "have stuck to the tail of the Hermitage lion to the end of his life; and . . . are still sticking to it, and drawing a loathsome sustenance from it, after he is dead." In fact, Lincoln himself, he humorously confesses with a touch of Mark Twain's "The True History of a Campaign That Failed," is as much a war hero as Cass:

By the way, Mr. Speaker did you know I am a military hero? Yes sir; in the days of the Black Hawk war, I fought, bled, and came away. Speaking of Gen: Cass' career, reminds me of my own. I was not at Stillman's defeat, but I was about as near it, as Cass was to Hulls surrender [in the War of 1812]; and, like him, I saw the place very soon afterwards. It is quite certain I did not break my sword, for I had none to break; but I bent a musket pretty bad on one occasion. If Cass broke his sword . . . he broke it in desperation; I bent the musket by accident. If Gen: Cass went in advance of me in picking huckleberries, I guess I surpassed him in charges upon the wild onions. If he saw any live, fighting indians, it was more than I did; but I had a good many bloody struggles with the musquetoes; and, although I never fainted from loss of blood, I can truly say I was often very hungry. Mr. Speaker, if . . . they [the Democrats] shall take me up as their candidate for the Presidency, I protest they shall not make fun of me, as they have of Gen: Cass, by attempting to write me into a military hero.

Within the rambling structure of this and more explicitly in his only other major speech during his two years in Congress, in late June 1848 on "Internal Improvements," he had two issues in mind: limiting executive power and creating economic prosperity through infrastructure improvements. On the political level, they were connected. The Democrats, with Jackson as their totemic model, believed that the president should use the veto to kill any congressional legislation of which he disapproved. The Whigs believed that the veto should be exercised only in extraordinary circumstances, not as a weapon to advance presidential desires and never as a tool to prevent Congress from exercising the will of the people. "That the constitution gives the President a negative on legislation, all know," Lincoln told his colleagues, "but that this negative should be so combined with platforms, and other appliances, as to enable him, and, in fact, almost compel him, to take the whole of legislation into his own hands, is what we object to, is what Gen: Taylor objects to, and is what constitutes the broad distinction between you and us." The role of the president is to administer the laws passed by Congress, not to initiate legislation or budgets. He should not exercise the veto against the will of Congress except in instances in which he believed it was being subverted by corruption or the bill at hand was unconstitutional. To Lincoln, this approach "appears like principle, and the best sort of principle at that— the principle of allowing the people to do as they please with their own business."

To the argument that federal funding of infrastructure improvements was unconstitutional, he assured his colleagues that "no one . . . needs be much uneasy in his conscience" about that. The Constitution gave Congress the power to use federal funds to advance the well-being of the nation. To embellish his call to boldness, he quoted the Renaissance poet Robert Herrick: "Attempt the end, and never stand to doubt; / Nothing so hard, but search will find it out." Congress should establish a list of projects that met the test of national advantage, even if indirectly, the way the Illinois-Michigan Canal benefits New Orleans as well as New York and every place between. Having learned his lesson in the Illinois debacle, he "would not borrow money. . . . Suppose, that at each session, congress shall first determine *how much* money can, for the year, be spared for improvements; then apportion that sum to the most *important* objects." To determine which are most important, the government should collect statistics about every aspect of produce, products, surpluses, and needs, so that it "would readily appear where a given amount of expenditure would do the most good." Such statistics would be made available to the states also, "and the whole country put on that career of prosperity, which shall correspond with its extent of territory, its natural resources, and the intelligence and enterprise of its people." If the collection of such statistics should be judged to be unconstitutional, the Constitution should be amended. "As a general rule," though, "we would do much better to let it alone. No slight occasion should tempt us to touch it. Better not take the first step, which may lead to a habit of altering it. Better, rather, habituate ourselves to think of it, as unalterable. It can scarcely be made better than it is. . . . New hands have never touched it. The men who made it, have done their work, and have passed away. Who shall improve, on what *they* did?"

Reluctantly, gradually, under the pressure of circumstances beyond his control, he was later to find it desirable to provide exceptions to the "general rule" and to become the instrument of recalibrating the Constitution. But he could not, in 1848, envision that the triumph of his moral principles about slavery would require changing it, and, if he had, the thought would have been awesomely frightening, a tectonic shift in the landscape—a change of boundaries, a removal of fences, and a redistribution of property almost on a cosmic scale.

Congress provided Lincoln few opportunities to exercise his gift for language, and Washington life for the freshman congressman had at best few advantages. He appreciated the long absences of his wife, whose arrogant sourness alienated some of their fellow lodgers, all fellow congressmen without their families, at Mrs. Sprigg's boardinghouse. He sometimes felt lonely, though, and especially missed his two sons. As a father, he had few or no standards of discipline, sparing the rod with the unhappy assurance that Mary would be liberal with it, and with a sense that an unforgiving world would provide his sons with severe discipline soon enough. At happy moments the family joined crowds of Washingtonians listening to the weekly band concerts. Mostly, though, Lincoln worked at congressional papers related to his two committees, added his voice to the daily politicking and late-night discussions with his Whig messmates in his Capitol Hill boardinghouse, and wrote occasional letters, many of which were devoted to attempting to get federal jobs for his Whig supporters. "If you collect," he wrote to an indiscriminate autograph collector, "the signatures of all persons who are no less distinguished than I, you will have a very undistinguished mass of names." Beneath the surface was his continuing ambition. He felt restless and displaced.

His most engrossing engagement was with the effort to elect a Whig president. From his little position, he worked in his mind on big things, catalyzed by the mental exercise of his ambition. As the campaign heated up in spring 1848, he put in writing what he would say to the country if he were running for the presidency, which reads partly as advice to Zachary Taylor, partly as a speechwriter's creation of a political credo for his candidate, and to some extent as an indirect assertion that he himself had the words and ideas that a president requires. No one had asked him to create such a document. And, apparently, no one saw it, though the logical result of its creation should have been its distribution to his colleagues, with the hope that Taylor might make use of it. In the document, Lincoln's intellect and nervous system projected him into the presidential subjunctive. It was role creation by a man not yet on the stage and hardly even in the wings.

"Were I president," he wrote, he would highlight four policies: he would not pressure Congress to legislate a national bank into existence, though he would not veto such legislation if Congress were to initiate it; he would modify the existing tariff to raise revenue to eliminate the Mexican War debt and to protect home industry; he would conclude the war with a treaty of peace that would take from Mexico only the limited amount of territory necessary to provide the United States with a defensible boundary, without acquiring territory "so far South, as to enlarge and aggravate the distracting question of slavery. . . . Finally, were I president, I should desire the legislation of the country to rest with Congress, uninfluenced by the executive in its origin or progress, and undisturbed by the veto unless in very special and clear cases." As a Whig, he would insist that the president be the administrator, not the policy creator. Congress and political parties represented the people's will; the president had been given the authority to uphold, not create, the law. Like his fellow Whigs, he saw Andrew Jackson's usurpation of power reborn in Polk's exercise of the veto and in his war policy, which threatened the balance between the branches of government.

If he and Mary had favorite Washington activities, they did not include visiting one of its best-known tourist sites, the infamous "Georgia Pen . . . where negroes were bought and sold within sight of the National Capitol," then "taken to Southern markets, precisely like droves of horses," which, he later remarked, had begun "to grow offensive in the nostrils of all good men, Southerners as well as Northerners." The slave market's daily bustle gave physical reality to the most stressful topic before Congress. Each party faced the difficulty of drawing both Northern and Southern votes should its candidate's position on slavery became central to his national campaign. The slaveholding Southerner, Zachary

Taylor, acceptable to the South by birth and class, was known *not* to be a defender of slavery, which made him palatable to the North. The non-slaveholding senator from Michigan, Lewis Cass, embodied the Democrats' general indifference to slavery. Both parties contained both slavery-enthusiasts and abolitionists, with much in between. But most Northern Whigs, unlike Northern Democrats, opposed slavery expansion, some for political more than moral reasons. Many, like Lincoln, hoped for gradual emancipation. Though he agreed that it would be wise for Taylor to say nothing about the issue, he and other congressional Whigs strongly opposed expansion, and Lincoln voted at least five times in support of a resolution, introduced by David Wilmot of Pennsylvania, banning slavery in any territory acquired from Mexico. The center of both parties, squeezed by proslavery expansionists on one side and Northern abolitionists on the other, struggled to maintain the status quo. Anything else seemed threateningly dangerous. The battlegrounds were the Senate, dominated by Southerners, and the House, with a slim Whig majority.

Lincoln's visceral abhorrence of slavery made him queasy at the sight of the Washington slave market. Twice, though, he had visited Lexington, where his wife's slave-holding family found him trustworthy enough to appoint him executor of Mary's father's estate, which probably made him responsible for the disposing of slaves. In a fiduciary capacity, he would always do his legal duty, as required by the law and, eventually, by the Constitution. As a lawyer, he had participated in two cases involving slaves. In one of them he had successfully defended a slave girl's claim to emancipation because of her residence in Illinois. In another, he gave counsel to a Kentucky slave owner whose slaves worked his Illinois farm half the year. This prevented Lincoln, when approached by antislavery advocates, from representing them. He then agreed to defend the slave owner, most likely on the principle that every accused deserves adequate legal representation. The claim that the slaves actually resided in Kentucky had been attacked as a charade to evade Illinois law. When the Illinois court decided that the slaves at issue "shall be free and remain free . . . from henceforward and forever," Lincoln had to have felt morally satisfied but professionally disappointed. He had lost on the question of fact. The law itself he completely supported.

In January 1849, his term in Congress close to an end, he injected himself into an aspect of the slavery issue about which he had, twelve years before, expressed his legislative intent: slavery in the District of Columbia. Its existence was a sore point for those who thought slavery an "injustice," as Lincoln had described it in his resolution to the Illinois legislature in 1837. Bad as it was for slavery to be legal in the South and unpleasant as it was that Southerners, visiting in the North, could be accompanied by slaves as long as residence was not at issue, the legality of slavery and a bustling slave market in the capital, where legislators and foreign representatives necessarily resided, was a different matter. It seemed to many an affront to the nation's image, a statement inconsistent with its claim to be a republic, an intolerable deviation from the underlying principle of the republic's founding declaration.

Lincoln took the opportunity on January 10, 1849, to try to play a constructive role in a tense congressional conflict between those who opposed any diminution of the rights of slaveholders in the District of Columbia and those, from moderate Whigs to abolitionists, attempting to eliminate slavery in the capital. The disagreement about how to treat runaway and recaptured slaves also had become particularly volatile. Taking advantage of ongoing parliamentary maneuvering on what was considered an extreme bill, Lincoln proposed a compromise, a substitute bill "to abolish slavery in the District . . . by the consent of the free white [citizens] . . . and with compensation to owners." It took the form of a concise, well-framed resolution with eight sections, which he asked the House to instruct the Committee on the District of Columbia to take up and then report to the full House. For Lincoln to introduce these resolutions there needed to be a reconsideration of the vote on the previous bill. A variant on numbers of compromise bills, Lincoln's resolution mandated that any slaves hereafter brought into the District would be free except those imported by government officials during their service; that all children born to slave mothers in the District after January 1, 1850, would be free; that all slaves currently in the District would remain slaves, but slave owners would receive from the government full value for those they chose to emancipate; that the District authorities would be required to "deliver up to their owners, all fugitive slaves escaping into said District"; and that an election would be held in which "every free white male citizen above the age of twenty one years" residing in the District for a year would be eligible to vote to determine whether or not these resolutions would become law.

When, a few days later, Lincoln announced that he would himself introduce his resolutions as a bill, the silence was deafening. Years later he explained that "finding that I was abandoned by my former backers and having little personal influence, I *dropped* the matter knowing that it was useless to prosecute the business at that time." Abolitionists soon raised the fugitive slave provision of his bill against him. Over the next decade it became increasingly clear that it would be difficult to get the center to hold. In early 1849, Lincoln still believed there was one.

But when he left Washington in March—as far as he knew, forever— he could not point to a single legislative accomplishment in regard to which his name had any prominence, let alone a bill dealing with slavery in the district. He had, though, dutifully voted in good conscience for his party's bills and resolutions. And when Taylor, for whose election he had worked so hard, became president in March 1849, Lincoln expected that he would share in the spoils by having a major influence on the distribution of patronage in Illinois and by a position for himself. He was, though, undecided about what he wanted. The interplay between his sense of propriety on the one hand and his ambition on the other distorted his focus. To his disappointment, he soon found himself with little to dispense to others and caught up in a patronage drama with elements of role-playing and betrayal that ended in his going, hat in hand, and attempting to get the job he decided he did want and believed he deserved.

He had indeed done the state some service, whether or not that line from *Othello* came to his mind. He had fought hard for the Taylor triumph. Though the election did not result in a Whig victory in Illinois and though he ended his congressional term less popular at home than when he started because of his resolutions on the origin of the war, he had on his own initiative energetically taken to the campaign trail for Taylor. With Mary and his sons, he traveled by train to New England via New York City early in September 1848, and then, at the end of the month, to Albany, where he met the Whig political impresario Thurlow Weed and the vice-presidential candidate, Millard Fillmore. After touring Niagara Falls, he traveled to Springfield via a Great Lakes steamer from Buffalo to Chicago. It was eye-opening for him, and useful for New England Whigs to have their presidential candidate represented so favorably by a Westerner whose power with language made him a formidable campaigner, emphasizing the national rather than the regional strength of Whig views.

For an obscure congressman, Lincoln was a noticeable success at rallies in Worcester, where he was a last-minute addition to the program, and then in New Bedford and Lowell. In effect, he had invited himself to New England in the hope that if a congressman were known to be in town, he would be asked to speak. His luck held. After Worcester, invitations came. He spoke in Boston and various towns in the Boston area, emphasizing executive overreaching, the tariff, and the Mexican War. He defended Taylor's qualifications and decried the spoiler role that the newly formed antislavery Free Soil Party, which had nominated Van Buren, might play by drawing votes away from Taylor. The Free Soil argument that "old party lines" needed to be broken down and a new party formed that made "opposition to slavery the leading idea" would harm Taylor, Lincoln argued, and probably elect the slavery-tolerant Cass. At a mass meeting in the Tremont Temple, Boston's largest auditorium, famous for hosting New England's most impressive events, he followed the main speaker, New York's governor William Henry Seward, who represented the moderate abolitionist attack on slavery. Years later, Seward recalled that Lincoln remarked to him, "I reckon you are right. We have got to deal with this slavery question, and got to give more attention to it hereafter than we have been doing." Seward may have been embellishing or creating history from his post-Lincoln vantage point. Concerned about the danger to Whig prospects that the extreme position represented, Lincoln emphasized the exclusion of slavery from the territories and the District of Columbia, not the abolition of slavery in the South.

Partisan Whig newspapers covered Lincoln's appearances favorably. The Worcester paper noted that he "has a very tall and thin figure, with an intellectual face, showing a searching mind, and a cool judgment." A Boston newspaper admiringly remarked that his speech contained "sound reasoning, cogent argument and keen satire." Another noted the difference between Eastern and Western oratorical styles: Lincoln's colloquial casualness, his reliance on humor and anecdote, his mixture of logic, sarcasm, and satire. An opposition newspaper gave him credit for sincerity while disparaging his humor as clownlike, though funny, and his honesty as suspect: "It was reviving to hear a man speak as if he believed what he was saying. . . . The speaker was far inferior as a reasoner to others who hold the same views; but then he was more unscrupulous, more facetious and with his sneers he mixed up a good deal of humor. His awkward gesticulations, the ludicrous management of his voice and the comical expression of his countenance, all conspired to make his hearers laugh at the mere anticipation of the joke before it appeared." Lincoln urged that "all those who wished to keep up the character of the Union; who did not believe in enlarging our field, but in keeping our fences where they are and cultivating our present possession, making it a garden, improving the morals and education of the people," should vote for the Whig ticket. Cultivate your own garden, protect and improve the property that you have. Lincoln's use of images drawn from the Western literary storehouse, from the Bible to Voltaire's *Candide*, gave cultural resonance to his defense of Whig policies and his attacks on the Democrats.

Immensely relieved by Taylor's election, he returned to Washington in December 1848. The question of his own future was much on his mind. Three months of his congressional term remained. The lengthy election-period visit home had reunited him with friends and native soil; it had also reminded him, if he needed it, that there was little to no possibility of a political future for him in an elected office in Illinois. "I am not a candidate for re-nomination or election," he wrote to potential supporters, honoring his pledge not to run for a second term. There was the possibility of a return to Congress at some distant date, but Illinois's political demography and the dismal Whig showing in the Illinois election made such a prospect unlikely. To his disappointment, the Taylor administration distributed little political patronage to Illinois, partly because the state had minimal clout in the Whig power structure in Washington. Also, Taylor decided to reward some Whigs who had not supported him. Naturally, various Illinois factions competed for the available spoils, which limited Lincoln's effectiveness on behalf of friends such as Anson Henry, about whose prospects he was "*exceedingly* anxious." With a few exceptions, he was unable to reward his supporters and, to add insult to Illinois's injury, when he and others backed Edward Baker for a cabinet position, they were rebuffed. It seemed to him self-defeating that, though every Democratic administration immediately dumped all Whig patronage holders, the Whig president should take the high road. In the end, he feared, such an approach would irreparably weaken the party. It was also a personal embarrassment.

With his congressional salary to end in March, he needed to be concerned about himself. In regard to a major appointive office, Lincoln told Joshua Speed, who had been urging an influential Kentucky Whig to help Lincoln get an appointment, that "there is nothing about me which would authorize me to think of a first class office; and a second class one would not compensate me for being snarled at by others who want it for themselves." The commissionership of the General Land Office had its attractions, and he believed that "so far as the whigs in congress, are concerned, I could have [it] almost by common consent." It came with an annual salary of three thousand dollars, and control over the disposition of all western public lands. But at least four prominent Illinois Whigs, including his friends Orville Browning and Cyrus Edwards, "all want it." Lincoln agreed to give his support to Edwards. Still, he told Speed in February 1849, "while I think I could easily take it myself," he feared that he would "have trouble to get it for any other man in Illinois." In the light of later events, his expectation that he could get the position was either unwarranted overconfidence or a search for encouragement to pursue it himself.

When Edward Baker, elected to replace Lincoln in Congress, pushed another candidate for the Land Office job, Lincoln agreed that he and Baker unite to support whichever candidate did not withdraw, unless Lincoln himself decided to be a candidate. "Baker has at all times been ready to recommend me, if I would consent," he told his supporters in April, but he would do so only if the people he and Baker had committed themselves to withdrew. "In relation to these pledges, I must not only be chaste but above suspicion." If neither of these men withdrew but could clearly be seen as unlikely to be appointed, he would reconsider.

It was too late. By the end of April, the Lincoln-Baker strategy was in shambles. An office that might have been his if, from the start, he had promoted his own candidacy, was now promised to a Chicago Whig, Justin Butterfield, partly as an olive branch to Henry Clay, whom Butterfield had supported for the nomination. "Of the quite one hundred Illinoisians, equally well qualified, I do not know one with less claims to it," Lincoln wrote to an Illinois friend working in the Land Office in Washington. It would be "an egregious political blunder." If the administration did not award those who had helped elect it, the party would be damaged and the Democrats strengthened. As for himself, "It will mortify me deeply if Gen. Taylors administration shall trample all my wishes in the dust merely to gratify these men." Lincoln's pleading letters on behalf of Anson Henry and others did no good. When, in the middle of May, still loyal to Cyrus Edwards's candidacy, he learned that the appointment was slated to go to Butterfield, he sent a barrage of letters to Washington, hoping to "get the ear of Gen: Taylor." Washington did not respond.

In early June 1849, having convinced himself that the job should rightfully be his rather than Butterfield's, he decided to go to Washington himself. He urged that letters in his support be addressed to him there. Either while traveling or on his arrival, he composed a memo advancing his candidacy. Since he had reason to believe that the secretary of the interior was supporting Butterfield and withholding Lincoln's supporters' letters, he hoped to get his arguments directly to the president. Taylor's inclination to delegate authority to the heads of departments, which Lincoln had made a virtue of during the campaign, he now had reason to criticize as an avoidance of responsibility. In his memo, he outlined why, since he was "preferred by the Whigs of Illinois" and since Illinois, like other states, should have the determining say in such appointments, he should be given the position. As to Illinois Whig politics, "I am in the center. Is the center nothing?—that center which alone has ever given you a Whig representative?" And, he argued, assuming that the claims of the north and the center of the state had equal validity, the other factors leaned heavily toward a reward for the center.

It is doubtful that Taylor got to read Lincoln's memo. Larger political and personal forces than Lincoln could muster had made Butterfield's appointment a fait accompli. Within a week, Lincoln learned that the Chicagoan had gotten the position. It was a bitter disappointment. Returning to his Washington boardinghouse, he threw himself onto his bed and stared "an hour or more" at the ceiling. A week later, in Springfield, it was additionally galling to Lincoln to learn that Cyrus Edwards believed Lincoln had betrayed him. He drew on his talent for compensatory stoicism, his predilection for the retrospective assertion that he had not cared very much whether or not he himself got the appointment. "Let it be understood I am not greatly dissatisfied," he wrote to his friend Charles Gillespie. But he wished the office had been used to "encourage our friends in future contests, and I regret exceedingly Mr. Edwards' feeling toward me. These two things away, I should have no regrets—at least I think I would not." He was certainly not speaking for his wife. A powerful office and three thousand dollars a year would have represented a down payment on Mary's expectations. Lincoln was indeed, though, speaking for himself out of the depths of his capability to renounce and regroup, to turn inwardly toward his long-cultivated stoic melancholy, with an element of the resentment that he almost always successfully concealed. When offered the secretaryship of the Oregon Territory, he said no. When the compensatory ante from Washington was raised with the offer of the governorship, he tersely declined. In this situation, brevity contained the world: the fewer words, the better.

Traveling from New England to Illinois in late September 1848, he had visited Niagara Falls, at the time America's best-known natural wonder. His literary sensibility, stirred by Niagara's "power to excite reflection, and emotion," expressed itself in an unfinished two-paragraph essay. It falls within a well-established eighteenth- and nineteenth-century literary sub-genre, an evocation of and a meditation on an awesome natural phenomenon. It also represents Lincoln's particular philosophical inflection, his personal sense of relationship to the national landscape, and his mastery of words, one of his occasional attempts to do what professional writers do regularly, to find appropriate language for experience and feeling, though he had no audience in mind and was writing for himself.

As a boy, he had read Oliver Goldsmith's description of the Falls in Lindley Murray's *English Reader*. "It is not easy to bring the imagination to correspond to the greatness of the scene," Goldsmith concluded. British and French eighteenth-century writers about beauty and nature, such as Goldsmith, had not needed to visit the New World to find Niagara a wondrous embodiment of the aesthetic of the sublime. Romantic poets, particularly Wordsworth and Shelley, made such natural phenomena central to their understanding of the relationship between the visible and the invisible, between physical beauty and the moral self. Niagara's magnificence provoked both reverent silence and effusive expressiveness. "What voices spoke from out the thundering waters," Dickens wrote, preceding Lincoln to the Falls by six years, "What faces, faded from the earth, looked out upon me from its gleaming depths; what Heavenly promise glistened in those angels' tears, the drops of many hues, that showered around, and twined themselves about the gorgeous arches which the changing rainbows made." By the 1840s it had become a major attraction to travelers. Christians saw the face of Jesus in the rainbow mists. Naturalists and geologists measured and compared. Philosophers meditated.

American writers, from Longfellow to Henry James, made an encounter with Niagara's dynamic power a test of the imagination's ability to encompass the sublime. Frederick Church's landmark painting gave ethereal power to Niagara as a Romantic image of America before the settlement, a sacred place of primal freshness. Sometimes the imagination failed. Mark Twain concentrated his satiric wit on the commercial exploitation of the Falls. Literate visitors from every walk of life wrote their sentiments into the guest book at Table Rock, a flat surface near the Falls, often "poetic effusions," as Dickens noted, sometimes "miserable profanations upon the very steps of Nature's greatest altar."

The essayistic inscription of the tourist from Illinois was neither effusively poetic nor humorously profane, though he kept faith with a convention of the nineteenth-century evocative essay in his opening invocation, the simple exclamatory "Niagara-Falls!" and the immediate statement of the key question that would determine the structure of his meditation: "By what mysterious power is it that millions and millions, are drawn from all parts of the world, to gaze upon Niagara Falls?" "Millions and millions" expresses Lincoln momentary attraction to relevant hyperbole, not a usual feature of his literary style: here factual exactness is less important than an evocation of the emotive power of everything connected with Niagara. This is the ordinary observation of an extraordinary man. The language is matter-of-factly succinct. The simple statement of the natural wonder's name establishes the hugeness of his subject. The exclamation point is both redundant and expressive. The question highlights the mysterious power of the Falls. Still, Lincoln immediately observes, "There is no mystery about the thing itself." When a great deal of river water meets these particular physical-topographical arrangements, of course "there will [be] a violent and continuous plunge," the water "will foam, and roar, and send up a mist," and "there will be perpetual rainbows." This is "the mere physical," by which he means the visible, effect that every tourist sees.

One sort of scientific observer, he notes, who has read enough to be knowledgeable about cause and effect and to appreciate the tools of scientific measurement, will hypothesize about the age of the earth by measuring how fast the water has been eroding the physical features of the land and the lake. A different sort of scientific observer will estimate the amount of water pouring down and be "overwhelmed in the contemplation of the vast power the sun is constantly exerting in quiet, noiseless operation of lifting water *up* to be rained *down* again." But the scientific dimension, though part of what makes Niagara so impressive to the human observation, is "a very small part of that world's wonder. Its power to excite reflection, and emotion, is its great charm." Such an informed awareness of the processes of nature will, inevitably, he believes, "excite reflection," and reflection and emotion are inseparable, the dynamic symbiosis between what we think and feel. The mystery of the natural world lies in its power to evoke a human response, and in the variety of the potential responses.

Lincoln did not fear that science and technology had been or ever would be an enemy to a humanistic civilization. His contemporaries, Victorian writers such as Emerson, Thoreau, Darwin, Tennyson, Browning, and Ruskin, exemplified the connection Lincoln also made between keener observation, "finer optics," and the inner eye of reflection and imagination. The Victorian world that he had now technically resided in for eleven years took as one of its themes the link between precise naturalistic observation and the conceptualization in intellectual and poetic language of the relationship between nature and human significance. Indeed "there is more," Lincoln continued in his second paragraph, than what can be counted and measured; much more. There is what the meditative mind brings to bear in its attempt to find human significance in natural phenomena. And in that "more" he finds the essence of his subject, the connection between the past and the present, his sense of how far back the past goes, his awareness of the fossil record, his belief in the constant processes of nature and evolutionary change, and, by analogy, his sense that he himself is a part of this process, a hint of personal self-exploration that captures Lincoln's awareness of his own fluidity. And he does this with a precision that is both poetically evocative and intellectually vivid:

> But still there is more. It calls up the indefinite past. When Columbus first sought this continent—when Christ suffered on the cross—when Moses led Israel through the Red-Sea—nay, even, when Adam first came from the hand of his Maker—then as now, Niagara was roaring here. The eyes of that species of extinct giants, whose bones filled the mounds of America, have gazed on Niagara, as ours do now. Contemporary with the whole race of men, and older than the first man, Niagara is strong, and fresh to-day as ten thousand years ago. The Mammoth and Mastodon—now so long dead, that fragments of their monstrous bones, alone testify, that they ever lived, have gazed on Niagara. In that long— long time, never still for a single moment. Never dried, never froze, never slept, never rested,

Stopping in mid-sentence, Lincoln gives his essay an eerie though unintended similarity to the many purposeful fragments in Romantic poetry, evoking the most controversial Romantic process poem, Coleridge's "Kubla Khan," a type that exemplifies the Romantic belief that process is all there is. That which is incomplete and unfinished signals the necessary dominance of change within nature and the human condition.

Lincoln's fascination with Niagara Falls had of course numbers of sources. It is the most famous feature of the mid-nineteenth-century American landscape. It is also a representation of his fascination from an early age with the human, the mechanical, and the natural, how things work in this world. And the Falls' ceaseless flow is both reinforcement of and counterpoint to his sense of naturalistic determinism, of endless time and individual temporality. There is not, in Lincoln's evocation and meditation, a hint of God or divine providence. Theological and cosmological speculations about first causes do not apply. The biblical references are temporal markers, apparently no different in function from Columbus's discovery of America. That Niagara was there before the creation of Adam transforms the biblical account of the creation into another marker, like the fossil record, in a naturalistic calendar. Niagara serves as a signpost in human history and prehuman time, and also as a time-keeper of "the indefinite past," an unascertainable beginning of less interest than the ongoing ceaseless changes. Just as "the mammoth and mastodon" have passed away, Niagara will witness the passing of the human species. All is change, all is flux, all is process, and he too, he implies, has within himself the inner clock that nature provides, the biological process that brings death to each individual, as it had to his mother and to Ann Rutledge, and inevitably to him and those he loves.

In this same exercise of imaginative meditation, Lincoln reached for a correlative for another aspect of himself. It is a useful stretch to say that in his ambition and in his sense of inner energy he identified, as he created the phrase, with a force that has "never dried, never froze, never slept, never rested," which will continue to be there as a marker when he no longer exists. Niagara's uniqueness provides both a measure for and a potential affirmation of human character and the human situation. And it stands apart as an image that affirms both strength and self-annihilation; it accentuates the limits of human history in contrast to nature's comparative timelessness. Such ceaselessness had its parallel in his own life, sponsored by the inner demand to make something of himself against the sluggish countercurrents of birth and family; to swim upstream against formidable obstacles—limited means, painful loss, emotional angst, and political discouragement. From the start, he needed to overcome internal and external opposition by willful acts of self-definition, the ambitious farm-boy autodidact becoming a splitter of words and ideas rather than fence rails.

Standing at the edge of Niagara Falls in September 1848, his term as a congressman coming to an end, Lincoln had to have had in mind: What next? Conservative by nature, he clearly had no plans to go over the Falls, despite his attraction to dark moods and dreams of death: the attraction was in the correlative, not the termination. And the opportunities that the powerful falling and rising waters might have suggested could encompass a national as well as a personal destiny. With irreconcilable issues seared into his Washington experience, he would have wondered whether the nation was soon to go over the falls, so to speak, whether in a barrel or not. Two days later, a Great Lakes steamer carried him to Springfield, via Chicago. And as he wrote his impressions, he stopped in mid-sentence.

CHAPTER 6

"Honest Seeking"

1849–1854

In March 1849, Abraham Lincoln appeared for the only time before the United States Supreme Court, Chief Justice Roger Taney presiding, to argue a case before it. The relatively obscure congressman whose single term was about to end probably did not attract particular attention, though his distinctive appearance may have been noticed as a minor irregularity in an ordinary day at the Court. His words before the Court, long obscured in the pages of Benjamin C. Howard's *Reports of the Supreme Court of the U.S. Jan. Term 1849* (1884), have recently been made available by the Lincoln Legal Papers project. The case was to resolve litigation regarding property ownership that had come to the Court because the two justices assigned to the Midwest circuit had disagreed. It was a federal matter because it involved a statute of limitations in an Illinois law affecting non-residents: the property originally at issue was in Ohio. In its obvious features it was a dry-as-dust case about how to interpret an Illinois law of 1827 and its 1837 repeal, which regulated the time a potential litigant had to initiate a lawsuit. Beneath the surface, though, there were larger issues.

In 1819 Matthew Broadwell, who was an Illinois resident and whose estate was Lincoln's client, sold William Lewis a parcel of land in Ohio. It turned out that Broadwell was not the rightful owner. The rightful owner legally ejected Lewis in 1825. In 1827, the Illinois legislature passed a statute stating that a suit for damages of the sort that Lewis had suffered had to begin within sixteen years of the cause of the action. Non-Illinois residents, though, were exempt from the limitation. In 1837 the legislature repealed the exemption for non-Illinois residents. In December 1843, Lewis sued Broadwell's estate for three thousand dollars in damages. Did Lewis, at this late date, still have the right to sue? Both parties and the court agreed that the starting date for the sixteen-year exemption was either 1827 or 1837. If 1827, then Lewis had no right to sue, since he had missed the sixteen-year exemption by some months. If 1837, then he did.

As with many cases Lincoln had argued in Illinois, this was about property rights, about the ownership of land, about the country-old necessity to establish legitimate title, suggestive of his father Thomas Lincoln's problems with the perplexities of title legitimacy in Kentucky. The issue touched on his family's travails and the nation's settlement and extension, an aspect of which he had directly experienced in the Black Hawk War in which he had fought in 1832—the problem of contested territory, the necessity to adjudicate conflicting claims about ownership. Its deep background distantly referenced the question of what rights American citizens had in the newly opened western territories, including whether the right of a resident of South Carolina to own human property, authorized by the Constitution and the laws of his state, was valid in territories that were federal property.

In the foreground, the issue was a technical one. Both the pro-slavery chief justice, who was to rule for the majority and against Lincoln's client, and Justice John McLean, an antislavery evangelical Christian from Ohio, who was to dissent, agreed that the technical issue should be resolved by an appeal to precedent. Taney (pronounced Taw-ney) argued that the Court had decided previously that "limitations would not begin to run until the time of the repeal" unless the law specifically indicated otherwise. But his argument in this case disregarded the precise language of the precedent and some of its major points, as if they did not exist. Citing the same precedent, McLean claimed the opposite. Closely examining its language, he argued that the words in the precedent actually said that "if [statutes] make no exceptions . . . the courts can make none. And when the exceptions of a statute are repealed, the act stands as though it had been originally passed without them." Precedent, in other words, determined that exemptions or exceptions in a law that had been repealed were governed by the date of the original law, except when there was an obvious unfairness. And, McLean stressed, the six years that Lewis had between the repeal in 1837 and the inception of his suit in 1843 had been ample time to meet the test of fairness. With three additional precedents to buttress his argument, he parsed the language and the arguments of earlier rulings.

A Democratic politician, Taney had been appointed in 1836 by Andrew Jackson to succeed the Federalist John Marshall. Like many of his opinions defining the authority of the Court, the chief justice's decision in *Broadwell v. Lewis* strengthened the Court's power in relation to state legislatures and Congress in order to protect Southern interests. As the arbiter of constitutionality, the Court embodied for Taney the ultimate bulwark against legislative attempts to interfere with property rights, a crucial concern for the Southern-born chief justice. Eight years later, the Dred Scott decision made clear that Taney, as an advocate for increasing the Court's power over legislatures, had in mind throughout that a Southern-leaning Court would be able to perpetuate slavery in the Southern states and perhaps extend it to the western territories. As long as it was controlled by justices like him (and five of his colleagues were Southern partisans), the more power the Court had over legislatures in regard to property issues, the better. And in order to protect slavery, the adjudication of property issues of any sort needed to be decided in strict contractual terms, without regard for fairness or morality. A contract was a contract, its terms not to be mitigated by issues that were not explicitly a part of the contract.

Lincoln probably had no sense of the chief justice's agenda. In fact, he agreed with Taney that the Constitution guaranteed the right of a state to legislate in favor of slavery by protecting and extending property rights. Lincoln took as a guiding principle, as did Taney, that both the courts and the executive owed deference to the legislature's precise language unless that language was incompatible with the Constitution, a criterion that Taney espoused in general but acted in exception to whenever there were overriding ideological factors. Like McLean, Lincoln believed that the relevant precedents in this case supported his client's defense, and he concisely presented the citations and references. But then, characteristically, he evoked what he believed should be the basis of the determinative argument, the underlying philosophical, political, and linguistic guidelines of a pragmatic society: that a realistic view of human nature needs to be a factor in judicial decision-making; that common sense, as the distillation of rationality, is the best guide to thought and action; that language, whose integrity must be maintained, is the supreme tool of civilized discourse; that prudence and restraint should dominate government; and that the balance of power established in the Constitution between the branches of government, and especially the role of the people's voice in their state legislatures and in Congress, should be given the highest respect.

Lincoln's brief was terse, carefully phrased, lucidly precise, a linguistic as well as substantive appeal to common sense as the gatekeeper to higher principles. In its combination of personal voice and rational discourse, it was framed with literary skill within the narrow limits that a thoughtfully crafted text for oral presentation required. "The dictate of common sense," he argued, "which seems to be the perfection of reason, would be that the law should only operate from its passage, as its terms import, and if the legislature had intended otherwise, they were competent, and it was their duty to say so." Neither extra-legislative voices nor "*judicial discretion*" should override the language of the legislation.

> In my judgment, each would leave the impress of mischief in its pathway, and therefore neither should be tolerated.—The question is not whether the legislature is competent to make a law of limitations of six years; but whether the court has discretionary power over the subject,

to make a law long or short at its pleasure. And besides, different Courts would exercise various *discretionary powers* and the decisions would be dissimilar and perhaps capricious according to the standards of discretion. To avoid such a state of things, should be the object of every honest mind; but nothing can pre [vent?] such a result, except adhering to the statute as passed. Hence the conclusion seems to follow, that it is most prudent to construe statutes as to give them effect from their date or otherwise, according to their terms, without any metaphysical or hair splitting distinctions in order to make them operate *retroactively*.

So the issue was—did any court have the right to manufacture legislative intent out of thin air or substitute judicial judgment or desire for legislative fact? If the Court could in effect rewrite legislation, then it would have the authority, Lincoln feared, to rewrite the founding legislative document, the Constitution, and the political ideologies and sectional loyalties of the judges would determine what statutes meant, without regard for their actual language.

As a Whig and a conservative reverentially respectful of the power of language as an instrument of precision and a force for empowerment, Lincoln desired no judicial tampering with the sacred texts and the highest respect for the voice of the people as embodied in their legislatures. Common sense, which is "the perfection of reason," rational analysis, and a sincere attempt at objectivity were the tools to determine meaning. In arguing his case, he believed that precedent, language, and principle were on his side. As a Democrat and an adherent of legislative popular sovereignty, Taney shared Lincoln's respect for the exact language of legislation, with one exception: when significant Southern interests such as slavery were at stake. Lincoln, though, unlike Taney, found moral considerations relevant enough to cast his legal argument in a humanistic and experiential frame, giving priority to an honest use of language and commonsense reasoning, which his strictly legal argument embodied.

In the end, neither Taney nor McLean paid any attention in their written opinions to Lincoln's main argument. Each argued narrowly on the basis of his interpretation of the precedent, McLean for the 1827 date, Taney for the 1837 date. Lewis had a right to sue, the Court decided. The chief justice adhered to the Taney Court's general preference for the amoral enforcement of contracts, which McLean often dissented from. In this case, to favor his view, Taney read into the legislation what it did not contain. The convergence of common law interpretation and political ideology paradoxically resulted in the antislavery Ohio judge dissenting in favor of Lincoln's strict language argument and the chief justice writing a majority opinion that in its local effect valued fairness over strict interpretation. In the overview, though, Taney's decision in this relatively unimportant case strengthened the ability of the Southern majority to protect slavery, providing a potential precedent for Taney's jurisprudence ten years later in the Dred Scott case.

Soon after the Court's adverse decision, the ex-congressman returned to the relative obscurity of his Springfield life, resuming his duties at the firm of Lincoln and Herndon. Six years later, his philosophical principles and his linguistic abilities were to be put to the test of national prominence. He was to get the opportunity to argue before huge audiences the issues that had been implicit in the case that he had lost. And the pro-slavery chief justice who wrote the decision against him administered his oath of office in 1861.

At home in Springfield in spring 1849, Lincoln resented his failure to obtain patronage for himself and other Illinois Whigs. He had done the party service, he believed, and his reward as a politician was to be passed over for the position he wanted, even after making a special trip to Washington to plead his case, and to have his impotence made public by the rejection of his recommendations. He continued to write letters on behalf of two of his supporters, his close friends Simeon Francis and Anson Henry, ratcheting the target down as the plums went to other people. "Not one man recommended by me has yet been appointed to any thing, little or big, except a few who had no opposition," he complained in May 1849.

The complaint became a muted litany during the next two years, intensified by his conviction, based on news supplied by an informant, that he had been stabbed in the back by someone, probably the secretary of the interior, who had withheld some of Lincoln's supporting letters. Lincoln declined opportunities to criticize Thomas Ewing, since he still hoped to get the secretary's support for Anson Henry, who "has done more disinterested labor in the Whig cause, than any other one, two, or three men in the state." The secretary's "position has been one of great difficulty," Lincoln wrote to the *Chicago Journal*, attempting to create for public consumption the pretence of Whig harmony. "I believe him . . . to be an able and faithful officer." Whether Ewing had in fact betrayed Lincoln is unclear. Lincoln's informant lost his clerkship, though not necessarily for leaking information, and Ewing himself was soon replaced.

Lincoln's anger, though, seeps through the calm surface of his response in November 1850 to the rumor that Justin Butterfield intended to resign as land office commissioner and that Lincoln would now be offered the appointment. His words seem even the more acidic coming from a politician usually eager to cast himself as a stoic moderate who did not take such things personally and who did not look back. He would not "accept the office, even if it should be offered to him," he told the *Illinois Journal*, which printed the comment without direct quotation. He would, though, the *Journal* reported, support Cyrus Edwards if Butterfield resigned, an attempt to remove the taint of Edwards's charge that Lincoln had betrayed him in the original competition because he had from the first intended to get the job for himself. All this had become a wretched business. It made him especially sensitive thereafter to the difficulty of patronage considerations.

Disappointed, he returned vigorously to his law practice, which was, anyway, a financial necessity. Herndon had done a reasonably good job of maintaining the practice during Lincoln's absence. An outspoken, politically engaged Whig, the junior partner had sufficient presence in Springfield to be elected clerk and city attorney in April 1850. But as an increasingly influential figure, it was the forty-one-year-old senior partner who provided both the anchor and influence of the two-man firm. As an ex-congressman and a force in Illinois Whig politics, Lincoln commanded entrée and attention, particularly with the legislature. Numbers of businessmen advocating bills favorable to their interests obtained his services. Lobbying his former colleagues, he combined his clients' interests with his own attraction to the political game. Mostly, though, his and Herndon's income came from the daily slog of small cases with small fees, the usual range of ordinary business. He soon renewed his fall and spring circuit court pilgrimages, while Herndon minded the office.

Politics, though, was never far from his mind, despite the lingering bad taste of his patronage disappointments. The troublesome, unresolved question was: What form could his political interests and ambitions take in an environment in which his possibilities were curtailed by the dominance of the Democratic Party and his limited usefulness to his Whig colleagues? Meanwhile, the 1849–1850 debate in Washington, the swan song of a debilitated and ill Henry Clay, attempted to resolve the slavery issue in a series of compromises that most hoped would be a permanent solution but many suspected would not. It proceeded to its conclusion without a public word from Lincoln on the subject. He had no role to play and no forum in which to express his views. His most prominent competitor for political power in Illinois, Stephen Douglas, now occupied its senior seat in the United States Senate, an achievement Lincoln must have viewed with resigned envy. And in January 1849 his antagonist in the dueling fiasco of 1840, James Shields, now an ex–brigadier general, was elected to the Senate by the Illinois legislature. "How do you suppose this, as a fruit of the glorious Mexican war, tastes" to the Illinois Whig aspirants who had supported the war, Lincoln asked with a touch of rhetorical bitterness. "Do you suppose they are in a mood of *blessing* the war about now?"

The unpopularity of his opposition to the war still weighed against his own candidacy for office even in June 1850 when for other reasons as well he informed his party by public announcement in the *Illinois Journal* that he would not be a candidate for the Whig nomination for a congressional seat. When the rumor circulated in 1852 that he was the likely Whig nominee for governor, he scuppered it, recognizing that this was an administrative office unsuited to his legislative, linguistic, and oratorical talents. Anyway, his ambition was set on national service. The Senate seat that the legislature would fill in early 1855 may have been on his mind. His wife particularly would have found biding time frustrating, waiting for the high-level career she had expected him to have. Returning to the state legislature or even to the United States House would have seemed regressive to both of them. By supporting Whig candidates and ideas, he could act both on principle and self-interest. When the Whigs wanted a skilled writer, a persuasive orator, and an adept organizer of political strategy, they turned to Lincoln. Otherwise, he was out in the cold, mainly because rival candidates and Illinois political demographics put him there.

In July 1850 his profession and one of his particular interests brought him to Democratic-dominated Chicago. A magnet for immigrants and entrepreneurs, the city was now the urban focus in the shift of economic and voting power from central to northern Illinois. When asked to act for the defense in *Parker v. Hoyt*, a case for infringement of a waterwheel patent, he happily agreed. His lifelong interest in inventions reflected his fascination with the practical technology of making things work. It was inseparable from his ideological commitment to the premise that advancement for the individual and for a democratic society was best served by "improvements." He indeed had some experience with water-related inventions. When the raft he had helped construct in 1831 got stuck at New Salem, he had put his inventive mind to work to solve the problem. In March 1849 he registered a patent for "An Improved Method of Lifting Vessels over Shoals," with a detailed drawing of an apparatus that, through the use of "adjustable buoyant air chambers," eliminated the necessity of removing cargo to lighten load and decrease draft.

In Chicago, arguing against the validity of a patent for an invention that he and his client believed was based on available commonsense technology and that inhibited the profits of businessmen by raising costs, he had occasion for advancing an underlying ideological preference. Just as he advocated a protective tariff, he favored the least possible restriction on domestic industry, especially small businesses: the possibility of advancement for the small mill owner and his hope for profit from his labor and investment should be encouraged. The defendant represented the interests of hundreds of small mill owners throughout the state. "This patent," the *Chicago Daily Democrat* reported, "has run since the year 1829, and thousands of dollars have been obtained from men, who had not the remotest idea, when building their mills of any infringement, but who paid damages rather than go into the expense and trouble of a suit at law." The United States Circuit Court, reversing a Springfield court decision, decided for Lincoln and the defendant. "The public will reap an advantage, and mill owners will not be subject to the prying visits of agents, nor to pay any more 'black mail' for a principle as old as the arts," the *Chicago Democrat* concluded. Neither Lincoln's brief nor an account of his examination and cross-examination exists except in a newspaper summary of the defendant's position that has the feel of a redacted, condensed précis of Lincoln's argument and his pithy, balanced style when speaking about practical matters.

He was, as the unusually lengthy trial began, unexpectedly provided with an opportunity to exercise his literary and oratorical skills on a larger scale and before a wider public. The Chicago Whigs invited him to give the primary eulogy for President Zachary Taylor, who had died in Washington on July 9, the same day on which the Court began hearing arguments in the patent-infringement case. Lincoln was apparently inclined to accept the invitation, though he did not know when the trial would end; there might be little time to prepare his eulogy before 4:00 P.M. on July 25, the time appointed for the address. Fortunately, the trial ended on July 24. Lincoln responded to the formal invitation, delivered two days earlier, that though "the want of time for preparation will make the task, for me, a very difficult one to perform, in any degree satisfactory to others or myself. . . . I do not feel at liberty to decline the invitation." He doubtless recognized that it was in his interest to take center stage on what would be a well-attended, widely reported Chicago occasion.

That he had only about a day and a half to create his text may have pushed him to burn the midnight oil, but his literary skills and his ability to balance narrative and moral exemplar resulted in the creation of one of his least-appreciated but most formally interesting literary achievements. Lincoln had worked hard on Taylor's behalf in 1848, and though he was careful to deflect his post-election disappointments away from the president by maintaining that Taylor had been above the fray and also probably had been misled, he faced the challenge of eulogizing a man he admired but who had not supported him in his time of need. And the situation had the additional limitation of the shortness of Taylor's service in the presidency. Lincoln easily met both challenges, the solution to the first inherent in the magnanimity of his personality, the second in his strategy of emphasizing Taylor's pre-presidential military career rather than his presidential accomplishments. A biographical narrative would allow Lincoln to exercise his talent for vivid evocation of place and action and at the same time indirectly counter the claim that as a Whig congressman he had failed to support the troops.

Since Taylor's military victories were the events without which his presidency would have been impossible, Lincoln determined that he could serve Taylor best by making his Mexican War triumphs one of the two structural centers of his eulogy. As idealized war narrative, the description is remarkable:

> Again the battle commenced, and raged till toward nightfall, when the Mexicans were entirely routed, and the General with his fatigued and bleeding, and reduced battalions marched into Fort Brown. There was a joyous meeting. A brief hour before, whether all *within* the fort had perished, all *without* feared, but none could tell—while the incessant roar of artillery, wrought those *within* to the highest pitch of apprehension, that their brethren *without* were being massacred to the last man. And now the din of battle nears the fort and sweeps obliquely by; a gleam of hope

flies through the half imprisoned few; they fly to the wall; every eye is strained—it is—it is—the stars and stripes are still aloft! Anon the anxious brethren meet; and while hand strikes hand, the heavens are rent with a loud, long, glorious, gushing cry of victory! victory!! victory!!!

The movement of point of view from those attempting to liberate the fort to those within the fort and then back to those outside, with balanced phrases and italicized emphases for clarity, creates a panoramic scenic and psychological tension. Not until "and now the din" does the prose becomes colored by patriotic purple, concluding with rhetorical flourishes and exclamation marks from the textbooks of patriotic oratory. Even the purple prose, though, is excellent of its kind.

Lincoln next neatly segues to the second center of his essay: the fundamentals of Taylor's character, the virtues that Lincoln desired to promote for both generals and presidents, the characteristics that enabled Taylor to triumph when defeat seemed likely if not inevitable. They are the same virtues that Lincoln believed would have made Taylor's presidency successful if it had not been so brief, though he leaves the details of Taylor's presidency unremarked on, except to the extent of a general comment about presidencies that anticipates his own later experience: "The Presidency, even to the most experienced politicians, is no bed of roses; and Gen. Taylor like others, found thorns within it. No human being can fill that station and escape censure," though he expects that history will judge Taylor "to have *deserved* as little as any who have succeeded him." Lincoln's prediction, more eulogistically generous than historically realistic, disregarded the likelihood that Taylor's presidency would be more forgotten than judged.

Yet, by what he chose to emphasize, Lincoln acknowledged that Taylor's value as a paradigm for leadership resided in his personal qualities rather than his presidential achievements, and in Taylor Lincoln found a mirror image of the characteristics he valued in himself. As a leader, especially as a military commander, Taylor triumphed by "a combination of negatives—absence of *excitement* and absence of *fear*. He could not be *flurried*, and he could not be *scared*." In all his activities, he "was alike averse to *sudden*, and to *startling* quarrels; and he pursued no man with *revenge*." His "*wisdom* and *patriotism*" earned the "confidence and devotion of the people," and his virtues were implemented in his public life by his assiduous devotion to his "*duty,*" a word that Lincoln proceeds to define. His definition is work-based and descriptive. It resonates with elements of his own future performance and fate: "He indulged in no recreations, he visited no public places, seeking applause; but quietly, as the earth in its orbit, he was always at his post. Along our whole Indian frontier, thro' summer and winter, in sunshine and storm, like a sleepless sentinel, *he* has *watched*, while *we* have *slept*, for forty long years. How well might the dying hero say at last, 'I have done my duty, I am ready to go.'"

The heroic Taylor's sudden death provided the synthesizing conclusion, changing the mood from celebration to melancholy. In the elegiac tradition that he knew so well, Lincoln elevated the individual death into universal significance. Taylor had provided a model of the triumph of service in the public interest, of ambition directed toward elevating national discourse by example. "But he is gone. The conqueror at last is conquered. The fruits of his labor, his name, his memory and example, are all that is left us." His character and achievements "give assurance" of his "country's gratitude," the reward of well-placed and constructive ambition, the inferential model for Lincoln of the plaudits that he hoped his own ambition would attain. Such honors make "a dying bed, soft as downy pillows are," he told his audience, slightly misquoting the last stanza of Isaac Watts's Hymn 31, familiar to Lincoln from his childhood reading and his parents' evangelical piety:

> *Jesus can make a dying bed*
> *Feel soft as downy pillows are,*
> *While on his breast I lean my head,*
> *And breathe my life out sweetly there.*

Lincoln characteristically substitutes a secular concept for the hymn's Christian consolation, retaining the poem's Christian resonance while eliminating its reference to Jesus. Taylor's death was "soft" because of his character and public service, not his religious belief or heavenly reward.

Mostly important, Lincoln tells his audience, Taylor's death usefully reminds us of the universality of death. As always, mutability, expressed in quotations from the textbooks of his childhood, like the verse from Dilworth's *New Guide to the English Tongue*, man's life "like an empty shadow glides away / And all his life is but a winter's day," or in Gray's "Elegy Written in a Country Church-Yard," or in the six relatively obscure stanzas of a poem Lincoln frequently quoted from memory, William Knox's "Mortality," had a tight grip on his personality and his melancholy moods. From this attraction to what he believed the ultimate reality, the end game and final story of a shared human destiny, he drew strength; and elegiac prose and poetry gave him the pleasure of constructing himself with a combination of beautiful language and philosophical realism.

> The death of the late President may not be without its use, in reminding us, that *we*, too, must die. Death, abstractly considered, is the same with the high as with the low; but practically, we are not so much aroused to the contemplation of our own mortal natures, by the fall of *many* undistinguished, as that of *one* great and well known, name. By the latter, we are forced to muse, and ponder, sadly.

The death of a president in office provides the ultimate national occasion for such meditation, and Lincoln, soon to become the third president to die in office and in circumstances that intensified the considerations that Taylor's death had prompted, was to provide the most powerful exemplar of his own analysis. His eulogy concludes with his reciting in full, from memory, Knox's poem:

> So the multitude goes, like the flower or the weed,
> That withers away to let others succeed;
> So the multitude comes, even those we behold,
> To repeat every tale that has often been told.

For we are the same, our fathers have been.
We see the same sights, our fathers have seen;
We drink the same streams and see the same sun
And run the same course our fathers have run.

They loved; but the story we cannot unfold;
They scorned, but the heart of the haughty is cold;
They grieved, but no wail from their slumbers will come,
They joyed, but the tongue of their gladness is dumb.

They died! Ay, they died; we things that are now;
That work on the turf that lies on their brow,
And make in their dwellings a transient abode,
Meeting the things that they met on their pilgrimage road.

Yea! hope and despondency, pleasure and pain,
Are mingled together in sun-shine and rain;
And the smile and the tear, and the song and the dirge,
Still follow each other, like surge upon surge.

'Tis the wink of an eye, 'tis the draught of a breath,
From the blossoms of health, to the paleness of death.
From the gilded saloon, to the bier and the shroud.
Oh, why should the spirit of mortal be proud!

It had to have been an impressive moment, the tall, homely, avid lover of poetry reciting an accessible poem that had the power in its simple direct-ness to touch the feelings of his audience. He had better poems than this one in his memory but "Mortality" was perfect for the occasion.

Though Lincoln had remarked on his "great devotion to Gen. Taylor per-sonally," the melancholy passion of the last section of his eulogy came from a man whose long-accustomed attraction to the language of loss had recently focused on a death far from the public stage but far closer to his heart. In December 1849, his second son, Edward Baker Lincoln, became ill with pulmonary tuberculosis. He died on the first of February 1850, a month less than four years old. "We miss him very much," Lincoln tersely wrote to his stepbrother, John Johnston. His poetic evocation of transience and death in his public eulogy in July took its personal resonance from the death of "Little Eddie," the title of a poem published anonymously in the *Illinois Journal* soon after the funeral, rather than from Taylor's. Lincoln is unlikely to have been the author, if only because the poem exhibits literary skill far inferior to his and its conventional Christian references are incompatible with his usual selectivity in using religious language. He would have embraced the poem's claim "that affection's wail cannot reach thee now," though to him the source of the disconnection was the finality of the grave rather than the separation between earth and heaven.

Early in January 1851, he received from his second cousin Harriet Hanks the news that his father was mortally ill. If the record is both accurate and complete, very few direct words had passed between father and son since Lincoln's departure in 1831 from his father's home, now in Farmington, near Charleston, about ninety-five miles from Springfield, though he possibly visited on two occasions in the 1840s. Thomas Lincoln's thirty-seven-year-old stepson, John Johnston, farmed the elderly Thomas's eighty acres. At the same time, he aggravated his stepfather's financial exigency by lackluster work habits and indebtedness in their intertwined business and domestic economies. In October 1841, Abraham had lent his father two hundred dollars, which was also a loan to Johnston, to secure which Thomas and Sarah legally transferred to Abraham ownership of forty acres that Thomas had bought from Johnston the previous year for fifty dollars. Lincoln gave his parents life tenancy, bonding himself to convey the land at their death to Johnston for the amount of the repayment of the debt. In May 1845, Lincoln made a thirty-five-dollar gift to his father, the money from a case he had transacted at the

County Court in Charleston, which he left at the courthouse for Thomas to pick up at a later date, perhaps only a monetary connection rather than a meeting. Johnston expressed disappointment at Lincoln's unwillingness to be more generous.

In December 1848, Lincoln responded by letter to a new request for financial help from his father and stepbrother, particularly his father's request for twenty dollars "to save [his] land from sale." "It is singular," Abraham wrote, "that you should have forgotten a judgment against you; and it is more singular that the plaintiff should have let you forget it so long. . . . I very cheerfully send you the twenty dollars. . . . Give my love to Mother, and all the connections"; he signed off with the endearment with which he ended his family letters, "Affectionately." To Johnston's request for eighty dollars, Lincoln responded with stern advice, the self-made man lecturing the wastrel.

> This habit of uselessly wasting time, is the whole difficulty; and it is vastly important to you, and still more so to your children, that you should break this habit. . . . You are now in need of some ready money; and what I propose is, that you shall go to work, "tooth and nails" for some body who will give you money [for] it. . . . And to secure you a fair reward for your labor, I now promise you, that for every dollar you will, between this and the first of next May, get for your own labor, either in money, or your own indebtedness, I will then give you one other dollar [in effect doubling your wages]. . . . Now if you will do this, you will soon be out of debt, and what is better, you will have a habit that will keep you from getting in debt again.

Lincoln chose to ignore the likelihood that Johnston, the improvident father of eight children, was incapable of such a transformation of character.

His affection for his stepmother was instrumental in motivating, in May 1849, Lincoln's one documented visit to his father's home. It's questionable that he would have made that visit if his attendance at various county courts had not brought him close enough to make it convenient to spend three days with his parents, his Hank family relatives, and his stepmother's son. During his visit, the ex-congressman entertained them with tales of exotic Washington and New England, though it's unlikely that he would have told them about his patronage disappointments, particularly his hope for the land office commissionership, much on his mind at the time. It had to have been noted by Thomas Lincoln that none of Abraham's children had been given one of the traditional Lincoln family names. His son's resentment of the limitations his father had attempted to impose on his education and vocation, his alienation from Thomas's backwoods values, and his need to replace an unsatisfactory father with better paternal models, provide the best but still inconclusive explanation for a man otherwise committed to duty distancing himself from an elderly, harmless parent.

Even his seventy-five-year-old father's impending death in January 1851 did not stir Lincoln beyond his judgmental alienation. In his response to his stepbrother's puzzlement, conveyed by Harriet, that he had not responded to the bad news, Lincoln wrote directly to Johnston, in formulaic terms, the coldest elegy he was ever to write, explaining that he had not answered his letters "not because I have forgotten them, or been uninterested about them—but because it appeared to me I could write nothing which would do any good."

> I sincerely hope Father may yet recover his health; but at all events tell him to remember to call upon, and confide in, our great, and good, and merciful Maker; who will not turn away from him in any extremity. He notes the fall of a sparrow, and numbers the hairs of our heads; and He will not forget the dying man, who puts his trust in Him. Say to him that if we could meet now, it is doubtful whether it would not be more painful than pleasant; but that if it be his lot to go now, he will soon have a joyous [meeting] with many loved ones gone before; and where [the rest] of us, through the help of God, hope ere-long [to join] them.

Whether or not the son expected that such conventional sentiments would be comforting to his pious father, even that possibility of generosity is cramped by the cold impersonality of "I sincerely hope," considering it is his father's life in question. The message counsels the dying man to put his trust in the belief system that he has always trusted in. But the substance of that system's claims had been so thoroughly rejected by the son that the invocation of a loving God who engages with all the affairs of the world, who cares for every human being, and has provided an afterlife in which people are united with lost loved ones has the feel, at best, of a pious fraud. At worst, it seems blatantly hypocritical. And the underlying meaning of "say to him that if we could meet now, it is doubtful whether it would not be more painful than pleasant"—which doesn't attempt to clarify whose pain this would be, that of the son or the father or both—is that this would not be a deathbed meeting at which the son would forgive the father for those things the son held against him. It is a rare performance for Lincoln: a manipulative use of language and signs of an unforgiving heart.

Almost two years later, in July 1852, the death of the seventy-five-year-old Henry Clay provided Lincoln the opportunity to write a eulogy of a man he more fully thought of as his progenitor, the contemporary patriarchal figure in a political lineage that began with Washington. The distance he had removed himself from his biological father inversely reflected the closeness he felt between himself and his political forebears. A eulogy of Clay, though, inevitably required at its heart an assessment of Clay's importance in relation to the issues that dominated his public life, and the speaker could not avoid expressing, directly or indirectly, his own views on the two inescapable topics, nationalism and slavery. That Clay's life had been devoted to the attempt of the second generation of Americans to validate the promise of the Revolution and that his death had occurred so close to July 4, required some of the aura if not the fact of an Independence Day oration. Chronological accident made that task easy, for "The infant nation, and the infant child began the race of life together. . . . They have been companions ever." The challenge, though, of combining an account of Clay's achievements with the controversial topics of nationalism and slavery put Lincoln's literary skills to a test that he did not completely meet. His genius with language is more evident in occasional passages than in the speech as a whole. He had little time in which to compose it, though that was also the case with other more structurally cohesive examples of his writings. The fault line was the difficulty of combining a eulogy with an effective discussion of the two key issues; and the absence of an emotional focus for genuine grief, or perhaps the sacrifice of that focus to political ideas, resulted in a disjointed, impersonal presentation.

Lincoln had it in mind to emphasize Clay's role as a unifying national figure. There may have been little exaggeration in the *Illinois Weekly Journal*'s comment that "during the proceedings business was suspended, stores closed, and everything announced the general sorrow at the great national bereavement." Reverence for Clay took on a nonpartisan idealization to which Lincoln's contribution perfectly matched his lifelong hero worship. Clay's apotheosis as the "great compromiser," eliciting sacrifices and reconciling opponents in order to preserve the Union, matched the role with which Lincoln felt most comfortable. In that spirit, and apparently with the notion of letting the opposition do some of his work for him, he incorporated into his eulogy a long quotation, about 15 percent of the entire composition, from a populist Democratic pro-Union newspaper, which lauded Clay's non-sectional nationalism and his attempt to keep intact the "sacred circle" of the Union. Much of the quotation's rhetoric is cliché and sentimental. But by pleasing or at least neutralizing the Democrats in his audience, the quotation allowed Lincoln to introduce his major theme: Clay as an advocate of liberty at home and abroad and as an enlightened nationalist, advocating a practical solution to the problem of slavery in his leadership of the American Colonization Society.

In gracefully direct prose, characterized by logical force and rhythmic precision, he efficiently summarized Clay's career, reflecting, in his comments on Clay's lack of formal education, his own early years: "Mr. Clay's lack of a more perfect early education, however it may be regretted gen-

erally, teaches at least one profitable lesson; it teaches that in this country, one can scarcely be so poor, but that, if he *will*, he *can* acquire sufficient education to get through the world respectably." Clay, like himself,
Lincoln knew, had an excessively powerful *will* that resulted in *can*. But
the lesson is not an affirmation of Romantic individualism but of democratic opportunity in a society in which education promotes upward mobility, at a minimum getting "through the world respectably." Lincoln's
complaint about his father was that he had barely gotten through, and
about Johnston, that he was not doing so at all. Clay's career provided
a shining epitome of such ascension and embodied the Whig version of
American values. Consequently, "there has never been a moment since
1824 till after 1848 when a very large portion of the American public did
not cling to him with an enthusiastic hope and purpose of still elevating
him to the Presidency." Wisely, Lincoln did not try to explain why Clay
and his supporters had failed in this purpose, perhaps because it seemed
inappropriate to a eulogy but almost certainly because he had no convincing explanation. And if Clay had not been successful, how could any
Whig leader of talent, who was not a general like Harrison and Taylor,
ever expect to be? "With other men, to be defeated, was to be forgotten; but to him, defeat was but a trifling incident, neither changing him,
or the world's estimate of him." It is doubtful that Lincoln believed this
about Clay or anyone else.

Instead of asking why Clay failed, Lincoln, reversing the unexplored
subtextual question, asked: How is it that he kept the loyalty of so many
for so long? Indeed, "the spell—the long enduring spell—with which
the souls of men," including his own, "were bound to him, is a miracle."
It is a miracle, he argued, that defies definitive explanation. Carefully
and thoughtfully, Lincoln now treads on the ground on which he himself currently stands as eulogist: the ground from which, Antaeus-like,
he continued to draw strength—his own dependence on and embrace
of language as the force that makes and moves people and nations. Clay
"was surpassingly eloquent; but many eloquent men fail utterly. . . . His
judgment was excellent; but many men of good judgment, live and die

unnoticed. His will was indomitable; but this quality often secures to its owner nothing better than a character for useless obstinacy. These then were Mr. Clay's leading qualities. No one of them is very common; but all taken together are rarely combined in a single individual; and this is probably the reason why such men as Henry Clay are so rare in the world."

It is Clay's "eloquence," though, rather than his judgment and will-power, to which Lincoln devotes his analysis. Two of its features, he tells his audience, need to be emphasized as keys to Clay's oratorical genius: the impassioned sincerity of his tone and manner, and his dramatic power to evoke vivid scenes and stir the emotions. "Mr. Clay's eloquence did not consist, as many fine specimens of eloquence [do], of types and figures— of antithesis, and elegant arrangements of words and sentences; but rather of that deeply earnest and impassioned tone, and manner, which can proceed only from great sincerity and a thorough conviction . . . of the justice and importance of his cause. This it is, that truly touches the chords of human sympathy. . . . All his efforts were made for practical effect. He never spoke merely to be heard." Clay imposed a tone and manner on his language, and he spoke entirely of practical issues and outcomes, never to philosophical presuppositions, Lincoln implies. His genius was in his personality, not his intellect, and Lincoln, the craftsman of words and sentences, of balance and antithesis, demonstrates one of the distinctions between Clay and himself in the very language of his eulogy.

Measuring himself against Clay, Lincoln is aware that he, too, avoided "fine specimens," pursuing sincerity through the agency of conviction. In contrast, though, he has the writer's mission to craft his language; Clay had the actor's to move his audience. Clay had been an inspired, vatic, spontaneous orator; Lincoln carefully calibrated his text and read from his manuscript. With "that noble inspiration, which came to him as it came to no other," Clay "aroused and nerved, and inspired his friends, and confounded and bore-down all opposition." His speeches were emotionally powerful and topically local, his words intended to be heard, not read. To stress that point, Lincoln concluded his praise with a cliché of oratorical history, the extemporaneous speech lost to posterity when local scribes are too struck by its brilliance to move their pens. "During its delivery reporters forgot their vocations," Lincoln remarked of Clay's legendary lost speech, "dropped their pens, and sat enchanted from near the beginning to quite the close. The speech now lives only in the memory of a few old men; and the enthusiasm with which they cherish their recollection of it is absolutely astonishing." Though its "precise language" is lost, "we do know" that it pled the cause of its subject "with deep pathos," that "it invoked the genius of the revolution," that it apostrophized Washington and others, that it "appealed to the interest, the pride, the honor and the glory of the nation—that it shamed and taunted the timidity of friends—that it bearded and defied the British Lion—and rising, and swelling, and maddening in its course, it sounded the onset, [un]till the charge, the shock, the steady struggle, and the glorious victory, all passed in vivid review before the entranced hearers."

The eulogy to Clay represents Lincoln's homage to Clay's style of oratory and to his brilliance; the language of the eulogy and its analysis of Clay's style represent by inference the distinction between Clay and Lincoln as masters of language. Clay's hortatory emotionalism required a use of language that Lincoln had from the start felt unsuited to himself and his ideas. Leaving behind his own grandiloquent tendencies, such as his apostrophes to Washington in his Lyceum and Temperance addresses and his evocation of the attack on Fort Brown, Lincoln praised in Clay what he no longer valued for himself. The parting of ways, though, was never complete, for Lincoln's admiration for Clay's oratorical achievements had as its binding connective tissue Lincoln's having early on committed himself to Clay's ideological agenda. Clay's advocacy of compromise on all political matters as the only strategy compatible with a democratic polity and a republican government provided Lincoln the model for his own approach. At moments of national peril, Clay's language was in the service of results, not effects. "Brightly, and captivating as it had previously shown [before the Missouri Compromise in 1820], it was now perceived that his great eloquence, was a mere embellishment, or, at most, but a helping hand to his inventive genius."

The key issue that pushed Clay and his contemporaries twice into crises that threatened national survival was the extension of slavery. More than half Lincoln's eulogy summarizes the threat to national unity created by slavery and the impermanence of any solution that perpetuated it. In a paragraph-long quotation about the danger of dividing "the country by geographical lines," as did the Missouri Compromise, Lincoln let Jefferson's analysis of the situation express his own. The loss of slave property, Jefferson had written, he could well accept as a minor matter, "if, in that way, a general emancipation, and *expatriation* could be effected; and gradually, and with due sacrifices I think it might be. But as it is, we have the wolf by the ears and we can neither hold him, nor safely let him go. Justice is in one scale, and self-preservation in the other." Could, in the short run, the Union adjudicate the distribution of power between slave and free states and could, in the long run, a nation committed to human freedom free itself of the burden of slavery as a legally protected institution? Both Clay and Lincoln hoped that the Compromise of 1850 would give the nation enough time to eliminate slavery gradually. Would the concept of the Union as a sacred entity temper the divisive passions that threatened its existence? It had done so twice already. And Clay's most significant acts of political leadership had been devoted, Lincoln reminded his Springfield audience, to sustaining national unity by compromise and to advancing the most practical resolution, the creation of a state in Africa for the newly freed slaves.

But the wolf, in Clay's and Lincoln's view, needed to be humanely handled, not kept in captivity or killed. And the expulsion could be viewed as liberation, a gathering of the dispersed tribes back to the land of their origin. Since they were legal property, their owners should be compensated. Once free men, the former slaves would govern themselves in the land of their ancestors. Clay "was, on principle and in feeling, opposed to slavery" and in "favor of gradual emancipation. . . . He did not perceive, that on a question of human right, the negroes were to be excepted from the human race. And yet Mr. Clay," like Jefferson, "was the owner of slaves. Cast into life where slavery was already widely spread and deeply seated, he did not perceive, as I think no wise man has perceived, how it could be at *once* eradicated, without producing a greater evil, even to the cause of human liberty itself." The greater evil would be four million uneducated ex-slaves whose existence would be a heavy burden to the nation and the source of social discord.

Like Clay, Lincoln did not believe that the interests of emancipated blacks and white Americans could be reconciled, and he saw no reason why the difficult but better solution was not separation. He had no cause, he felt, to believe that emancipated slaves and white Americans could live together harmoniously. Whereas he readily embraced America as the melting pot in which European immigrants were reshaped into American citizens, he concluded that the chasm between blacks and whites was too great to make that realistically plausible. Race prejudice and historical wounds would make black-white relations distressing. Harmonious integration was unimaginable. That was not to deny the humanness of the enslaved. It was not to deny their equal right to personal autonomy and communal liberty. It was, in the context, a widely held vision of significant difference between the races and a pragmatic approach to resolving an otherwise intractable problem. If emancipation could come only as the by-product of a civil war, and Clay and Lincoln could have foreseen the situation in those terms, they would have thought that horror a confirmation of the wisdom of their reliance on gradual emancipation and colonization. For Clay "there is a moral fitness in the idea of returning to Africa her children, whose ancestors have been torn from her by the ruthless hand of fraud and violence . . . to transform an original crime, into a signal blessing to that most unfortunate portion of the globe . . . May it indeed be realized!" Lincoln exclaimed, approaching the conclusion of his eulogy. That would be "a glorious consummation."

Neither man thought of black slaves as Americans, with a stake in and a right to possess the country. Slaves were due liberty, not citizenship; and, even if an argument could be made on the basis of the free black population that there were exceptions to that view, the impracticality of expanding that population to include almost four million additional blacks seemed insurmountable. Establishing a state for ex-slaves in the land of their ancestors was the best available solution. For "Pharaoh's country was cursed with plagues, and his hosts were drowned in the Red Sea for striving to retain a captive people who had already served them more than four hundred years. May like disasters never befall us!" And just as "Divine Providence" provided us with Henry Clay, let us "strive to deserve . . . in future national emergencies" that Providence will provide new "instruments of safety and security."

Characteristically, Lincoln draws on the Bible as the text of reference most widely shared by nineteenth-century Americans, and his "Divine Providence" is his deistic preference to any specifically sectarian God. The basis for success was works, not faith. And if the ways of Divine Providence are inscrutable, a theme Lincoln was to emphasize in the last memorable speech of his life, it was also unclear to the nation and to Lincoln who the new instrument of "safety and security" might be. He did not believe it would be Stephen Douglas. The whole force of Lincoln's eulogy affirmed the speaker's identification with Clay and exclaims a confidence in the futurity of Clay's ideas that encourages, in the retrospect of history, those with keen ears to hear in Lincoln's words his hope to be Clay's successor.

Within a single year Lincoln had lost a son and a father. Within two years he had lost a political model and also a rare political phenomenon, a president of his own party. This was less, though, a test of his capacity for mourning than it was a demonstration of his resilience. The president the Whigs had lost did not seem to Lincoln likely to be the last they would elect, though indeed it was. Lincoln had some sense of himself waiting in the wings as a replacement for Clay, and the ideological and pragmatic vision that Clay embodied as a statesman lived on in Whig mythology and in Lincoln's values, though his only hope for political advancement inhered in the next Whig nomination for a senatorial seat, for which there would be numbers of competitors. The death of his son, of course, hurt him most, and also intensified the alternating depressions and irritability to which his wife was prone.

Six weeks after Eddie's death, the couple conceived again, a son to be born in December 1850, a compensatory replacement for Eddie that marked for Lincoln the necessary affirmation of life's patterns. The pain of Eddie's death intensified Mary's emotional fragility and anxiety-ridden foreboding. Robert Todd died in 1851, and Mary considered the deaths of her father and her son twin disasters aimed particularly at her. Her husband had his work to immerse himself in. Necessity and preference kept him away from home on the court circuit. His ambition also kept him alert, and he had been developing a keen sense of what offers to turn down. Mary had no alternative to domesticity, which kept her even closer to painful memories, frustrated hopes, and the difficulty of maintaining an orderly house, at which she was only partly successful. She needed domestic help, but was peremptory, explosive, and cheap. She spent money on frills, mostly to feel good about herself, a mood advanced by dressing fashionably. She both doted on and was harshly punitive with her eldest son, and her temperament had her both dependent on and uncontrollably angry at her husband. Some of his habits got on her nerves: his lack of formal manners, his disregard for personal appearance, his long silences, his absorption in reading, his stoic imperturbability, his long working hours, his absences from home. She fell into the role of the shrew. He became a practitioner of patience, forbearance, and withdrawal.

Marital equilibrium was a daily challenge. Lincoln played the long-suffering Victorian husband-father figure to a spoiled child-wife who threw temper tantrums and thought herself better than others. Friends and neighbors told ugly stories. Mary gained a reputation as a difficult wife. "I think he would have been very fond of a wife had he one to suit," a friend later remarked. But he was no doubt fond of her, indeed loved her, and each had strengths and weaknesses that enabled the other. They rarely entertained, and Lincoln seemed reluctant to bring friends home.

It could not be predicted whether at any one time Mary would be explosively angry or wittily charming. She took sharp dislike to some of her husband's associates, particularly his junior partner, William Herndon. A paranoid streak made her imagine detractors and enemies, which enlarged the number of people who felt hostile to her. Her inability to manage servants was a constant problem. She wheedled and threatened them into lower-than-market wages, and regularly fired them or found they had quit. Lincoln sometimes negotiated a cook or a housemaid's hiring or retention by offering additional wages to be paid without Mary's knowledge. The taciturn, privacy-loving Lincoln was forced into the role of providing bribes.

Mary's temper sometimes became violent, particularly with servants and children. A housemaid, Margaret Ryan, recalled that she "often struck other girls." Mary was quick to punish her children corporeally, especially her oldest son. "Ms L would whip Bob a good deal. She was half crazy." She regularly lashed out at her boys with hand or whip. She also "flailed out physically at her husband." Once, both of them half-dressed, she chased him out of the house with a broom. Margaret brought him his clothes. Lincoln devised stratagems to avoid incidents. "When he returned in evening would come in through kitchen and find out from M. if ML was all right before going in front of house—At another time saw Mrs L strike L. on head with piece of wood while reading paper . . . cut his nose—lawyers saw his face in Court next day but asked no questions." A neighbor heard screams from the Lincoln house—"'Murder'. 'Murder'—turned round—Saw Mrs Lincoln up on the fence—hands up—Screaming—went to her—she said a big ferocious man had Entered her house—Saw an umbrella man come out—I suppose he had Entered to ask for old umbrellas to mend. He Came out and Said—'Should be sorry to have such a wife. . . .'" The same neighbor, observing Lincoln arrive home very late on a cold night, heard an axe and saw him in the yard chopping wood, "I suppose to cook his supper." Cutting wood after midnight seemed characteristic of his role in the marriage. He did what had to be done and let Mary be Mary. At the death of her father and son, he empathized with her inconsolable misery, her ceaseless crying and absence of appetite. Though her presence was often troublesome, when they were apart he missed her, and his commitment to their life together was irrevocable.

Living in a tense household, he was often happier at work, both a necessity and a pleasure. The overlap between legal and political activities made it efficient for him to attend to them both, often at the same time. In Springfield and traveling on the judicial circuit, he was still a public man, though he held no political office, widely known and immediately recognized for both activities. He won and lost his fair share of cases. His physical presence, gawky, irregular in dress and accessories, without any touch either of fashion or of self-consciousness, marked him as a familiar, comfortable sight, made even taller outdoors by his stovepipe hat. In small groups, his homely face, high-pitched voice, and pithy stories made him the quintessentially accessible man. His idiomatic sincerity before juries and audiences made him trustworthy. He had the comfortable fit of an old shoe to colleagues. It was a shoe that fit no one else.

Fellow lawyers remarked on how committed Lincoln was to the circuit court experience. By all reports he enjoyed the fellowship established between the circuit regulars with whom he dined and sometimes shared a bed in crowded inns. If he had reason or inclination to limit the traveling life, he could have sent Herndon to work some of the cases, but he never did. His much-exercised horse and buggy needed frequent maintenance and repair. Perhaps it helped his political career to be seen regularly in towns throughout central Illinois, and he apparently never complained that these travels kept him away from home. The schedule was often grueling, the caseload heavy, the demands on his energy formidable. In early spring 1853, for example, he and Herndon litigated about sixty cases in Springfield, including a murder case. Less than a week after the birth of his fourth son, in early 1853, he began a tour of county courts that kept him moving throughout central Illinois for two months. He returned to Springfield for the summer term of the United States circuit and district courts. In early September he left for another two months of circuit court appearances. If he missed his wife and sons, the advantages of circuit life for four months of the year outweighed the losses. Late at night, sitting by the fireplace in an inn or hotel, he was often observed reading Shakespeare, Byron, Burns, or the Bible, or meditating, lost in reflection, so it seemed to his lawyer-friends.

His Whig colleagues relied on his oratorical skills. On August 14 and 26, 1852, he spoke at length in Springfield in support of Gen. Winfield Scott, the Whig candidate for the presidency. He repeated the speech the next month in Peoria, mainly rebutting, point by point, Stephen Douglas's charges. The senator's condemnation of Whig political strategies as dishonorable seemed to Lincoln hypocritical, especially Douglas's accusation that Scott used language duplicitously in his attempt to court both Northern and Southern votes. Turning the tables, Lincoln dissected, with satiric bite, Douglas's language, sarcastically referring to him by the title he had attained after spearheading the self-interested expansion of the Illinois Supreme Court. "What wonderful acumen the Judge displays on the construction of language!!!" In his critical analysis of Scott's statements, Douglas, Lincoln pointed out, had used "the word 'with' as if equivalent to 'not withstanding' . . . 'although I defy,' and 'although I spit upon.' Verily these are wonderful substitutes for the word 'with.'"

When the builders of the tower of Babel got into difficulty about language, if they had just called on Judge Douglas, he would, at once, have construed away the difficulty, and enabled them to finish the structure, upon the truly democratic platform on which they were building. Suppose, gentlemen, you were to amuse yourselves some leisure hour, by selecting sentences, from well known compositions, each containing the word "with" and by striking it out, and inserting alternately, the Judge's substitutes, and then testing whether the sense is changed. As an example, take a sentence from an old and well known book, not much suspected for duplicity, or equivocal language; which sentence is as follows: "And Enoch walked *with* God; and he was not, for God took him." Try for yourselves, how Judge Douglas' substitutes for the word "with" affect this sentence.

Whether Lincoln spoke from notes, as he did with stump speeches, or a prepared text, as he did with formal addresses, the conciseness of his argument and its literary allusions suggest careful preparation. His honesty in "the construction of language" was intended to contrast with Douglas's duplicity. Lincoln highlighted his own skill and Douglas's banality when he quoted Oliver Goldsmith's "An Elegy on the Death of a Mad Dog," explaining why Scott had no reason to regret Douglas's attack: "The man recovered of the bite, / The dog it was that died," an ironic reversal that he would also have reason to apply to Douglas's attacks on him in the 1858 senatorial campaign. The base constructions of language that the Democrats are limited to are exemplified, Lincoln observed, by a "democratic battle hymn," an examination of which revealed that while Democrats glorified the working man, their opposition to internal improvements made the life of the working man more difficult than it need be. It was a witty though overly broad accusation, considering that Douglas supported a transcontinental railroad.

Lincoln's penchant for humor both lightened and intensified his partisan jousting. Defending Scott, he created an extended comic riff on amateur military ludicrousness, grounding it for his audience in the reality of their shared Springfield experiences. The Democrats, in exaggerating Franklin Pierce's military record, were attempting, Lincoln extrapolated half-seriously, to render all military experience ludicrous. It is a tactic "to ridicule and burlesque the whole military character out of credit; and thus to kill Gen. Scott with vexation." Lincoln countered with an inventive literary burlesque of his own, exemplifying his delight in using language for comic and serious purposes simultaneously:

> Being philosophical and literary men, they have read, and remembered, how the institution of chivalry was ridiculed out of existence by its fictitious votary Don Quixote. They also remember how our own "militia trainings" have been "laughed to death" by fantastic parades and caricatures upon them. We remember one of these parades ourselves here, at the head of which, on horse-back, figured our old friend Gordon Abrams,

with a pine wood sword, about nine feet long, and a paste-board cocked hat, from front to rear about the length of an ox yoke. . . . Now, in the language of Judge Douglas, "I submit to you gentlemen," whether there is not great cause to fear that on some occasion when Gen. Scott suspects no danger, suddenly Gen. Pierce will be discovered charging upon him, holding a huge role of candy in one hand for a spy-glass; with B U T labeled on some appropriate part of his person; with Abrams' long pine sword cutting in the air at imaginary cannon balls, and calling out "boys there's a game of ball for you," and over all streaming the flag, with the motto, "We'll fight till we faint, and I'll treat when it's over."

With an election at stake, Lincoln hammered away at Douglas and Pierce with his usual combination of satiric wit, literary allusion, practical politics, and issues of principle, the speech a rallying of the faithful. In regard to principle, Douglas had criticized the response of Millard Fillmore, Taylor's vice-president and successor, to the execution by the Spanish of a group of Americans who had invaded Cuba in 1851, intending to overthrow Spanish rule and prepare for American annexation, a mission tacitly supported by the Democrats. "They were fighting against one of the worst governments in the world," Lincoln unhesitatingly admitted. "But their fault was, that the real people of Cuba had not asked for their assistance; were neither desirous of, nor fit for civil liberty." And if "Judge Douglas thought it cause for war," his was the responsibility to bring "a proposition before the Senate to declare war. I suppose he knows that under the Constitution, Congress, and not the president, declares war."

In response to Douglas's criticism of Senator William Seward's argument that slavery be excluded from California by virtue of a "higher law," Lincoln granted that if, indeed, this is what Seward had said, then "in so far as it may attempt to foment a disobedience to the constitution, or to the constitutional laws of the country, it has my unqualified condemnation." An extra-constitutional appeal to "a higher law" or "natural law" seemed to him dangerous: different interest groups held conflicting tenets of "higher law"; and the law of the land was the Constitution, not "higher law." National survival, let alone prosperity, depended on adherence to the Constitution.

In regard to practical politics and Whig electoral strategy, Lincoln reminded his audience that Douglas's criticism of Seward's speech was not the real grounds of Douglas's hatred of Seward; that derived from the electoral realities of the presidential race in New York. In order to win the election, the Democratic candidate, Franklin Pierce, needed to win New York's electoral votes. For that he needed the votes of most of the New York Democrats, who in 1848 had strayed to the third-party candidate, Martin Van Buren, the Free Soil Party nominee. Many of those might now be influenced by Seward to support the Whig candidate, Gen. Winfield Scott. The more radical on the slavery issue Seward could be made to appear, the better for Franklin Pierce and the Democrats. In Lincoln's analysis, if Scott took but a small number of Free Soil votes, he would win New York and the presidency. The Democrats had, Lincoln believed, nominated Pierce because he had taken a stand agreeable to the Free Soil Party and against the Fugitive Slave Law but at the same time Pierce would not contradict reports in the South that he favored the law. He would hold the Democratic vote in New York by distancing himself from the unpopular requirement that slaves who had fled to the North be returned to their masters and at the same time hold Southern Democratic votes by allowing his Southern supporters to affirm his support of the law.

With the unselfconscious explicitness with which he and his contemporaries used race imagery, Lincoln concluded his attack on Pierce: "Why Pierce's only chance for presidency, is to be born into it, as a cross between New York old hunkerism, and free soilism, the latter predominating in the offspring. Marryat, in some one of his books, describes the sailors, weighing anchor, and singing:

Sally is a bright Mullatter,
Oh Sally Brown——

Pretty gal, but can't get at her,
  Oh, Sally Brown.

Now, should Pierce ever be President, he will, politically speaking, not only be a mulatto; but he will be a good deal darker one than Sally Brown."

The possibility that Lincoln had read the English writer Frederick Marryat's *Diary in America* rather than only heard and memorized the refrain of the sailors preparing to depart from the London docks suggests that he had earned the use of a quotation that in its full extent affirms that Sally is beautiful, smart, and desirable. In Marryat's version, she is proposed to and courted for "seven years" by a white admirer. In the end, though, she loves someone of her own race and "won't wed a Yankee sailor." Eros, not racism, drives the dynamic of the lyric. Still, the language of race and its political usefulness was just as much Lincoln's as his contemporaries.

Though politics compelled his interest more than the practice of law, he practiced assiduously between 1852 and 1856; and between 1852 and 1860 he tried numbers of cases and earned fees for legal work and lobbying that provided an income greater than he had ever had and a net worth, from savings and interest, that made him for the first time financially comfortable. As suited his temperament, he lived a debtless life, with sufficient money available for the things he considered important, including a day servant and a cook. The major strain of the household arose from his wife's erratic temperament, not her spending habits. Without the inclination or ambition to become rich, he avoided investments, whether in land or markets, except for a Springfield real estate purchase in October 1852 and two land acquisitions that cost him nothing, the reward for his service in the Black Hawk War. These came from a grateful nation, 40 acres to be selected from available government land in Iowa under the congressional act of September 28, 1850, and another

120 acres under the act of March 3, 1855. He selected 40 acres in Tama County and 120 in Crawford County, both recommended by a highly placed lawyer for the Illinois Central who was also investing there. Probably he had information that led him to believe the land would increase in value because of railroad projects.

Between the start of his legal career and the early 1850s, Lincoln accrued income from volume rather than high fees, though his fees matched those charged by other lawyers, codified in 1852 in a well-publicized schedule adopted by the Chicago bar. Competition between the plethora of lawyers in central Illinois kept fees modest, and there were instances in which he sacrificed part of what he might have charged because he insisted that his fees reflect the number of hours he had worked. He lost as many cases as he won, and the claim that he worked more effectively for clients whose cases he believed in may have some truth to it, though indeed, even if unconsciously, he may also have calibrated his energy and modulated his enthusiasm relating to whether he thought a case winnable. He was not, as a lawyer, any more honest, self-sacrificing, or idealistic than most of his contemporaries. But his talent for logical analysis, his folksy language, and his anecdotal persuasiveness, compensating for flaws in his legal knowledge and combined with his political activities, made him well known in the legal profession throughout the state.

It also made him the lawyer of choice, beginning in the early 1850s, of some of the newly formed corporations, particularly railroads, that wanted an attorney with strong analytical powers and who also had the common touch. Such a lawyer could put an attractive human face on corporate anonymity and power. He also had political presence, a reputation for fairness, and influence with the legislature, which in December 1852 appointed him one of two commissioners to take testimony in Chicago in an investigation of the Illinois and Michigan Canal company. For corporate services he could expect higher fees than from individuals; the fees could be calculated in relation to what amounts of money, especially if he won the case, were at issue for the corporation. He embraced the opportunity to represent the railroad companies that were in the process of transforming the infrastructure of the state. He had no bias against railroads. In fact, he was deeply sympathetic to that industry. Its combination of invention, initiative, and capitalism had all the features of the Whig vision of what would make America prosperous. It would especially benefit the western states. For the ex-legislator who had helped bring his state to the verge of bankruptcy by government-sponsored transportation projects, this new combination of land grants, private capital, and engineering brains seemed a vindication of his support of Clay's "American System."

In February 1849, a month before the end of his congressional term, he had responded on the House floor to objections to a bill favored by his Western constituency that granted portions of U.S. government land "in aid of the several States in the construction of railroads and canals" but did not require that they be built. With a characteristic appeal to human nature and human experience, he asked, "What motive would tempt any State Legislature, or individual, or company of individuals, of the new States to expend money in surveying roads which they might know they could not make?" It was understandable that a state like Ohio that had at one time favored "granting lands to the new States" and "had now grown to be a giant" should fear "that the public lands were in danger of being wrested from the General Government by the strength of the delegation in Congress from the new States. But that apprehension . . . was utterly futile. There never could be such a thing. If we take these lands . . . it will not be without your consent. We can never outnumber you."

The passage of the bill helped transform the infrastructure of the nation, especially of the western states, and hence much else, through easements, land leases, and sale of government property. It gave railroads the opportunity to change the topography and demography of the country. Lincoln contributed to creating these corporate economic powerhouses, one of which, the Illinois Central, became his most remunerative employer. Railroads united the nation, were engines of progress for American nationalism; they carried Western goods to the east and brought amenities westward, supplementing and supplanting north-south commerce, opening new territories to settlement; they made a small number of owners and investors multimillionaires; they created new towns and industries, turning a few cities, such as Chicago, into giant metropolises; and they enabled Henry Clay's Whig vision to become the paradigm for a changing America that Lincoln welcomed.

As a lawyer and politician, he worked for various railroad interests, mostly representing the defendant in litigation for damages. In 1851, he lobbied the legislature for the incorporation of the Illinois Central Railroad. By 1854, he was one of its core lawyers, to whom it semi-guaranteed regular employment. His largest fee ever, five thousand dollars, came from the Illinois Central for saving it hundreds of thousands of dollars by his successful defense against McLean County's claim that the railroad owed county taxes on its assets even during the grace period granted by the legislature on the railroad's state obligations, "the largest law question that can now be got up in the state." If the railroad had lost, it would have been obliged to pay all taxes accruing during the grace period to every county in Illinois. When railroad executives in Chicago needed cover against raised eyebrows in the New York office because of Lincoln's unusually high legal fee, they signaled him that they would not seriously oppose a suit against them for collection. The court decided for Lincoln.

Between 1849 and 1854 there was no sharp distinction between Lincoln's legal and his political career. His law practice had always been compatible with his political life and the later claim that he had been only a country lawyer before he became president misrepresents the nature of his practice, his long-time association with the sophisticated Springfield bar, and the close relationship between the Illinois legal and political communities. If Lincoln was in any way noticeably different from his colleagues, it was that he added very little of the investor-businessman to the mix. To the extent that there was any "country" in Lincoln's lawyering, it was in his strategic colloquial tone and his predilection for traveling the circuit, which made him such a familiar presence in legal and political forums. His style as a lawyer reflected his deeply embedded preference for the language of egalitarian sincerity. That preference provided the voice for his logically analytical mind and the tone for his tightly balanced, sometimes poetic language.

That he made few political speeches between 1849 and 1854 had little to do with any disinclination to engage in public political discourse. He had not hesitated to speak at length for Scott and the Whigs in the 1852 campaign. If he was discouraged with politics, the election in 1852 of the statewide and national Democratic tickets made that inevitable. Everywhere the Whigs were in disarray. There was neither an issue nor a leader for them to rally around. In Illinois, Lincoln's party had little reason to think it would ever again elect either a governor or a senator.

Unhappy at the narrowing of opportunities and the likelihood that his desire to attain national distinction might never be realized, Lincoln soon had the chance to hear a message of empowerment from America's most charismatic exponent of the power of individual genius. In mid-January 1853, he sat in the audience in the largest hall in Springfield, the chamber of the House of Representatives, for the second of Ralph Waldo Emerson's three Springfield lectures that winter. It had the simple but evocative title, "Power." There is no evidence that Lincoln had yet read any of Emerson's essays published in his 1841 and 1844 volumes or in *Nature; Addresses and Lectures* in 1849 or in *Representative Men* in 1850. And there is no evidence that the two American originals were introduced that night, though that may have happened at the supper after the lecture, hosted in the Senate chamber by the ladies of the First Presbyterian Church, one of whom was Mary Lincoln.

Nine years later, when Emerson came to the White House, it may have seemed to him their first meeting. It was now with a man who could be readily recognized and identified in the framework of Emerson's description, in his January 1853 lecture, of "men whose magnetisms are of that force to draw material and elemental powers, and, where they appear, immense instrumentalities organize around them." Within a few days of that White House meeting, Lincoln borrowed from the Library of Congress the 1858 edition of *Representative Men: Seven Lectures*. The logic and history of Lincoln's life as a reader suggests that he read at least the first essay, "Uses of Great Men," probably the entire volume. "It is natural to believe in great men," the first essay begins. "Nature seems to exist for the excellent. The world is upheld by the veracity of good men: they make the earth wholesome." Aware of the elements that constituted his body and his life, Lincoln would have recognized the applicability to who he was and where he now stood of Emerson's view that "a man is a center for nature, running out threads of relation through every thing, fluid and solid, material and elemental. The earth rolls; every clod and stone comes to the meridian: so every organ, function, acid, crystal, grain of dust, has its relation to the brain. It waits long, but its turn comes."

To whatever extent Lincoln could have predicted the success of the endangered enterprise he led in 1862, he could not have believed in 1853 that he would ever have the chance to be tested on that level. He had always hoped that his turn would come. Much of his life had been a self-conscious as well as an intuitive preparation for high service. Though the immediate signs were not encouraging, Emerson's words that January night *were*. They exemplified the power of language, affirming the power inherent in the human mind. If he listened to Emerson's lecture as carefully as one has reason to suppose, it must have seemed that Emerson's subject had been chosen with Lincoln in mind, that his words were directed at the particular surfaces *he* needed to engage at this point in his life.

"Who shall set a limit to the influence of a human being?" Emerson asked.

> There are men, who, by their sympathetic attractions, carry nations with them, and lead the activity of the human race. And if there be such a tie, that, wherever the mind of man goes, nature will accompany him, perhaps there are men whose magnetisms are of that force to draw material and elemental powers, and, where they appear, immense instrumentalities organize around them. Life is a search after power; and this is an ele-

ment with which the world is so saturated,——there is no chink or crevice
in which it is not lodged,——that no honest seeking goes unrewarded.

Lincoln's "honest seeking" had so far gone without reward, whereas
power had cooperatively responded to rivals such as Stephen Douglas.
Lincoln had become, in Emerson's terms, "a cultivated man, wise to
know and bold to perform." His preparation had been assiduous; his will
had been "educated" by the necessities into which he had been born. But
what power he would be able to harness within himself and implement in
the affairs of this world was a question perplexingly unresolved. It was a
perilously vital issue for him.

Unlike the multitude, which has "no habit of self-reliance or original
action," and from which Emerson distinguished the gifted leader, Lincoln
was a man of substantial self-reliance, with a capacity for agency within
the parameters of his constitutional conservatism and his preference for
analysis rather than Romantic assertion. As with Emerson, his ultimate
self-reliance inhered in his command of language to shape himself and
others; and his habit of "original action" resided especially in his faith in
words to make realities, to motivate thought and action. So, he must have
wondered, why had he not achieved what his ambition and talent from
early on had directed him toward? And from where or what explanation
was he to get direction, encouragement, even hope that he would still
have the opportunity to channel and merge the power of his individual
selfhood with a powerful social and political current, something of national if not cosmic importance? He would have recognized himself in
Emerson's assertion that

all successful men have agreed in one thing,——they were *causationists*.
They believed that things went not by luck, but by law; that there was
not a weak or a cracked link in the chain that joins the first and the last
of things. A belief in causality, or strict connection between every trifle
and the principle of being, and, in consequence, belief in compensation,
or, that nothing is got for nothing,——characterizes all valuable minds,

and must control every effort that is made by an industrious one. The
most valiant men are the best believers in the tension of the laws.

The "doctrine of necessity" that he had held in his youth and suppos-
edly renounced, at least insofar as it offended Christian sensibilities, had its
more sophisticated expression in Emerson's belief that "cause and effect"
is the law of nature, that everything is connected, that there is a cosmic
principle of compensation, or balance, determining outcomes in human
affairs, that there is always a price to be paid, and that brave human beings
embrace and live by the laws that are "the principle of being." This is the
universal law that Lincoln would refer to in his second inaugural address,
his belief that some power had shaped the outcome of the war, and we
come closest to understanding the laws that are the essence of that power
by finding effective words to refer to them. "All power," Emerson emphasized, "is of one kind, a sharing of the nature of the world." The challenge
for Lincoln was to find a way to increase his share in and to live that power
expressively. "The mind that is parallel with the laws of nature will be in
the current of events, and strong with their strength." How to get strong
with "the current of events" continued to be his concern in the year after
attending Emerson's lecture. He needed a compelling topic and a forum,
neither of which he had the capability to provide.

Almost a year to the day after Emerson's lecture in Springfield, Stephen Douglas, now a dominant national figure who had been competitive for the Democratic presidential nomination in 1852, provided a use
to which Lincoln could put his strengths. He introduced in the Senate a
bill containing the ground rules for admitting the territory of Nebraska
to statehood. As chairman, he had shepherded it through the "Committee on Territories." Like every effort since 1820 to bring new states into
the Union, Nebraska's candidacy immediately became subsumed into
North-South politics and the slavery issue. Douglas had anticipated that
it would. His object was to move statehood westward, to advance the
creation of a transcontinental railroad with Chicago as its hub, and to
position himself as the likely Democratic candidate in 1856. To Douglas,

the slavery issue was political, slavery an undesirable but permanent reality that touched very lightly on his moral register. He believed strongly in national expansion. And he wanted to lead the country toward a better disposition about the balance between pro- and antislavery interests, particularly in regard to the admission of new states to the Union.

In the bill's attempt to recast the issue of slavery in the territories, it voided a key provision of the 1850 Compromise. The Compromise had recommitted the country to excluding slavery from all states north of an irregular line drawn east to west, from the Atlantic to the Pacific. Nebraska was north of that line. So, too, was Kansas, whose statehood aspirations were soon included in an amended bill, dubbed the Kansas-Nebraska Act. Previously, the Compromise's north-south balance had been maintained by coupling the admission of a slave and a free state. Douglas believed he had a better idea, which he called "popular sovereignty." Settlers would be permitted to bring slaves with them to any territory in the country, which, he argued, the Constitution gave them the right to do. At the time of admission to statehood, the residents would vote on whether to make slavery legal or illegal in their newly formed state. The people of the state would make the decision, the proper and best expression, Douglas argued, of representative government, states' rights, and democracy. The federal government would play no role in the process, and neither the North nor the South would have any legitimate ground for complaint about the way the result had been determined. It would be the democratic resolution of what had heretofore been an irreconcilable sectional conflict. The bill passed the Senate by a vote of 37 to 14, and the House by a narrower margin, 113 to 110. President Franklin Pierce signed it into law on May 30, 1854.

Sometime soon after, Lincoln attempted to clarify his thoughts about the principles the issue raised. Fragments of his essayistic analysis survive. Two of the four items, describing the nature of government and the rationale for its existence, may have been written having in mind the possibility of a public lecture. There is no reason to think he wrote these with the Kansas-Nebraska bill in mind. Still, the two items that his editor calls "Fragment on Government" are underpinned by a philosophic concern about the role of government that has political implications and that segues intellectually into the other two fragments, both of which are "On Slavery" and written in direct response to Douglas's bill.

Government, Lincoln posits, has two necessary functions: to do for the people as a whole what they cannot individually do for themselves and to administer justice in a community in which "the injustice of men" is an inevitable feature. "If one people will make war upon another, it is a necessity with that other to unite and cooperate for defense. . . . If some men will kill, or beat, or constrain others, or despoil them of property, by force, fraud, or noncompliance with contracts, it is a common object with peaceful and just men to prevent it." The necessity for the larger force of government inheres in the tendency in human nature to be unjust in the furtherance of self-interest. The function of government is to ensure and promote justice.

Such an attempt to define government in terms of human nature and justice required a definition of the human and of human rights, particularly in regard to the obligations of government. Lincoln's progress toward a sharper delineation of the slavery issue took mature focus now in the two fragments on slavery. The logic and language he brought to its expression connect his view of "natural law," based on observation and experience, to his belief that the path of common sense and logic leads to a true understanding of justice. This is the view of a man who has been raised on a wisdom literature that at every level posits first principles or moral laws, requiring only the evidence of deeply held conviction. For example, it is a self-evident truth, understood by every living creature, that the worker has a right to "the fruit of his labor," Lincoln wrote. This is, in fact, "so plain, that the most dumb and stupid slave that ever toiled for a master, does constantly *know* that he is wronged" and "although volume upon volume is written to prove slavery a very good thing, we never hear of the man who wishes to take the good of it, *by being a slave himself.*" And to the argument that "some men are too *ignorant*, and *vicious*, to share in government," that may be so; but "by your system, you would always keep them ignorant, and vicious. We proposed," referring to the Founding Fathers and the Declaration of Independence, "to give *all* a chance; and we expected the weak to grow stronger, the ignorant, wiser; and all better, and happier together."

That was the founding conception, the affirmation of the "equal rights of men." By the test of self-evident moral law, giving every creature the desire to protect and enjoy the fruits of his labor, and by the fact of every person's awareness of injustice when deprived of that, slavery exemplifies injustice. The logic of its justification is flawed and dangerous. If A argues that he has the right to enslave B, then B can use the same argument to claim his right to enslave A.

> You say A. is white, and B. is black. It is *color*, then; the lighter, having the right to enslave the darker? Take care. By this rule, you are to be the slave to the first man you meet, with a fairer skin than your own. You do not mean *color* exactly?—You mean the whites are *intellectually* the superiors of the blacks, and, therefore have the right to enslave them? Take care again. By this rule, you are to be slave to the first man you meet, with an intellect superior to your own. But, say you, it is a question of *interest*; and, if you can make it your *interest*, you have the right to enslave another. Very well. And if he can make it his interest, he has the right to enslave you.

The philosophy, the logic, and the language that Lincoln combined in his solitary and personal reflections on the subject in mid-1854 give the sense of a man preparing to bring a "mind that is parallel with the laws of nature" into consonance with "the current of events, and strong with their strength." The language and the argument of this search for expression on the subject of human rights were to be the basis of all he was to write on the subject in the future.

CHAPTER 7

"The Current of Events"
1855–1861

The Kansas-Nebraska Act had given national prominence and tension to a topic on which Lincoln knew he could be a formidable spokesman. He immediately took his search for power as a sharing of "the nature of the world" to the only forum available to him: the Whig Party electoral rallies throughout Illinois in the fall of 1854. A presidential election was two years off. As always, though, the Illinois electoral pot was stirring, especially concerning the election in early 1855 of a junior senator to replace James Shields. It was the position Lincoln had had his eye on for some time and desperately wanted. His persuasive articulation of the widely shared outrage at the likelihood that territorial sovereignty would make slave states of Nebraska and Kansas made it reasonable for him to hope that he would be a viable candidate, given his popularity among Illinois Whigs. A substantial number of antislavery Democrats might enter into a coalition with antislavery Whigs to elect someone with Lincoln's views.

His speeches in the fall of 1854 made him the most prominent anti-Kansas-Nebraska voice in Illinois and established the subject, substance, and rhetoric of what was to be, in effect, a six-year-long political campaign that included his election to the Illinois House in the summer of 1854, his campaigns for an Illinois Senate seat in 1854–1855 and 1858, and his election to the presidency in 1860. Throughout, his major antagonist was his decades-long Democratic counterpart and inverse alter-ego, Stephen Douglas, the architect and defender of "popular sovereignty," who struggled to maintain his doctrine against proslavery and pro-Buchanan Democrats on the one side and, on the other, a loose coalition of anti-Nebraska forces.

In this whirlwind transformation of the political landscape, the Democrats were splitting into two sectional parties, Northern and Southern, and the Whigs were also splitting, absorbed in the North by splinter parties and the newly formed but still unstructured Republican Party. In 1854, the Republicans began to form as a coalition of disaffected Democrats, anti–Kansas-Nebraska Whigs such as Lincoln, and third-party antislavery, free-soil advocates whose common bond was disapproval of slavery. Many, like Lincoln, had as their target the institution's containment and eventual elimination. A minority advocated immediate abolition. Lincoln would join the Republicans in Illinois, he gradually concluded, provided their anti–Kansas-Nebraska views agreed with his, including the restoration of the Missouri Compromise and gradual emancipation. "I have no objection to 'fuse' with any body provided I can fuse on ground which I think is right," he told the only abolitionist member of the Illinois legislature in August 1855. He was still a Whig, he wrote to Joshua Speed at the same time, "but others say there are no whigs, and that I am an abolitionist." When he decided in May 1856 to associate himself with the new party, his challenge was to help keep its disparate elements politically cohesive and to bring in as many outriders as possible.

As a student of American history, Lincoln was aware of the vitriolic environment in which political parties had originally been created and that the framers of the Constitution had not desired their existence. He appreciated the inherent danger to effective government in political parties: the manipulation of language to advance their agendas. Political campaigns embodied the inevitable discord between the linguistic nuance of rational discussion and the blunt rhetoric of partisan politics.

Consequently the founders, eschewing faction, had rejected political parties, making no provision for them in the Constitution. They soon, though, found themselves dividing into parties, despite being aware that they would thus be drawn, directly or by surrogate, into a dishonest use of language that campaigns in a democratic ethos encourage and almost require. The ultimate Whig Party man, Lincoln now found himself organizing partisanship into the framework of a new party that needed linguistic structure and substance to delineate its positions. He needed to find language that would define and rally his constituency. He wanted to avoid lies and he wanted to undermine the efficacy of negative campaigning. He had, between 1854 and 1859, the advantage of the discussion being dominated by one issue only, and that an issue with a strong moral dimension about which he felt passionate.

The argumentative underpinning of his view of the Kansas-Nebraska Act was that slavery was so unjust and destructive of core American values that its unacceptability preceded all decisions arrived at by popular sovereignty; that common sense and human experience revealed that once slaves were allowed into a territory, powerful interest groups, factionalism, and greed would keep them there; that popular sovereignty thus increased the likelihood that slavery would spread; and that if public opinion became indifferent to slavery, its presence would become normative. Slavery might then be reintroduced into states that had previously banned it. Since slavery and free labor were incompatible, at some future time the nation would be, he concluded, either all one or the other. And if slavery were to become a normalized nationwide institution, the Founders' claim that all men are created equal and endowed with inalienable rights would be forever unrealized. It would be a denial of government by the people, and a reversion to injustice, barbarism, and tyranny.

His six-year-long campaign had a number of turning points. The first was his failure to be elected, in February 1855, junior senator from Illinois, a position that he felt in his grasp and almost his. He expected it to be his launching pad into national visibility. Like all alert politicians, he counted heads. In the fall of 1854 and early 1855, widely soliciting support, he called in, gently but firmly, the outstanding obligations that his goodwill, reputation, and party loyalty had created. "I really have some chance," he proclaimed to a Whig politico whose support he wanted. "I have got it into my head to try to be U.S. Senator, and I wish somehow to get at your Whig member," he told another. With some anti–Kansas-Nebraska Democrats unwilling to vote for a Democrat who supported the Kansas-Nebraska Act, "it has come round that a Whig may, by possibility, be elected . . . and I want the chance of being the man."

In summer 1854, he had allowed himself to be nominated for the Illinois legislature, perhaps to encourage positive thoughts about a possible candidacy for the United States Senate. When elected, he declined the office. That he had ever intended to resume a state legislative career seems unlikely. "I only allowed myself to be elected," he weakly explained, in order to help the Whig candidate for Congress. "My friends are now asking me to make the race" for Shields's Senate seat, he coyly wrote to a legislator whose vote he hoped for, the result to be determined by a legislative, not a popular, referendum. And he was soon defending himself against the accusation by anti–Kansas-Nebraska Democrats and Northern Illinois Whigs that his strong loyalty to central Illinois would prevent him from fairly representing the entire state. "It is not within my recollection," he responded, "that the Northern members ever wanted my vote [as a state legislator] for any interest of theirs, without getting it."

He hoped that the Kansas-Nebraska furor would create enough passion to override party loyalty and shift the usual alignments. There were three major constituencies, each represented by a prominent candidate: the Whigs, the pro–Kansas-Nebraska Democrats, and the anti–Kansas-Nebraska Democrats. The Whigs did not stick together, primarily because the pro-Buchanan governor, maneuvering behind the scenes for the position, exacerbated long-standing antagonisms. A small group on each side vowed never to vote for a candidate the other supported. Consequently, it became impossible for either Lincoln or Shields to be elected. To mend matters, the anti–Kansas-Nebraska Whigs and anti-Buchanan Democrats coalesced in favor of the anti–Kansas-Nebraska Democratic candidate, Lyman Trumbull, who had started with five votes. Lincoln had started with forty-five, Shields forty-one. "I do not know that it is much advantage to have the largest number of votes at the start," Lincoln sensibly observed. When he realized that the pro-Buchanan governor might be elected unless he withdrew, Lincoln released his votes to Trumbull. "The agony is over," he wrote on February 21, 1855. "I am *not* Senator. I have to content myself with the honor of having been the first choice of a large majority of the fiftyone members who finally made the election." But he had wanted the office, not the honor. "I could not, however, let the whole political result go to ruin, on a point merely personal to myself." Mary Lincoln, who had been counting on a return to Washington, gave bitter expression to their mutual disappointment. He put it in the best light possible. "A less good humored than I perhaps would not have consented to it." But to have resisted the "current of events" would have been destructive to himself and his principles.

Starting in the fall of 1854, when he composed his foundation antislavery text, his talent as a writer and speaker brought him to center stage in Illinois. His value to himself and to the emerging Republican Party between 1854 and 1858 was not in the likelihood of his election to high office, and in the two decades prior to 1860 he held no office at all. In the larger scheme of things, he desperately wanted the power of his words to be accompanied by the power to implement them, which only holding high office could provide. After all, he acknowledged, a party at its basic level needed to offer alternatives and win elections, and the Whig campaign platform in 1854 and the new Republican Party stage in 1855 provided the forum in which he could perform and excel. But what Emerson referred to as becoming "strong with the current of events" had as its enabling source within Lincoln not political office but intellect, moral insight, and superior language skills. They were in the service of a vision more than of an election campaign; though in the end the vision and the power of office to advance it were inseparable. As a practical politician, he never undervalued that connection. The creation of a text that could serve as the philosophical and political exposition of his coalition, and which would make him ultimately the leader of the movement, became his dominant preoccupation.

As usual, he combined his Circuit Court perambulations with political speechmaking. In August 1854 he spoke in Winchester and Carrollton; in September in Springfield, in Peoria, in Bloomington twice; and in October in Chicago. All were in essence one speech, adapted for the particularities of the occasion, often a direct response to a Democrat who had spoken to the same audience. Occasionally he was pushed forward by supporters at a Democratic political meeting, an early version of a dog-the-opponent strategy that four years later so infuriated Douglas that he agreed to regularize these unscheduled appearances into a series of debates. In the second of his Bloomington speeches, Lincoln responded to a speech by Douglas immediately preceding his. The *Illinois Journal* reported in October that after Douglas, "by appointment, addressed a large audience" in Peoria, "the crowd then began to call for Lincoln, who, as Judge Douglas had announced was, by agreement, to answer him."

Cautious by personality and vocation, Lincoln was unlikely to risk misspeaking spontaneously on as charged and complicated a subject as Kansas-Nebraska, which had become shorthand for everything to do with the topic of slavery. He had a lifelong preference for not speaking extemporaneously, and though no manuscript of any of the 1854 to 1858 speeches survives, he regularly had his pen in hand during the 1854 preelection months. The *Illinois Journal* published an early effort in mid-September 1854 as an unsigned editorial on the Kansas-Nebraska Act, which quoted the Act's exact language to establish that it did indeed repeal the Missouri Compromise. Lincoln attacked by comic illustration the hypocrisy of those who claimed that Kansas-Nebraska did not legislate slavery into the territories, an illustration that was to become a staple of his foundation speech. Characteristically, it was logically sharp and colloquially vivid. As often, his literary skills sustained appropriate devices, in this instance a rhetorical question to convey moral outrage and an imaginary dialogue in which the terms in which he had framed the fiction required that he identify himself as one of the speakers:

> To illustrate the case—Abraham Lincoln has a fine meadow, contain-ing beautiful springs of water, and well fenced, which John Calhoun [a Central Illinois Democrat active in the 1854 campaign] had agreed with Abraham (originally owning the land in common) should be his, and the agreement had been consummated in the most solemn manner, re-garded by both as sacred. John Calhoun, however, in the course of time, had become owner of an extensive herd of cattle—the prairie grass had become dried up and there was no convenient water to be had. John Cal-houn then looks with a longing eye on Lincoln's meadow, and goes to it and throws down the fences, and exposes it to the ravages of his starving and famishing cattle. "You rascal," says Lincoln, "what have you done? What do you do this for?" "Oh," replies Calhoun, "everything is right. I have taken down your fence; but nothing more. It is my true intent and meaning not to drive my cattle into your meadow, nor to exclude them therefrom, but to leave them perfectly free to form their own notions of the feed, and to direct their movements in their own way!"
>
> Now would not the man who committed this outrage be deemed both a knave and a fool,—a knave in removing the restrictive fence, which he had solemnly pledged himself to sustain;—and a fool in sup-posing that there could be one man found in the country to believe that he had not pulled down the fence for the purpose of opening the meadow for his cattle?

Since part of his argument against the Kansas-Nebraska Act would be based on the historical record, Lincoln needed to be sure he was rep-resenting the record accurately. Aware that Douglas often subordinated accuracy to verbal fireworks, he wanted to be certain that his own his-torical presentation was sustained by fact and by the plain meaning of the language of the documents. As a one-man enterprise, he acted as his own researcher as well as speechwriter, except for the assistance that

Herndon provided. Lincoln worked from his own books, adding volumes available from other sources in Springfield. To demonstrate that documentary evidence supported his claim that the Founders had been ashamed of slavery and had worked within practical limits to prevent its extension required specific citation of a large number of events, dates, and documents. His intention was to create a valid alternative to what seemed to him the false history of legal and public opinion about slavery circulated by those favorably or indifferently disposed to it. The absence of references to slavery in the Declaration of Independence and the Constitution seemed grounds for claiming that its existence embarrassed the Founders. Its exclusion from the relevant territories by the Ordinance of 1787 provided Lincoln statute and verse in support of his argument that Congress had believed it had the right to determine slavery's disposition within federally owned land and had intended to limit its spread. His analysis of documents from the Revolutionary period and the first forty years of the nineteenth century indicated that slavery was a declining backwater in the current of history. European and American standards of justice had determined that it was a temporary stigma rather than a permanent institution.

This was, he recognized, an optimistic reading, an alternative vision that took its force from his increasing commitment to the power of narrative to create the truth that comes from belief in the narrative itself. His temperament, legal training, and rational values required that history and law support his moral passion. And, no doubt, in its selectivity and its value-inflected determination, he attempted to provide an account that would be more attractive and have greater appeal than the alternatives, one of which was that Negroes, since they were subhuman, were not entitled to any rights at all. At the same time, he needed a narrative that would not contradict the widely held belief, which he shared, that the white race was superior and that the Declaration did not affirm black social and political equality, only legal equality based on the universal right to personal liberty.

As an historian, he looked to the past to support the views he

desired to promote in the present. The effort was a prodigious one precisely because he recognized that human experience provided powerful
oppositional arguments. Slavery and slaveholding were an indisputable
historical reality. The tendency of people to promote their own well-
being as the primary consideration in issues of power and justice, and
the prevalence of an innate aggression in its preservation, seemed un-
deniable facts, making optimism and idealizations difficult to sustain.
The narratives that advanced the better angels, even in the reduced
state in which "the Divine image in [man's] Mind is quite changed and
altered" that *Dilworth's Speller* had impressed on the young Lincoln,
needed every advantage of history and language to sustain themselves
against the reality of human nature and historical fact. Lincoln had
memorized too much Shakespeare not to have absorbed that into his
bones and his language. Even Byron's and Burns's Romantic idealizations keenly recognized the power of the countervailing forces. Injustice and tyranny were internal as well as external givens, and any attempt to oppose them, a struggle with the self as well as with others.
Lincoln had learned from his literary masters that language was the
instrumental weapon in the struggle. The victory, even if temporary,
went to the best creator and teller of tales.

But was there no indisputably true story, no universal set of givens
built into the fabric of creation, unvaryingly true always and everywhere?
And if there were, how were we to know it and how were we to adjudicate between claims of alternative or conflicting higher truths? The
proslavery forces had just as much confidence and found just as much
evidence in the record (especially the Bible) for their claims about "natural law" as did slavery's opponents. And history showed that what was
widely accepted as natural law at one time was denied at another. Early
on, he recognized that the persuasiveness of claims about natural law and
universal truths resided in the ability of words and narrative to generate
widespread concurrence. If there was indeed a predisposition to believe
what he believed, he needed to find the language that expressed what the
majority preferred as operative feelings and beliefs. He could not create

that majority, but he could find it, he could search it out. He and his contemporaries could find coherence in the widely shared conviction that Americans prefer justice to injustice, that they are generous in their extension of beneficence to others, that self-interest can be discovered in the assertion that "all men are created equal," and that greed, folly, aggression, and lust for domination can be subordinated to better impulses and more constructive narratives. "All men are created equal" is a claim in a belief system, Lincoln recognized, not a rationally verifiable proposition. So is its opposite. One is born and educated into one's belief system, though it seems that even in a largely deterministic universe the possibility for choice sometimes exists. Lincoln, whatever the causal determinants and to whatever limited degree he was self-consciously purposeful, had made his choice. He now desired to find the best language to harness and implement this belief system in a country whose alternative narrative would lead, he believed, to betrayal and disaster.

The Peoria audience to which Lincoln addressed an early version of his foundation speech in October 1854 had heard Douglas talk for three hours. With a humor that both affirmed and denied Douglas as the main attraction, Lincoln postponed his response from the late afternoon to the evening, probably the only unscripted words he spoke that day:

It is now several minutes past five. . . . If you hear me at all, I wish you to hear me thro'. It will take me as long as it has taken him. That will carry us beyond eight o'clock at night. Now every one of you who can remain that long, can just as well get his supper, meet me at seven, and remain one hour or two later. The Judge has already informed you that he is to have an hour to reply to me. I doubt not but you have been a little surprised to learn that I have consented to give one of his high reputation and known ability, this advantage of me. Indeed, my consenting to it, though reluctant, was not wholly unselfish; for I suspected if it were understood, that the Judge was entirely done, you democrats would leave, and not hear me; but by giving him the close, I felt confident you would stay for the fun of hearing him skin me.

The tactic had the colloquial tone and directness that made Lincoln so effective with juries. The irony of his comment that human nature would compel the audience to reassemble, anticipating the delight it would take in seeing him skinned, capitalized on his awareness of the bond between the victim and the victimizer. His would be a self-interested self-sacrifice. And the implicit warning was humorously clear: he expected to turn the tables and he desired the largest audience possible. If, while at a structural disadvantage, he could "skin" Douglas, his own arguments would seem even the more formidable.

Reassembled in the glare of torchlight, the audience heard a loosely structured presentation divided into four sections: a statement of theme and purpose; a history of slavery in relation to the territories; an analysis of the ramifications of the Missouri Compromise and its revocation; and a discussion of the relationship between slavery, self-government, and what it is to be human. These were to be the elements that would carry Lincoln through at least a hundred more speeches in the next four years, supplemented by new documents and events. Like the writers he admired, he set out his theme at the start: "The repeal of the Missouri Compromise, and the propriety of its restoration, constitute the subject of what I am to say," and he would say it without questioning the patriotism or assailing "the motives of any man, or class of men; but rather to strictly confine myself to the naked merits of the question." It would be a speech about policy, his ideal of what all political discourse should be, and he would be "National in all the positions" he would take and not advance positions "narrow, sectional, and dangerous to the Union." Since this subject "is no other, than part and parcel of the larger general question of domestic-slavery, I wish to MAKE and to KEEP the distinction between the EXISTING institution, and the EXTENSION of it, so broad, and so clear, that no honest man can misunderstand me, and no dishonest one, successfully misrepresent me."

The only issue at hand, he stressed, was extension. Maneuvering toward the middle of his constituency, aware that abolition could not be the platform of a party that hoped to win an election in Illinois or nationally, he would sustain the flawed reality against powerful forces attempting to make it substantially worse. "Much as I hate slavery, I would consent to the extension of it rather than see the Union dissolved," he told his audience, "just as I would consent to any GREAT evil, to avoid a GREATER one." However, the extension of slavery to Nebraska, he emphasized, slightly misquoting a favorite line from *Hamlet*, would not contribute to avoiding the greater evil: "It hath no relish of salvation in it."

To Douglas and many Northern Democrats, Lincoln thus opposed the only viable solution, and to proslavery Southerners a limitation on extension logically implied a first step toward abolition. Limitation would increase discord rather than advance peace. Abolition would create economic and social problems. Why should white Americans act against their own material and national self-interest? Why should Southerners voluntarily divest themselves of valuable property and in some cases pauperize themselves? What would become of almost four million slaves once they had been freed? And who would pay for the measures necessary to provide redress? Indeed, was any redress possible, since slavery was a core constituent of Southern society's structure, the embodiment of a value system, a class-based worldview by which the society defined itself? And pervading every aspect of this discussion was the almost unanimous conviction, North and South, that Negroes were inherently inferior to whites.

Against all this, Lincoln appealed to reason, historical fact, and the sense of justice that he believed a constituent of human nature. The power of persuasive language, he hoped, could motivate America to become the agent of its own liberation. With respect for the historical basis of the appeal to reason, he began the Peoria address with a brief description of what had led up to the Missouri Compromise and what the Compromise had achieved. To Thomas Jefferson went the honor of having determined the key antecedents. He "was, is, and perhaps will continue to be, the most distinguished politician of our history," an implied contrast with Washington, who, for Lincoln, transcended political categories. Jefferson, in the ordinance of 1787, had originated "the policy of prohibiting slavery in new territory." "Thus, away back of the constitution, in the pure, free breath of the revolution, the State of Virginia, and the National congress put that policy in practice." Paradoxically, Jefferson also gave us the Louisiana Purchase, whose vast territories engendered the North-South competition that resulted in the Missouri Compromise of 1820, which even Douglas had praised, proclaiming that it "had been canonized in the hearts of the American people, as a sacred thing." Because of the acquisition of new territory in the Mexican War, the settlement of California, the fugitive slave problem, and the tension created by the slave trade in the District of Columbia, the measure had required the adjustments made by the Compromise of 1850. That was now being undone by "the *repeal* of the Missouri Compromise." "I think, and shall try to show, that it is wrong; wrong in its direct effect, letting slavery into Kansas and Nebraska—and wrong in its prospective principle, allowing it to spread to every other part of the wide world, where men can be found inclined to take it."

The history of slavery raised a practical question and a moral issue that he needed to address before engaging with the specific arguments that Douglas had made in favor of the Kansas-Nebraska Act. The practical question was: Who is responsible for the existence of slavery in America and what can be done to eliminate the institution? The moral question was: How and by what standard are we to judge slaveholders? To the first question Lincoln answered that the responsibility was nation-wide; and that no one had proposed a practical means of abolishing slavery, given the complicated difficulties. The repatriation of almost four million Negroes to Africa was as impractical, he granted, as it was un-likely, though his "first impulse would be to free all the slaves, and send them to Liberia. But . . . if they were all landed there in a day, they would all perish in the next ten days; and there are not surplus shipping and sur-plus money enough in the world to carry them there in many times ten days." Though he was to continue to support the colonization program, he recognized that it was a palliative, not a solution. And to "free them all, and keep them among us as underlings" would probably, he believed, hardly better their condition.

What, then, to do? "Free them, and make them politically and socially, our equals? My own feelings will not admit of this; and if mine would, we well know that those of the great mass of white people will not." Ever the realist, he feared the potential for race violence. "Whether this feeling accords with justice and sound judgment, is not the sole question, if indeed it is any part of it. A universal feeling, whether well or ill-founded, can not be safely disregarded." Southern and Northern race prejudice was too powerful a force to disregard. But "it does seem to me that systems of gradual emancipation might be adopted." The national will and treasury could be directed toward programs that would lead to slavery's eventual elimination. Persuasion was the only sensible and viable weapon of choice. Since neither history nor human nature could readily be changed, the best strategy was an appeal to an ideal moral standard and to gradual emancipation.

In the meantime, those for whom slavery was painful, in body or in conscience, would have to continue to bear their pain, as he explained the next year to Joshua Speed, reminding him of their steamboat experience in 1841: "You may remember, as I well do, that from Louisville to the mouth of the Ohio there were, on board, ten or a dozen slaves, shackled together with irons. That sight was a continual torment to me; and I see something like it every time I touch the Ohio, or any other slave-border. It is hardly fair for you to assume, that I have no interest in a thing which has, and continually exercises, the power of making me miserable. You ought rather to appreciate how much the great body of the Northern people do crucify their feelings" by accepting the Fugitive Slave Law "in order to maintain their loyalty to the constitution and the Union."

He knew, though, that this was not entirely true. On the one hand, there existed widespread Northern approval or indifference to slavery; on the other, abolitionist zeal without a practical program; in the middle, tortured temporizers. But it is human nature, he reminded his audience, to judge others more harshly than we judge ourselves. The Northern assumption of moral superiority and its holier-than-thou condescension were unwarranted. Indeed, condemnation of Southern iniquity needed to recognize the intractable difficulty of the Southern situation. "I surely will not blame them for not doing what I should not know how to do myself. If all earthly power were given me, I should not know what to do, as to the existing institution." Indeed, the Southern people "are just what we would be in their situation. If slavery did not now exist amongst them, they would not introduce it. If it did now exist amongst us, we should not instantly give it up. This I believe of the masses north and south." His awareness of the conflicting qualities of human nature disinclined him to judgmental condemnation; the moral imperative required the attempt to project oneself into the other person's position. As a reader of Shakespeare, he had learned empathetic identification with a wide range of human feelings and thoughts. In his own mind, he could dramatically project what it meant to be somebody else, even a slaveholding Southerner, especially about moral issues and the complications of the human situation.

Still, he had no doubt that Douglas and Southern-sympathizing Democrats mistook the will of the nation. They were wrong on the facts and unwise in their policies. Their claims were "no other than a bold denial of the history of the country." The American public no more wanted the extension of slavery into the territories than it desired "reviving the African slave trade by law." Every one of Douglas's arguments, Lincoln maintained, was factually wrong or distorted by omission or carried such momentous practical consequences that those needed to be made explicit. It is false, he argued, that slavery will not go where climate and soil are unfit for cotton, sugar, or rice production. Slaves can labor in shops and factories; opening new territories for slavery increases the demand for and the monetary value of slaves. America can, he argued, successfully expand to the Pacific without spreading slavery to the territories. "I conclude then, that the public never demanded the repeal of the Missouri Compromise."

To counter Douglas's equation of popular sovereignty with "the sacred right of self-government," Lincoln clarified his view of the relationship between democratic institutions and first principles, those that are so basic that without them democracy cannot exist. Douglas, he perceived, had cleverly taken the high ground. The disjunction between what that first principle of self-government required and Douglas's application of it needed to be exposed. Popular sovereignty in the territories, Lincoln argued, promises one thing but delivers another. It presents itself as a moral argument based on a core first principle of American political philosophy but is in fact an immoral obfuscation. By misusing democratic language and processes, it allows a small group of self-selected inhabitants in a sparsely settled territory to determine the legality of slavery by majority vote, but prior to statehood and without regard to due process or voting standards or constitutional legitimacy. It is a dishonest use of language in which something is made to appear that which it is not, a deceitful creation of the shell but not the substance. "Near eighty years ago we began by declaring that all men are created equal; but now from that beginning we have run down to the other declaration, that for SOME men to enslave OTHERS is a 'sacred right of self-government.' These principles can not stand together. They are as opposite as God and mammon; and whoever holds to the one, must despise the other." The threat was to the perpetuation of America as a democracy. "Let no one be deceived. The spirit of seventy-six and the spirit of Nebraska, are utter antagonisms; and the former is being rapidly displaced by the latter."

Since popular sovereignty had the potential to introduce slavery into the states generated from the territories, that result would be incompatible, Lincoln believed, with the Declaration of Independence, the Ordinance of 1787, the Constitution, the termination of the African slave trade, and the Missouri Compromise. It would abuse the secularized "natural law" that our inherent sense of justice demanded be widely implemented: "that no man is good enough to govern another man, *without that other's* consent. I say this is the leading principle—the sheet anchor of American republicanism," and that those entitled to self-governance cannot be disposed of as slaves. "The doctrine of self-government is right . . . but it has no just application, as here attempted. Or perhaps I should rather say that whether it has such just application depends on whether a negro is *not* or *is* a man."

If a Negro is a human being, Lincoln argued, that would predetermine the territorial question and void the issue of "territorial sovereignty." Judge Douglas believes that he is not, "and consequently has no idea that there can be any moral question in legislating about him." "The great mass of mankind [the Caucasian race] take[s] a totally different view," Lincoln insisted, though the sweep of this claim is more passionately rhetorical than statistically probable in the mid-nineteenth century. "They consider slavery a great moral wrong; and their feeling against it, is not evanescent, but eternal. It lies at the very foundation of their sense of justice; and it cannot be trifled with." Opposition to slavery has as its underlying belief the humanity of the Negro. The "sense of justice and human sympathy" inherent in human nature, both North and South, tells us "that the poor negro has some natural right to himself . . . that, after all, there is humanity in the negro." He is a human being, and the first principle of self-governance applies to him as well. Without that recognition, "our republican robe is soiled, and trailed in the dust."

Let us repurify it. Let us turn and wash it white, in the spirit, if not the blood, of the Revolution. Let us turn slavery from its claims of "moral right," back upon its existing legal rights, and its arguments of "necessity." Let us return it to the position our fathers gave it; and there let it rest in peace. Let us re-adopt the Declaration of Independence, and with it, the practices, and policies, which harmonize with it. Let north and south— let all Americans—let all lovers of liberty everywhere—join in the great and good work. If we do this, we shall not only have saved the Union; but we shall have so saved it, as to make, and to keep it, forever worthy of the saving. We shall have so saved it, that the succeeding millions of free happy people, the world over, shall rise up, and call us blessed to the latest generations.

Subsequent events of course made clear that Lincoln's sense of the re-alistic failed him in this appeal to let slavery "rest in peace" in the status established for it from the founding to the Compromise of 1850. The ex-tremes on both sides had too much energy and commitment to permit that, and the moral implication of his belief that Negroes are human beings and hence entitled to self-governance resides uneasily and in-consistently with his call to maintain the status quo. In appealing to the human heart's innate abhorrence of slavery and locating this first prin-ciple not in transcendent super-reality but in human nature, he knew he was making a questionable claim for which the feeling itself is presented as the proof. Still, it was the only appeal he could make, the only strategy compatible with his sense of the practical. The success of the argument was necessary, he believed, in order to keep the Union from falling apart. The phrase "rest in peace" in a situation that wouldn't permit peace pro-vides retrospectively one of the only ironies in a speech in which the an-tislavery moral vision is expressed with eloquent passion.

Lincoln had no other recourse but an appeal to first principles, in-cluding his fellow citizens' sense of justice; and his only tool for persua-sion was language: the most effective words he could find to stir minds and hearts. His language is sharp, the phrasing and balance are mostly effective; the literary allusions strengthen tone and argument. As a com-position, it suffers from being less polished and practiced than the care-fully composed speeches of his presidential years. It is the antecedent to the seven loosely structured Lincoln-Douglas campaign debates of 1858. Though large subsections of the Peoria speech have tight cogency, on the whole it rambles, with parts out of place, a rarity in the Lincoln oeuvre, partly because it is a second test run of a foundation speech in the process of being created. The substance is right, but the structure falters.

Each speech he gave after the Peoria address used some of its ma-terials to advance his ideas. The process of revision increased fluidity, argumentative concision, structural tightness, and sharpness of expres-sion. After all, he had, like so many, been taken totally by surprise in 1854 by "territorial sovereignty." If in Peoria he fumbled to find the center and smooth the outreach of his argument, he had the excuse that he had been "astounded" by Douglas's new approach. "We were thunderstruck and stunned; and we reeled and fell in utter confusion," he told his audience. He grabbed the blunt cutting instruments of daily life for his metaphors, suggesting revolutionary insurrection by outraged citizens. "But we rose[,] each fighting, grasping whatever he could first reach—a scythe—a pitchfork—a chopping axe, or a butcher's cleaver. We struck in the direction of the sound; and we are rapidly closing in upon him. He must not think to divert us from our purpose, by showing us that our drill, our dress, and our weapons, are not entirely perfect and uniform."

Confronting Douglas challenged Lincoln with the formidable obstacle of insidiously plausible lies. Douglas, he believed, debased public discourse by inventing and denying facts; by constant repetition, he misinformed and confused public opinion. His claims were "a bold denial of the history of the country."

> If we do not know that the Compromises of '50 were dependent on each other; if we do not know that Illinois came into the Union as a free state—we do not know any thing. If we do not know these things, we do not know that we ever had a revolutionary war, or such a chief as Washington. To deny these things is to deny our national axioms, or dogmas, at least; and it puts an end to all argument. If a man will stand up and assert, and repeat, and re-assert, that two and two do not make four, I know nothing in the power of argument that can stop him.

Yet argument was all that he had at his disposal, and the challenge of opposing Douglas's linguistic shiftiness and outright falsifications kept Lincoln assiduously at the task of correction. Ultimately, there seemed only two ways in which to counter Douglas's vision—to overcome his arguments in the court of public opinion or to defeat him in an election, depriving him of his Senate seat. Lincoln was about to emerge as the dominant Western spokesperson for the centrist Republican Party view partly because he had superior skills and also because the over-confident senator soon gave him the opportunity to share his national spotlight.

A hardscrabble ex–Border State Southerner who had raised himself through hard work into the professional middle class and who had embraced the ideology of national growth through immigration, education, monetary expansion, and technological progress, Lincoln was familiar with Kentucky, not the Deep South. Between 1854 and 1861, he underestimated the willingness of the Southern leadership to go to war, if necessary, to preserve their social and economic structures, including slavery. Without the advantage of the three-fifths constitutional provision, which counted every five Negroes as the equivalent of three whites in determining congressional districts, the South's influence in Congress would become subordinate to that of Northern majorities. With immigration swelling northern populations, the South was already losing the demographic competition. Lincoln expected that an honest use of language, the power of reason, the strength of historical bonds, and an appeal to an innate sense of justice would keep the Union together. Douglas believed that the ploy of territorial sovereignty served more effectively what he thought Lincoln's honesty could never achieve: to assuage the South and prevent disunion, which would terminate the western and international expansion of American power. The extension of slavery did not seem too great a price to pay. Since territorial sovereignty was in the national interest, verbal sleight of hand would provide the mechanism to sway public opinion toward a desirable political goal.

Lincoln, in the process of discovering that verbal dishonesty often holds the advantage in the court of public opinion, was reluctant to accept, despite all the evidence he acknowledged to the contrary, that some conflicts are immune to discourse. The language of persuasion fails when first principles clash and one side is willing to take up arms. The South's cultural conservatism, regional bravado, and greater loyalty to native state than to the Union had the potential to be lethal on the national stage as well as in the backwoods or on the dueling ground.

In the two years following the Peoria address, Lincoln hoped a consensus could be formed around the principle of self-governance, acknowledging the right of the individual, defined to include the Negro, to control his own employment. He spent much of his energy attempting to influence public opinion in Illinois. He continued to travel the Eighth Judicial Circuit, slogging through the daily requirements of the law practice he was dependent on for his income. Some cases he found interesting and self-educating, particularly a patent case that brought him to Cincinnati in 1854. The Eastern lawyers, including a short, heavily bearded Pittsburgh dynamo, William Stanton, with whom he had expected to serve on a team of equals, shuffled him aside as an irrelevant country lawyer who had gotten the mistaken impression that he had a role to play in the trial. Lincoln had been brought on board on the assumption that he would have local influence in Illinois, if needed. His treatment would have humiliated a less stoically graceful man.

His work for the Illinois Central provided regular income, including his huge fee in 1857 for his successful defense against the 1853 McLean County tax claim. As late as 1857, he tried and won the Effie-Afton bridge case in Chicago, a significant conflict between railroad and riverboat interests whose underlying issues fitted perfectly the mercantile and east-west transportation ideology that Lincoln and the Republican Party embraced. "There is a travel," he told the jury, "from East to West, whose demands are not less important than that of the river. It is growing larger and larger, building up new countries with a rapidity never before seen in the history of the world." His mind and pen still sought effective ways to express his political and philosophical ideas. He expanded an apt expressive paradigm when, in August 1855, he responded to Joshua Speed's request to tell him where he stood on Kansas-Nebraska and slavery. Was he a "black Republican?" Was he a Whig? Was he a Know-Nothing, who desired to keep America Anglo-Saxon, Protestant, and white, particularly by blocking Irish Catholic immigration? Characteristically, Lincoln found principles and ideas more attractive than party pigeonholes. Where he now "stood" in the party sense was "a disputed point. I think I am a whig; but others say there are no whigs, and that I am an abolitionist. . . . I now do no more than oppose the *extension* of slavery. I am not a Know-Nothing. That is certain. How could I be? How can any one who abhors the oppression of negroes, be in favor of degrading classes of white people?"

Denying equal rights under human and natural law to any group of people greased the slippery slope down which those in power could push any other group whose subordination or exclusion served its economic and ideological interests. A seething Lincoln paraphrased the mind-set and the words of Byron, Burns, and Tennyson, and projected himself imaginatively into the language of political exile dear to nineteenth-century republicanism, which frequently cited czarist Russia as a paragon of despotic tyranny:

Our progress in degeneracy appears to me to be pretty rapid. As a nation, we began by declaring that *'all men are created equal.'* We now practically read it 'all men are created equal, *except negroes.'* When the Know-Nothings get control, it will read 'all men are created equals, except negroes, *and foreigners, and catholics.'* When it comes to this I should prefer emigrating to some country where they make no pretence of loving liberty—to Russia, for instance, where despotism can be taken pure, and without the base alloy of hypocracy.

By early 1856, Lincoln had become the likely anti–Kansas-Nebraska nominee against Douglas, though who would nominate him was not completely clear. Introduced at an anti–Kansas-Nebraska editors' convention as "our next candidate for the U.S. Senate," Lincoln responded that theirs was a "sentiment I am in favor of." "Our" referred to a fusion of various parties and positions gradually taking the name Republican. That was not what Lincoln's conservative Whig supporters, who assumed that Republicans were abolitionists, wanted to hear. That he would have to join the Republicans to have any chance at office, however, was probably clear to him. In May 1856, he made his commitment, alienating some of his conservative Whig supporters. After William Herndon signed Lincoln's name to a call for Sangamon County to appoint delegates to attend the first statewide Republican convention, in Bloomington, Lincoln allowed his name to stand. At the convention, he took to "the platform amid deafening applause," so the pro-Republican Alton *Weekly Courier* reported. "He enumerated the pressing reasons of the present movement. He was here ready to fuse with anyone who would unite with him to oppose the slave power; spoke of the bugbear disunion which was so vaguely threatened. It was to be remembered that the *Union must be preserved in the purity of its principles as well as the integrity of its territorial parts*. It must be 'Liberty and Union, now and forever, one and inseparable.'"

In spring 1856 he began the first stage of two years of campaigning during which he gave more speeches than he had ever before given in such a contained time, perhaps more than he had given in his lifetime. After the June 1856 nomination of the western explorer John Frémont, a national celebrity with military credentials, as the first Republican presidential candidate, and with a statewide Republican ticket in place, Lincoln campaigned assiduously. He learned, to his surprise, that when his name had been placed before the Philadelphia convention for the vice-presidential nomination as a moderate Westerner, he had received 110 votes, giving him additional prominence as a Republican voice. He seemed to be moving, if at a moderate pace, with "the current of events." Between May 1856 and the election in November, he gave some fifty speeches. As strategy, it meant staying to the center to bring anti–Kansas-Nebraska Whigs into the Republican fold. Fortunately, the Illinois Republicans had no prominent radical voice, as Ohio and New York Republicans had. Lincoln stuck to his middle ground, emphasizing that while slavery was unjust and abominable, its eradication could be only gradual.

If he thought, though, that he could escape the charge that he was an abolitionist and the Republicans a sectional party, he soon found he was mistaken. The Democratic newspapers in Illinois contributed the kind of vituperative rhetoric that Lincoln had pledged not to use. He did "not propose to question the patriotism, or assail the motives of any man, or class of men," he had promised his Peoria audience, but to confine himself "to the naked merits of the question." His opponents called Lincoln's exposition of what he believed to be the historical fact about American slavery corrupt hyperbole and political dishonesty. He soon had a reputation among Illinois Democrats as the ablest "black Republican," part insult, part praise. The anti-Republican *Illinois State Register* recast the language in which Lincoln expressed his fear that the slavery controversy would result in the dissolution of the Union into language close enough to Lincoln's to convey the uninflected substance but changed enough to cast it as a threat rather than a worrisome extension of the logic of the situation. Not only did Lincoln believe, the *Register* claimed, that there could be "no Union with slavery" but that "agitation would be ceaseless until it shall be swept away . . . the mode of its eradication he left to inference from his own antecedents and those of the ruling spirits of black-republicanism— Garrison, Greeley, Seward, Sumner, and others of that genus."

No matter how forcefully he stressed that his only political aim was to prevent extension, the logic of his underlying abomination of slavery was rephrased as radical opposition to the existence of slavery anywhere. Hence his attempt to distinguish himself from radical Republican abolitionists was presented as deceitful campaign rhetoric. Behind it, many believed, was a commitment to abolish slavery by whatever tactics necessary—by congressional votes, by constitutional mandate, by fomenting slave rebellions, or by military force, if necessary. The company that he kept made Lincoln's denials suspect. In reporting on a speech he delivered in late August 1856, the *Register* summarized its view of "that great high-priest of abolitionism" who had raved and ranted on the platform until, in the face of an unresponsive audience, he "became disgusted at his own impudence. And here quietly vanished away the *post mortem* candidate for the vice presidency of the abolition political cock-boat, the depot master of the underground railroad, the great Abram Lincoln. He left no traces of his appearance, and has now 'gone to be seen no more.'"

The invective emphasized differences that no use of language or reason could bridge. Lincoln had a vested interest in not acknowledging this to his audiences. After all, he had faith in language and reason; he had a new political party to rally; and he had to prepare the ground for the 1858 senatorial campaign. In addition, the price of acknowledgment would be to decrease the chance that he and his colleagues could persuade the opposition to return to the pre–Kansas-Nebraska status quo. Since Lincoln's operative assumption was that in a democracy public opinion shapes decision-making, the political challenge was to convince the majority. Though he hoped for the resolution of the ballot box, he also recognized that the ballot box might not be the final determinant.

The 1856 election probably would not favor the Republican presidential candidate anyway. Three candidates vied for the Northern vote: Millard Fillmore, the former president whom Lincoln had supported as Taylor's running mate in 1848 and who was now the Know-Nothing Party nominee; James Buchanan, the pro-Southern Pennsylvanian who had been President Polk's secretary of state, now the Democratic Party nominee; and John C. Frémont, whom the Republicans had nominated. Fillmore could take enough Northern votes, particularly from conservative ex-Whigs and those hostile to immigrants and Catholics, to block Fremont, whose constituency was exclusively Northern. Buchanan could expect the votes of most Southern Democrats and those Northern Democrats who had not become Republicans because of their support of Kansas-Nebraska. The *Illinois State Register* had good reason to be confident that "the political death-knell of John C. Fremont" would ring "next November." Savvy, realistic Republicans such as Lincoln realized that the election provided the opportunity to lay the ideological and electoral groundwork for 1860. That view was confirmed when the combined votes of Fillmore and Fremont exceeded those of Buchanan. If Fremont had gotten Fillmore's votes, he would have been elected.

Could the Union survive the election of a Republican president, Fillmore asked during the campaign. "His charge," Lincoln responded in July 1856, "is that if we elect a President and Vice President both from the Free States, it will dissolve the Union. This is open folly." Those who claimed that anti–Kansas-Nebraska Northerners encouraged the breakup of the Union by attempting to force on the South conditions it could not accept were themselves the culprits. "We, the majority, would not strive to dissolve the Union; and if any attempt is made it must be by you, who so loudly stigmatize us as disunionists. But the Union, in any event, won't be dissolved. We don't want to dissolve it, and if you attempt it, *we won't let you*." The federal government would keep it together by force. "With the purse and sword, the army and navy and treasury in our hands and at our command, you *couldn't do it*. This Government would be very weak, indeed, if a majority, with a disciplined army and navy, and a well-filled treasury, could not preserve itself, when attacked by an unarmed, un-disciplined, unorganized minority. All this talk about dissolution of the Union is humbug—nothing but folly. *We* won't dissolve the Union, and *you* SHAN'T."

In this bellicose response to the charge that the Republicans were sectionalists whose election would destroy the Union, Lincoln struck a note inconsistent with his intent to mold public opinion by sound argument and calm reason. If the Union was in danger, who was threatening it? he challenged the Buchanan Democrats. "A majority will never dissolve the Union. Can a minority do it?" Unwarrantedly and against his own historical knowledge, Lincoln implied that it could not. His appeal to physical force as the final arbiter registered the degree of his frustration in dealing with the charge. It resulted partly from the pressure of a political campaign in which he regularly attempted to turn the argument. But the charge from the opposition had enough presumptive truth in it to be a potent political accusation against his party and surely one to be used against him in his senatorial campaign in 1858. His evocation of the iron fist expressed his unhappy awareness that the power of fact and reason might be insufficient. He did make explicitly clear what only the most obtuse could not have seen—that a Republican administration would use force, if necessary, to prevent secession and perpetuate the Union. During the next five years, he would never say this again quite as explicitly, mostly because, given Southern machismo, it was dangerously counterproductive, and perhaps also because, though it indulged his talent for eviscerating sharpness, he tactically disavowed the iron fist for public discourse.

The issue, though, would not go away. The "ablest black Republican" needed to find a less threatening way to assure Illinois voters, without undercutting the principles of his antislavery position, that he and his party would not use force to eliminate slavery. But if there "could be no Union with slavery," as the anti-Republican *Illinois State Register* reported Lincoln saying in June 1856, every argument that he made opposing the extension of slavery could reasonably be seen as a coded statement that the Republican Party would fulfill the most precipitate demands of the antislavery coalition. Even if the *Register* had not slanted a nuanced state-ment by Lincoln into a reductive paraphrase, his point still would have been seen that way. Every avowal that he opposed only slavery's extension increased his opponents' conviction that this could not possibly be true. Southern and Southern-sympathizing views found the non-extension ar-gument inherently deceitful. Lincoln was vulnerable to the charge. With those who thought as he did, he was persuasive and confirmatory. With those who did not, he was inevitably unsuccessful. That, in the end, the determination of the issue might be made by the sword he rationally un-derstood as early as 1856. But emotionally he could not accept that it would come to that.

On the occasion of a banquet at the Tremont House in Chicago in De-cember 1856, the three hundred assembled Illinois Republicans, having elected a governor and a near majority of state legislators, expressed in a toast their uneasy confidence that the South would not dare leave the Union: "THE UNION—the North will maintain it—the South will not depart therefrom." Lincoln gave the main response. He emphasized electoral persuasion, the search for a majority: "Our government rests in public opinion. Whoever can change public opinion, can change the government. . . . Public opinion . . . always has a *'central idea.'*. . . That 'central idea' in our political public opinion, at the beginning was, and until recently has continued to be, 'the equality of men.'" To those who would not join in the forthcoming Republican electoral majority,

> can we not come together, for the future. Let every one who really believes, and is resolved, that free society is not, *and shall not be*, a failure, and who can conscientiously declare that in the past contest he has done only what he thought best . . . let bygones be bygones. Let past differences, as nothing be; and with steady eye on the real issue, let us inaugurate the good old "central ideas" of the Republic. We *can* do it. The human heart *is* with us—God is with us . . . to renew the broader, better declaration [than the equality of states and the equality of citizens] . . . that "all *men* are created equal."

It was a stirring speech, enriched by the Shakespearean resonance of "let past differences, as nothing be," its plea for unity designed to invigorate Republicans and bring Fillmore ex-Whigs and Know-Nothings into the fold. And, still, between the lines was the threat of the toast.

It seemed likely to Lincoln that the Supreme Court and the administration were conspiring to protect and extend slavery, and that Chief Justice Taney's Southern-dominated Court would soon decide against a widely publicized suit on behalf of Dred Scott, a black man who claimed that he had been made free by being taken to reside in a free state. As usual, Lincoln searched for a metaphor or an analogy, something anecdotal and specific, whose language would be drawn from daily life, to make this point:

> We can not absolutely *know* that all these exact adaptations are the result of preconcert. But when we see a lot of framed timbers, different portions of which we know have been gotten out at different times and places and by different workmen—Stephen [Douglas], Franklin [Pierce], Roger [Taney] and James [Buchanan], for instance—and when we see these timbers joined together, and see they exactly make the frame of a house

or a mill, all the tenons and mortices exactly fitting, and all the lengths and proportions of the different pieces exactly adapted to their respective places, and not a piece too many or too few . . . or, if a single piece be lacking, we can see the place in the frame exactly fitted and prepared to yet bring such piece in—in *such* a case, we find it impossible to not *believe* that Stephen and Franklin and Roger and James all understood one another from the beginning, and all worked upon a common *plan* or *draft* drawn up before the first lick was struck.

If he was to suffer from the plausible accusation that he and other "black Republicans," if elected to national office, would make slavery illegal everywhere, then it would be best to accept the logic of the Southern argument that opposition to "extension" was actually opposition to the existence of slavery by going on the attack, by turning the tables. The proslavery forces, he argued, with the Court and the administration behind them, were actively implementing the logic of their position: slavery and the international slave trade should be legal everywhere. If that were the intention, which for the sake of argument Lincoln believed it plausible to maintain, then he could very well again make the point, in the same language he had used in March 1843, again paraphrasing Matthew 12.25, "'A house divided against itself cannot stand,'" followed by the most quoted line from the speech: "I believe this government cannot endure, permanently half *slave* and half *free*." It would be either all one or the other. The activities of the proslavery forces made that inevitable. The implications of the likely *Dred Scott* decision made a more sophisticated version of the earlier blunt coercion threat well worth making now, especially if he could make the case in the language of rational argument rather than of inflammatory threat.

The occasion on which he chose to make this point so emphatically that it would attract attention was his acceptance of the Republican nomination for the United States Senate in Springfield in June 1858, in a speech that, in historical retrospect, was also the start of the 1860 presidential campaign. It could only have been made by a man who knew that he and his party would never be elevated to office by Southern votes. It concentrated on the one issue that made a Republican victory possible. His advisors, to whom he read the speech before delivering it at the state convention, worried that the Democrats would claim that at last the Illinois Republicans had admitted their intent to eradicate slavery everywhere. Despite Lincoln's explanatory gloss thereafter that he and the Republicans would never take action to initiate eradication, the anti-Republican forces had good reason to be incredulous. The Kansas-Nebraska "agitation . . . *will* not cease," Lincoln predicted, "until a *crisis* shall have been reached, and passed." Given his speeches of 1855–1856, it would be reasonable to infer that this "crisis" might very well require physical coercion.

A rigorously crafted and compact composition, the speech was an argumentative essay whose intent was to raise the ante, to close rather than open the door of compromise. Unlike the foundation speech that had served him well between 1854 and 1858, this address was brief. Not a word is out of place or excessive. The structure is simple and tightly organic. Divided into three parts, the speech begins with a proem, or preliminary discourse, proceeds to the descriptive and evidentiary argument, and concludes with a statement of mission. Its memorable segment, the proem, is predictive, the restrained prophetic voice proclaiming a future that has to be. The details of the historical process that will result in the triumph of one or the other are reserved for the evidentiary argument. "I do not expect the Union to be *dissolved*—I do not expect the house to *fall*—but I *do* expect it will cease to be divided. It will become either *all* one thing, or *all* the other. Either the *opponents* of slavery, will arrest the further spread of it, and place it where the public mind shall rest in the belief that it is in the course of ultimate extinction; or its *advocates* will push it forward, till it shall become alike lawful in *all* the States, *old* as well as *new—North* as well as *South*." The two cultures cannot coexist indefinitely as distinct cultures.

The proem and the evidentiary argument are effectively bridged by the question "Have we no *tendency* to the latter condition?" Is there indeed reason to believe that a proslavery conspiracy is in progress? Conspiracy rivets the imagination, rational as well as paranoid. Lincoln's account portrays how formidable are the wiles of the proslavery enemy, how devious its plan to make slavery universal. In the body of the composition, the masterful storyteller weaves together the strands of the narrative: "Let any one who doubts, carefully contemplate that now almost complete legal combination—piece of *machinery*, so to speak—compounded of the Nebraska doctrine, and the Dred Scott decision." The narrative's factual accuracy, he grants, is unverifiable. Still, it compels belief, though "we can not absolutely *know* that all these exact adaptations" result from a conspiracy.

Speaking to the Republican faithful, he knew his account had the power to inspire those who desired to visualize themselves as moving with "the current of events." His words had irresistible psychological and mythic cogency. Connecting the dots, his expository strategy made clear the theme of the narrative. What the country can expect in the future, he posits as the story's climax, is that a combination of malleable public opinion and the next Supreme Court decision, extrapolating from *Dred Scott* that "the Constitution . . . does not permit a *state* to exclude slavery from its limits," will result in slavery "being alike lawful in all the States. . . . Welcome or unwelcome, such decision *is* probably coming, and will soon be upon us, unless the power of the present political dynasty shall be met and overthrown."

It is implicit in the logic of Lincoln's evidentiary narrative that it transition into a statement of the Republican mission, which is the eventual defeat of the conspirators' plot. "To meet and overthrow the power of that dynasty, is the work now before all those who would prevent that consummation. That is *what* we have to do. But *how* can we best do it?" He had two answers. The first targeted a subsidiary conspiracy related to his own candidacy for the Senate. It drew on one of the standard tropes of conspiracy theory, the notion that there is a devil in the parlor, a Judas, or more than one, in the camp of the righteous, whispering into the ears of the susceptible that the Republicans ought to support Douglas as "the aptest instrument" to defeat the Taney-Buchanan conspiracy.

There was indeed substance behind Lincoln's charge. Various Eastern Republicans, led by Horace Greeley, had been advocating Douglas's merits and the possibility of bringing him into the Republican camp. The expendable Lincoln would once more be out in the cold. He again found in the Bible his aptest metaphor for communicating vividly the core of his opposition, this time in Ecclesiastes 9:4: "They remind us that *he* is a very *great man* and that the largest of *us* are very small ones. Let this be granted. But 'a *living* dog is better than a *dead lion*.' Judge Douglas, if not a *dead* lion for *this work*, is at least a *caged* and *toothless* one. How can he oppose the advances of slavery? He don't *care* anything about it. His avowed *mission is impressing* the 'public heart' to *care* nothing about it." If Douglas should indeed have a change of heart and principle, Lincoln would place no obstacle to his becoming the Republican standard-bearer. "But clearly, he is not *now* with us—he does not *pretend* to be—he does not *promise* to *ever* be."

That the pro-Douglas activity within the Republican Party had the potential to damage Lincoln's own candidacy or, at worst, make it impossible, he well knew. What his party needed to do to block the pro-Southern conspiracy, he argued, was, first, to reject Douglas, and second, to elect Lincoln, and by so doing energize itself throughout the nation to grasp power by itself becoming a force of nature, "sharing," in Emerson's words, " the nature of the world." The party "that is parallel with the laws of nature will be in the current of events, and strong with their strength." In Lincoln's words, the party needed to remember that two years before it had "mustered over thirteen hundred thousand strong," his metaphor now turning to the military sphere, as if revitalizing the connection between moral fervor and physical force.

With his linguistic template derived from models like Henry V rallying his troops at Agincourt, Lincoln emulated the distinctive intensity of Shakespearean language. His italicized emphasis of particular words gives the passage the feel of soliloquy, the best of literary English from Shakespearean oration to Tennyson's "Ulysses."

> We did this under the single impulse of resistance to a common danger, with every external circumstance against us. Of *strange*, *discordant*, and even *hostile* elements, we gathered from the four winds, and *formed* and fought the battle through, under the constant hot fire of a disciplined, proud, and pampered enemy. Did we brave all *then*, to falter now?— *now*—when that same enemy is *wavering*, dissevered and belligerent? The result is not doubtful. We shall not fail—if we stand firm—we shall not fail. *Wise councils* may *accelerate* or *mistakes* delay it, but sooner or later the victory is *sure* to come.

The syntactical reversal of the sentence that begins "Of *strange*, *discordant*, and even *hostile* elements*, the alliteration of "four," "formed," "fought," and "fire," and the distinctively original use of "discordant" and "dissevered" make this mission statement the most distinctively powerful by any American president.

What became known as the Lincoln-Douglas debates, as well as additional campaign speeches, required most of Lincoln's time and energy between June and November 1858. What he had to say he had said before, with variations to meet the debate exigencies of the moment, with the conspiracy issue added to the moral and historical arguments. The campaign trail allowed little opportunity for considered composition, though he revised and tweaked the verbatim newspaper transcriptions for later publication in a volume that contributed to his increased visibility in national Republican circles. He carried a notebook that contained newspaper accounts of previous speeches and documents from which he might want to quote, such as his Peoria address, some of Douglas's speeches, and the Declaration of Independence. He also kept extensive notes, like the one of late August 1858 that its modern editor has labeled "Fragment: Notes for Speeches." With this notebook, aided by his prodigious memory, he was well prepared for the campaign grind.

No sooner did the language of his "House Divided" speech extend beyond its convention auditors than it began to be closely parsed by friends and enemies. His friends wanted clarification. The opposition would never believe him. The abolitionists within and outside his party had little to no alternative. Still, he wanted to keep old and gain new friends. "I never . . . intended" that the phrases at issue assert or intimate "any power or purpose, to interfere with slavery in the States where it exists." He would "not cavil about language," he told the editor of the Chicago *Daily Democratic Press*. "I declare that whether the clause used by me, will bear such a construction or not, I never intended it. I have declared a thousand times, and now repeat that, in my opinion, neither the General Government, nor any other power outside of the slave states, can constitutionally or rightfully interfere with slaves or slavery where it already exists." The denial had its tactical usefulness as an evasive device, and it did indeed reflect his view. It did not, though, deny or rationalize the iron logic that his "House Divided" speech had highlighted: somehow, through some means or other, slavery would be eradicated in the slave states, which nervous Northerners and proslavery Southerners understandably assumed would result from a constitutional or military crisis. Douglas would soon make variations on this point central to his debate attacks, to which Lincoln's best response was deflection, evasion, and counterattack.

Neither candidate had a series of debates in mind when the campaign began in June 1858. Both expected that they would, as usual, speak on different days in many though not all the same venues, charging and countercharging to the extent that seemed appropriate. With more incentive than Douglas to dramatize the campaign and attract public attention, Lincoln began by attending his opponent's speeches and responding soon afterward, usually the next day. This inevitably had some of the elements of a debate rebuttal. In July, the day after Douglas spoke in Chicago, Lincoln constantly referred to his opponent by name. It was a speech, as most of the debates were to be, not of new ideas but of thrust and counter-thrust, of explanation, clarification, and evasion, and of center stage review of the key issues that had been stated often and widely publicized between 1856 and 1858, including the assurance, to "great applause," that "we have no right to interfere" with slavery in the states where it already exists.

In Springfield late in July 1858 Douglas spoke in the afternoon, Lincoln at night, prefacing his usual points with an assessment of the disadvantage he was at in the election because the most recent legislative apportionment had given the Republicans fewer seats than actual population numbers warranted. An effort to add seats to reflect the population increase in Republican-leaning northern Illinois had been beaten back. Also, there were Democratic holdovers in districts the Republicans had reason to believe they could now carry. "We have some cause to complain," he told his audience, "of the refusal to give us a fair apportionment." It made a Lincoln victory in November even the more unlikely. "Our State ticket," he wrote to Lyman Trumbull, "will be elected without much difficulty. But, with the advantages they have of us, we shall be very hard run to carry the Legislature." Since the Senate election was to be decided by legislative vote, it would be possible for the party of the candidate who would not be elected to have gotten more votes in total than the party of the winning candidate but to have lost the election because his party had not won a majority of legislative seats. The man elected by the legislature would, in that sense, have gotten fewer votes than his opponent.

In a comic "poor me" riff, the theme of which was that we Republicans have only principle and truth on our side, Lincoln made capital of his disadvantage, especially Douglas's fame and his own comparative obscurity:

Senator Douglas is of world wide renown. All the anxious politicians of his party . . . have been looking upon him as certainly, at no distant day, to be the President of the United States. They have seen in his round, jolly, fruitful face, postoffices, landoffices, marshalships, and cabinet appointments, chargeships and foreign missions, bursting and sprouting out in wonderful exuberance ready to be laid hold of by their greedy hands. [Great laughter.] And as they have been gazing upon this attractive picture so long, they cannot, in the little distraction that has taken place in the party, bring themselves to give up the charming hope; but with greedier anxiety they rush about him, sustain him, and give him marches, triumphal entries, and receptions beyond what even in the days of his highest prosperity they could have brought about in his favor. On the contrary nobody has ever expected me to be President. In my poor, lean, lank, face, nobody has ever seen that any cabbages were sprouting out. [Tremendous cheering and laughter.]

What Lincoln had that Douglas lacked was wit, and the skill to use it with calculated restraint. As a language device, it was particularly potent. In two speeches in July, he was at his most buoyantly witty and humorously relaxed. Douglas, he scoffed, was advertised wherever he went by his proprietary slogan "Popular Sovereignty." "It is to be labeled upon the cars in which he travels; put upon the hacks he rides in; to be flaunted upon the arches he passes under, and the banners which wave over him. It is to be dished up in as many varieties as a French cook can produce soups from potatoes . . . the whole thing is the most arrant Quixotism that was ever enacted before a community." Lincoln's description of Douglas's hyperbolic branding alluded by inversion to the contrast between the candidates' physical appearances: Don Quixote resided in Lincoln's own lean, lank face and body, the idealistic knight raising the lance of principle against a low-minded opponent, the stubby peasant-like Douglas.

With no subject profane enough to escape his satire, Lincoln performed as if humor had the power to redeem the profane. The humor continued through August, with one of its most salient thrusts countering the charge that he favored miscegenation. His own dark complexion hovered shadow-like between the lines of the accusation, foreshadowing the later charge that he himself had black blood. If he favored a policy that would lead to black-white amalgamation, how could he not favor miscegenation? "I protest, now and forever, against that counterfeit logic which presumes that because I do not want a negro woman for a slave, I do necessarily want her for a wife. [Laughter and cheers.] My understanding is that I need not have her for either. . . . Why, Judge, if we do not let them get together in the Territories, they won't mix there. [Immense applause.]" His words had a tint of dark humor in a community aware that miscegenation was widespread in the South.

His strategic Christianity made Christian references particularly useful to him. They were sharply at the forefront of his memory and his reading. Apparently, he had that spring supplemented his mental storehouse with a perusal of the entire Bible for a lecture, the first version of which consisted mostly of a list of the inventions referred to in the Old Testament. In late August 1858, in a memorandum to himself which he drew on for later speeches, he framed a response to Douglas's charge that Lincoln advocated disobeying the *Dred Scott* decision. He desired, he explained, not disobedience but revocation through judicial reconsideration or the political process. "I point out to him that Mr. Jefferson and General Jackson were both against him on the binding political authority of Supreme Court decisions. No response. I might as well preach Christianity to a grizzly bear as to preach Jefferson and Jackson to him." That Lincoln's own Christianity had been widely questioned made the thrust cut two ways, though more sharply into Douglas, especially since the humor of the "grizzly bear" comparison to the physical Douglas would have been noticed.

When Douglas used boxing imagery to describe the contest between the two men, Lincoln again found an effective way to reduce his opponent's appearance to a humorous metaphor for a crucial difference between them. Since some auditors had taken Douglas's words as a challenge to an actual physical match, Lincoln used deflationary humor to emphasize that the contest was one of words:

I am informed, that my distinguished friend yesterday became a little excited, nervous, perhaps, [laughter] and he said something about *fighting*, as

though referring to a pugilistic encounter between him and myself. . . .
I am informed, further, that somebody in *his* audience, rather more excited, or nervous, than himself, took off his coat, and offered to take the
job off Judge Douglas' hands, and fight Lincoln himself. Did anybody
here witness that warlike proceeding? [Laughter, and cries of yes.] Well,
I merely desire to say that I shall fight neither Judge Douglas nor his
second. [Great laughter.] I shall not do this for two reasons. . . . In the
first place, a fight would *prove* nothing which is in issue in this contest. It
might establish that Judge Douglas is a more muscular man than myself,
or it might demonstrate that I am a more muscular man than Judge Douglas. But this question is not referred to in the Cincinnati platform, nor in
either of the Springfield platforms. Neither result would prove him right
or me wrong. . . . My second reason for not having a personal encounter
with the Judge is, that I don't believe he wants it himself. [Laughter.] He
and I are about the best friends in the world, and when we get together
he would no more think of fighting me than of fighting his wife.

When Douglas made an appeal for Republican votes because he opposed the Buchanan administration's proslavery Kansas constitution, which
rejected popular sovereignty, Lincoln attacked him with a reworking of
the biblical parable of the repentant sinner. There was no subject sacred
enough to escape Lincoln's humor, and humor had the power to absorb
the sacred into the logic of everyday life. Why does the Judge, he scoffed,
expend his energy arguing against the unarguable view that the Constitution permits a newly formed state to decide such issues "without outside
interference?" Douglas's self-delusion and egomania are so great, Lincoln
scathingly exaggerated, that he does that most un-Christian of things and
thinks himself a God. "Does he expect to stand up in majestic dignity, and
go through his *apotheosis* and become a god, in the maintaining of a principle which neither a man nor a mouse in all God's creation is opposing?"

He says I have a proneness for quoting scripture. If I should do so now,
it occurs that perhaps he places himself somewhat upon the ground of

the parable of the lost sheep which went astray upon the mountains, and when the owner of the hundred sheep found the one that was lost . . . it was said that there was more rejoicing over the one sheep that was lost and had been found, than over the ninety and nine in the fold. [Great cheering, renewed cheering.] The application is made by the Saviour in this parable, thus, "Verily, I say unto you, there is more rejoicing in heaven over one sinner that repenteth, than over ninety and nine just persons that need no repentance." [Cheering.] And now, if the Judge claims the benefit of this parable, *let him repent.* [Vociferous applause.] Let him not come up here and say: I am the only just person; and you are the ninety-nine sinners! *Repentance*, before *forgiveness* is a provision of the Christian system, and on that condition alone will the Republicans grant his forgiveness. [Laughter and cheers.]

The seven debates to which Douglas agreed as the lesser of two evils on condition that his opponent cease trailing him and benefiting from his large audiences began in Ottawa, in northwestern Illinois, at the beginning of the fourth week of August 1858 and concluded in Alton on October 15. Two longtime combatants and friendly political enemies became sustained verbal antagonists. Held outdoors before audiences mostly if not entirely of men, numbering as few as about five thousand and as many as almost twenty thousand, the debates were attended by partisans who came by train from other parts of the state and by the local able-bodied who could stand for three hours in whatever the weather. Exemplifying the best and worst of nineteenth-century political circuses, from rampant drunkenness to sober and serious consideration of moral issues and political interests, the debates' alternating arrangement favored Douglas's skills. Each candidate had an hour to open, an hour and a half to respond, and a half hour for rebuttal. Lincoln, who found his parameters framed by the necessity to repeat what he had said a hundred times before, inevitably fell back on the Peoria speech, its recent variations, and the documents in his notebook. Since the speakers mainly confirmed the base rather than extended the argument, there was little room for originality of idea or language. Though Lincoln managed some brilliant passages, the lengthy debates were repetitive, with each candidate running in the latter stages on rhetorical steam rather than energy and enthusiasm. No paragraph or even sentence was memorable enough to become embedded in the American memory.

Whatever coherence the debates had derived from each speaker's attempt to create and then clarify his competing narrative. Each had an abundance of material at hand that needed to be shaped into a story containing drama, unity, and persuasive power. Each reached for a narrative that would speak to human nature and partisan passions, attempting to instill in his audience an inclination to frame the issues in terms favorable to his interests. Their tactics converged: Each recognized the attraction of the conspiracy narrative as a genre, the chill inherent in exposing the attempt of pernicious forces to have their way by deceit and deception. Each grasped that human nature, at least in Western culture, would always be drawn to the explanatory narrative that made sense out of confusion.

The story line that gave Douglas's narrative coherence was simple: The Republican Party had come into existence to attain power by dividing Democrats and creating a coalition of sectional opportunists without regard to the welfare of the country as a whole; Lincoln, an ambitious and duplicitous politician, had been the chief plotter in Illinois, his platform constructed to elevate him to high office rather than advance principles; and Lincoln and Lyman Trumbull had engaged in a series of secret agreements in an effort to pull the abolitionist wool over the voters' eyes. To justify themselves, they played the superior-than-thou antislavery moral card, a poor and improper excuse for self-serving and divisive policies. Lincoln tailored his moral message to suit different constituencies in different parts of the state. Behind it all was the lust for power.

Lincoln's competing narrative began with historical background: the origin of slavery; its importation to the colonies; the practical obstacles to its elimination at the time of the country's creation; the twists and turns of the history of slavery between 1776 and 1850; and the views of the various Founding Fathers and the next generation from Thomas Jefferson to Henry Clay. The next stage began in 1854, with the passage of the Kansas-Nebraska Act, which exposed the long-standing cabal between proslavery Southerners and Northern collaborators to implement their expansionist ideology—the United States would extend from the Atlantic to the Pacific and southward to encompass Cuba, the Caribbean, and even much of South America. "Popular Sovereignty" would make the new territories slave-friendly, at least to the extent that territories could vote not to exclude slavery. Once slavery was in place, it would be difficult if not impossible for newly formed states to make it illegal. The plot darkened in 1857 when Douglas, Buchanan, and Taney conspired to produce the *Dred Scott* decision. Its purpose was to make the United States a nation in which slavery was permitted everywhere by Supreme Court decree, without regard to the wishes of individual states, and eventually to allow the revival of the importation of slaves. The American republic would be transformed into an immense empire. Slavery would be one of its basic constituents.

Douglas's narrative required that an examination of Lincoln's career reveal that he had been and continued to be driven by political ambition, not principle, a claim that Lincoln attempted to discharge by admitting that he was not untouched by ambition but that he had never spoken or acted with ambition as his primary motive. Douglas pointed to the agreement among the Illinois Whigs to alternate running for office in order to maximize their chances of success, claiming that Lincoln's withdrawal from the Senate race in 1855 in favor of Trumbull was part of a plot in which Trumbull, hitherto a Democrat, agreed to support Lincoln against Douglas in 1858. Thus Lincoln and his colleagues were unprincipled pursuers of political power. And how could any responsible Unionist support abolition or even gradual emancipation, given the price that would have to be paid, except as a cynical ploy for personal and political advancement? Douglas's narrative also took force from his claim that Lincoln's tendency to support American expansion only selectively, expressed in his opposition to the Mexican War, revealed that he was not fully committed to the country's manifest destiny. "I tell you to increase, to multiply, to expand, is the law of this nation's existence. You cannot limit this great country by mere boundary lines, saying thus far thou must go and no further." The Republicans, Douglas concluded, were too tolerant of America's competitor for power in the new world, Great Britain, and Lincoln's divisive ideology existed only to serve personal ambition.

Lincoln's narrative required that he take the moral high ground. He had long been seeking the opportunity simultaneously to do that and to win elections. The requirements of his narrative now allowed him to give priority to both. For the first time he had his fullest charge of the power that came from being strong with "the current of events." The conjunction of self-identity and ideology on the one hand, and external events on the other, enabled him to become a force of nature in Emerson's sense. When he reached, as he did in his Chicago speech in July 1858, for an image to dramatize the continuity of liberty and to connect the men who had proclaimed that "all men are created equal" with himself and his contemporaries, he found it in the new language of electricity, "the electric cord . . . that links the hearts of patriotic and liberty-loving men together . . . as long as the love of freedom exists in the minds of men throughout the world." As the debates proceeded, he rewrote Douglas's narrative-in-progress, arguing that the moral aspect of the slavery issue should be the controlling standard.

Each made his claim based, in the context, on first or foundational principles. Lincoln reworked the Jeffersonian claim that "all men are created equal"; Douglas, the populist credo that the Constitution requires, as a sacred principle, that each state have the right to decide every issue by popular vote and that nature's God has made the white race superior to the black. "It does not become Mr. Lincoln, or anybody else, to tell the people of Kentucky that they have no consciences—that they are living in a state of iniquity, and that they are cherishing an institution to their bosoms in violation of the law of God. . . . 'Judge not, lest ye be judged,'" he preached in the sixth debate, at Quincy. In Douglas's view the Constitution required that the powers reserved to the states continue to be reserved to them. Nothing about the slavery issue transcended that principle. The moral issue was irrelevant to the practical problem at hand. And he did not think it sensible or wise to run the ship of state onto the rocks by pursuing equality for an inferior race.

Lincoln, in fact, agreed, making his argument against the *Dred Scott* decision on the basis of its unconstitutional abrogation of states' rights. His only aim, he constantly repeated, was to reaffirm that territories, unlike states, do not have the right to make a proslavery or an antislavery decision. The difference between his and Douglas's approach "springs from a sentiment in the mind, and that sentiment is this: on the one part it looks upon the institution of slavery as being wrong, and, on the part of another class, it does not look upon it as wrong." He did not favor granting voting or any other political rights to Negroes. But "if we cannot give freedom to every creature, let us do nothing that will impose slavery upon any other creature."

Naturally, the competing conspiracy narratives were factually incompatible, but both were powerful explanatory mechanisms. They drove the political emotions and ideological convictions of the voters. Like many incompatible narratives, they readily coexisted, occupying the same national and historical space, part of a dialectic directing passions and framing ideologies. They were energizing stories, both for leaders and followers. Though neither man won the debates by any obvious evaluative standard, the election was to be a Douglas victory, since the Democrats maintained their majority in the legislature. That the debates occurred at all resulted from Douglas's political weakness, his need to reposition himself in his own party after alienating pro-administration Democrats. What had been a shrewd strategy to keep the Union together and advance Douglas's presidential prospects was in the process of becoming moot and even disadvantageous. Popular sovereignty came increasingly under attack from Republicans and from proslavery Democrats. To become president, Douglas needed Southern votes. Republican power in the North was growing, its demographics increasingly favorable. It was clear the tide was turning toward them.

* * *

If, under the pressure of intense campaigning between 1856 and 1858, Lincoln had little time for the creation of much more than variations on his foundation speech and depended heavily on what he had already written, he still engaged occasionally with pen and paper in an attempt to work out his ideas and find even better ways to express them. Away from home, he wrote and read at odd hours, often late at night in inns frequented by his legal and political colleagues. In Springfield, the division of labor and time was much the same. At his expanded but modest residence at the corner of Eighth and Jackson, his life focused on domestic survival and on his sons, the eldest soon to begin his elevation into the gentry via Philips Exeter and Harvard, eager to escape a demanding mother and an indulgent father. Lincoln found his own escape routes—absence on the road and withdrawal at home. When pushed, his taciturn patience never seemed to fail. At times, there was merriment in the parlor and an occasional party, when Mary decided that she needed to entertain to support and advance their rise in the world. And despite the tensions and volatile flare-ups, it remained an intimately loyal relationship.

Mary gave no indication that she appreciated her husband's literary talent and may have resented his constant reading. She expressed her opinion about political ideas in their private conversations, but hardly in terms that commanded his serious attention. More interested in people and position than ideas, she allowed her views on Kansas-Nebraska to be inflected by her Lexington background, her temperamental noblesse oblige, and her criticism of her husband's rivals as obstacles to advancement rather than as representatives of policy differences. Her paranoid resentments dominated her political consciousness. It is also unlikely that slavery raised a moral issue for her. Her Kentucky family's Whig elitism and her Know-Nothing dislike of foreigners distanced her from moderate Republican principles. That she ever complimented her husband on an effective turn of phrase or composition or made the connection between his gift for language and his political advancement seems unlikely. There are no references in her letters to his written and spoken words, as if she regarded his as simply another political voice, though the one to which she had hitched her star. Later, some of his colleagues concluded, as did Joshua Speed, that "when gems of American literature come to be selected from great Authors as many will be selected from Lincolns speeches as from any American author." Mary, though, seemed unresponsive to this aspect of her husband's talent.

Since Lincoln was unable to conceive of political discourse as separate from the written word, his compositional energy was directed mostly by political ideas and exigencies. At some periods the pressure in this regard was greater than at others; it was at one of its apogees between 1854 and 1858. Only a few fragments of the many handwritten elucidations and fine-tunings of his arguments and advocacies survived the loss of his campaign notebook. Fragments on sectionalism, on the struggle against slavery, on the *Dred Scott* decision, and notes for particular speeches survived accidentally in manuscripts. Others, it's reasonable to surmise, were haphazardly discarded or destroyed. Even some of the 1858 debate speeches might have been lost when entire newspaper files were discarded or lost to fire if Lincoln, after the last debate, had not collected them into a scrapbook.

In April 1858, accepting an invitation to address the Bloomington Young Men's Association, he decided on a subject, "Discoveries and Inventions," which had nothing directly to do with politics, an exemplification of the strength of his residual literary energy. The subject's distance from contentious topics was part of its attraction. The lecture, though, resonates with a basic tenet of Lincoln's political philosophy: material and cultural progress through free labor and inventive genius. Emulating the essayists of his early reading and his most prominent American contemporary, he started his own essay with an abruptly effective metaphor, evoking the widespread mid-nineteenth-century fascination with the silver and gold mines of the west. Like Emerson, he had the gift of aphoristic vividness in arranging linguistic tropes into effective combinations and shifting viewpoints:

All creation is a mine, and every man, a miner.

The whole earth, and all *within* it, *upon* it, and *round about* it, including *himself*, in his physical, moral, and intellectual nature, and his susceptibilities, are the infinitely various 'leads' from which, man, from the first, was to dig out his destiny.

In the beginning, the mine was unopened, and the miner stood *naked*, and *knowledgeless*, upon it.

The earth and its possibilities are a vast mine and human beings the miners who can work it for their mutual improvement:

Fishes, birds, beasts, and creeping things, are not miners, but *feeders* and *lodgers*, merely. Beavers build houses; but they build them in nowise differently, or better now, than they did, five thousand years ago. Ants, and honey-bees, provide food for winter; but just in the *same way* they did, when Solomon referred the sluggard to them as patterns of prudence.

Man is not the only animal who labors; but he is the only one who *improves* his workmanship. This improvement, he effects by *Discoveries*, and *Inventions*. . . .

What distinguishes human beings in regard to the creation of a civilization, Lincoln emphasizes, is their capacity to apply cerebral power to observation and remediation, to invent techniques and devices that raise the quality of human life. Theological distinctions are irrelevant. If God is the originator, he has no role to play, or presence to make felt, in the implementation. The nineteenth-century American can-do engineering aesthetic that proclaims confidence in man's capacity to make improvements is at the heart of Lincoln's human self-definition. That vision includes the national scale of Henry Clay's American plan and the local scale of Thomas Jefferson's small craft improvements at Monticello. It implies the application of craft and technology, from individual artisanship to large-scale agricultural and industrial production, to improve the quality of life for large numbers of people.

Unfinished or only partially extant, the essay proceeds to use the biblical record, treating it as quasi-history, as the source for evidence of how and when man's inventive capacity first manifested itself. The skein of the essay becomes a listing, with biblical citations, of the discovery of clothes (Adam and Eve), weaving (Abraham), boat building (Noah), the wheel and transportation (Joseph), water power, agriculture, the use of camels and horses, the harnessing of the powers of nature, especially the wind for windmills—all ancient discoveries and inventions mentioned in the Bible. It concludes with a short mention of the discovery of steam power for mechanical use, "unquestionably a modern invention." The truncated ending gives the impression that Lincoln had run out of intellectual steam. In terms of interest and ideas, the essay dries up quickly. The baldly enumerative structure is flat; the language has the mechanical matter-of-factness of a legal brief. For those aware of trends in nineteenth-century historical methodology, the Bible as a history of inventions would have seemed the wrong text for a subject that required extra-biblical documentation, mainly from the archaeological record.

Aware that he had gone off in a wrong direction, he gave it a second try in early 1859, with an expansion of scope and depth as well as a change of focus, a revision that in effect created a new essay on the same subject. It is one of his most brilliant and revealing compositions. Between April 1858 and February 1859, despite a demanding legal and political career, he found time to compose an intellectually sharp, philosophically engaging essay, charged with connections between the past and present that had personal resonance for him as well as contemporary cultural significance. It emphasizes the invention that he cared most strongly about and believed should matter passionately to everyone, especially in a modern democracy: "*Writing*—the art of communicating thoughts to the mind, through the eye," which, he had no doubt, "is the great invention of the world." He found time to read it as a lecture on February 11 to the Phi Alpha Society of Illinois College at Jacksonville. He gave it again in Decatur, and then to the Springfield Library Association before declining invitations that well might have resulted in an extensive lecture tour.

In the new essay, the Bible plays a minimal role, an occasional reference for intellectual positioning and universalizing inclusion. Rather than providing a semi-comprehensive list of important inventions, the essay has a contemporary thesis and selective focus, and its searches for the underlying frame of mind and the tools of intellectual conveyance that make possible any particular invention, past and future. The metaphor of the "mine" makes a subordinate appearance, still effective but neither controlling nor the main focus. It is adapted to the new emphasis, which is the mind of man, particularly its initial primary invention, its invention of "the art of invention," and the inventions and discoveries that follow thereafter. The human brain and its rational and creative faculties, Lincoln maintains, are the source of the most meaningful wealth; the treasures of most value to humankind come from the interaction between human capacities and the observable natural world. "There are more mines above the Earth's surface than below it. All nature—the whole world, material, moral, and intellectual,—is a mine. . . . Now, it was the destined work of Adam's race to develope, by discoveries, inventions, and improvements, the hidden treasures of this mine." To do that, mankind first needed to develop "the art of invention," based on "the *habit* of observation and reflection," and then the key tools, speech and writing, by which to communicate and exchange ideas.

The initial framework of the essay focuses on the contrast between contemporary "Young America" and "Old Fogy," a semi-humorous, semi-satiric play on a standard nineteenth-century essayistic trope in which old ways of thinking are compared to new ones by personifying each, a variant on the popular topic of "the spirit of the age." "We have all heard of Young America," the essay begins. "He is the most *current* youth of the age. Some think him conceited, and arrogant; but has he not reason to entertain a rather extensive opinion of himself?" Young America, Lincoln says, gets cotton from England, linen from Ireland, wool from Spain, furs from the Arctic, his food from various countries, his whale oil from the Pacific, his diamonds from Brazil, his cigars from Havana.

He has a global reach, and he reaches always for more. He is the "unques-
tioned inventor of *Manifest Destiny*."

> He owns a large part of the world, by right of possessing it; and all the
> rest by right of *wanting* it, and *intending* to have it. As Plato had for the
> immortality of the soul, so Young America has "a pleasing hope—a fond
> desire—a longing after" territory. He has a great passion—a perfect
> rage—for the *"new"*. . . . He is a great friend of humanity; and his desire
> for land is not selfish, but merely an impulse to extend the area of free-
> dom. He is very anxious to fight for the liberation of enslaved nations
> and colonies, provided, always, they *have* land, and have *not* any liking
> for his interference. As to those who have no land, and would be glad of
> help from any quarter, he considers *they* can afford to wait a few hundred
> years longer. . . . His horror is for all that is old, particularly "Old Fogy";
> and if there be anything old which he can endure, it is only old whiskey
> and old tobacco.

Undoubtedly an expansionist Democrat, "Young America" fails to appreciate that Western civilization is the cumulative product of what "Old
Fogies" of the past have discovered, invented, and improved.

Lincoln was less interested in making political points than in epito-
mizing a particular political philosophy, even if the reference to "whiskey and tobacco" might have brought to mind Stephen Douglas, and "Old
Fogy" the now widely used "Old Abe." The satiric criticism is prelude to
the essay's main point: human progress is not the result of any inherent
superiority of human beings in the present to those in the past but of the
gradual accumulation, through observation, reflection, and experiment,
of discoveries, inventions, and improvements that have been transmit-
ted from one generation to another by the key tool of Western development: the art of writing. Was the inventor of the steam engine "wiser or
more ingenious," Lincoln asks, "than those who had gone before him?
Not at all." The intellectual processes that made modern America possible began to be developed in ancient times with the invention of "the art

of invention." And the benefits of that invention would have been comparatively limited if not for the development of the two essential tools of transmission without which our civilization would not exist: speech and writing.

While speech was and is essential, it is writing, Lincoln emphasized, which is the supreme artifact of human genius. "Speech alone, valuable as it ever has been, and is, has not advanced the condition of the world much." This is a noteworthy hierarchy of values for a man whose achievement was seen, during his lifetime and to some extent thereafter, to be based on his oratory rather than on the writing process that created the words he spoke. And in the historical retrospect, Lincoln's own analysis gets at the heart of why the words of Henry Clay, his "beau ideal" of a statesman and an orator, have not survived the occasions of their articulation while his own have:

> *Writing*—the art of communicating thoughts to the mind, through the eye—is the great invention of the world. Great in the astonishing range of analysis and combination which necessarily underlies the most crude and general conception of it—great, very great in enabling us to converse with the dead, the absent, and the unborn, at all distances of time and of space; and great, not only in its direct benefits, but greatest help, to all other inventions. . . . Its utility may be conceived, by the reflection, that, to *it* we owe everything which distinguishes us from savages. Take it from us, and the Bible, all history, all science, all government, all commerce, and nearly all social intercourse go with it.

The reach of writing, Lincoln argues, was extended by three additional inventions and discoveries: the art of printing, which made writing widely available; "the introduction of Patent-laws," which "added the fuel of *interest* to the *fire* of genius"; and "the discovery of America," which gave new impetus to discoveries and inventions.

His argument takes its autobiographical force from his career as a lawyer and politician. As an autodidact, he was enabled to rise in the world by the written word that printing made widely available. Without the written word, few aspects of the life he valued would have been possible for a poor farmer-carpenter's son. Concerned, as a lawyer, with legal structures that protected property and provided the incentive inherent in ownership, he believed patent laws to be essential to securing the relationship among ideas, language, and communication. Legal title, whether to land or to an invention, promotes individual labor and new ideas, creates wealth and stability, and spreads civilization through the language of contracts. And of equal importance, America, he believed, provided a fresh context in which to break away from old habits of mind into a new freedom of thought and investigation. "A new country is most favorable—almost necessary—to the immancipation of thought, and the consequent advancement of civilization and the arts." Deeply committed to that vision, he valued immensely the central role of writing in America's distinctiveness, both in the dissemination of ideas and in the formative texts that he revered.

An anxious but self-confident Lincoln attempted now to apply the fire of his own genius as a writer-speaker to the desperate issues of his world. American democracy required skillful and honest use of the written language. From childhood on, the written word had meant everything to him, an avid reader of literary anthologies, and of Shakespeare, Byron, Burns, and the Bible, creating in his memory a storehouse of heightened language to enrich his mental and emotional life. As a lawyer and politician, he had struggled with the precise use of language to communicate ideas, keenly aware of the potential by venal politicians to corrupt it for self-serving purposes. His service in the state legislature had provided almost daily examples of that. Douglas's speeches, culminating in the 1858 debates, had exemplified linguistic shiftiness, hyperbole, and disregard for the integrity of fact. As a congressman, Lincoln took a stand against the verbal obfuscation used to disguise American aggression against Mexico, and unscrupulous opponents still pursued him with the taint of his Mexican War speeches. It had taken more than ten years for that charge to lose most of its bite. And between 1854 and 1859, his position on the issue that overwhelmed all others had been inseparable from his effort over more than twenty years to find effective, accurate language to express his ideas about a complicated reality that readily lent itself to evasion, self-deceit, and linguistic trickery. Language mattered immensely. And in the possible uses of language, the written word came first.

CHAPTER 8

The Master of Language and the Presidency

1861–1865

When, in February 1859, Lincoln read his expanded essay on discoveries and inventions to an audience at Illinois College, his presence had begun to be charged with a charismatic aura through the power of his language skills and the sincerity of his moral vision. Together, they had brought him into alignment with Emerson's "current of events." His physical presence and colloquial characteristics contributed. It was not a new Lincoln by any means; it was an intensified Lincoln. The debates had given him national exposure for the first time. Like a photograph in the process of becoming fully developed, his public presence had become fuller, sharper, and clearer to those who were motivated to pay attention. That was still mainly a segment of the Republican Party, mostly Illinois friends and loyalists and some in Indiana and Ohio, but also elements within the eastern center of the party in New York, Pennsylvania, and New England eager to hear the party spokesman from the West who had given Douglas a run for his money. He had also found the words to create a discourse that cogently expressed Republican antislavery extension principles. Was he, they wanted to know, endowed—in his own phrase—with "the fire of genius"?

That he was a sophisticated Westerner who carried his learning lightly and mediated shrewdly between ideas and idiomatic casualness put people at ease. His jokes, anecdotes, and analogies made him the center of verbal attention in small groups, private and public. He had antagonized very few of his constituents or fellow politicians. He carried hardly any baggage, both literally and materially. His presence resonated almost tangibly with a folksy Western charisma. If he towered over people, he did not do so in ways that exaggerated his stature or dominated spaces. On the contrary, he had a way of folding and stretching himself when seated that relaxed his body into amusing implausibility. Though his height made him stand out oddly in a crowd, it had a touch of the comic that humanized it. The very short Stephen Douglas used his powerful voice and bombastic rhetoric to expand his stage presence. Lincoln had a way of hunkering down, growing through words rather than voice, though ideas rather than physical presence.

Despite a busy court schedule, Lincoln's philosophical mind and literary inclinations found a productive focus in mid-August 1859 when he received an invitation to speak at the end of September to the Wisconsin State Agricultural Society at its annual fair in Milwaukee. Throughout September, political invitations took him farther than usual from Springfield, delivering up-to-date versions of his foundation speech in Iowa, Indiana, Ohio, and eventually Wisconsin and Kansas. Directed toward rallying Republicans for local and state elections and positioning him for the 1860 campaign, the speeches covered the rhetorical ground he had occupied since 1854, with emphasis on the superior efficiency of Northern free labor to Southern slave labor. The message was specifically political, the tone witty and polemical in regard to the usual issues, especially popular sovereignty and the fear that Republican ascendancy meant Northern suppression of Southern institutions. In mid-September, in Cincinnati, he attempted to discharge that accusation. With autobiographical good humor, he made clear, looking across the river to Kentucky, where he stood on the claim that as a black Republican he favored miscegenation: "We mean to recognise and bear in mind always that you have as good hearts in your bosoms as other people, or as we claim to have, and treat you accordingly. We mean to marry your girls when we have a chance—the white ones I mean—[laughter] and I have the honor to inform you that I once did have a chance in that way."

With his drive to examine basic definitions and values, Lincoln had for some time been thinking about the nature of wealth and the relationship between labor and capital. That issue, usually the concern of political and economic theorists rather than roll-up-your sleeve politicians, would be his subject in Milwaukee. In the first half of September, before his Ohio trip, he found time to write the essay. In Cincinnati he devoted a section of a long political speech to the subject, which he omitted from the printed version, probably having decided to confine his published comments on the economic issue to the less political Milwaukee presentation. Again in the autobiographical mode, he offered himself as an effective example of the superiority of free over slave labor. A hired worker, he argued, does not of necessity have to remain so. In fact,

> the general rule is otherwise. I know it is so, and I will tell you why. . . . I was myself a hired laborer, at twelve dollars per month. . . . A young man finds himself of an age to be dismissed from parental control; he has for his capital nothing save two strong hands that God has given him, a heart willing to labor, and a freedom to choose the mode of his work and the manner of his employer; he has got no soil nor shop, and he avails himself of the opportunity of hiring himself to some man who has capital to pay him a fair day's wages for a fair day's work. . . . He works industriously, he behaves soberly, and the result of a year or two's labor is a surplus capital. Now he buys land on his own hook; he settles, marries, begets sons and daughters, and in course of time he too has enough capital to hire some new beginner.

As handy illustration rather than as self-dramatizing narcissism, Lincoln's own experience, he states, represents the system at its successful best, the hired man who has risen to become simultaneously worker and capitalist. This, he claims, is "the true condition of labor in the world." Ever the realistic student of human nature, no individual, he argues, is chained "throughout life to labor for another . . . unless he be of that confiding and leaning disposition that makes it preferable for him to choose that course, or unless he be a vicious man, who by reason of his vice, is, in some way prevented from improving his condition, or else he be a singularly unfortunate man." These three categories of exception prove the universal rule:

> I hold that if there is any one thing that can be proved to be the will of God by external nature around us, without reference to revelation, it is the proposition that whatever any one man earns with his hands and by the sweat of his brow, he shall enjoy in peace. I say that whereas God Almighty has given every man one mouth to be fed, and one pair of hands adapted to furnish food for that mouth, if anything can be proved to be the will of Heaven, it is proved by this fact, that the mouth is to be fed by those hands, without being interfered with by any other man who has also his mouth to feed and his hands to labor with. I hold if the Almighty had ever made a set of men that should do all of the eating and none of the work, he would have made them with mouths only and no hands, and if he had ever made another class that should do all the work and none of the eating, he would have made them without mouths and with all hands. But inasmuch as he has not chosen to make man in that way, if anything is proved, it is that those hands and mouths are to be co-operative through life and not to be interfered with. That they are to go forth and improve their condition . . . is the inherent right given to mankind directly by the Maker.

Consistent with his lifelong denial of revelation as a source of knowledge, Lincoln's conviction of God's intention on this matter derives only from his observation of material reality. If the argument is strained as rational evidence, it is rhetorically and emotionally powerful, drawing into a single passage his faith in natural law, the self-evident truths expressed in the Declaration of Independence, and in human experience. Lincoln the lawyer-logician certainly knew that nothing was proved by this argument from design, though the dark humor inherent within the image of alternative physiologies carried seductive conviction. But the argument embodies a view of fairness so passionately and deeply held that it is experienced as a belief system, and it allows Lincoln this rare instance in which to claim God as an ally.

Though the Cincinnati speech contained some of Lincoln's most concise, powerfully eloquent writing on the subject, the Milwaukee occasion prompted him to focus explicitly and at greater length on the theoretical aspects of the labor and wealth question. Like his February 1859 essay on "Discoveries and Inventions," the emphasis was only indirectly political, but its controlling trope expressed the values of his Northern constituency, especially its free-soil, antislavery, small business, and entrepreneurial appreciation of individual opportunity. It stated the intellectual and humanistic ground rules from which his political actions were derived.

Labor, rather than capital, he argued, was the source of all wealth. In the creation of wealth, labor came first, whether the labor of the field or factory worker or of the man who worked with his mind. What man makes with his hands and his head creates value and civilization. Consequently, the highest respect should be given not to the accumulation of capital, a worthy and necessary end, but to labor, brains, and creativity. His main argument focuses on the economic sphere, and emphasizes that neither discoveries nor inventions could have become the dominating factors in developing a sophisticated modern culture without the written word. "A capacity, and taste, for reading, gives access to whatever has already been discovered by others. It is the key, or one of the keys, to the already solved problems. . . . It gives a relish, and facility, for successfully pursuing the [yet] unsolved ones." Consequently, "Free Labor insists on universal education." A labor theory of value requires an educated citizenry. It denies impermeable and inflexible class distinctions. It is socially dynamic, not static. Labor produces capital, and the accumulation of capital allows the worker to rise to ownership.

Dividing his essay into two main sections, each with a brief theoretical overview and a hortatory conclusion, Lincoln made use of the standard essay structure learned from his childhood literary anthologies. He first positions and celebrates the fair as a socializing event addressing the innate tendency within human beings to be suspicious of strangers and hostile to outsiders. Agricultural fairs have many uses, he observes. At their highest level of civilizing utility, which sets the context for all their practical uses, they address an age-old universal problem: "They bring us together, and thereby make us better acquainted, and better friends than we otherwise would be." Ever the realist, with no illusions about tribal clannishness amplified into divisive regionalism, he sought the right perspective and tone to describe the tendency within human nature to dehumanize the "stranger."

> From the first appearance of man upon the earth, down to very recent times, the words *'stranger'* and *'enemy'* were *quite* or *almost*, synonymous. Long after civilized nations had defined robbery and murder as high crimes, and had affixed severe punishments to them, when practiced among and upon their own people respectively, it was deemed no offence, but even meritorious, to rob, and murder, and enslave *strangers*, whether as nations or as individuals. Even yet, this has not totally disappeared.

The origin of war and of enslavement resides, he posited, in the innate human tendency to dehumanize those who do not belong to one's own clan, nation, or race. "The man of the highest moral cultivation, in spite of all which abstract principle can do, likes him, whom he *does* know, much better than him whom he does *not* know. To correct the evils, great and small, which spring from want of sympathy, and from positive enmity, among *strangers*, as nations, or as individuals, is one of the highest functions of civilization." Fairs contribute to this process of socialization, to making more pleasant, durable, and strong "the bond of social and political union among us." By implication, and with a distinctive lightness of touch, Lincoln expressed in broad humanistic terms the dark and the bright sides of the human condition. Like other socializing devices, from local markets to national legislatures, from language to law, from psychology to philosophy, state fairs exist, he proposed, to help make strangers into neighbors, to create sympathy between regions and nations, and, by inference, between the North and South. They help transform tribal loyalty into identification with all things human.

If Lincoln was whistling in the dark in regard to American affairs, his optimism resonates with a philosophical sweetness that reflects his abiding hope that realism about human nature and self-awareness about the balance between morality and self-interest will prevail. Universal self-interest made fairs and unions possible. As a holiday from work and strife, the fair provides a time and place for recreation, defined as the opportunity to be liberated from the destructive tensions that interfere with the fullest realization of "inalienable rights . . . life, liberty, and the pursuit of happiness." With that phrase in mind, Lincoln quotes one of his favorite literary alternatives to the Declaration. "If, as [Alexander] Pope declares," he told his audience, quoting *Essay on Man*, "'happiness is our being's end and aim,' our Fairs contribute much to that end and aim, as occasions of recreation—as holidays." True happiness, Lincoln implies, resides in being in consonance with the values that fairs promote, and happiness can best be construed philosophically as promoting the processes and values of civilization, one of whose "highest functions" is to eliminate enmity and promote sympathy "among *strangers*, as nations, or as individuals." Self-interest at its most enlightened, he argued, is always other interest as well.

Aware that his audience of farmers had less tolerance than he for the philosophic overview, he turned from theory to his first practical consideration: What can farmers do to help themselves and their fellow citizens? Since they are the most numerous "it follows that their interest is the largest interest." Since the population of the nation was increasing rapidly, and the amount of arable land was finite, what farmers could best do was increase their yield per acre to produce more food from the same amount of land. "The cost of land is a great item, even in new countries," and small farms, he believed, the most efficient. Scientific agriculture should emphasize producing the largest possible number of bushels per acre. Under any conditions, the more thoroughly a man cultivates his acreage, Lincoln believed, the better he would feel about his work. Human nature dictated this. "Every man is proud of what he does *well*; and no man is proud of what he does *not* do well. With the former, his heart is in his work; and he will do twice as much of it with less fatigue. The latter performs a little imperfectly, looks at it in disgust, turns from it, and imagines himself exceedingly tired. The little he has done, comes to nothing, for want of finishing." Without pride in work, Lincoln concluded, such work gets done poorly or inconclusively. The lesson of *"thorough cultivation,"* he thought, had universal application. He knew himself to be an exemplification of what he preached.

No substantial disagreement existed, he believed, about the value of labor, for "the world is agreed that *labor* is the source from which human wants are mainly supplied." But disagreement did exist about the relationship between hired labor and capital on the one hand and slave labor and capital on the other. All agreed that slave labor precluded the laborer accumulating capital. But the slave owners of the South claimed that the Northern laborer was just as much restricted "to that condition for life" as the slave. Yet, Lincoln argued, even in the slave states "a majority of the whole people of all colors, are neither slaves nor masters," and in the North "the prudent, penniless beginner in the world," as he himself had been, "labors for wages awhile, saves a surplus with which to buy tools or land," works "on his own account . . . and at length hires another new beginner to help him. This, say its advocates, is *free* labor—the just and generous, and prosperous system, which opens the way for all—gives hope to all, and energy, and progress, and improvement of condition to all." By inference, a society in which capital mostly resides in the value of land and slaves, and which manipulates social, economic, and cultural restrictions to discourage non-slave laborers from accumulating capital, by its essence inhibits discoveries, inventions, and improvements. It has no ideological room for the application of technology and science to agriculture. And in the slave economy, labor and education are incompatible. Free labor, though, "insists on universal education." In class-fluid capitalism, both for the individual and for the general welfare, "heads and hands should cooperate as friends."

In the pursuit of happiness, nothing, Lincoln continued, gives as much pleasure as the application of human energy to individual and communal improvement. Returning to the educated farmer as the embodiment of free labor, he lightly echoes Jefferson in evoking the ideal combination of knowledge, inventive energy, and agricultural commitment. "I know of nothing so pleasant to the mind, as the discovery of anything which is at once *new* and *valuable*—nothing which so lightens and sweetens toil, as the hopeful pursuit of such discovery. And how vast, and how varied a field is agriculture, for such discovery. The mind, already trained to thought, in the country school, or higher school, cannot fail to find there an exhaustless source of profitable enjoyment."

Synthesizing the dominant themes of his philosophic and his political-social interests, Lincoln, as a creator of wisdom literature himself, now found a level of literary expressiveness that he had never before fully achieved. He celebrates, with something of the tone of Walt Whitman and anticipating the title of the poet's 1882 volume *Specimen Days*, the beauty and excitement of agricultural plenitude:

> Every blade of grass is a study; and to produce two, where there was but one, is both a profit and a pleasure. And not grass alone; but soils, seeds, and seasons—hedges, ditches, and fences, draining, droughts, and irrigation—plowing, hoeing, and harrowing—reaping, mowing, and threshing—saving crops, pests of crops, diseases of crops, and what will prevent or cure them—implements, utensils, and machines, their relative merits, and [how] to improve them—hogs, horses, and cattle— sheep, goats, and poultry—trees, shrubs, fruits, plants, and flowers— the thousand things of which these are specimens—each a world of study within itself.

Rearranged typographically, the paragraph reveals a free-verse poem of sophisticated triadic phrases, alliteration and assonance, and a delayed

climactic phrase that remembers the first sentence, providing both recognition and unity:

> *Every blade of grass is a study;*
> *And to produce two,*
> *Where there was but one,*
> *Is both a profit and a pleasure.*
> *And not grass alone;*
> *But soils, seeds, and seasons*
> *Hedges, ditches, and fences,*
> *Draining, droughts, and irrigation—*
> *Plowing, hoeing, and harrowing—*
> *Reaping, mowing, and threshing—*
> *Saving crops, pests of crops, diseases of crops,*
> *And what will prevent or cure them—*
> *Implements, utensils, and machines,*
> *Their relative merits,*
> *And [how] to improve them—*
> *Hogs, horses, and cattle—*
> *Sheep, goats, and poultry—*
> *Trees, shrubs, fruits, plants, and flowers—*
> *The thousand things*
> *Of which these are specimens—*
> *Each a world of study within itself.*

It is Lincoln's best poem.

There are such glittering prizes for the labors of the mind and the
body. Inherent, though, within the application of human activity to the
reality of the world, Lincoln concluded, is the need to accept limitations. In the competition, some will be successful and many more will
lose. The winners will need "but little philosophy to take them home in
cheerful spirits." The others should keep in mind that "the vanquished
this year, may be victor the next, in spite of all competition." Life calls

for careful definition of success and failure. It requires, on the one hand, the fullest engagement with effort and, on the other, stoic acceptance of limitation. The wise, he emphasizes, know the source both of chastening rebuke and pleasurable consolation. In the tradition of both Jefferson and Henry Clay, he brought to his stoic engagement with mutability the conviction that the good works of those who labor help to secure a better world for themselves and their posterity. "It is said," he concluded, in an admirable combination of realism and optimism, that

> an Eastern monarch once charged his wise men to invent him a sentence, to be ever in view, and which should be true and appropriate in all times and situations. They presented him the words: *"And this, too, shall pass away."* How much it expresses! How chastening in the hour of pride!—how consoling in the depths of affliction! "And this, too, shall pass away." And yet let us hope it is not *quite* true. Let us hope, rather, that by the best cultivation of the physical world, beneath and around us; and the intellectual and moral world within us, we shall secure an individual, social, and political prosperity and happiness, whose course shall be onward and upward, and which, while the earth endures, shall not pass away.

In the fall and early winter of 1859, Lincoln turned down more invitations to speak than he accepted, limited by his need to earn a living and determined not to create the impression that he was campaigning for the 1860 Republican presidential nomination. Speeches of principle would be indistinguishable from speeches for self-advancement. A network of Lincoln enthusiasts, radiating out from Springfield, lit small fires here and there. The publication of the 1858 debates in early 1860 ensured, whereas before it had been only likely, that wherever Republicans discussed possible standard-bearers for 1860, Lincoln's name was mentioned, though rarely with the enthusiasm or sense of inevitability that accompanied well-known names such as William Seward of New York and Salmon Chase of Ohio.

His prospects were never far from his own mind. What better consolation for his 1858 defeat and what more satisfying a triumph over Douglas than to be elected president. In correspondence and conversation, he played the modest mouse, especially on the issue of qualifications. At the same time he was also the cat, and the rhetoric of modest reserve did not fully disguise the attack crouch of the ambitious politician. It would not be to his advantage to be seen as an active candidate. When an Illinois newspaper editor solicited approval to push his candidacy, Lincoln's modesty was both real and strategic. "I must, in candor, say I do not think myself fit for the presidency. I certainly am flattered, and gratified . . . but I really think it best for our cause that no concerted effort . . . should be made." But he would not support any candidate already in the field, he wrote a competitor's supporter. "I shall labor faithfully in the ranks, unless, as I think not probable, the judgment of the party shall assign me a different position." That judgment, he knew, could be influenced. By February 1860 the calendar required direct expression of his self-interest. "I am not in a position where it would hurt much for me to not be nominated on the national ticket," he told his influential friend Norman Judd. "But I am where it would hurt some for me to not get the Illinois delegates."

"Some" meant a great deal. For other states to support him if their candidates fell short, he needed Illinois solidly behind him. To keep his rivals' constituencies amenable to him in case "the current of events" came his way, he also needed to be seen as a favorite son rather than a national rival. His chances would also be improved, he and his supporters realized, if the Republican National Committee could be persuaded to hold the party's nominating convention in Chicago. That would happen only if Lincoln continued to be perceived as a nonthreatening candidate. How to get the advantage of appearing to be an unlikely nominee while also impressing potential supporters? The most viable approach suited him: he would take the high road of ideas and ideology as the rationally analytic but also morally passionate spokesman for his party, his literary and oratorical gifts serving both principle and partisanship.

An unexpected opportunity came in October 1859 when a small

group of New York City Republicans who had kept their eyes westward during the 1858 debates invited him to present himself and his message for East Coast consideration. Ex-governor and now senator William Seward dominated New York Republican politics and presidential consideration. Some worried that his reputation for antislavery extremism might alienate enough Northern voters to undermine Republican chances in 1860. Seward's opposition to the proslavery features of the Compromise of 1850 and his use of the phrase "irrepressible conflict" in a speech in 1858 had stirred up even more anxiety than Lincoln's "a house divided against itself cannot stand," partly because of Seward's position as front-runner for the nomination, and also because Lincoln had gone to great trouble to explain that he meant his statement as descriptive, not predictive. It was widely hoped by abolitionists and feared in the South that a Seward presidency would use the power of the federal government to emancipate the slaves. Lincoln's moderation seemed potentially less damaging than Seward's radicalism.

In late February 1860, Lincoln took the opportunity offered by the New York invitation to demonstrate his qualifications, including his moderation. Though one of the least memorable, it was one of the most important speeches of his career, precisely because it established his credentials before a rigorous audience, including reporters for the major Eastern newspapers, as a man whose intellect and leadership had to be taken seriously. He could indeed be cast as an alternative to Seward. His most intensely researched essay, his exposition attempted an airtight, detailed, evidentiary argument in support of the claim that a majority of those who had originated the republic and created the Constitution opposed the extension of slavery, desired its eventual elimination, and believed only Congress had the power to govern the territories. Characteristically, the address had at the start a statement of theme, followed by a tight evidentiary argument and a rhetorical conclusion, its basic framework the high-toned, logically structured essay form and political discourse that Lincoln most admired. What had become characteristically his own, and what he had gotten better at with practice and maturity, was on the one hand a fine interweaving of precise language, concision of phrasing, and logical tightness, and, on the other, a personal voice that was sincere, colloquial, anecdotal, and humorous, projecting a persona of dignified but amiable authenticity. The balance between the logical emphasis and the narrative individualization could be adjusted to suit subject and occasion.

At Cooper Union, he adjusted his exposition heavily in favor of the evidentiary argument, the lawyerly and scholarly presentation of a brief so airtight it would convince an intellectually demanding audience. His auditors would have no doubt that they were in the presence of a man of formidable intellect and linguistic talent. The usual touches of humor, anecdote, and the colloquial are mostly absent. A brief introduction provides the thematic questions without any pause, digression, or stylistic bow toward the personal or the informal. Much of the essay is weighted toward the heavy center of evidence and argument, relieved but not diverted by occasional jabs of irony. Late in the essay, the historical argument is subsumed into political explicitness, the measured scholarly tone into touches of outrage and even anger. The political sinews of the speech palpitate into explicit and direct confrontation with the ideological enemy who had launched two outrageous accusations against the Republican Party—that it advocated lawless disregard of the *Dred Scott* decision and that it was responsible for John Brown's attack at Harpers Ferry. "You will not abide the election of a Republican President! In that supposed event, you say, you will destroy the Union; and then, you say, the great crime of having destroyed it will be upon us! That is cool. A highwayman holds a pistol to my ear, and mutters through his teeth, 'Stand and deliver, or I shall kill you, and then you will be a murderer!'"

Lincoln's timing is perfect. The anecdotal voice, the colloquial tone, the recourse to the power of narrative experience and storytelling asserts itself. The balance between that and logical analysis finds its effective level: "To be sure, what the robber demanded of me—my money—was my own; and I had a clear right to keep it; but it was no more my own than my vote is my own; and the threat of death to me, to extort my money, and the threat of destruction to the Union, to extort my vote, can scarcely be distinguished in principle." If only, he anguished, the South would confine itself to a practical accommodation. If it would trust the North to honor the slave states' right to maintain slavery indefinitely and would accept the law of the ballot box as the ultimate arbiter, all might be well for the Union.

What he could not promise and consequently would not address directly was that the rule of the ballot box would not, at some time in the future, eliminate slavery nationwide. If the power of the vote was the ultimate determinant of political conflicts, persuasion and historical process made eventual emancipation likely. Though for tactical reasons he would not acknowledge it explicitly, Seward was right: there was an "irrepressible conflict" of ideologies in which the South embodied a thin version of democracy—an hierarchical structure in which decision-making was in the hands of an elite; a distrust of democracy as the tyranny of the majority; and a predisposition toward a local nationalism that rejected the concept of the nation as a single entity with the power to control sectional interests. Lincoln could accept that the interests of many Southern states differed significantly from those of the rest of the country. He also could claim that they were not about to be challenged, let alone abridged, in any practical way. But, he reminded his Cooper Union audience, the South made additional demands on the North: that it forgo the election of a Republican president; that it renounce its belief that slavery was morally wrong; and that it end its effort to prevent slavery's spread to the territories.

In response, all Lincoln could offer was the status quo. "Wrong as we think slavery is, we can afford to let it alone where it is, because that much is due to the necessity arising from its actual presence in the nation; but can we, while our votes will prevent it, allow it to spread into the National Territories, and to overrun us here in these Free States?" Why, he asked, were voices both North and South "reversing the divine rule, and calling not the sinners, but the righteous to repentance—such as invocations to Washington, imploring men to unsay what Washington said, and undo what Washington did?" It was one thing to claim that the Constitution forbade slavery's elimination except by a change in the Constitution, an almost impossible task under the circumstances. It was another to falsify the words of Washington and the historical record.

The iron fist now burst through the velvet glove, the image of force that partly justified Southern fears, despite the elusive distinction between force as a means to sustain the Union as a single entity and force as an instrument to eliminate slavery, even if the force of a majority vote. "Neither let us be slandered from our duty by false accusations against us, nor frightened from it by menaces of destruction to the Government nor of dungeons to ourselves. LET US HAVE FAITH THAT RIGHT MAKES MIGHT, AND IN THAT FAITH, LET US TO THE END, DARE TO DO OUR DUTY AS WE UNDERSTAND IT." The assertion had resonance and political advantage, the rhetorical equivalent of stiffening spines and rallying troops. It seems unlikely, addressing his own constituency, that Lincoln had an abiding or deep sense of the impact of his language on a South that also thought that it was in the right, and that its commitment to duty and its belief in the rightness of its cause would overcome superior wealth and numbers. If right makes might, the South had faith that it would prevail.

The next day, watching the countryside spurt by him in fits and starts from the window of his train to Providence, Rhode Island, Lincoln probably had in mind that a good many of his countrymen did not share his basic premise that natural law dictated that slavery was morally wrong and that many others did not believe that that moral claim required either the division of the Union or the shedding of blood or both. The assertion that "RIGHT MAKES MIGHT" was one he would never make again in so emphatic a form, partly because it was not always readily sustainable in the face of facts and history, and also because it began to have less and less political utility. On the contrary, like "a nation divided against itself" and "irrepressible conflict," the phrase was divisive, not part of the solution but part of the problem. If there was a solution short of military force, Lincoln continued to believe that it was political, the goodwill of reasonable and prudent people working within a democratic and constitutional framework. And he and his party could best advance that interest by persuading the country to elect him to its highest office and his party to congressional dominance. To that end, he needed to move his language from that of force back to that of political persuasion, though by early 1860 the national division could no longer be addressed by rational discussion. Lincoln's appeal was mainly to his Northern base, contributing to its consolidation. The South had already made up its mind about the black Republicans, though Lincoln could not believe that his election in itself would require the South to take action. He expected words only.

Traveling from one New England political venue to another, he essentially repeated his updated foundation speech. He found it tough going, though apparently his audiences did not. Many felt they were hearing the persuasive words of an articulate, logically powerful, and awkwardly endearing charismatic Western moderate who could almost certainly unite a Northern and Western coalition to deliver the presidency to the Republican Party. On a Sunday in Exeter, New Hampshire, under "orders" from his conventional son Robert, Lincoln grumblingly agreed "to go to church once to-day," he wrote to his wife, a place he absented himself from except under family pressure or political necessity. Exhausted after speeches in Providence, Manchester, and Dover, he still had ahead of him speaking engagements in Hartford and New Haven. "I have been unable to escape this toil," he wrote to Mary with weary resignation. Unlike his usual Western crowds, these were sophisticated audiences, familiar with at least portions of his previous speeches, especially the Cooper Union address. "If I had foreseen it I think I would not have come East at all. The speech at New York being within my calculation before I started, went off passably well, and gave me no trouble whatever. The difficulty was to make nine others, before reading audiences, who have already seen all my ideas in print."

As always, extemporaneous speech placed him in peril of misspeaking. His every word was being scrutinized. Even with his prodigious memory, the danger was there, his wariness aggravated by his dispiriting awareness that these auditors already knew everything he had to say.

He could not of course have prepared ten separate speeches. At Cooper Union, reading from a text whose words he had chosen and shaped himself, he could exercise his artistry. He could not control the national distemper, but he could maintain creative control. Nine additional speaking appearances, though, risked a fall from literary craftsmanship and high standards into extemporaneous spontaneity, frustrating his passion for careful writing and revising. His literary artistry existed in uneasy tension with the language of political campaigning. To his and the nation's surprise, he was soon to be relieved of the necessity for the latter.

Relief came unexpectedly in March 1860 when it became clear, soon after his return from New England, that he was a viable contender, though not the front-runner, for the Republican presidential nomination. Tactics and tradition required that he do little to no direct campaigning. Spearheaded by his legal and political friends, who had his reserved but unequivocal encouragement, his supporters in Illinois had been advancing his candidacy. In 1854, when he had been the front-runner for a Senate seat, the shifting fortunes of political accommodation had taken him from near-victory to painful defeat. Now "the taste *is* in my mouth a little," he confessed to Lyman Trumbull at the end of April, asking him to be alert to missteps and cabals. Being the second choice of many of the other candidates' supporters, acceptable to most and anathema to none, had an advantage, especially in a time of passionate intensity about the issues and about winning. "I have not heard that any one makes any positive objection to me." It was not to his advantage to give speeches before the convention. His positions were well known, his moderation an asset. The less of a threat he seemed to his rivals, the better his chances. His supporters worked behind the scenes to keep as many state delegations as possible friendly to his contingent attractions and to the illusion that Chicago would be a neutral location for the nominating convention in May. It would also, they argued, augment Republican fortunes in the increasingly important western states.

The choice of Chicago allowed his partisans to generate a strong field of pro-Lincoln energy around and in the convention hall. Seward's supporters expected Seward to come so close on the first ballot as to influence enough delegates to nominate him on the second. "Be careful to give no offense, and keep cool under all circumstances," Lincoln urged his operatives. While the hoopla of Abe the rail-splitter, Honest Abe, and log cabin populism provided imagistic myth-making, Lincoln's adept coterie of insiders who had laid the groundwork for his candidacy by traveling to key states, strengthening his position as a backup candidate, now worked the hallways, hotel rooms, and convention floor. The message was that Lincoln could hold moderate voters; Seward could not. Those Republicans on either side of Lincoln would have no other place to go. With the Democrats in disarray, having divided into two separate candidacies, one pro-Southern, the other an attempt at a national ticket led by Douglas, Lincoln could hold the entire North. With Seward, there would be defections to Douglas. With the likelihood of even a fourth party and a three- or four-candidate race, a Republican who could hold the North would most likely be elected.

On the first ballot, Lincoln had little more than half Seward's numbers but more than anyone else. On the second he was only a few short of Seward. After the third, the country discovered that the three-term state legislator and one-term moderate antislavery congressman, who had held no other office, who had no executive experience, who was resented for his opposition to the Mexican War, and whom many considered a clumsy Western primitive without formal education or drawing-room manners, was almost certain to be elected president.

At home in Springfield, Lincoln's response to this startling likelihood had to have been occasional withdrawal into meditative moments that found their language in his favorite poems, especially the lines from Gray's "Elegy," carried in his memory since his early days:

The boast of heraldry, the pomp of power,
And all that beauty, all that wealth e'er gave,

Awaits alike th' inevitable hour:——
The paths of glory lead but to the grave.

His debates with Douglas had made it unlikely that he still feared his own grave site would elicit from some future poet what Gray had concluded about "the youth to fortune and to fame unknown," or at least the first part of the epitaph: "some mute inglorious Milton here may rest, / Some Cromwell guiltless of his country's blood." Lincoln was Milton enough to know that he had achieved some glory with his language, which had been considerably responsible for getting him where he now was. As a prose writer, he had confidence in his mature capacities. As a poet, he had skill but had left ambition behind, inspired to write verse only rarely and by specific occasion. Two examples from the late 1850s are dedicated to young women he had met on the campaign trail. His eight lines "To Rosa" are a characteristic variant, echoing Burns and particularly Herrick's "Gather ye rosebuds while ye may" on the mutability theme that had preoccupied his habitual melancholy and its stoic vision:

You are young, and I am older;
  You are hopeful, I am not——
Enjoy life, ere it grow colder——
  Pluck the roses ere they rot.

Teach your beau to heed the lay——
  That sunshine soon is lost in shade——
That now's as good as any day——
  To take thee, Rosa, ere she fade.

The young lady's father, an innkeeper, may have had a literal enough mind not to see, or a broad enough one not to object to, the poem's sexual resonance.

In the political arena, convention required that others speak on Lincoln's behalf. Once nominated, tradition pressured candidates to respect the nation's preference that they make no public statements between the nomination and the election, though surrogates were delegated to speak in every contested venue. The long-standing practice of energizing the base by mass demonstrations, with marching bands and torchlight parades, contributed to the usual nationwide electoral circus, though the fiery rhetoric and the literal fireworks on Lincoln's behalf were confined to the Northern states. He greeted delegations and demonstrations with carefully chosen words, his participation confined to consultations and pulse-taking. "It is the opinion of friends, backed by my own judgment, that I should not really, or apparently, be showing myself about the country." Occasional off-the-record support from Southerners encouraged unrealistic optimism. "I receive from the South [many assurances] that in no probable event will there be any very formidable effort to break up the Union. The people of the South have too much of good sense, and good temper, to attempt the ruin of the government. . . . At least, so I hope and believe." His optimism provided the necessary precondition for evading consideration that his election could result in civil strife. When, in October, three uncertain states, Ohio, Indiana, and Pennsylvania, elected Republicans to statewide offices, he wrote to Seward, "It now really looks as if the government is about to fall into our hands."

Though he avoided writing or speaking publicly between April 1860 and mid-February 1861, he allowed himself privately the good-humored expression of an imaginary dialogue between his two main electoral opponents, Douglas, the nominee of the Northern Democrats, and John Breckinridge, the candidate of the proslavery Southern Democrats, "Meeting and Dialogue of Douglas and Breckinridge." As always, he found Douglas vulnerable at the junction between character and language, the dynamic point at which trust is to be determined. In the dialogue, Douglas accuses Breckinridge of "breaking up the Democratic party," while the latter disputes the contention, claiming that he in fact represents the real Democratic Party. The real issue, Breckinridge continues, is why Douglas, who broke with Breckinridge's faction because it "insisted on Congressional protection of slave property" whereas Douglas insisted on nonintervention, is now forming coalitions with the other Southern faction, the Constitutional Union Party, led by John Bell, which also is in favor of the congressional protection of slavery.

> DOUG—Bell is a good Union-man; and you, and your friends, are a set of disunionists.
>
> BRECK—Bah! You have known us long, and intimately; why did you never denounce us as disunionists, till since our refusal to support *you* for the presidency? Why have you never warned the North against our disunionist schemes, till since the Charleston and Baltimore sessions of the National convention? Will you answer, Senator Douglas?
>
> DOUG—The condition of my throat will not permit me to carry this conversation any further.

By framing his attack on Douglas's linguistic duplicity in the form of a dialogue, Lincoln reaffirmed his belief in the richness of language as a vehicle of truth, able to capture the conditions of the moment and to address character and values. The dramatic framework appealed to the obsessive reader of Shakespeare as he extended his literary self-definition into drama, even if only in this small way, and the lasting touch of the history plays that had so absorbed him is apparent in his creation of dialogue for actual historical figures. Just as the condition of Douglas's throat fortuitously does not allow him to carry the conversation any further, it also expressed Lincoln's view of Douglas's character: another exemplification of why he, not Douglas, should be elected.

Inevitably, Lincoln's nomination elicited requests that he provide information to campaign biographers to help satisfy an electorate about a man likely to be president about whose life prior to 1854 not even the basic facts were known. He expressed his disinclination to cooperate in a form letter, dictated to his newly employed secretary, that "applications of this class are so numerous that it is simply impossible for him to attend to them." But the obligation to provide material for an official campaign biography was inescapable. He did what he would have preferred to avoid when the request came to assist John L. Scripps, an editor at the pro-Republican Chicago *Press and Tribune*, whose biography of Lincoln would also be published in New York by Horace Greeley as a supplement to his newspaper and then in book form. It was followed by eighteen separate campaign biographies, including three in German and two in Welsh.

As the only one to which Lincoln directly contributed, Scripps's biography has special interest, partly for its factual and sympathetic view of Chief Black Hawk's anti-Americanism, mostly for its primal role in creating the mythic Lincoln who "never uses profane language" and "is a regular attendant upon religious worship." It also censors Lincoln's description of his father. Whereas Lincoln's narrative does not mention religion at all, his parents' or his own, Scripps wrote that Lincoln had "the religious element within him . . . thoroughly awakened" by his parents' Baptist piety, shaping his character, for "there can be no true and lasting greatness unless its foundation be laid in the truths of the Bible." Scripps presents a minimalist portrait of Thomas Lincoln, stressing his hard start in life, his piety, his lack of education, and his "wisdom" in leaving Kentucky for Indiana because of his opposition to slavery, contradicting Lincoln's explanation that he left "chiefly on account of the difficulty in land titles." The qualified empathy of Lincoln's lovely phrase that his father in his childhood was "a wandering labor boy" Scripps did not use; and the bitter power of Lincoln's phrase "He never did more in the way of writing than to bunglingly sign his own name" Scripps apparently found too acerbic to be appropriate in a campaign biography whose intent was to be iconic, not revelatory.

That Scripps absorbed most of the basic facts provided by Lincoln in an approximately four-thousand-word sketch into a bland and pietistic narrative is hardly surprising: it is the prose of a journeyman carefully decorating his subject with the conventions the situation required. Lincoln's own account, though, has a sharpness of style and mind and an occasional frankness on matters of personal and political resonance that exemplify his passion for the point at which language and sincerity are inextricably bonded. Words mattered so much, if you will, whether the occasion of expression was public or personal, that his autobiographical sketch inevitably became an exemplification of the existential self, its style and focus part of a self-definition that even a self-serving situation could not entirely undermine. The needs of conventional public portraiture were less compelling than the compulsion to write well, which also meant to write honestly. Part of the conflict between formal occasion and artistic demand could be resolved by making the sketch as fact-based as possible. Still, it was part of Lincoln's personality and skill to select and arrange facts so that they spoke of the real world in the fullest sense, the observed and the observer simultaneous and inseparable. The objective positioning of his third-person autobiographical narrative gives its factual emphasis an emotional register while also charging the personally revealing statements with a power they might not otherwise have.

At the same time, in creating the autobiographical sketch Lincoln did put up brakes and boundaries. He would go this far and no farther, taciturnity and concision serving both censoring and stylistic values, narrative itself providing shape, direction, and inference. The word "bunglingly" carries the full but restrained force of Lincoln's real judgment of his father's character. The single factual sentence that concludes the genealogical history, "The present subject has no brother or sister of the whole or half blood," speaks volumes about familial loneliness. That "there were no children of this second marriage" can be read as a statement about Thomas and Sarah Lincoln's relationship. No statement at all would have communicated the bare fact. The only statement about his own marriage is whom he married and when. There is nothing about his children except that he had four of them, one of whom died. Apparently the few facts in Scripps's single paragraph devoted to Lincoln's domestic life came from another source, and included a politely fictional description of Mary Lincoln that might have made her husband uneasily anticipate the actual future: "Mrs. Lincoln is a lady of charming presence, of superior intelligence, of accomplished manners, and, in every respect well fitted to adorn the position in which the election of her husband to the Presidency will place her. The courtesies and hospitalities of the White House have never been more appropriately and gracefully dispensed than they will be during the administration of Mr. Lincoln."

Lincoln, of course, said nothing about either his wife's lifelong aspiration or her qualifications to become First Lady, especially since his own were decidedly at issue in the minds of many. Much else was on his mind in creating the autobiographical sketch that directed this always reticent man away from the personal, especially when it was hazardous. Other than the account of his family background, early years, and rise to the legal profession, the sketch is mainly devoted to two political matters that were threatening Lincoln's credibility as a candidate: the inaccurate claim that he had failed to support the troops in the field during the Mexican War and the accusation that he had come lately, and solely for political expediency, to his antislavery views. Both seemed to him painful slanders that attacked both his political viability and his character. It was important for the voters to know that the likely next president had as early as 1837 coauthored a resolution, appearing in the record of the state legislature, denouncing slavery as unjust. "His position on the slavery question . . . was then the same that it is now," Lincoln wrote, instructing Scripps to include the full text of the 1837 statement.

In the three paragraphs devoted to rebutting the charge, about which "much has been said," that he had failed to support the troops, he directed readers to consult his votes in the *Congressional Globe*, and to distinguish between those votes and his conviction that "the act of sending an armed force among the Mexicans, was *unnecessary*, inasmuch as Mexico was in no way molesting, or menacing the U.S. or the people thereof; and that it was *unconstitutional*, because the power of levying war is vested in Congress, and not in the President." The war had been politically motivated, he explained, by an administration drawing attention away from its capitulation to Great Britain in the Oregon boundary dispute. This insistence on his integrity in place, he brought the sketch to an abrupt end, the autobiographical intensity apparently absorbed into self-defense. He, too, he asserts, is a law-abiding, humane, and loyal patriot, a man of character who believes in the Constitution and the law.

In May 1860 an old friend congratulated Lincoln, after years of silence between them, on his nomination. "You can hardly imagine, and
I cannot describe my feelings when I saw by the papers this morning
that you were a candidate for the Presidency," Joshua Speed wrote from
Lexington. Having inherited four of his father's fifty-seven slaves, Speed
had become a businessman who, among other items, advertised "Valuable Slaves for Sale." Recollections of his visit in 1841 to the Speed family
plantation must have come vividly to Lincoln's mind: the intimacy of the
friendship, Mary Speed's attractiveness, and the experience of visiting
briefly among people who accepted slavery as a permanent institution.
Speed himself had always believed that slavery did not meet standards
of Christian morality in the abstract. In practice, though, he lived com-
fortably with it as an institution. If the citizens of Kansas were to vote to
exclude slavery, he would "rather rejoice" as a Christian but, he had written to Lincoln in 1854, he would defend their right to make slavery legal
if they so chose, even if it meant the dissolution of the Union. Still, he
wrote in 1860, "allow a warm personal friend, though as you are perhaps
aware, a political opponent, to congratulate you. Should you be elected
and I think you have a fair chance for it—I am satisfied that you will
honestly administer the government—and make a lasting reputation for
yourself. . . . My wife is warmly for you." Won't you visit us?

Though he would like, Lincoln responded, "to see Kentucky generally, and you in particular," a visit was impossible. "Could not she and
you visit us here?" The Speeds joined the president-elect for a reunion in
Chicago. "As a friend, I am rejoiced at your success—as a political opponent I am not disappointed," Speed had written to him. Lincoln asked
if Speed, a Southerner who much desired the continuation of the Union,
would accept a cabinet-level appointment in his administration. Speed
declined. Now and in the war that was to come, with some hesitation
and much regret he gradually became his old friend's valuable ally in the
effort to keep Kentucky in the Union, an exemplification of that Southern
constituency, especially in the Border States, that preferred the Union
to slavery, if one had to go, though continuing to hope that both could
be retained. From early in their relationship, aware of Lincoln's literary

interests, Speed had appreciated his gift for language. Some part of his certainty that Lincoln as president would achieve "a lasting reputation" came from his conviction that Lincoln would use this talent to conciliate and inspire, and that his leadership in the terms provided by both art and honesty would endure on the page and in historical memory.

What the nation could not have anticipated as Lincoln left Springfield for Washington on February 11, 1861, the day before his fifty-second birthday, was that his lifelong development as a writer had brought it a president with the capacity to express himself and the national concerns more effectively than any president ever had, with the exception of Thomas Jefferson, although nothing Jefferson wrote during his presidency, not even his dramatic first inaugural address, has a permanent place in the literary or political canon. The degree to which presidents before Lincoln, with the exception of Jefferson and John Adams, composed their own speeches is not entirely clear. The other Virginian presidents, Washington, Madison, and Monroe, had of course attained the basic literary fluency expected of gentlemen educated in the classical tradition valued by the eighteenth century, and Madison certainly had a strong hand in his written pronouncements. But if, as is often claimed, Alexander Hamilton helped George Washington write his Farewell Address, our first president was also the first to use a speechwriter. By personality and education, his successor, John Adams, wrote sharply focused prose in the New England and Unitarian Enlightenment tradition. His son, John Quincy Adams, perhaps the most literary and learned of presidents, a master of many languages, a translator of classical poetry, a poet himself, and an obsessive writer, wrote his own public communications. The seventh president, Andrew Jackson, used language with effective efficiency, leading by force of character rather than literate persuasion; a general used to issuing orders as commander in chief. It is likely that large parts if not all of the final drafts of Jackson's inaugural addresses were written by a cabinet member; the ideas were Jackson's, but not the final language.

Before Jackson, presidents were products of a culture that assumed that presidents would come from an elite and educated class. (After Jackson, it hardly mattered whether a president was educated, let alone literary.) Until Lincoln, there were few instances of presidents speaking memorably to the country or to Congress, whether as authors of their own words or not. As presidents, their language skills were hardly put to the challenge. Inaugural addresses solemnized the oath of office, ceremonial and celebratory except at times of crisis, and were likely to be the only occasions on which presidents directly addressed the public. The annual summary of the state of the nation, to which cabinet members contributed reports and language, was delivered by messenger to the clerk of the House, a precedent established by Jefferson, who disliked giving public addresses. The absence of electronic communication and speedy transit kept presidents focused on their duties as Washington-based administrators. Except for Washington's Farewell Address and Jefferson's pre-presidential Declaration of Independence, few presidents' words before Lincoln and very few after have presence, let alone residue, in the American national memory.

Three presidents after Lincoln wrote well: Grant, Theodore Roosevelt, and Woodrow Wilson, the latter two, products of the educated elite. Grant was a natural wordsmith; nothing Roosevelt or Wilson wrote made a memorable imprint. Presidents after Wilson hardly wrote anything, especially their own speeches, perhaps with the possible exception of Jimmy Carter, a writer of competence but not literary talent, and William Jefferson Clinton, the best-educated post–World War II president, with a gift for spontaneous oratory rather than disciplined writing. The post–World War II genre of the presidential memoir has mostly produced drab voluminousness. Some of Franklin Roosevelt's words have struck deeply into the American consciousness, not because he wrote them but because at a time of national crisis he assembled the best team of speechwriters of any modern president and worked closely with them. After Roosevelt, less talented speechwriters took over, and the president's own language hardly mattered to the process: at best, he became editor in chief of the final draft of what others wrote.

In 1861 language as an agent of consensus and persuasion to shape the national will found its most skillful embodiment in presidential history in the newly elected Lincoln. He was, though, a president who almost half the country had so emphatically rejected as to keep him off the ballot entirely. Much of the South never had the opportunity to hear him, and many with access to newspapers that reprinted his words had already made themselves impervious to him. The country as a whole knew little about him other than his Republican principles. Hagiographical Republican biographers rushed in to fill the gap. Still, the educated elite of the Northeast expected little from the formally uneducated autodidact; and the Copperhead North, represented by a Democratic Party eager to accommodate the South, detested him. Only sectional fractiousness, especially the South's conviction that it could sustain independence, had made Lincoln's election possible. Consequently the immense obstacles to a successful presidency were so different from those any other president had faced that they came close at times to making even his great language skills inadequate.

Leaving Springfield for Washington in February 1861, Lincoln recognized that the national divisions that had made his election possible required that his highest priority be reconciliation. He needed, though, to pursue it without compromising core Republican principles. For the time being, the only weapon he had at his command was language. If intellectual readiness is everything, he was ready, as he well knew when he said goodbye to his Springfield world, having prepared himself over a lifetime to become a well-read master of the human narrative. If that narrative was to have its tragic dimension in Lincoln's failure, despite his talents, to prevent the South's secession, shorten the inevitable war, or alleviate Northern racism, it was to be an object lesson in the limitations of language rather than a failure in preparation. At the same time, the unfortunate givens of the narrative provided the context for his two greatest achievements, the Gettysburg Address and the second inaugural address, in which he did what great writers do: create useful texts from which readers can derive inspiration, literary pleasure, and universalizing direction.

He had a sense of that part of his mission as he left Springfield. In a brief farewell from the railway platform to a crowd that included many longtime friends, he eulogized his past life, emphasizing the danger of what lay ahead. It was partly confessional autobiography, every word in the end carefully revised for publication, even to the call for the prayers of well-wishers and the assistance of the "Divine Being," a deistic motif that as president he relied on as compatible with the religious sentiment of the country and his own non-Christian beliefs. The speech echoes some of his favorite poetry and its theme of mutability, the loss and bereavement that time brings. The hope that the worst will be averted, which he needed to sustain for himself and provide for his countrymen, is in the tense of contingency, the negative undercurrent of the subjunctive, its emphasis on "confidently" an indirect confession that in this circumstance it was indeed difficult to be confident:

My friends—No one, not in my situation, can appreciate my feeling of sadness at this parting. To this place, and the kindness of these people, I owe every thing. Here I have lived a quarter of a century, and have passed from a young to an old man. Here my children have been born, and one is buried. I now leave, not knowing when, or whether ever, I may return, with a task before me greater than that which rested upon Washington. Without the assistance of that Divine Being, who ever attended him, I cannot succeed. With that assistance I cannot fail. Trusting in Him, who can go with me, and remain with you and be every where for good, let us confidently hope that all will yet be well. To His Care commending you, as I hope in your prayers you will commend me, I bid you an affectionate farewell.

Traveling eastward by a circuitous route, he fulfilled his intention to let his countrymen see him. Secreted in his luggage was the draft of his inaugural address, to be further revised once he reached Washington, the contents of which he declined to reveal in the brief speeches and greetings he extended in Indianapolis, Cincinnati, Columbus, Cleveland, Syracuse,

Albany, Trenton, and Philadelphia, among other cities, though he made certain not to speak without a carefully prepared text. His words, though, did brush up against the speech he had prepared for installation into office. Before the New Jersey Senate, he was touchingly and substantively autobiographical in a graceful segue from the impression that Weems's *Life of Washington* had made on him as a child to his commitment to perpetuate the Union and its liberties "in accordance with the original idea for which that struggle was made" by the founding generation. "I shall be most happy indeed if I shall be an humble instrument in the hands of the Almighty, and of this, his almost chosen people, for perpetuating the object of that great struggle." For this, "I am exceedingly anxious."

The intersection between autobiography and national narrative highlighted a crucial point, one that he had internalized and now attempted to revivify in the memories of his countrymen, some of whom had read the same books, many of whom knew the facts of Valley Forge and the New Jersey battles: "I remember all the accounts there given of the battle fields and struggles for the liberties of the country, and none fixed themselves upon my imagination so deeply as the struggle here at Trenton, New-Jersey. The crossing of the river; the contest with the Hessians; the great hardships endured at that time, all fixed themselves on my memory more than any single revolutionary event; and you all know, for you all have been boys, how these early impressions last longer than any others." Struggle was much on his mind, the word appearing five times in the brief speech. The effort to preserve the Union, he implied, might create as much hardship as the struggle to create it. The advantage of qualifying the self-serving misconception held by many Americans that they were God's chosen people was also on his mind. Americans had been blessed with much, but not everything, he delicately stated: they were "the Almighty's . . . *almost* chosen people." These imperfect, less than fully chosen people were now creating for themselves the possibility that they would not be even a single people anymore. If they forsook "the liberties of the people" embodied in the founding documents, their already noteworthy distance from the ideal of a chosen people would be increased considerably.

To all Americans he advised patience and prudence, the leitmotif of his inaugural address before an audience of thirty thousand on a cloudy cold March 4. He took the oath of office from a chief justice who had decided twice against his interests, once in 1847 in his one appearance before the Supreme Court and later in the *Dred Scott* decision. Now the consequences of secession counted more heavily for Lincoln than any indefinite extension of slavery in the South. He did not desire that the nation embark on a civil war to emancipate the Negro, and all his lessons in human nature had led him to believe that as individuals Northerners were no better than Southerners: faced with the same historical and economic realities, they too would be slaveholders. He insisted only that the Southern elite accept his election and that it contest Republican efforts to prevent slavery's extension only at the ballot box. The status quo did not harm the South, he emphasized. And those who desired the end of slavery, he advised, could afford to wait for its inevitable demise by attrition, in the expectation that the forces of history required its eventual elimination, the conviction that its incompatibility with humane democratic values numbered its days.

Having revised his composition during his ten days in Washington before the inauguration, he now had in hand a text that emphasized reconciliation rather than federal enforcement, to which his earlier draft had given more prominence. It was, he may have realized, almost out of the question that the states that had already declared secession would revoke it in response to reassurances that the government would not interfere with established legal institutions, let alone violate the constitutional rights of any state. His appeal was to the border states and to the North: "That there are persons in one section, or another, who seek to destroy the Union at all events, and are glad of any pretext to do it, I will neither affirm nor deny; but if there be such, I need address no word to them. To those, however, who really love the Union, may I not speak?" Recognizing that passionate extremes often determined political results, his appeal was to the center that he feared might not hold. He needed to inspire pro-Union passion by emphasizing that the entire nation had flourished under the Constitution, that "with its institutions, [the country] belongs to the people who inhabit it," who have the power to change it lawfully, and that "nothing valuable can be lost by taking time." Americans, he assured his countrymen, have the competence "to adjust, in the best way, all our present difficulty." Since the government would not assail the South, "you can have no conflict, without being yourselves the aggressors. *You* have no oath registered in Heaven to destroy the government, while *I* shall have the most solemn one to 'preserve, protect, and defend' it," he said, standing a few feet from Chief Justice Taney.

William Seward, soon to be sworn in as secretary of state, had urged an additional paragraph and provided its first draft, which Lincoln found useful. It was the only significant portion of any essay that Lincoln ever had or would compose that he had not written entirely himself. The thrust of Seward's thought and phrases gave Lincoln a starting point, with the talented Seward providing the trigger for creative editorial revision, resulting in a poetic and passionately expressed call for reconciliation. Seward's paragraph had been flat at the start, both in voice and rhythm, rising in the final sentence but not soaring, and pedestrian in its climactic image. Using much of Seward's language, Lincoln's recasting was inspired. He revised "The mystic chords which proceeding from so many battlefields and so many patriot graves pass through all the hearts and all the hearths in this broad continent of ours will yet again harmonize in their ancient music when breathed upon by the guardian angel of the nation" to "The mystic chords of memory, stretching from every battle-field, and patriot grave, to every living hearth and hearthstone, all over this broad land, will yet swell the chorus of the Union, when again touched, as surely they will be, by the better angels of our nature."

The changes transformed the adequate to the brilliant. Seward's uninflected "I close" Lincoln revised to "I am loathe to close," adding personal emotion and the reminder that the current peace, perpetuated by the suspension of time which the speech required, was likely to end soon after the speech concluded. Adding rhythm, alliteration, and balance to Seward's banal phrasing, Lincoln provided orchestration to bare notes. More significantly, in the change from the sentimental "guardian angel of the nation" to "the better angels of our nature" Lincoln rejected a nineteenth-century literary cliché that evoked external forces of protection for an image familiar to him from his early reading in Protestant guidebooks, directing responsibility for the national condition and all human activity to the fact that human nature contained both good and evil. Salvation depended on human beings recognizing and drawing on the best within themselves.

Noble and beautiful as the words are, including his willful, unrealistic expression of confidence that these "mystic chords of memory" will be widely heard, "as surely they will be," this was little to offer extremists on either side. There were few "better angels" in the human nature of the people in either camp, or, if so, they were mostly out of sight; to the extent that there *were* "better angels," each side believed it had considerably more of such heavenly grace in its values than the other. The South condemned as enemies even those who claimed that slavery would be ended over time and without bloodshed. Abolitionists were appalled at the prospect of so long a wait. And, as at most times, the extremes drove the center. Those willing to act rather than talk initiated change, and Lincoln's inaugural address inevitably failed in its primary purpose of maintaining things as they were. Before he spoke and as he spoke, Southern initiatives on the ground were narrowing Lincoln's options and determining, despite his desire to the contrary, that he would be a wartime president.

Words could not prevent the war, and by themselves words could of course not fight the war. Their value was on the home front, as an instrument to attain enough of a consensus to keep the center from falling apart, which it came perilously close to doing at the very start and numbers of times throughout a war longer than either side had anticipated. Overestimating the amount of Union loyalty in the South, Lincoln miscalculated. Southern-state patriotism was easily inflamed, and the non-landed and small farm interests in a rural and often barter economy had little economic incentive to give their allegiance to an almost invisible federal government. Lincoln showed little understanding of Southern grievances, fears, and political realities. The degree to which economics and demographics created a Southern nightmare appears to have had little force in his analysis, partly because it was against his party interest, perhaps because he could do little about it, and also because he hoped the status quo could be maintained. But how little purchase such considerations would have on Southern analyses of the situation, and how they failed to address the main issues, he seems not to have realized, as if slavery as a moral issue could be addressed independent of the Southern economy and social fabric, and as if secession were mainly an expression of extreme sectional nationalism rather than of political-economic anxieties. Neither in his inaugural nor in his special message to Congress on July 4, 1861, did he confront the deeper issues. He implied, with no indication of serious analysis, if any analysis at all, that the forces represented by the Republican Party were benign in regard to the interest of those Southerners who determined policy.

They were not. Northern capitalist and free-labor interests required a single national market, a nation unified by banking, manufacturing, and transportation networks, with government revenue derived from and industry protected by an import tariff, a variant of Henry Clay's American system, a centralized state in whose economy the role of the South would be to contribute raw materials for which it would trade, often at disadvantageous prices, for financial services and finished goods. Separatism, of course, would make such a system impossible, and, as a truncated state, the North would be more vulnerable to foreign pressure, its economy weakened, its ability to play a major role on the international stage more limited. The expectation of an imperial America from coast to coast, shared by many Democrats and most Republicans, would be severely undermined. From the Southern point of view, however, secession came because "the political economic foundation for unity was extremely weak and any attempt to strengthen [it] by increasing economic integration threatened the long-term interests of the plantation economy." Secession was opposed by a North represented by a political party intent on consolidating its economic power, which it now aligned with its moral and political vision.

The election of a Republican president gave certainty to the Southern elite that the forces for single-state hegemony had indeed gained control of the country. The long-standing stalemate had been broken in the North's favor. The passage of congressional acts strengthening the central state, including tariff legislation and a transcontinental railroad route disadvantageous to the South, confirmed Southern fear of relative disenfranchisement and seemed a foretaste of what was to come. After almost eighty years of wielding congressional power by virtue of seniority and the three-fifths rule, and presidential power by virtue of Virginia's genius, the South now faced, sooner than later, the loss of political dominance. Leaving Washington in order to implement self-government at home seemed not only reasonable but principled. In a quasi-democratic environment in which the ballot box counted less than the power of local oligarchs, a small number of Southerners could determine policy.

Southern leadership also miscalculated, not in its analysis of the reasons for secession or its timing, but in its confidence that the remedy would cure the disease. Lincoln's argument, in his first two presidential speeches, that as independent states the South and North could not live peacefully alongside one another and that an independent South would be worse off than as part of the Union seemed hogwash to Southerners, who observed very little federal presence in the South, mostly embodied in the post office; there were no federal personal or business taxes other than the tariff collected at ports; and many of the federal soldiers stationed in the South were Southerners. Lincoln's fear that secession would lead to more spin-off—with each state in the Confederacy and the Union potentially becoming a new country by the same principle that rationalized the South's secession—expressed the outcome that many Southerners desired. Each state, they believed, had the right to follow its own interests. That, after all, was why they were not Republicans. By July 1861, the argument was irrelevant to the South: secession had occurred;

armed conflict, though minor, had begun; and the South felt it had made its move at a propitious time.

The mystery is not when or why the South seceded, but why it thought it could do so successfully. Two of the reasons did impress Lincoln, causing him great anxiety: the belief that internal dissent would weaken Northern response and that the new president would be a chief executive incapable of taking decisive action. It was widely believed in the South that under the pressure of internal opposition and due to weakness of character, Lincoln would most likely allow the South to go its own way. Many Northern and international observers thought this assessment accurate.

But even if it were not, there were other factors weighing heavily in the South's calculation. Some were based on questionable assumptions, but all were informed by geostrategic realities, adding rational ballast to bellicose patriotism. The South believed that its men were superior fighters; that, at the leadership level, they were better military strategists; that with much of the officer corps of the minuscule Union army being Southerners, they would be loyal to their home states; that with comparatively few immigrants, Southerners were more patriotic, attached to the local soil, and ethnically unified, hence more willing to make sacrifices if required; and that, with their superiority in martial character, it would be a short war, which would offset their demographic and industrial disadvantages. While the North faced logistical obstacles in invading the South, Southerners needed only to defend their own territory—in fact, Confederate forces could harass, if not occupy, Washington, D.C., from nearby Virginia. And the South controlled the country's vital natural resources, particularly cotton and sugar cane. It also had foreign sympathizers, economic partners, and potential allies, such as Great Britain, which made diplomatic recognition and material support likely if the scenario developed favorably.

If this Southern reckoning miscalculated the significance of the North's superiority in manpower, industrial production, and capital resources, it seemed solidly enough based on rational analysis to persuade those who saw their world at greatest risk from inaction to pledge their sacred fortunes and secede. The South's misestimate of Lincoln was understandable—partly wishful thinking, partly overconfidence, and also an inevitable ignorance about a president little known even by many of his supporters, though he had taken pains to tell the country he would act to preserve the Union and that he had full confidence it would prevail. That he was not able over the next four years consistently to sustain this confidence at the same high level as at the start, that divisions within the Union sometimes undermined the war effort, and that widespread doubt arose about his strength of character, does not abrogate the fact that his confidence was solidly based in political-economic realities and in self-knowledge.

Four months after his inauguration, Lincoln summarized to a special session of Congress what had occurred since, the prelude to his analysis of the illegality of the rebellion. His pithy narrative had explanatory vividness. His arguments were far from new, but they were presented with a biting combination of lawyerly contempt for rationales that would wither under rigorous analysis and an impassioned explanation to his Northern constituency of why they were morally and legally bound to suppress the rebellion and make the country whole again. He wanted his words to be heard by the border states also, an appeal to their loyalty to the principles of American government. Despite evidence to the contrary, he still thought "there is much reason to believe that the Union men are the majority in many, if not in every other one, of the so-called seceded States," a locution he maintained in one form or another throughout the war. Since it was illegal to secede, "secession" was a misnomer. The Confederacy was not a legal government, hence no government at all unless it would determine itself to be so by victorious force of arms. And he remained convinced, partly because of his belief in the power of language to affect public opinion, that the Confederacy's leaders had been able to persuade Southerners to rebel only by virtue of three decades of linguistic dishonesty, a barrage of verbal propaganda that corrupted the relationship between language and truth: "With rebellion thus sugar-coated, they have been drugging the public mind of their section for more than thirty years; and, until at length, they have brought many good men to a willingness to take up arms against the government the day *after* some assemblage of men have enacted the farcical pretence of taking their State out of the Union, who could have been brought to no such thing the day *before*."

Under such circumstances, a discussion of the nature of revolutions of the sort that he had explored as a young man in his Springfield Lyceum address would have seemed irrelevant to him. In 1776, the colonists had rebelled against a government to which they had neither voluntarily pledged their enduring commitment as equal partners nor given their consent by the ballot box. In signing the Constitution, the states had entered into a contract based on shared principles of representative government that forbade withdrawal except by mutual consent, and had pledged themselves to settle disputes by the mechanisms provided by that compact. In 1776, the colonists had rebelled against an arbitrary master in an authoritarian culture. From Lincoln's perspective, what uniquely distinguished the republic its founders had created was its commitment to political equality and equality of opportunity for every human being. "This is essentially a People's contest," he told the Congress on July 4. "On the side of the Union, it is a struggle for maintaining in the world, that form, and substance of government, whose leading object is, to elevate the definition of men—to lift artificial weights from all shoulders—to clear the paths of laudable pursuit for all—to afford all, an unfettered start, and a fair chance, in the race of life."

Ironically, some of the libertarian values that underlay Southern secession were impossible to maintain during a war. To fight effectively, the South, with fewer resources, had to institute measures that made it an even more unified central state than the North, including a compulsory draft, price controls, high personal taxation, control of the labor supply, nationalization of the railroads, a central court system, and state-controlled manufacturing plants. The war effort required it to act contrary to the values it advocated. Otherwise, it would not have a chance of winning. Such measures actually were easier to implement in the more demographically uniform, politically rigid Confederacy, which forbade opposition parties or a free press, than in the diverse, politically contentious North, which maintained a free market and constitutional protections throughout the war, except for a temporary suspension of habeas corpus as constitutionally authorized "in Cases of Rebellion." The North's greater wealth, market resources, and manpower made it possible to fight *and* maintain relative economic normalcy. What Lincoln needed most was to keep internal political differences from interfering with the prosecution of the war. He also needed military victories. Poor training, deficient leadership, and a structural flaw in which individual states raised, financed, appointed officers, and maintained some control over the vast bulk of Union forces—which consisted of two parallel armies, a large amateur force of state militia and a small professional one—contributed to making the Union trial by battle long and hazardous, despite superior resources. After much humiliation and anguish, Lincoln finally, in 1863, got victories at Gettysburg and Vicksburg.

Between his special address to Congress in July 1861 and his address at Gettysburg in November 1863, he was aware that the Union's poor battlefield record made inspirational rhetoric temporarily irrelevant. The public wanted successful action, not words. In his 1861 annual message, he provided a conventional account of diplomatic, domestic, and budgetary matters, inflected by the subject that dominated all others, to which he now added a new phrase: "The Union must be preserved, and hence, all indispensable means must be employed." Some disposition of slavery to weaken the South, which used slave labor to support the war effort, may have been on his mind in a sketchy way. For the bold or the desperate imagination, the category "all indispensable means" could very well include emancipation. Emancipation inhered in his argument that "the insurrection is largely, if not exclusively, a war upon the first principles of popular government—the rights of the people," and that the Southern elite believed that "large control of the people in government, is the source of all political evil."

That emancipation, refracted by evasion and medium distance, was on his mind can be deduced from the particular focus of his deviation from his usual commitment to logical essay structure, introducing in the last half-dozen paragraphs a subject heretofore irrelevant to the presentation: the relationship between capital and labor, which had been the subject of his 1859 speech to the Milwaukee agricultural fair. He now revisited it in the context of "all necessary measures." "Labor is prior to, and independent of, capital," he again asserted, emphasizing that free labor is essential to a dynamic economy and to a Republic. Implicit in the context is that all labor, including black labor, must be free if there is to be upward mobility for white labor and if democratic institutions are to survive.

In September 1862, he reflected on the divine will in a paragraph-long private meditation of heartaching perplexity, prompted partly by the claims of Christian representatives on both sides that God favored them, that Jehovah and Jesus were the Union's sanction and ultimate weapon. Using words as agents of cogitation and clarification, he lucidly evaluated the intellectual and theological basis of the widespread clerical demand that he rally the nation in more intensely Christian and sectarian terms. He did not doubt that there was some power or force in the universe determining final outcomes and even initiating processes. That was consistent with his deistic beliefs, conditioned by his Calvinistic temperament and his never fully relinquished determinism. On the highest level, free will was an illusion. For the actors in the daily drama, there were indeed decisions to be made, but their disposition (and, by implication, their origin) had been shaped by larger forces. "The will of God prevails. . . . In the present civil war it is quite possible that God's purpose is something different from the purpose of either party—and yet the human instrumentalities, working just as they do, are of the best adaptation to effect His purpose. I am almost ready to say this is probably true—that God wills this contest, and wills that it shall not end yet." The "almost" now merges into declarative certainty. "He could have either *saved* or *destroyed* the Union without a human contest. Yet the contest began. And having begun He could give the final victory to either side any day. Yet the contest proceeds."

Why that was so was not a question Lincoln was ready to answer explicitly, although an answer, even if not fully satisfactory, seems implicit in the context of his increasing preoccupation with the disposition of slavery in regard to the war effort. It is likely that by September 1862 he had begun to associate the length of the war, evidence that God had not yet affirmed the moral superiority of either side, with his view that the North also was complicit in perpetuating and profiteering from the republic's primal sin. The war had begun to have the feel of atonement through blood and repentance, a Calvinistic explanation that had psychological utility, especially since no alternative explanation provided satisfaction.

In October 1862, a newspaper account of an interview he had granted to the widow of a well-known religious writer quoted his response to the prayer she had offered at the White House for "light and wisdom . . . to be shed down from on high, to guide our President." "If after endeavoring to do my best in the light which he affords me, I find my efforts fail, I must believe that for some purpose unknown to me, He wills it otherwise." But since the war continues, "we must believe that He permits it for some wise purpose of his own, mysterious and unknown to us." On the one hand, all he could do was keep trying to find the right combination of generals and strategies. On the other, accepting that an inscrutable power with its own purposes had responsibility for the overall course of events was useful. If those events were at least partly determined by the need for expiation, then both expiation and national interest could best be served by resolving the slavery issue.

At the end of March 1863, Lincoln responded to a Senate request that he declare a day of "national prayer and humiliation" with a proclamation cleverly embodying his ability to play the role of tactful presidential clergyman with a bent toward Calvinistic literalism. The war effort required it. With references to Christian specifics that he rarely used, such as "the Holy Scriptures," the proclamation was calibrated to evoke the tone of the biblical prophets, chastising national pride and materialism, like Isaiah preaching to the Hebrews. At the same time, it was a state document. But the underlying argument and the dominant rhetoric were a variant on the "Meditation on the Divine Will," the private document he had written in September 1862. Lincoln now tactfully avoided explicitly charging that the North was as responsible for slavery as the South or even responsible at all, as he had done in the 1862 "Meditation." The nation's sins were unspecified, the charge put in the hypothetical. "May we not justly fear that the awful calamity of civil war, which now desolates the land, may be but a punishment, inflicted upon us, for our presumptuous sins, to the needful end of our national reformation as a whole People?" The charge was cast in the biblical vagueness of "we have forgotten God," an indictment that Lincoln in other circumstances would not have found compelling. But to make public at this point in the war his private meditation that charged the North with complicity in the perpetuation of slavery would have been counterproductive.

A month before writing the 1862 "Meditation," Lincoln had met with a "Committee of colored men" who came at his invitation "to hear what the Executive had to say to them." Whatever else was in his mind, he devoted his remarks entirely to his long-held hope, modeled after the program initiated by Henry Clay, that the slavery problem could be resolved by separation and colonization. Cogently and gracefully eloquent, it is Lincoln's fullest exposition of the colonization program, the expectation of a Liberian homeland for American blacks. His argument to the free blacks who had prospered was that they should unselfishly "do something to help those . . . not so fortunate" as themselves, those who had not prospered. The reality was that "there is an unwillingness on the part of our people, harsh as it may be, for you free colored people to remain with us." But if the Negro free citizens of the North would show the way toward colonization, much might be accomplished, an argument he elaborated on in terms that the committee probably found bizarre, including the proposition that, for logistical reasons and also because proximity to the United States would provide emotional solace, a Central American colony would be more satisfactory than Liberia. "It does not strike me that you have the greatest reason to love [white Americans]. But still you are attached to them at all events." Were there no volunteers? "I want you to let me know whether this can be done or not."

The newspaper summary of Lincoln's argument for colonization concludes, "The Chairman of the delegation briefly replied that 'they would hold a consultation and in a short time give an answer.' The President said: 'Take your full time—no hurry at all.' The delegation then withdrew." It was an adroit performance by a man who, a week after his discussion with the Negro committee, wrote to the influential, cantankerous, and critical newspaper editor Horace Greeley, who advocated that the president immediately declare all Negroes emancipated, that "My paramount object in this struggle *is* to save the Union, and it is *not* either to save or to destroy slavery. If I could save the Union without freeing *any* slave I would do it, and if I could save it by freeing *all* the slaves I would do it; and if I could save it by freeing some and leaving others alone I would also do that."

For almost a year and a half he had stuck to his premise that the disposition of slavery need not and should not be addressed until the rebellion had been defeated. And if a speedy resolution of the war required a renewed commitment to gradualism, he would settle for that, especially if it were the only price to pay for a return to the situation prior to secession. A recent congressional appropriation for colonization and Lincoln's realistic report on the subject in his December 1862 annual message focused on Northern free Negroes. But harshly mistreated by Northern racism though they were, the real issues were slavery, the South, and the war. Aware that no practical implementation existed, Lincoln soon acknowledged that the time for colonization as a solution to slavery had passed, if it had ever been viable.

By mid-September 1862, refining in words and speech his thoughts on the issue, he was being directed by events to the hitherto unthinkable. Concerned that the constitutional division of powers be adhered to, he had legal reservations about the chief executive mandating emancipation. But, he implied to a delegation of Chicago Christians whose petition claimed that emancipation was God's will, such an act could be justified in his role as commander in chief as essential to the war effort. Still, he told them, "I hope it will not be irreverent for me to say that if it is probable that God would reveal his will to others, on a point so connected with my duty, it might be supposed that he would reveal it directly to me. . . . *And if I can learn what it is I will do it!* These are not, however, the days of miracles, and I suppose it will be granted that I am not to expect a direct revelation. I must study the plain physical facts of the case, ascertain what is possible and learn what appears to be wise and right. The subject is difficult, and good men do not agree." The worst thing he could do would be to use words that he could not enforce, since how "would *my word* free the slaves, when I cannot even enforce the Constitution in the rebel States?" The Border States provided "fifty thousand bayonets in the Union armies. . . . It would be a serious matter if, in consequence of a proclamation such as you desire, they should go over to the rebels." He could not afford to view the matter other than "as a practical war measure, to be decided upon according to the advantages or disadvantages it may offer to the suppression of the rebellion."

The delegation of clergymen gathered in Chicago were respectful and conciliatory, though Lincoln's theological materialism must have been distancing: here was a president who noticed that those who claimed God spoke to them disagreed about what he said; who admitted unhesitatingly that God did not speak to him; and responded to the language of religious faith with a reference to logical probabilities. A decision on emancipation, Lincoln maintained, could not and should not be determined by revelation, religious faith, or moral certitude. Such a decision was a matter of state. What was relevant was a factual, realistic assessment of the best interests of the nation as a whole, which at the moment meant the defeat of the Confederacy. But words mattered, the clergymen argued in response. "'No one can tell the power of the right word from the right man to develop the latent fire and enthusiasm of the masses.' 'I know it,' exclaimed Mr. Lincoln," who brought the hour-long interview to a close with the request that he not be misunderstood. "I have not decided against a proclamation of liberty to the slaves, but hold the matter under advisement," and the clergymen could leave with the assurance that "the subject is on my mind, by day and night, more than any other." The biblical resonance of "by day and night" was a typical Lincoln touch. He assured them, as they departed, deferring to the clerical rhetoric while maintaining his intellectual independence, that "whatever shall *appear* [author's italics] to be God's will I will do."

Whatever God's will and whatever the rhetoric that would satisfy his various constituencies, it was Lincoln's decision. Having weighed the arguments on both sides, he concluded that the war effort could best be served by limited emancipation. On September 22, he presented to his cabinet a proclamation: as of January 1, 1863, the slaves in those states that were on that date in rebellion were to be emancipated by presidential proclamation; that he would recommend that Congress provide all states not in rebellion pecuniary aid to pay for emancipation; and that Congress continue to provide financial encouragement to those of African descent to emigrate. It was simultaneously a radical and a conservative proclamation, minimally idealistic and substantially pragmatic, a small stick with numbers of coercive carrots, emancipation in a minor key. It was an effort to keep the Border States stable for the Union, to address the concern of Negro-phobic Northerners, especially within his own party, to weaken the Confederacy, to reduce Northern resistance to Negroes serving in the Union army, to give heart to abolitionists, and to inspire his Republican constituency.

A practical measure, it also had symbolic power. It had been slowly prepared for and pressured into existence, with high downside risk for the Union. After cabinet discussion, the proclamation was held back for later release, when it might be seen less as an act of wartime desperation than of bold forward movement. On January 1 a streamlined, less-legalistic version, to which Seward and Chase made helpful contributions and on which Seward's name also appeared, was published. There was now no going back. Lawyerly, concise, and unliterary, it was admirably suited to its purpose, and, paradoxically, perhaps the single most consequential document of Lincoln's presidency, an act of dictate rather than of commentary or persuasion. At the same time as he composed the final draft, he recommended to Congress a constitutional amendment to abolish slavery throughout the United States, the gradual process to be completed by the year 1900. Slave owners would be compensated by the federal government, the exact amount to be determined by Congress. The amendment would require a two-thirds majority vote in the Congress and the approval of three-fourths of the states. Voluntary colonization would be encouraged and supported. All slaves who had been freed by the fortunes of war would remain free. "In *giving* freedom to the *slave*, we *assure* freedom to the *free*—honoring alike in what we give, and what we preserve."

"*We* cannot escape history," Lincoln wrote in his 1862 annual message, partly in the context of pro-Confederate activities by some Indian tribes on the southwestern frontier and the rebellion of Sioux Indians in Minnesota. The subject had personal and political interest to him. His paternal grandfather had been killed by Indians. He had fought as a young man in the Black Hawk War, fated neither to kill nor participate in a battle but to come upon mangled corpses, both white and red. The history he and his contemporaries could not escape included their occupation, by force or by treaty, of the entire country. In Kentucky, Indiana, and Illinois, the Lincoln and Hanks families had benefited from the assumption that white settlers had the right to possess any and all of the land of the New World. Of course not every Indian tribe peacefully accepted dispossession; and Lincoln, in mid-1862, had to deal with tribes that had become, in modern terminology, "enemy combatants" providing aid, directly or indirectly, to the Confederacy, either fighting against Union interests or asserting their own. It was another one of the burdens of history that could not be escaped.

As with most of his contemporaries, questions of conscience about the Indian expulsion apparently never arose in Lincoln's mind, at least partly because the white world could little afford what would have seemed a self-indulgent moral luxury while the dispossession was still in process. On this matter, moral values and self-interest were inseparable twins. His frontier background influenced his adherence to the almost universal belief that the Indian did not possess the land, at least in any sense that the white world could accept. Nomadic, comparatively few in numbers, they rarely appeared in any place they claimed to have rights to; they had no documents delineating boundaries or establishing ownership. To the settlers, they were an alien, warlike race, responsible for their own annihilation since they did not have the will or intelligence to leave their hunting life for an agricultural existence. They were not, and it was thought could never become, citizens of the United States. And since they were not slaves, there need be no movement to free them. There were no idealists or lobbyists to represent them; they played no role in the American economy. And preoccupation with Negro emancipation, which challenged the moral imagination of nineteenth-century white America, left little to no room for the assumption of moral responsibility for the Indian situation. One sin or debt to be repaid seemed to Lincoln and his contemporaries enough.

The tribes also had the distinctive feature of their ambiguous status: sovereign but in fact feudal or tribute nations, existing under the thumb or the threat of military force, pushed westward by imposed treaties and the federal army to make way for white settlements. Secessionists and Copperheads unquestionably had the right to land and citizenship. The relationship between Negroes and the land was in the process of being reconfigured, though demographics already gave blacks limited possession. But Indian tribes had no place in the national territory other than on reservations, segregated from the white population into loose quasi–prison camps. It was a question of land and its ownership. "A nation may be said to consist of its territory, its people, and its laws," Lincoln told Congress in December 1862. "That portion of the earth's surface which is owned and inhabited by the people of the United States, is well adapted to the home of one national family; and it is not well adapted for two, or more." Just as it could not endure divided between the Union and the Confederacy, the nation could not exist divided between white settlers and Indian tribes.

Lincoln now found himself trapped by military and political conditions into complicity in executing Indians. The factors that created the trap were similar enough to those of the Black Hawk War to provide images of painful déjà vu to a sensitive man already disturbed by nightmares about the blood being shed in a war for which he had some responsibility. In 1851, the Santee Sioux Indians of Minnesota had been forced to cede to the government their twenty-four-million-acre hunting ground. In 1852, they were corralled into a reservation on the Minnesota River. In 1858, they were swindled of half that land. In August 1862, when the government failed to pay the $1.4 million compensation provided by treaty, and its agents and politicians stole most of the supplies that the treaty granted, the Indians rebelled. When Chief Little Crow complained that despite stacks of provisions in clear sight, supposedly theirs by treaty, his people had nothing to eat, the government agent responded, "So far as I'm concerned . . . let them eat grass or their own dung." Minnesota political leaders, led by Governor Alexander Ramsey, in league with commercial interests, advocated expelling all Indians from Minnesota.

The Sioux took to arms, murdering eight hundred settlers, "killing, indiscriminately, men, women, and children," attacking "with extreme ferocity," Lincoln told Congress. As always, barring some tactical blunder, federal forces eventually dominated the battlefield by virtue of superior numbers, discipline, and firepower. By December 1862, the Sioux had been defeated. Of the 2,000 captured, a military board sentenced 303 to be hanged. Governor Ramsey and most white Minnesotans approved. Ramsey demanded that the federal government order all remaining Indians be removed or exterminated and that Washington pay Minnesota $2 million in reparations, $600,000 more than what had been owed the Sioux. Congress and the Lincoln administration complied, part of a series of agreements that, enriching some and compensating others, eliminated all Indians from the state and kept Minnesota dedicated to the Union war effort.

When he received the names of those scheduled to be hanged, Lincoln telegraphed for the trial transcripts. At the same time, he received appeals for and against clemency. As in all such instances and especially this one, given the number at issue, he approached the exercise of the power of pardon with painful deliberateness. "Anxious to not act with so much clemency as to encourage another outbreak on the one hand, nor with so much severity as to be real cruelty on the other, I caused a careful examination of the records of trials to be made." His first priority was to confirm the execution of those who had committed rape, the primal crime that an Indian could commit against the white community. To his surprise, he found only two instances. "I then directed a further examination," he wrote in response to a request for a report from the Senate, the venue that had jurisdiction over Indian affairs, "and a classification of all who were proven to have participated in *massacres*, as distinguished from participation in *battles*." The number was down to forty. It appears from his phrasing—exact, concise, balanced, delicately qualified, and also coldly utilitarian—that he had had someone analyze the documents for him. The language, though, is clearly his own. One of the forty had been strongly recommended for commutation to ten years' imprisonment. "I have ordered the other thirty-nine to be executed." The general in charge requested a postponement: there were "secret combinations . . . embracing thousands of citizens pledged to execute all the Indians." Under strict military security, the thirty-nine were hanged. Neither executions nor clemency, however, impinged on Lincoln's view of the inexorable right of the Union to secure Indian property for free labor. He submitted to the Senate an Indian "reconstruction" plan which, he reassured Minnesotans, contained "stipulations for extinguishing the possessory rights of the Indians to large and valuable tracts of land."

In March 1863, he had a formal audience with the chiefs of seven prominent Western tribes. That they were in Washington involuntarily seems likely, the guests of a government intent on impressing them with its power, extending a diplomatic carrot while at the same time demonstrating its military power and national wealth. Their appearance attracted a crowd, squeezing into the East Room, peering over the shoulders of cabinet secretaries and other dignitaries, who were seated in a circle. Into its center stepped the president, prepared to listen to speeches and to address his guests. The *Daily Morning Chronicle* described the Indian chiefs as "fine-looking," with "the hard and cruel lines in their faces which we might expect in savages; but they were evidently men of intelligence and force of character." That the principals neither spoke nor understood the other's language made interpreters necessary. Apparently no record exists of what the two chiefs who addressed Lincoln said, or how they said it, either by transcription in their own language or in the interpreter's English.

It may have been impossible for there to have been any stranger sound than Lincoln addressing the Indian chiefs in a gentle version of Indian-inflected pidgin English, which the translator then rendered into one or more of the Indian languages, which the President could not understand let alone vet for accuracy. Lincoln participated in the convention that white people somehow were better understood by Indians by speaking the way a native English speaker would speak to a foreigner who had difficulty with the language, adding here and there a white version of Indian phrases. The audience for such language was not the assembled chiefs, especially in the mind of someone as linguistically sophisticated as Lincoln, but the American public, who would have expected him to reinforce their own cultural prejudices in regard to the Indian tribes that pidgin Indian repre-sented. The interpreter, presumably, found the words that conveyed the president's message, which the Indian nations already had had preached at them for much of the nineteenth century.

Such words emphasized the powerlessness of the tribes in the face of white supremacy. Even Lincoln's conciliatory personality could not have softened the message, though the more substantive parts reached a digni-fied preciseness of language that by training and talent he was almost in-capable of slighting. The explicit and implicit messages, though, occupied the slippery slope between realpolitik and genocide. This president had recently shown that as the vehicle of his people he was pledged to affirm the national will by military force. For the Indian tribes to survive, they had to become more like the white man.

There is a great difference between this pale-faced people and their red brethren, both as to numbers and the way in which they live. We know not whether your own situation is best for your race, but this is what has made the difference in our way of living.

The pale-faced people are numerous and prosperous because they cultivate the earth, produce bread, and depend upon the products of the earth rather than wild game for a subsistence.

This is the chief reason of the difference; but there is another. Although we are now engaged in a great war between one another, we are not, as a race, so much disposed to fight and kill one another as our red brethren.

You have asked for my advice. I really am not capable of advising you. . . . I can only say that I can see no way in which your race is to become as numerous and prosperous as the white race except by living as they do, by the cultivation of the earth.

As to the alleged treaty violations, the government is not at fault "if our children should sometimes behave badly. . . . You know it is not always possible for any father to have his children do precisely as he wishes them to do."

It is impossible to know what the chiefs made of Lincoln's comparison between Indian tribal warfare and the American Civil War or between the relative disposition of the two cultures in regard to fighting and killing one another. The *Daily Morning Chronicle* reported that "the President's remarks were received with frequent marks of applause and approbation," apparently from the white audience. "'Ugh,' 'Aha' sounded along the line [of chiefs] as the interpreter proceeded, and their countenances gave evident tokens of satisfaction."

Lincoln spent most of his long work days plagued by sleep deprivation and bad dreams, administrating the war and the Republican domestic agenda, often involved in patronage decisions and contentious appointments, pained by lost battlefield opportunities and the high cost of the war, especially in lives, anguishing over whom to pardon and whom to have executed—what he called "the butchering business"—and, in 1864, worrying that he would not be reelected and that, consequently, everything for which the Union had sacrificed would be lost by a compromise that would end the war on damaging terms. His opportunities to address the public were few, and there was little tradition for and less political sense in manufacturing such occasions. "In my position it is somewhat important that I should not say any foolish things," he told a crowd requesting an impromptu speech. "It very often happens that the only way to help it is to say nothing at all." Even if he were not a heavily burdened wartime president, he was precluded from campaigning in 1864.

At the rare moments he had reason to be hopeful his language reflected the momentary lightening of his burden, an exuberance that turned him to poetry, the métier natural to his expression of emotion. He was rarely without a volume of the mid-nineteenth-century dialect humor he favored for comic relief, whether for nighttime reading or for reciting at lugubrious cabinet meetings. Comic verse had lightened his mood as early as his 1829 "Chronicles of Reuben." Two weeks after the Union victory at Gettysburg, his notion of Sunday morning prayer was celebratory poetic frivolity for private amusement, a spontaneous eight-line combination of dramatic monologue and comic lyric titled "Gen. Lees invasion of the North written by himself," which concluded with the less-than-immortal line "we skedaddled back again, / and didn't sack Phil-del."

Despite the press of duties, he found time to read, especially the Bible and Shakespeare, the only president, other than John Quincy Adams, for whom literature and life were inseparable. Though his early reading was narrow, it was expanded by increased access to books beginning in the late 1840s and even more so during his presidency. With the Library of Congress at hand, a gift from Jefferson to him, so to speak, he borrowed from its large collection Horace's poetry, *Plutarch's Lives*, Samuel Butler's *Hudibras*, and Ralph Waldo Emerson's *Representative Men*, among other volumes, and he added books to the White House library, including editions of two of his constantly reread favorites, Thomas Hood and Oliver Goldsmith, and popular contemporary poets such as Elizabeth Barrett Browning. An intense re-reader, both on the page and in his memory, he found minutes and sometimes hours between snatches of business, often in the evenings or late at night, to read poetry for solace and pleasure, returning to his favorites in the canon as well as sampling American contemporaries, especially comic versifiers. He also, in July 1862, read Longfellow's *Song of Hiawatha,* at the same time, a suggestive conjunction, that he borrowed *The History of Minnesota; from the Earliest French Explorers to the Present Time.* He was soon to be responsible for the execution of thirty-nine of Hiawatha's descendants, so to speak, and he signed in August 1864 an order "for the sale of Valuable lands in the late Winnebago Indian Reservation, in Minnesota," more than fifty thousand acres to be made available for purchase by settlers and businessmen. Hiawatha's "departure," with which Longfellow's poem ends, as "Westward, westward Hiawatha / Sailed into the fiery sunset," provided poetic anaesthetizing and stoic inevitability to dispossession.

Lincoln's most-read volume was Shakespeare's plays, his secular Bible. As often as he attended performances, he still preferred Shakespeare in the theater of his own mind, his book in hand, his favorite lines often read aloud to himself or to others. Particular characters and situations compellingly embodied personal parallels, the unchanging reality of human nature and the human situation. "Human-nature will not change," he wrote in November 1864. "In any future great national trial, compared with the men of this, we shall have as weak, and as strong; as silly and as wise, as bad and good." He found a wealth of varied particularity in Shakespeare's characters, paradigms for his own world. Shakespeare's scenes of ambition, murder, regicide, and civil war resonated for him with his and his country's situation, his voice trembling, as he gazed down, so to speak, to imagine the blood on his own hands. Even if it had been shed for right purposes, it was still blood. Shakespeare's history plays now had special purchase, even more than they had always had, as exemplars of the drama of national destiny, great leaders contesting for dominance, the clashing of ambitions and wills, and the attempt to assert contradictory national visions. The second part of Shakespeare's Henry VI sequence, dramatizing the brutal war between the houses of York and Lancaster, provided a linguistic equivalent of his own torn soul, his civil war also increasingly spinning out of control, the military murders, including the legal butchery, amplified for both sides.

So deeply absorbed was he as a reader of Shakespeare that quotations from the plays came as naturally to him as breathing. Writing from memory in June 1864, he slightly misquoted Henry VI. "This war," he told an audience gathered in Philadelphia to raise money to tend the wounded, "has carried mourning to almost every home, until it can almost be said that the 'heavens are hung in black'" In Shakespeare's theater, when stage curtains were hung in black, it informed the audience that a tragedy was about to be performed. Shakespearean tragedy and the American national tragedy were to Lincoln correlatives. Shakespeare's vivid language made the consonance between imagination and reality devastatingly powerful.

That power of language resides, Lincoln believed, in its honest and particularized use, its persuasiveness determined by its adherence to the linguistic ground rules of a moral lexicon. He made and exemplified the point in an address to a Sanitary Fair, the name given to fairs to raise funds for the United States Sanitary Commission, in Baltimore in April 1864. The dispute between the North and the South had at its essence, he proposed, a disagreement about definitions, particularly how to define the word "liberty. . . . The world has never had a good definition," and though both sides in the war "declare for liberty," each means a different thing by the use of the word. And each calls what he declares for "liberty" and calls what the other declares for "tyranny." As he often did, Lincoln found his example in animal imagery and the tradition of the animal fable. "The Shepherd drives the wolf from the sheep's throat, for which the sheep thanks the shepherd as a *liberator*, while the wolf denounces him for the same act as the destroyer of liberty, especially as the sheep was a black one. Plainly the sheep and the wolf are not agreed upon a definition of the word liberty." The claim that white liberty requires black servitude is a definition of liberty, in Lincoln's telling phrase, from "the wolf's dictionary," and that dictionary must be repudiated.

A few writers, such as Shakespeare, had burned their lines and their imaginative patterns into Lincoln's receptive consciousness with an inscribing power that made them inseparable from his own ability to speak and write, and even to think, about human beings and human affairs. Their texts he had selectively raised to the level of a secular sacredness. His early passion for Burns had not diminished, and it is likely that Burns's influence, not in language but in feeling and ideology, informed Lincoln's passionate emphasis on the war as the assertion of the principle that the people govern, that the republic is dedicated to the dominance of the common man. When invited to attend the annual celebration of Burns's birthday in January 1865, hosted by the Burns Club of Washington, he sent a toast honoring the people's poet: "I can say nothing worthy of his generous heart, and transcendent genius. Thinking of what he has said, I can not say anything which seems worth saying," though, in retrospect, he did just that in his many poetic evocations in his speeches of the principles to which the republic was dedicated. Those had evolved in the cauldron of creative history and literature, from ancient times to the present, and were vividly available in the prose and poetry of British writers. In a few weeks in March 1863, he read volumes three and four of Hume's *History of England*, the first two of which he had borrowed in January, attended performances of Shakespeare's *Henry IV* and *Hamlet*, and took turns at the White House reading aloud with Senator Charles Sumner an *Introduction to the Study of International Law*.

The war itself, and its surrounding incidents and activities, was a text, Lincoln told a Washington audience soon after his reelection in November 1864, to be studied and to learn from. The causes of all wars inhere in human nature, he believed, which his experience and deterministic philosophy led him to conclude would never change. The American history that he and his contemporaries had forged in blood provided a textbook whose lessons might again, at other times and over other causes, be relevant to the destiny of the republic. "In any future great national trial, compared with the men of this, we shall have as weak, and as strong; as silly and as wise; as bad and good. Let us, therefore, study the incidents of this, as philosophy to learn wisdom from, and none of them as wrongs to be revenged." And these words that he is contributing to the effort to retain and re-create the republic more fully in the spirit of the Declaration of Independence are themselves texts to be studied as part of the heritage. He himself, he implies, is an exemplification of the oppositional varieties of human nature, of which there have been and will be others, all actors on this varied stage on which imagination and truth are the constituents of an honest style and the character of a leader. His own words, becoming part of the universal text, he created with the care and craftsmanship typical of writers who combine their immersion in language and life with the inspiration of the moment and the artistry that creates literary masterpieces.

A lifetime of reading wisdom literature thoroughly informs the two Lincoln essays that have most permeated the American historical consciousness, and which continue to shape our sense of ourselves when we look in the mirror of language and history. Both the Gettysburg and the second inaugural addresses were forged by his advice to himself and his country to study what had happened for helpful lessons rather than retribution, and at the same time to engage with issues of national identity. Expressive of how difficult it is in any intellectually honest assessment to know why such a war has occurred and who is responsible, these two essays also engage with the problem now paramount in Lincoln's mind: how to bring the South back into a united nation. He heard the vengeful voices of his Republican constituency, and desired to urge constructive and rational forgiveness, not retribution. Hardly a Christian in terms of any of the nineteenth-century orthodoxies, and only in the ethical sense, Lincoln could sincerely appeal, even if indirectly, to Christian charity, as well as to enlightened self-interest, in the search for a language and logic that would prevent counterproductive retribution.

He began his formulation of reconstruction policy in his annual message in December 1863, to which he appended a proclamation setting out conditions for amnesty and reconstruction, the results of which he reported to Congress a year later. It was a war policy in that it encouraged those in the rebellious states who had had enough of war or who had been pro-Union from the start to take over the government of their states and thus weaken the Confederacy. It was a peace policy in that it established ameliorative ground rules for the rebellious states to rejoin the Union as self-governing entities and as partners in national government. Citizens of those states would be pardoned, except for high-ranking military, governmental, and judicial officers—particularly those who had left positions in the federal government to join the rebellion—provided that three conditions were met: that residents swore allegiance to the Constitution and the Union, recognizing its indivisibility; that a republican form of government was established; and that emancipation was legally acknowledged and enforced.

With memorializing indirection and poetic subtlety, Lincoln set the tone of reconstruction in November 1863 in his Gettysburg Address, that oft-analyzed literary masterpiece that dwells on the dynamic crux of the relationship between the dead and the living, particularly "the unfinished work" and "the great task remaining before us." That task was, explicitly, the completion of the war. It was also the perpetuation of the republic as a text constantly being rewritten, particularly the extension of the basic principles of that unique experiment, a government "of the people, by the people, and for the people," pushed beyond the limits that its eighteenth-century founders had established to a more open and inclusive embrace of democratic equality. The task, by the logic of its paradigm, required creating a policy and a set of conditions the result of which would be national reconciliation and a stronger union. To the degree to which Gettysburg was a battle-worshipping and mournfully triumphal occasion, it was also, through Lincoln's words, a celebration of life, particularly the regeneration of the geographical and ideological wholeness of the nation. And those in the South who had died so that the Union might perish were not proper objects of this commemoration. But the living Southerners, whose lives were inseparable from the deaths of their own sons, brothers, and husbands, were part of the necessary work of the future. Without their commitment, the "new birth of freedom" would be delayed or even denied.

Addressing an audience that could barely hear him and that hardly had time to focus its attention before the speech was over, Lincoln encapsulated a lifetime of experience in the dynamic interconnection between life and death, the elegiac apostrophe that speaks out of the stoic temperament, compelled by its attraction to melancholy and mutability to find wisdom and inspiration in loss. It affirms that the poetry of loss is, by virtue of its poetic essence, also the poetry that makes sense out of life. It makes reality the basis of the wisdom that heals and renews. For Lincoln, the dead were all around him, at the battlefield, in his nightmares, and in the daily tasks of office, including the "butcher business," which he anguished over whichever side appeals for pardon came from. It elicited from him, despite the press of official business, occasional letters of sympathy and condolence, heart-wrenching in their combination of empathy and precision, the exact word and the plain style. His own dead were more precious to him than Confederate dead, the inevitable narrowing of sympathy that war requires of both sides.

But at Gettysburg he would not go so far as to exclude from the sacredness of the ground the fact that many of the corpses were Americans from the other half of the nation. If they had not "nobly carried on" the cause of the Union, they had nonetheless also given their "last full measure of devotion" in a cause whose defeat was necessary in order to "resolve that these dead shall not have died in vain." The challenge was to turn *all* that carrion flesh into new life, "a new birth of freedom." A reading selection from his childhood textbook, *Dilworth's Speller*, echoes in his language:

> From every corner of th' extended earth,
> The scattered dust is called to second birth;

The fever'd body now unites again,
And kindred atoms rally into men;
The various joints resume their ancient seats,
And every limb its form repeats.

This secular "second birth," connected by the long "electric chord" back to the founders, required all the dead to live in the new life of the recombined nation.

Given his brooding and philosophical temperament, he was again compelled to address, to the extent that his practical responsibilities permitted, questions of natural law underlying why the war had happened and who was responsible. The answers were relevant to the problem of amelioration and reconstruction. Who was to blame for the misery and the deaths? And if individuals and states had indulged in recklessly self-destructive folly, had not the war already sufficiently exorcised that regression on both sides? Basic human nature never changed, he was certain; the collective human text demonstrated that incontrovertibly. The culture's permanent mixture of folly and wisdom was there to see in the literary and historical records created by the writers he cherished. Reconstruction required forgiveness within reasonable rules. He had set those out, and would continue to argue for their flexible imposition, relative to local conditions in each state. At the same time, he had to have known that the deep core of Southern resentment would be exacerbated by defeat; that deep-seated attitudes and structures would survive emancipation: the mind-set of masters without the fact of slavery; and that the challenge of establishing equality before the law, given the nationwide deep prejudice against the Negro, was formidable.

Such issues he expected the Congress and the president to address in the months and years after the war, which, as he took the oath for his second term on March 4, 1865, he was pleased to say had recently shown "reasonably satisfactory and encouraging" progress. The explicit causes of the war, he reminded his audience, were obvious: though "both parties deprecated war . . . one of them would *make* war rather than let the nation survive; and the other would *accept* war rather than let it perish. And the war came." Behind the legal and constitutional debates, all knew that slavery "was, somehow, the cause of the war," the desire of part of the nation to extend it and part of the nation to restrict it, an admission that he had not found it politic to make, or at least to emphasize, previously. The question of how former slaves, now in some limited way automatically citizens in a nation in which most of the people did not accept them as equals but desired them either to be subordinated or, even better, gone from the land, could be made part of "a new birth of freedom" was difficult to answer, except that it would be with difficulty.

With his usual biblical resonance and Shakespearean inclusiveness, in one of the supreme dramatic monologues of American literature, he moved deeply, though concisely, into the heart of the historical darkness, the problem of first causes and why, and to the most famous peroration in the American literary canon. How, he asked in some of the same language he had used in his "Meditation on the Divine Will," was it possible for both sides, who prayed to the same God, to be right? And why did a "just God," belief in whose existence as a force for justice in the universe Lincoln aspired to and sometimes attained, allow the suffering of the war to last for so long? Yes, "The Almighty has His own purposes," and they are beyond human understanding, but "woe unto the world because of its offences!" And then the crucial and difficult sentence: "If we shall suppose that American Slavery is one of those offences which, in the providence of God, must needs come, but which, having continued through His appointed time, He now wills to remove, and that He gives to both North and South, this terrible war, as the woe due to those by whom the offence came, shall we determine therein any departure from those divine attributes which the believers in a Living God always ascribe to Him?"

It is indeed a real question, only vaguely rhetorical in the sense that he does not answer it, though he would if he could. It is in its entirety a hypothesis: let us for the moment, he proposes, speculate about these matters—"if we shall suppose"—without arguing whether the speculation is true or not. And the question contains two sub-questions: If God is indeed providential but is also just, why did he decree slavery at all, even if he decreed it for only a specific period of time? And if God had decreed it, why should God not take responsibility for its removal without requiring "this terrible war"? And, the main question asks, in regard to a God who has (hypothetically) decreed the "offence" of American slavery and who has required the deaths of those who participated in the offences He had initiated, is this God the same as or different from the God posited by those who believe in "a living God," as do Christians, by which Lincoln means a God who participates in and cares about the affairs of mankind? Is this a God of love and forgiveness, a God of mercy? And is this a just God? Since Lincoln did not doubt that justice was on the side of those who opposed slavery, why, then, if there is a just God, let alone a merciful one, have *both* North and South been made to suffer so horribly?

Lincoln had no answer, and it is probable to conclude from his carefully crafted language, especially its elaborate phrasing, that the answer that inheres in the question is that some power beyond the human, call it what you will, determined that the historical event of slavery and the givens of human nature would produce results that no recourse either to reason or to first causes, let alone to Christian definitions of deity, can explain. His own deism allowed for a God who, having made the world, did not participate in the working out of its ends, whose management of human destiny only inhered in his allowing the patterns and values established by His will to work themselves out in human affairs. Lincoln's response to his own question is to change his tone and focus. The question mark is followed by, "Fondly do we hope—fervently do we pray—that this mighty scourge of war may speedily pass away." And whether it does or does not is not entirely in human hands: "Yet, if God wills that it continue . . . until every drop of blood drawn with the lash, shall be paid by another drawn with the sword . . . so still must it be said 'the judgments of the Lord, are true and righteous altogether.'"

Thus if forces beyond human control, which we cannot understand but have faith in as an expression of natural law, determine that more blood should be shed by both sides, so be it. And so be it because the entire nation is responsible for slavery. And the duty of the president, the Congress, and the people of the nation as a whole is to undertake reconciliation and reconstruction: "With malice toward none; with charity for all; with firmness in the right, as God gives us to see the right, let us strive on to finish the work we are in; to bind up the nation's wounds; to care for him who shall have born the battle, and for his widow, and his orphan—to do all which may achieve and cherish a just, and a lasting peace, among ourselves, and with all nations."

On the evening of April 11, 1865, having returned from a visit to Richmond, which had been torched by the retreating Confederate army and government, Lincoln addressed a crowd that had gathered in the driveway of the North Portico of the White House. Washington was ecstatically celebratory. A friend stood behind him holding a candle as he read, "in gladness of heart," from a "carefully prepared manuscript." His mind was focused on reconstruction, which he defined as the "re-inauguration of the national authority," particularly Louisiana as a test case, and on the proposed constitutional amendment to give former slaves citizenship and all legal rights, a subject "fraught with great difficulty." He would, he expected, by constitutional responsibility, have the duty to speak and act on the subject in the months and years ahead. Four days later his ability to exercise his gift for language and his mastery of words on this and all other subjects ended.

ANNOTATED BIBLIOGRAPHY

Most of Lincoln's formal writing consists of speeches and lectures for public audiences. His private writing is composed of letters, some of them personal, many not, and occasional fragmentary memos to himself. All this has been collected into an eight-volume edition with two supplements, *The Collected Works of Abraham Lincoln* (New Brunswick: Rutgers University Press, 1953; 1974), edited by Roy P. Basler, which remains the scholarly edition of record. It is the edition I have cited throughout. A fully annotated edition, with explanatory notes and biographical identifications, is much needed. The two-volume edition of *Lincoln's Speeches and Writings* (New York: Library of America, 1989), based on Basler's texts, or the one-volume paperback version, are excellent Lincoln companions for the general reader. A complete collection of everything pertaining to Lincoln's career as a lawyer, *The Law Practice of Abraham Lincoln, Complete Documentary Edition*, edited by Martha L. Bennet and Cullom Davis (Urbana and Chicago: University of Illinois Press, 2000) has been published by the University of Illinois Press in an electronic edition. Among its documents is a transcription of Lincoln's only brief argued before the United States Supreme Court, which has not heretofore been discussed in any book about Lincoln, even in the two most recent (and helpful) books about Lincoln's legal career, Mark E. Steiner's *An Honest Calling: The Law Practice of Abraham Lincoln* (DeKalb: Northern Illinois University Press, 2006) and Brian Dirck's *Lincoln the Lawyer* (Urbana and Chicago: University of Illinois Press, 2007). I have relied on *The Law Practice . . . Documentary Edition* for all documents and facts about Lincoln's legal career.

In addition to the words authenticated as Lincoln's, recollections by his contemporaries of what he said in their presence or said to a third party have been preserved. When reading these, one doesn't know whom to trust, though some sources have been demonstrated to be more trustworthy than others, and some not credible at all. The best strategy would be to trust none, but that would leave one sailing on a small sea indeed, since a significant amount of what we know or think we know about Lincoln comes from his contemporaries. *Recollected Words of*

Abraham Lincoln (Stanford: Stanford University Press, 1996), edited by Donald E. Fehrenbacher and Virginia Fehrenbacher, is a reliable guide to what Lincoln's contemporaries claimed he said and the degree to which the claims have plausibility. In many cases they have little to none, especially in regard to his religious beliefs, unsupported and implausible accounts of which are still being perpetuated.

For example, the accounts of Lincoln's religious views in William J. Wolfe's *The Almost Chosen People: A Study of the Religion of Abraham Lincoln* (New York: Doubleday, 1959) and in John Meecham's *American Gospel: God, The Founding Fathers, and the Making of a Nation* (New York: Random House, 2006) cite second- and thirdhand recollections by self-serving parties about what Lincoln said as if they were reliable. In contrast, David L. Holmes's *The Faiths of the Founding Fathers* (New York: Oxford, 2006), focusing on the deism of Lincoln's predecessors, exemplifies a scholarly discrimination between reliable and unreliable source material. Mark A. Noll's discussion of Lincoln's religion in *America's God: From Jonathan Edwards to Abraham Lincoln* (New York: Oxford, 2002) is scholarly and sophisticated but skirts a direct answer to the most relevant question: Was Lincoln a Christian? So, too, does Ronald C. White's "Lincoln's Sermon on the Mount: The Second Inaugural" (in *Religion and the American Civil War*, ed. by Randall M. Miller, Harry S. Stout, and Charles Reagan Wilson [New York: Oxford, 1998]). There is evidence that Lincoln did not believe in the divinity of Jesus, the immortality of the soul, or the existence of an afterlife, but some recollections present him as a true believer. I have relied only on evidence that meets the usual scholarly criteria.

Among the large number of background books that I have benefited from, the most helpful have been: Richard Franklin Bensel, *Yankee Leviathan: The Origins of Central State Authority in America, 1859–1877* (New York: Cambridge, 1990); Don E. Fehrenbacher, *The Dred Scott Case: Its Significance in American Law and Politics* (New York: Oxford, 1978); William E. Gienapp, *The Origins of the Republican Party, 1852–1856* (New York: Oxford, 1997); Robert J. Johannsen, *Stephen A. Douglas* (New York: University of Illinois Press, 1973); Michael F. Holt, *The Rise and Fall of the American Whig Party: Jacksonian Politics and the Onset of the Civil War* (New York: Oxford, 1999); Merrill D. Peterson, *The Great Triumvirate: Webster, Clay, and Calhoun* (New York: Oxford, 1987); David M. Potter, *The Impending Crisis, 1848–1861* (New York: Harper and Row, 1976); Robert V. Remini, *Henry Clay: Statesman for the Union* (New York: Norton, 1991); Charles Sellers, *The Market Revolution: Jacksonian America, 1815–1846* (New York: Oxford, 1991); Sean Wilentz, *The Rise of American Democracy, Jefferson to Lincoln* (New York: Norton, 2005); and three excellent books that were published too recently for me to utilize them—Austin Allen, *Origins of the Dred Scott Case: Jacksonian Jurisprudence and the Supreme Court, 1837–1857* (Athens: University of Georgia Press, 2006); Robert Pierce Forbes, *The Missouri Compromise and Its Aftermath: Slavery and the Meaning of America* (Chapel Hill: University of North Carolina Press, 2007); and Daniel Walker Howe, *What God Hath Wrought: The Transformation of America, 1815–1848* (New York: Oxford, 2007).

The widely discussed "new burst of freedom" that Lincoln apostrophized in the Gettysburg Address has had its corollary in an explosion of books about every aspect of Lincoln, many of them exemplary in their analyses and scholarship. Two such volumes by Gabor S. Boritt, *Lincoln and the Economics of the American Dream* (Urbana and Chicago: University of Illinois Press, 1978; 1994) and *The Lincoln Enigma: The Changing Faces of an American Icon* (New York: Oxford, 2002), contain valuable bibliographical essays. Some of that burst appears in electronic form on the Internet, providing bibliographies, documents, chronologies, book reviews, and analysis regarding every aspect of Lincoln's career and his age, including the complete texts of now rare books that Lincoln studied, such as Thomas Dilworth's *New Guide to the English Language* (Philadelphia: Joseph Crukshank, 1747), widely known as *Dilworth's Speller*. The sites I have found most useful are: www.webpages.char ter.net/lincolnbooks; www.alincolnassoc.com; www.showcase.netins.net/web/ creative/lincoln.html; www.memory.loc.gov/ammem/alhtml/malhome.html; www.memory.loc.gov/ammem/index.html; www.thelincolnlog.org/view; www .cdl.library.cornell.edu/moa; www.hti.edu/m/moagrp; and www.digital.library .pitt.edu.

I have relied on numbers of general biographies and biographical studies, particularly four classics of Lincoln literature: William H. Herndon's and Jesse W. Weik's *Herndon's Lincoln: The True Story of a Great Life* (1888; 2006, ed. Rodney O. Davis and Douglas L. Wilson [Urbana and Chicago: University of Illinois Press]); Albert J. Beveridge's *Abraham Lincoln, 1809–1858* (2 vol., Boston: Houghton Mifflin, 1928); J. G. Randall's *Lincoln the President* (5 vol., New York: Dodd, Mead, 1945–1955); and the invaluable *Lincoln Day by Day: A Chronology, 1809–1865*, edited by Earl Schenck Miers et al., 4 vol. (Washington: Lincoln Sesquicentennial Commission, 1960); 1 vol. (Dayton: Morningside, 1991). The modern biographies most relevant to the context and demonstration of my thesis are David Herbert Donald's *Lincoln* (New York: Simon and Schuster, 1995), supplemented by *We Are Lincoln Men: Abraham Lincoln and His Friends* (New York: Simon and Schuster, 2003), particularly the chapter on William Herndon, which supplements Donald's *Lincoln's Herndon: A Biography* (New York: Knopf, 1948), and the chapter on Lincoln's friendship with Joshua Speed; Richard J. Carwardine's *Lincoln* (Harlow: Pearson Longman, 2003), which focuses on the theme of power in Lincoln's life; and Douglas Wilson's *Honor's Voice: The Transformation of Abraham Lincoln* (New York: Knopf, 1998). The latter is the most incisive general account of Lincoln's early life, with an indispensable chapter, "Wrestling with the Evidence," that provides a detailed overview of the problems that Lincoln biographers face in their use of sources.

As is the case with numbers of his biographical predecessors, Wilson's mission requires that he examine in his exposition the evidence regarding aspects of Lincoln's life that remain obscure and often controversial, particularly his relationship with his father, with Ann Rutledge, and with Joshua Speed, and his courtship of Mary Todd. Wilson relies heavily on Herndon's interviews with Lincoln's contemporaries, an indispensable edition of which he and Rodney O. Davis have edited, *Herndon's Informants: Letters, Interviews, and Statements About Abraham Lincoln* (Urbana and Chicago: University of Illinois Press, 1998). One aspect of the demythologizing of Lincoln begun by Beveridge (see John Braeman, "Albert J. Beveridge and Demythologizing Lincoln," *Journal of the Abraham Lincoln Association* 25, no. 2 [2004], 1–24, available at www.historycooperative.org) required discrediting Herndon's sources. In general, though not always, I find Herndon's informants reliable, especially when multiple contemporaries with little to no direct connection to one another and in ways consistent with other sources make variants of the same claims. For example, there seems to me no doubt that Lincoln's mother was an illegitimate child; that Lincoln loved Ann Rutledge and was deeply pained by her death (for a book-length account of this side of the argument, see John Evangelist Walsh, *The Shadows Rise: Abraham Lincoln and the Ann Rutledge Legend* [Urbana and Chicago: University of Illinois Press, 1993], and see also Douglas L. Wilson's essay "Abraham Lincoln, Ann Rutledge, and the Evidence of Herndon's Informants," *Lincoln Before Washington* [Urbana and Chicago: University of Illinois Press, 1997], 74–98, and Lewis Gannett, "'Overwhelming Evidence' of a Lincoln-Ann Rutledge Romance? Reexamining Rutledge Family Reminiscences," *Journal of the Abraham Lincoln Association*, Vol. 26, Issue 1 [2005], 28–41); that Lincoln was heterosexual, sharing a bed with Joshua Speed (and occasionally others) because of material rather than sexual circumstances (for the opposite view, see C. A. Tripp. *The Intimate World of Abraham Lincoln* [New York: Free Press, 2005]); and that Lincoln (under pressure) hesitantly backed into his marriage to Mary Todd (for the fullest recent discussion, see *Honor's Voice*).

The most incisive study presenting the intellectual Lincoln is Allen C. Guelzo's *Abraham Lincoln, Redeemer President* (Grand Rapids: Eerdmans, 1999). This and other studies of Lincoln as a thinker and theorist on a range of philosophical interests have perhaps made a dent in the long-standing myth of Lincoln as a relatively uneducated and unsophisticated country lawyer sentimentalized in Carl Sandberg's widely read biographies. Lincoln's inner life, particularly his melancholy, has been the subject of analysis beginning with Herndon's biography and his informants' comments. The modern attempt to unravel (or perhaps complicate) Lincoln's psyche and treat his culture in psychological terms has been interesting and sometimes revealing, particularly George B. Forgie's *Patricide in the House Divided: A Psychological Interpretation of Lincoln and His Age* (New York: Norton, 1979); Charles B. Strozier's *Lincoln's Quest for Union: Public and Private Meanings* (Urbana and Chicago: University of Illinois Press, 1982); *The Historian's Lincoln: Pseudohistory, Psychohistory, and History*, ed. Gabor S. Boritt and Norman O. Forness (Urbana and Chicago: University of Illinois Press, 1988); Michael Burlingame's *The Inner World of Abraham Lincoln* (Urbana and Chicago: University of Illinois Press, 1994); and Joshua Wolf Shenk's *Lincoln's Melancholy: How Depression Challenged a President and Fueled His Greatness* (Boston: Houghton Mifflin, 2005). Burlingame is particularly perceptive and forthright on the range of Lincoln's moods and the emotional stress of his relationships, especially with this wife. Mary Lincoln has been the subject of biographies, especially Justin G. Turner and Linda Levitt Turner's source volume, *Mary Todd Lincoln: Her Life and Letters* (New York: Knopf, 1972), and Jean H. Baker's *Mary Todd Lincoln: A Biography* (New York: Norton, 1987). The study of the marriage that seems to me the most accurate and perceptive is Michael Burlingame's "The Lincolns' Marriage: 'A Fountain of Misery, of a Quality Absolutely Infernal'" in *The Inner World of Abraham Lincoln*. I have benefited from all these volumes, even if only in some cases by disagreement.

One subdivision of Lincoln studies has focused on his eloquence, especially the rhetorical and stylistic qualities of his major speeches and particularly the speeches of his presidency, with emphasis on his persuasive powers, his careful revisions in the writing process, and the historical circumstances of his performances. The most recent of these is Douglas Wilson's excellent *Lincoln's Sword: The Presidency and the Power of Words* (New York: Knopf, 2006). It has a number of informative predecessors, including Ronald C. White's *The Eloquent President: A Portrait of Lincoln Through His Words* (New York: Random House, 2005) and John Channing Briggs's *Lincoln's Speeches Reconsidered* (Baltimore: Johns Hopkins, 2005), and there are valuable studies focusing on Lincoln's best-known individual speeches, especially Garry Wills's *Lincoln at Gettysburg: The Words That Remade America* (New York: Simon and Schuster, 1992), Ronald C. White's *Lincoln's Greatest Speech: The Second Inaugural* (New York: Simon and Schuster, 2002), Harold Holzer's *Lincoln at Cooper Union* (New York: Simon and Schuster, 2004), Alan Guelzo's *Lincoln's Emancipation Proclamation: The End of Slavery in America* (New York: Simon and Schuster, 2004), and Gabor Boritt's *The Gettysburg Gospel: The Lincoln Speech That Nobody Knows* (New York: Simon and Schuster, 2006). Some studies have focused exclusively on the Lincoln-Douglas debates, particularly Harry V. Jaffa's *Crisis of the House Divided: An Interpretation of the Issues of the Lincoln-Douglas Debates* (Chicago: University of Chicago Press, 1959); and David Zarefsky's *Lincoln, Douglas, and Slavery: In the Crucible of Public Debate* (Chicago: University of Chicago Press, 1990). Both Jaffa and Zarefsky recognize that unlike Lincoln's carefully crafted speeches, which have many of the qualities of literary essays, the debates were semi-spontaneous campaign addresses without any particular literary merit.

A number of essays and books have focused on my own subject, Lincoln as a writer, particularly Daniel Kilham Dodge, *Abraham Lincoln: The Evolution of His Literary Style* (Chicago: University of Chicago Press, 1900); Daniel Kilham Dodge, *Abraham Lincoln, Master of Words* (New York: Appleton, 1924); Roy O. Basler, "Lincoln's Development as a Writer," the introduction to *Abraham Lincoln: His Speeches and Writings* (New York: World, 1946), 1–49 (reprinted in Basler, A *Touchstone for Greatness, Essays, Addresses, and Occasional Pieces About Abraham Lincoln* (Westport: Greenwood, 1973); Jacques Barzun, "Lincoln the Literary Artist" (1959), reprinted in *A Jacques Barzun Reader: Selections from His Works*, ed. Michael Murray (New York: HarperCollins, 2002), 293–304; and Edmund Wilson, *Patriotic Gore: Studies in the Literature of the American Civil War* (New York: Oxford, 1962), 99–130. Barzun's essay is a sophisticated appreciation of Lincoln's literary genius.

The answer to the obvious question—why another book on Lincoln?—is that, with the exception of Basler's excellent essay, the length of which limits its scope and minimizes the subject's narrative potential, there is no modern study of the origin and development of Lincoln's literary sensibility and genius. This book focuses on Lincoln as a writer in a narrative that starts at the beginning. Barzun's and Wilson's essays, like the studies of the speeches of Lincoln's presidency listed here, are spatial rather than temporal, interested in prominent features of the moment rather than development over time, and touch only briefly on the connections between what Lincoln read, especially in his formative years, and what he thought and how he wrote. Lincoln's reading in the textbooks and literary anthologies of his youth, the literature that helped shape his mind and his prose style, is an essential part of the story. And the application of his gifts as a writer to his vocation and to his private life is also a necessary part of my narrative.

Throughout, I have referred to many, though not all, of Lincoln's prose compositions as essays, distinguishing between those he carefully composed with essay models and a philosophic worldview in mind and those that were the semi-spontaneous product of campaign situations: the difference, for example, between his second inaugural address and the Lincoln-Douglas debates. Just as some of the essays Emerson wrote were initially created for an oral occasion and delivered as public lectures, so, too, were some of Lincoln's essays. What makes them essays in addition to being speeches or addresses is central to my account of Lincoln as a writer. Like the other great canonical writers of American literature, a status that he is gradually attaining, Lincoln had a career as a writer, with a beginning, middle, and end. It parallels and is inseparable from his life story.

NOTES

Abbreviations

CW: Roy P. Basler, *The Collected Works of Abraham Lincoln* (New Brunswick: Rutgers University Press, 1953; 1974).

Beveridge: Albert J. Beveridge, *Abraham Lincoln, 1809–1858.* 2 vols. (Cambridge: Houghton Mifflin, 1928).

Dilworth: Thomas Dilworth, *A New Guide to the English Tongue* (popularly known as *Dilworth's Speller*) (London: 1740; Philadelphia: Joseph Crukshank, 1747).

DD: *Lincoln Day by Day: A Chronology, 1809–1865,* ed. Earl Schenck Miers et al., 4 vols. (Washington: Lincoln Sesquicentennial Commission, 1960), 1 vol. (Dayton: Morningside, 1991).

Donald: David Herbert Donald, *Lincoln* (New York: Simon and Schuster, 1995).

Grimshaw: William Grimshaw, *History of the United States from Their First Settlement as Colonies to the Cession of Florida* (Philadelphia: John Grigg, 1826).

HI: *Herndon's Informants: Letters, Interviews, and Statements About Abraham Lincoln,* ed. Rodney O. Davis and Douglas L. Wilson (Urbana and Chicago: University of Illinois Press, 1998).

LP: *The Law Practice of Abraham Lincoln: Complete Documentary Edition,* ed. Martha L. Bennet and Cullom Davis (Urbana and Chicago: University of Illinois Press, 2000).

Murray: Lindley Murray, *The English Reader: Or, Pieces in Prose and Poetry, Selected From the Best Writers, Designed to Assist Young Persons to Read with Propriety and Effect,* 11th Philadelphia edition (Philadelphia: Benjamin Johnson, 1814).

RW: *Recollected Words,* ed. Don E. Fehrenbacher and Virginia Fehrenbacher (Stanford: Stanford University Press, 1996).

Scripps: John Locke Scripps, *Life of Abraham Lincoln* (Chicago: 1860), ed. Roy P. Basler and Lloyd A. Dunlap (New York: Greenwood, 1968).

Scott: William Scott, *Lessons in Elocution: Or, A Selection of Pieces, in Prose and Verse, for the Improvement of Youth in Reading and Speaking and Writing* (Leicester: Honi Brown, 1820).

Wilson: Douglas L. Wilson, *Honor's Voice: The Transformation of Abraham Lincoln* (New York: Knopf, 1998).

1. "All the Books He Could Lay His Hands On"

3   *rudimentary life*   See Beveridge, vol. 1, 2–99; Louis A. Warren, *Lincoln's Youth* (Indianapolis: Indiana Historical Society, 1959), 15–25; for an illuminating discussion of the realities versus the myth of the agrarian West, see Henry Nash Smith, *Virgin Land: The American West as Symbol and Myth* (Cambridge: Harvard University Press, 1950); Charles Sellers's *The Market Revolution: Jacksonian America, 1815–1846* (New York: Oxford, 1991) details the subsistence culture of Lincoln's early years.

3   *rule of three*   RW, 370–71.

4   *the Deists rationalized*   For a basic primer on deism in colonial America, see David L. Holmes, *The Faiths of the Founding Fathers* (New York: Oxford, 2006), 39–51.

4   *perpetuated his illiteracy*   HI, 126.

5   *unidentified father*   HI, 445, 615; see Paul H. Verdun, "Appendix: Brief Outline of the Joseph Hanks Family," HI, 779–83, for an authoritative genealogy. Her prolific Hanks predecessors included a large number of illegitimate children.

5   *"not a lazy"*   HI, 113.

7   *save from his earnings*   For attempts to untangle Thomas Lincoln's complicated land dealings and debts, see Beveridge, chap. 1 *passim*, and Donald, 24.

7   *Aesop's fables*   see www.english.udel.edu/lemay/franklin/1747.html.

8   *"we had Spelling Matches"*   HI, 112.

10   *"Obedience comprehendith"*   Dilworth, 129.

10   *"Personal merit"*   Dilworth, 130.

10   *"Trade is so noble"*   Ibid.

10   *"in their mouths"*   Dilworth, 132.

11   *"Make no friendship"*   Dilworth, 139–50.

12   *"Christ's arms"*   Dilworth, 133.

12   *"Ah! Few and full"*   Dilworth, 132.

13   *"came by Lincolns"*   HI, 36.

14   *"I cannot remember"*   CW, 7.281.

14   *by a contemporary*   HI, 240.

14   *population of less than three thousand*   Donald, 24.

15	*"unbroken forest"* CW, 4.62.
15	*"a little two face"* HI, 39.
15–16	*"He has never since pulled a trigger"* CW, 4.62.
16	*"There was no physician"* HI, 40.
16	*"Man like an empty shadow"* Dilworth, 132.
17	*"Thomas Lincoln and Mrs Lincoln"* HI, 41.
18	*"He was always full of his Stories"* HI, 455.
19	*"would go out in the woods"* Ibid.
19	*"As Company would Come"* HI, 108.
19	*"Abe was not Energetic"* HI, 109.
19	*"devoured all the books"* HI, 455.
20	*"like physical labor"* HI, 106–107.
20	*"all he could get"* HI, 43.
20	*"I ought to leave them"* Warren, 68–69, 233.
21	*"mighty fine lies"* HI, 129; Warren, 69–70; Eleanor Atkinson, *The Boyhood of Lincoln* (New York: McClure, 1908), 25.
22	*Dombey and Son* DD (1857), 197; see David L. Rinear, *Sage, Page, Scandals, and Vandals: William E. Burton and Nineteenth-Century American Theater* (Carbondale: Southern Illinois University Press, 2004), 122–25, 127, 140, 126.
23	*"if he Ever got"* HI, 41.
23	*"short sentences against cruelty"* HI, 112.
23	*"full of fun"* HI, 41.
23	*"wrote a piece"* Ibid.
23	*"at this Early age"* Ibid.
24	*"often for amusement"* HI, 43.
25	schoolmate's father HI, 101. He became the owner of Weems's *Life of Washington* when his borrowed copy was damaged by water. Its owner would not accept its return and "insisted on Lincoln paying him for the Same which Lincoln agreed to do and as he had not the money to pay . . . he worked for Crawford a pulling corn blades at 25 cts a day and this paid for the Damaged Book."
25	mold him into the advocate See Daniel Walker Howe, "Why Abraham Lincoln Was a Whig," *Journal of the Abraham Lincoln Association*, 16, no. 1 (1995), 27–38; www.historycooperative.org.
25–26	was in Lincoln's hands HI, 109.
26	*"had a just claim"* Grimshaw, 71.
26	no violence was committed Grimshaw, 73.
27	Since the middle Grimshaw, 34–35, 300–301.
28	*"My proud-spirited"* James Riley, *An Authentic Narrative of the Loss of the*

American Brig Commerce, Wrecked on the Western Coast of Africa, In the Month of August, 1816, with an Account of the Sufferings of the Surviving Officers and Crew, Who Were Enslaved by the Wandering Arabs, On the African Desert; and Observations Historical, Geographical, and Made During the Travels of the Author, While a Slave to the Arabs, and in the Empire of Morocco (Hartford: S. Andrus and Son, 1817), 260–61.

29   "writing rude verses"   HI, 101.

2. Shakespeare

30   "He did not seem"   HI, 506.
31   "He would . . . say"   HI, 104.
31   "Abe would take"   HI, 109.
31   "He was a great talker"   HI, 169.
31   "that when he did good"   HI, 602.
31   "He said that"   HI, 127
32   "was better read"   HI, 132.
32   "Abe could Easily learn"   HI, 108.
33   "My mind is like"   RW, 413.
33   repeatedly read both volumes   On the basis of evidence from primary sources, particularly Herndon's Informants and Lincoln's own words, I have described the books Lincoln read and his reading practices, especially memorization. The evidence to support my claims about Lincoln's reading is persuasive, I believe, in all cases but not necessarily conclusive in every case. The sources do not provide a comprehensive list or, in many instances, an account of how much of any particular volume Lincoln read. For example, there is no certainty that Lincoln read the two anthologies at issue fully and intensely. But it seems to me a sustainable inference from what we know about his personality, his situation, his reading practices, and his passion for memorization that he applied himself to these two anthologies in the same way that he did to Aesop's Fables and the Bible. I have made the same assumption about James Riley's An Authentic Narrative and William Grimshaw's A History of the United States. When Lincoln got a book into his hands, he read it thoroughly, especially in his early years. The most recent attempt (as of this writing) to list the books associated with Lincoln and assess whether he read them or not is Robert Bray, "What Lincoln Read—An Evaluative and Annotated List," Journal of the Abraham Lincoln Association, Vol. 28, Issue 2 (2007), 28–81. My assessments are in agreement with his.
33   "We should cherish"   Murray, 55.
33   "near allied"   Murray, 312.

33   *"True liberty"*   Murray, 206, 327.

34   *"Do you count"*   Murray, 186–87.

34   *"We ought to distrust"*   Scott, 57.

35   *"Father of All!"*   Murray, 379.

35   *" for a cheerful countenance"* Scott, 57.

35   *"And Melancholy"*   Scott, 256.

36   *Abe wrote . . . often shown* HI, 11.

37   *"The Poetry of Abe"*   HI, 127–28.

37   *"Lincoln is my name"*   CW, 1.1.

37   *"Good boys"*   HI, 473.

37   *Addison . . . John Gilpin*   Scott, 120–21, 183–85, 268–73.

38   *"a Kind of quarrel"*   HI, 119–20.

38   *"The Satire was good"*   HI, 114.

38   *neighbors "burst their sides"*   HI, 41.

38   *"The Poem is Smutty"*   HI, 127.

39   *"Reuben & Charles"*   HI, 127, 152.

39   *"Adam and Eve's"*   Scott, 264–65.

40   *"this was . . . the first"*   HI, 119–20.

40   *"The production was witty"*   HI, 122–23.

40   *only what Scott provided*   Soliloquies or brief dialogues from *Romeo and Juliet, Henry VIII, Julius Caesar, Hamlet, Henry IV, Henry V, Othello, Richard III,* and *As You Like It.*

41   *"I charge thee"*   Scott, 359, 361.

41   *"Uneasy lies the head"*   Scott, 376, 388.

42   *"our quarrels fill'd"*   Scott, 372.

42   *"Shakespearean soliloquies"*   See James A. Stevenson, "A Providential Theology: Shakespeare's Influence on Lincoln's Second Inaugural Address," *Midwest Quarterly*, Vol. 43, Issue 1 (2001), 11–29.

42   *"this cursed hand"*   Scott, 377.

44   *silver half-dollar*   See F. B. Carpenter, *The Inner Life of Abraham Lincoln, Six Months at the White House* (New York: Hurd and Houghton, 1866), ed. Mark E. Neely, Jr. (Nebraska: University of Nebraska Press, 1995), 96–98. Carpenter quotes Lincoln that "it was a most important incident in my life" (97).

45   *"Poor Matthew!"*   CW, 1.368.

45   *"seven negroes"*   CW, 4.62.

45–46   *"Abe fought"*   HI, 131.

46   *"We stood"*   Warren, 176–86.

47   *"all hands were"*   CW, 4.63.

47   *"he was apt to be"*   HI, 518.

48   *"I turned down"*   HI, 456.

48   *"went & saw Abe"*   Ibid.

49   *"We Kept our victuals"*   DD, 14; HI, 457.

49   *"there it was we Saw"*   HI, 457.

50   *fifteen dollars a month*   Wilson says ten dollars; Harry E. Pratt, *The Personal Finances of Abraham Lincoln* (Springfield: Abraham Lincoln Association, 1943), says eight dollars.

51   *wrestling match*   Wilson, 21–51.

51   *debating club*   Wilson, 69–71.

52–53   *"I believe the improvement"* CW, 1.7.

53   *"the framers"* CW, 1.8.

53   *"But, Fellow-Citizens"* CW, 1.8.

54   *"too familiar with"* CW, 1.9.

55   Whigs . . . Clay   See Michael F. Holt, *The Rise and Fall of the American Whig Party: Jacksonian Politics and the Onset of the Civil War* (New York: Oxford, 1999); Sean Wilentz, *The Rise of American Democracy, Jefferson to Lincoln* (New York: Norton, 2005); and Daniel Walker Howe, *What God Hath Wrought: The Transformation of America, 1815–1848* (New York: Oxford, 2007).

55   *Little blood*   For a full account of the context and events of the war, see James Lewis, "The Black Hawk War of 1832," www.lincoln.lib.niu.edu/blackhawk/scholarshipindex.html.

56   *"Heads cut off"*   HI, 371.

57   *"He was acquainted with"*   HI, 555–56.

57   *"We passed our evenings"*   HI, 556.

57   *"a true Statement"*   CW, 1.12.

57   *"The only part"*   HI, 328.

58   *"the more I see"*   See James Lewis, "The Black Hawk War of 1832," www.lincoln.lib.niu.edu/blackhawk/p2d.html.

58   *formidable amount*   Pratt, *Personal Finances*, 12–15, and Dirck, 55–58.

58   *"too insignificant"*   CW, 4.65.

3. Burns, Byron, and Love Letters

61   *"he generally mastered"*   HI, 18.

61   *"laborious, and tedious"*   CW, 4.121.

62   *he "was a schollar"*   HI, 59.

62   *"Work, work"*   CW, 4.121.

62   *He never fully*   See Mark E. Steiner, *An Honest Calling: The Law Practice of Abraham Lincoln* (DeKalb: Northern Illinois University Press, 2006), 160–77; and Brian Dirck, *Lincoln the Lawyer* (Urbana and Chicago: University of Illinois Press, 2007), 154–72.

62   *"of good moral"*   DD, 56.

62   *swore the relevant oaths*   DD, 59.

62   *"He was not required"*   Albert A. Woldman, *Lawyer Lincoln* (New York: Caroll and Graf, 1936), 23.

62   *"he nearly knew"*   HI, 21.

63   *"I should say that Burns"*   HI, 141.

63   *"Conversation very often"*   HI, 429.

63   *by the 1830s*   HI, 354–55.

63–64   *"an Educated as well"*   HI, 66.

64   *"I can not frame"*   CW, 8.237.

64   *not strange to his ear*   HI, 355.

64   *"For prey"*   CW, 1.106.

65   *"repeated with great Glee"*   HI, 420.

66   *substantial essay*   Lincoln's formal speeches are carefully crafted prose compositions that, except for the occasional rhetorical devices that acknowledge listeners, fulfill the classical standards established by the essay tradition from Montaigne to Emerson. There can of course be overlap between the creation of a speech for an audience and a prose composition for readers, and in the case of Lincoln (as, for example, also with Emerson's Phi Beta Kappa address, "The American Scholar"), the literary creation may serve both the listening and the reading occasion. I distinguish throughout between Lincoln's semi-spontaneous campaign speeches, which are looser in structure and less modeled after traditional essays, and his carefully prepared formal addresses. The latter, I believe, deserve to be categorized as essays and belong to American literature as well as to American history and oratory.

66   *"was passionately fond"*   HI, 145.

66   *"No man could tell"*   HI, 182, 185, 187.

67   *"There was a strong"*   HI, 185.

67   *"an Englishman S-h-t"*   HI, 438.

67   *"In the morning after"*   Ibid.

67   *"once prosecuting a man"*   HI, 630.

68   *"Lincoln . . . had been telling"*   HI, 442–43.

68   *"I can't think"*   HI, 617.

68   *"The great majority"*   HI, 644.

69   *"mind was skeptical"*   HI, 21.

69   *"with great pleasure"*   HI, 251.

70   *"He held opinions"*   HI, 579.

71   *"he employed his intellectual"*   HI, 24.

71   *"He was an avowed"*   HI, 576.

71   *"heard Lincoln call"*   HI, 576–77.

72   *poetry of Byron*   See David J. Harkness, "Lincoln and Byron, Lovers of Liberty," *Lincoln Herald* 43, no. 4 (December 1941), 2–23.

72   *Byron "all extensively"*   HI, 141.

72   *"frequently heard him"*   HI, 497.

72   *"friends after this"*   HI, 21.

72   *"The effect upon"*   HI, 383.

72   *"As to the condition of"*   HI, 155–56.

73   *"He was staying"*   HI, 556–57.

73   *"ran off the track"*   RW, 111.

73   *"I do not think"*   HI, 156.

74   *"was a great admirer"*   HI, 156, 30.

76   *"in my office in 1854"*   HI, 632.

78   *"become the* political religion"   CW, 1.112.

78   *"That we improved"*   CW, 1.115.

79   *"Close thy Byron"*   Thomas Carlyle, *Sartor Resartus* (1831–1832), book II, chap. ix, "The Everlasting Yea."

79   *"Forsook Byron"*   HI, 30.

79   *"took from my library"*   HI, 404. *Childe Harold's Pilgrimage* III, 21.

81   *"It is the harp"*   HI, 617.

82   *"My education was"*   HI, 380.

82   *"proposed to me"*   CW, 1.117.

82   *"deficient in the nicer"*   HI, 610.

83   *"I have been sick"*   CW, 1.54.

84   *"The opposition men"*   Ibid.

85   *"I have commenced"*   CW, 1.78.

85   *"I am quite as lonesome"*   Ibid.

86   *"Whatever woman"*   Ibid.

86   *"You must write me"*   Ibid.

87   *"in all cases"*   CW, 1.94.

87   *"you feel yourself"*   CW, 1.94.

89   *"In a few days we had"*   CW, 1.118.

89   *"deeply wounded by"*   CW, 1.119.

89   *"I most emphatically"*   Ibid.

91   *"that he had traded off"*   RW, 145. Though Fehrenbacher judges Jesse K. Dubois's recollection of doubtful truth, this part of it seems to me credible.

91   *"destined to be"*   Beveridge, 1.210–11.

92   *"county government"*   See Paul M. Angle, *Here I Have Lived: A History of Lincoln's Springfield, 1821–1865* (Chicago: Abraham Lincoln Association, 1971), 35–82.

93   *"since 1823"*   Beveridge 1.213–18.

93	*"a fiery fighter"* Angle, *Here I Have Lived*, 65.
94	*"I have only sought"* Wilson, 177.
94	*"Handbill"* CW1.89–93. See Wilson, 173–79; Beveridge 1.212–29.

4. "How Miserably Things Seem to Be Arranged"

99	*"furniture for"* HI, 590.
100	*"It is probably cheap"* Ibid.
100	*"I have a very large"* Ibid.
100	*"almost without"* Ibid.
101	*With money to invest* David Donald, *We Are Lincoln Men: Abraham Lincoln and His Friends* (New York: Simon and Schuster, 2003), 31–32.
101	*promote its canal* Wilson, 126–29.
101	*"a pretty woman"* HI, 719.
102	*Stuart regularly traveled* Pratt, *Personal Finances*, 26–29; see LP, "The Law Practice of Abraham Lincoln: A Narrative Overview," and "A Statistical Portrait" (disk 1) for a comprehensive account of the facts of Lincoln's law practice.
103	*"So far as I now remember"* HI, 499–500.
104	*"In your paper"* CW, 1.48.
104	*"Whether elected or not"* Ibid.
104	*"alive on the first"* Ibid.
105	*"this young man . . . taken down"* HI, 478.
105	*"The gentleman has alluded"* Ibid.
106	*"His 'skinning' of one"* HI, 239.
106	*"frequently interrupted"* CW, 1.50.
107	*"Mr. Chairman"* CW, 1.65–66.
107	*"when an examination might be"* CW, 1.68.
108	*"I am opposed"* CW, 1.69.
108	*"black settlement"* See Sean Wilentz, *The Rise of American Democracy, Jefferson to Lincoln* (New York: Norton, 2005), 199, 652, 841, and Steiner, 110–11.
109	*"has no power"* CW, 1.75.
109	*"the promulgation of abolition"* Ibid.
109	*"the institution of slavery"* Ibid.
109	*"but that that power"* Ibid.
109	*"The difference between"* Ibid.
112	*"It is particularly embarrassing"* CW, 1.159.
113	*"And here, inasmuch"* CW, 1.165–66.
114	*"Washington is the mightiest"* CW, 1.279.

114   *"On that name"*   Ibid.

115   *"When all such of us"*   CW, 1.274.

116   *in which "there shall be"*   CW, 1.279.

116   *"The* preacher, *it is said"*   CW, 1.272.

116   *"Nor can his sincerity"*   Ibid.

116   *"To have expected"*   CW, 1.273.

117   *"Such is man"*   Ibid.

118   *"Temperance, by fortifying"*   Murray, 49.

118   *"The demon of intemperance"*   CW, 1.278.

118   *"The universal* sense*"*   CW, 1.275.

118   *"has given us a degree"*   CW, 1.278

119   *"And when the victory"*   CW, 1.279.

120   *"There was more difference"*   HI, 698.

120   *emotional withdrawal*   Almost every Lincoln biographer, beginning with Herndon, as well as many of Lincoln's contemporaries, has noticed and attempted to explain his "melancholy" or "sadness," the widely used nineteenth-century terms. The most recent discussions are Michael Burlingame's "Lincoln's Depressions," in *The Inner World of Abraham Lincoln* (Chicago and Urbana: University of Illinois Press, 1994), 92–122, and Joshua Wolf Shenck, *Lincoln's Melancholy: How Depression Challenged a President and Fueled His Greatness* (Boston: Houghton Mifflin, 2005).

121   *her actual home*   Justin G. Turner and Linda Levitt Turner, *Mary Todd Lincoln: Her Life and Letters* (New York: Knopf, 1972), 5.

122   *"a bright, lively"*   HI, 624–25.

122   *Like her father and family*   For a comprehensive examination of the Todd family and Lincoln, see Stephen Berry, *House of Abraham: Lincoln and the Todds, a Family Divided by War* (Boston: Houghton Mifflin, 2007).

122   *"a violent little Whig"*   Wilson, 215.

123   *"poetry, which she was"*   Wilson, 216.

123   *hovered about Mary*   Wilson, 217; HI, 624.

124   *"done nothing to make"*   HI, 197.

124   *killing himself*   HI, 197, 336. The attribution of the poem, for which there is only internal evidence, is in dispute. See Joshua Wolf Shenk, "The Suicide Poem," *The New Yorker*, June 14, 2004, 62.

124   *manly virtue*   See Wilson, 233–92.

124   *Byron that autumn*   DD, 145.

125   *"He was very sad"*   Wilson, 235.

125   *"so much affected"*   Ibid.

125   *"It would just kill me"*   Wilson 236.

125   *"I am now the most miserable"*   CW, 1.229

125   *"You see by this"*   CW, Supp. 1.6.

126   "that fatal first of Jany." CW 1.282.

126   "Miss Todd is flourishing" Wilson, 237. For the fullest account of Mary's emotional health, see Jason Emerson, The Madness of Mary Lincoln (Carbondale: Northern Illinois University Press, 2007).

126   "for the never-absent idea" CW, 1.282.

127   "We have had the highest" CW, 1.254.

127   "In the year 1841" CW, 1.371.

128   "Thus stands this curious" CW, 1.257–58.

128–29 "Thus ended this" CW, 1.376.

129   "it was too damned bad" CW, 1.258.

129   "It is not the object" CW, 1.376.

130   "one of the sweetest" CW, 1.261.

130   "We got on board" CW, 1.260.

133   "Richard should be" Turner, 27.

134   "Feeling, as you know I do" CW, 1.265.

134   I think it reasonable Ibid.

134   Speed is "naturally of a nervous" Ibid.

135   "What nonsense!" CW, 1.266.

135   "you well know that" CW, 1.267.

135   "forever banish" Ibid.

136   "You know" CW, 1.269.

136   "Miss Fanny and you" CW, 1.281.

136   "How miserably things seem" Ibid.

138   "Yes (if you must chaw)" CW, 1.295.

139   "wanted stackin" Ibid.

140   "Are you now" CW, 1.303.

140   He was not "entirely" HI, 430.

140   "If I had not been married" HI, 431.

141   "Jim—'I shall have'" HI, 251.

141   "that the marriage" Ibid.

141   "only meager preparation" HI, 251, 665–66.

141   "Lincoln looked" HI, 251.

141   "'with this ring'" HI, 665–66.

142   "Close thy Byron" Thomas Carlyle, Sartor Resartus (1831–1832), book II, chap. ix, "The Everlasting Yea."

142   "hug it the tighter" CW, 1.280.

5. "Were I President"

144   "wrinkled, wizened face" Woldman, Lawyer Lincoln, 40.

145   "half-interest" Personal Finances, 30.

145   *"damned abolitionist pup"*   Woldman, *Lawyer Lincoln*, 49.

147   *"Nothing new"*   CW, 1. 305.

147   *partners of a sort*   For an informed account of the limits of the partnership, see Michael Burkhimer, "Mary Todd Lincoln: Political Partner?" *Lincoln Herald* 105, no. 2 (summer 2003): 67–72.

148   *"Now if you should hear"*   CW, 1.367.

149   *"'union is strength'"*   CW, 1.315.

149   *"We had a meeting"*   CW, 1.319.

150   *"Surely no Christian"*   CW, 1.277–78.

150   *"To yield to Hardin"*   CW, 1.353.

151   *"If I am not"*   Ibid.

152   *"That I am not"*   CW, 1.382.

153   *"When [he] first"*   HI, 472.

153   *"I could myself"*   CW, 1.382.

154   *"Being elected"*   CW, 1.391.

155   *"carried Poe around"*   HI, 519.

155   *"His favorite way"*   HI, 407.

156   *"Seeing it"*   CW, 1.378.

156   *poem he admired*   See Wilson, "Abraham Lincoln and the Spirit of Mortal," *Lincoln Before Washington: New Perspectives on the Illinois Years* (Chicago and Urbana: University of Illinois Press, 1997), 133–48.

157   *"Feeling a little"*   CW, 1.366.

157   *"I would give"*   CW, 1.378.

157   *"By the way, how would you"*   CW, 1.367.

157   *"Let names be"*   CW, 1.392.

158   *"My childhood's home"*   CW, 1.378–79.

158   *"I am neither dead"*   CW, Suppl. 6.

161   *"lingering in"*   CW, 1.385.

162   *"When first my father"*   CW, 1.386.

165   *"the lightning-bug"*   Mark Twain to George Bainton, October 15, 1888. See *Art of Authorship: Literary Reminiscences, Methods of Work, and Advice to Young Beginners, Personally Contributed by Leading Authors of the Day*, compiled and edited by George Bainton (New York: Appleton, 1890).

165   *"In this troublesome"*   CW, 1.465.

166   *"more from a wish"*   CW, 1.431.

167   *Lincoln's views*   See Robert V. Remini, *Henry Clay: Statesman for the Union* (New York: Norton, 1991), 668–86.

169   *"I have ever regarded"*   Ibid, 693.

169   *"I implore"*   www.bartleby.com/268/9/7.html.

170   *"Discussion and experience"*   CW, 1.408.

171   *"Verry soon"*   CW, 1.411.

172   *"In the early days"*   CW, 1.411–12.

173   *"to each labourer the whole"*   CW, 1.412.

174   *"There is a good deal"*   CW, 1.422.

174   did not respond   Donald, 124.

176   *"most sacred right"*   CW, 1.438–39.

176   *"Let him answer"*   CW, 1.439.

177   *"not very unlike"*   CW, 1.437.

178   *"Any people"*   CW, 1.438.

178   *"This is a most valuable"*   CW, 1.439.

179   *"a bewildered"*   CW, 1.441–42.

179   *"the art of being"*   CW, 1.514.

179   *"Like a horde"*   CW, 1.508

179   *"By the way, Mr. Speaker"*   CW, 1.509–10.

180   constitution . . . own business   CW, 1.504.

181   *"needs be much uneasy"*   CW, 1.488.

181   *"Attempt the end"*   CW, 1.489. "Seek and Find," *Hesperides* (1648).

181   *"not borrow"*   CW, 1.489–90.

181   *"As a general rule"*   CW, 1.488.

182   *"If you collect"*   CW, 2.19.

183   *"Were I president"*   CW, 1.454.

183   *"Georgia Pen"*   CW, 2.237, 253.

184   *"shall be free"*   Beveridge 1.392–97; See Steiner, *An Honest Calling*, 103–36.

185   *"to abolish slavery"*   CW, 2.260.

186   to *"deliver up"*   CW, 2.20–22.

186   *"finding that I was"*   CW, 2.22.

187   *"opposition to slavery"*   CW, 2.9.

187   *"I reckon you are"*   DD, 321.

188   *"has a very tall"*   CW, 2.1.

188   *"sound reasoning"*   CW, 2.5.

188   *"It was reviving"*   CW, 2.6–7.

189   *"I am not a candidate"*   CW, 1.455.

189   *"exceedingly anxious"*   CW, 2.31.

189   *"there is nothing about me"*   CW, 2.28–29.

189   *"so far as the whigs"*   CW, 2.29.

189   *"while I think"*   CW, 2.29.

190   *"Baker has at"*   CW, 2.41.

190   *"In relation to these"*   Ibid.

190   *"Of the quite one hundred"*   CW, 2.43.

190   *"an egregious political blunder"*   Ibid.

190   *"get the ear of"*   CW, 2.50.

191   *"I am in the center"*   CW, 2.43.

191   *"an hour or more"*   DD (1849) 16.

191   *"Let it be understood"*   CW, 2.59.

192   *he tersely declined*   CW, 2.65.

192   *"It is not easy"*   Murray, 134.

192   *"What voices spoke"*   Charles Dickens, American Notes, chap. 14.

193   *"poetic effusions"*   American Notes, chap. 14.

193   *"By what mysterious"*   CW, 2.10.

193   *"There is no mystery"*   Ibid.

194   *"overwhelmed in the contemplation"*   Ibid.

194   *"a very small part"*   Ibid.

194   *"finer optics"*   The phrase, from Pope's *Essay on Man*, portions of which Lincoln memorized, became for John Ruskin and the Victorians a shorthand reference to a modern redefinition of human vision.

195   *"But still there is more"*   CW, 2.10–11. Some of the language and imagery and Lincoln's awareness of prehistorical time probably derive from his reading of Robert Chambers, *Vestiges of the Natural History of Creation* (London: John Churchill, 1844).

6. "Honest Seeking"

198   *the only time*   LP File ID L02339. Supreme Court January Term, 1849 *776: William Lewis, Who Sues for the Use of Nicholas Longworth, Plaintiff, v. Thomas Lewis, Administrator De Bonis Non of Moses Broadwell, Deceased. From Benjamin C. Howard, *Reports of the Supreme Court of the U.S. Jan. Term 1849* (1884).

200   *"make no exceptions"*   LP L02339 Document 68918. Howard 781–82.

201   *"The dictate of common sense"*   Ibid., "Brief."

203   *"Not one man"*   CW, 2.46.

204   *"has done more"*   CW, 2.78.

204   *secretary's "position has been"*   CW, 2.68.

204   *"accept the office"*   DD, 43.

205   *"How do you suppose"*   CW, 2.23.

205   *not be a candidate*   CW, 2.79.

206   *"An Improved Method"*   CW, 2.32.

207   *"This patent"*   LP File ID L02330. Parker v. Hoyt. Document 132926. *Chicago Daily Democrat*, July 25, 1850.

207   *"The public will reap"*   LP File ID L02330. Parker v. Hoyt. Document 132926. *Chicago Daily Democrat*, July 25, 1850.

207   *"the want of time"*   CW, 2.82–83.

208   *"Again the battle"*   CW, 2.85.

209   *"The Presidency"*   CW, 2.89.

209   *"a combination of negatives"*   CW, 2.87.

211   *"The death of the late"*   CW, 2.90.

211   *"So the multitude goes"*   Ibid.

213   *"We miss him"*   CW, 2.77.

213   *"that affection's wail"*   See Ruth Painter Randall, *Lincoln's Sons* (Boston: Little, Brown, 1955), 22–27; Jean Baker, *Mary Todd, A Biography* (New York: Norton, 1987), 126–28; Tom Emery, *Eddie: Lincoln's Forgotten Son* (Carlinville, Ill.: History in Prints, 2002); and Jason Emerson, "'Of Such Is the Kingdom of Heaven': The Mystery of 'Little Eddie.'" *Journal of the Illinois State Historical Society*, Vol. 92, No. 3 (Autumn 1999); see www.find articles.com/p/articles/mi_qa3945/is_199910/ai_n8862405.

214   *"It is singular"*   CW, 2.15.

214   *"This habit of uselessly"*   CW, 2.16.

215   *"I sincerely hope"*   CW, 2.97.

216   *"The infant nation"*   CW, 2.121.

217   *"during the proceedings"*   Ibid.

217   *"Mr. Clay's lack"*   CW, 2.124.

218   *"there has never been"*   CW, 2.125.

218   *"the spell"*   Ibid.

219   *"Mr. Clay's eloquence"*   CW, 2.126.

220   *"During its delivery"*   CW, 2.127.

220   *"Brightly, and captivating"*   CW, 2.129.

221   *"the country by"*   CW, 2.128–29.

221   *"was, on principle"*   CW, 2.130.

222   *"there is a moral fitness"*   CW, 2.132.

223   *"Pharaoh's country"*   CW, 2.132.

224   *"I think he would"*   HI, 617.

225   *"often struck other girls"*   HI, 597.

225   *"A neighbor heard screams"*   HI, 389–90.

227   *"often observed reading Shakespeare"*   See Henry Clay Whitney, *Life on the Circuit with Lincoln* (Caldwell, Idaho: Caxton, 1940), especially 61–188.

227   *"When the builders"*   CW, 2.141.

228   *"The man recovered"*   CW, 2.143.

228   *"Being philosophical"*   CW, 2.149–50.

229   *"They were fighting"*   CW, 2.153.

229   *"Judge Douglas thought"*   Ibid.

229   *"in so far as it may attempt"*   CW, 2.156.

230   *"Why Pierce's only chance"*   CW, 2.157.

232   *increase in value*   *Personal Finances*, 77–79.

233   *"in aid of the several"*   CW, 2.27.

234   *"the largest law question"*   CW, 2.202.

235   *"men whose magnetisms"*   Ralph Waldo Emerson, *Essays and Lectures* (New York: Library of America, 1983), 971.

236   *"It is natural"*   Emerson, *Essays and Lectures*, 615, 618.

236   *"Who shall set a limit"*   Emerson, *Essays and Lectures*, 971.

237   *"a cultivated man"*   Ibid.

237   *"all successful men"*   Ibid.

238   *"All power"*   Emerson, *Essays and Lectures*, 972.

238   *"The mind that is parallel"*   Ibid.

240   *"the injustice of"*   CW, 2.221–22.

240   *"so plain, that"*   CW, 2.222.

241   *"some men are"*   Ibid.

241   *"You say A. is white"*   CW, 2.222–23.

241   *"the current of events"*   Emerson, 972.

7. "The Current of Events"

242   *"the nature of"*   Ibid.

243   *"I have no objection"*   CW, 2.316.

243   *"but others say"*   CW, 2.323.

245   *"I really have"*   CW, 2.290.

245   *"I have got it into"*   CW, 2.289.

245   *"I only allowed"*   Ibid.

245   *"It is not within"*   CW, 2.295.

246   *"I do not know"*   CW, 2.303.

246   *"The agony is over"*   CW, 2.304–307.

247   *"by appointment"*   CW, 2.247.

248   *"To illustrate the case"*   CW, 2.230.

250   *"proslavery forces"*   See Mark A. Noll, *The Civil War as a Theological Crisis* (Chapel Hill: University of North Carolina Press, 2007), especially chap. 3, "The Crisis Over the Bible," 31–50.

251   *"It is now several"*   CW, 2.247–48.

252   *"The repeal of the"*   CW, 2.248.

253   *"Much as I hate"*   CW, 2.270.

253–54 *"was, is, and perhaps"*   CW, 2.249.

254   *"had been canonized"*   CW, 2.252.

254   *"I think, and shall try"*   CW, 2.255.

254   *"first impulse"*   Ibid.

255   *"free them all"*   CW, 2.255–56.

255   *"Free them, and make them"*   CW, 2.256.

255   *"Whether this feeling"*   Ibid.

255   *"it does seem"*   Ibid.

255   *"You may remember"*   CW, 2.320.

256   *"I surely will"*   CW, 2.255.

256   *"are just what we"*   Ibid.

256   *"no other than"*   CW, 2.282.

256   *"Reviving the African"*   CW, 2.256.

256   *"I conclude then"*   CW, 2.261.

257   *"Near eighty years ago"*   CW, 2.275.

257   *"Let no one be"*   Ibid.

257   *"that no man is good"*   CW, 2.265–66.

258   *"and consequently"*   CW, 2.281.

258   *"The great mass of mankind"*   Ibid.

258   *"They consider slavery"*   CW, 2.281–82.

258   *"sense of justice and human"*   CW, 2.264–65, 276.

258   *"Let us repurify"*   CW, 2.276.

260   *"We were thunderstruck"*   CW, 2.282.

260   *"If we do not know"*   CW, 2.282–83.

262   *"There is a travel"*   CW, 2.415.

263   *"a disputed point"*   CW, 2.322–23.

263   *"Our progress in"*   Ibid.

263   *"sentiment I am"*   CW, 2.333.

264   *"The platform amid"*   CW, 2.341.

264   *"not propose to"*   CW, 2.248.

265   *"black Republican"*   CW, 2.345.

265   *"no Union with slavery"*   Ibid.

265   *"that great high-priest"*   CW, 2.366, 368.

266   *"the political death-knell"*   Ibid.

266   *"His charge"*   CW, 2.354–55.

267   *"With the purse"*   CW, 2.355.

267   *"A majority will"*   CW, 2.366.

268   *"The UNION—the North will"*   CW, 2.383, 385.

269   *"can we not come"*   CW, 2.385.

269   *"We can not"*   CW, 3.465.

270   *"I believe this government"*   CW, 1.315; CW, 3.461.

271   *"agitation . . . will not"*   CW, 2.461.

271   *"I do not expect"*   Ibid.

272   *"Let any one"*   CW, 2.462, 465.

272   *"the Constitution . . . does not"*   CW, 2.467.

273   *"They remind us"*   Ibid.

273   *"that is parallel"*   Emerson, *Essays and Lectures*, 972.

273   *"mustered over"*   CW, 2.468–69.

274   *"We did this under"*   Ibid.

275   *"I never intended"*   CW, 2.471.

276   *"we have no right"*   CW 2.494.

276   *"We have some cause"*   CW, 2.506.

276   *"Senator Douglas is"*   Ibid.

277   *"It is to be labeled"*   CW, 2.507.

278   *"I protest"*   CW, 2.498.

278   *"I point out"*   CW, 2.552.

278   *"I am informed"*   CW, 2.541–42.

279   *"Does he expect"*   CW, 2.509.

279   *"He says I have"*   CW, 2.510–11.

283   *"I tell you to increase"*   Robert W. Johannsen, *Stephen Douglas* (Urbana and Chicago: University of Illinois Press, 1973), 671–72.

283   *"all men are"*   CW, 2.499–500.

283   *"It does not become"*   CW, 3.275.

284   *"if we cannot give freedom"*   CW, 2.501.

286   *"when gems"*   HI, 500.

287   *"All creation is"*   CW, 2.437.

287   *"Fishes, birds"*   Ibid.

288   *"the art of communicating"*   CW, 3.360.

289   *"There are more mines"*   CW, 3.358.

289   *"We have all heard"*   CW, 3.356.

290   *"He owns a large"*   CW, 3.357.

290   *"wiser or more"*   CW, 3.358.

291   *"Speech alone"*   CW, 3.360.

291   *"Writing—the art"*   CW 3.360–61.

292   *"A new country"*   CW, 3.363.

8. The Master of Language and the Presidency

295   *"We mean to recognise"*   CW, 3.453.

296   *"the general rule"*   CW, Supp. 1.43–44.

296   *"the true condition of labor"*   Ibid.

297   *"I hold that"*   CW, Supp. 1.44–45.

298   *"A capacity"*   CW, 3.480–81.

299   *"They bring us"*   CW, 3.471.

299   *"From the first"*   Ibid.

299   *"The man of"*   CW, 3.471–72.

299   *"the bond of social"*   CW, 3.472.

300   *"inalienable rights"*   CW, 2.266, *passim.*

300   *"it follows that"*   CW, 3.473–74.

301   *"Every man"*   CW, 3.475.

301   *"the world is agreed"*   CW, 3.477.

301   *"a majority"*   CW, 3.478–79.

301   *"insists on universal"*   CW, 3.480.

302   *"I know of nothing"*   Ibid.

302   *"Every blade"*   Ibid.

303   *"but little philosophy"*   CW, 3.481.

304   *"an Eastern monarch"*   CW, 3.481–82.

305   *"I must, in candor"*   CW, 3.377.

305   *"I shall labor"*   CW, 3.491.

305   *"I am not in a position"*   CW, 3.517.

306   *"irrepressible conflict"*   For an account of Seward, his relationship with Lincoln, and "irrepressible conflict," see Doris Kearns Goodwin, *Team of Rivals: The Political Genius of Abraham Lincoln* (New York: Simon and Schuster, 2005), 191–92, 324–26, 364–65, and *passim.*

307   *"You will not abide"*   CW, 3.546–47,

307   *"To be sure"*   CW, 5.547.

308   *"Wrong as we think"*   CW, 3.550.

308   *"reversing the divine"*   Ibid.

309   *"Neither let us be"*   Ibid.

310   *"to go to church"*   CW, Supp. 1.49.

310   *"I have been unable"*   Ibid.

311   *"the taste is in"*   CW, 4.45.

311   *"I have not heard"*   CW, 4.47.

312   *"Be careful"*   CW, 4.49.

313   *"You are young"*   CW, 3.203.

314   *"It is the opinion"*   CW, 4.103.

314   *"I receive from"*   CW, 4.95.

314   *"It now really"*   CW, 4.126–27.

315   *"DOUG—Bell"*   CW, 4.123–24.

315   *"applications of this"*   CW, 4.60.

316   *"is a regular"*   Scripps, 165.

316   *"the religious element"*   Scripps, 39.

316   *"chiefly on account"*   CW, 4.61–62.

316   *"He never did more"*   CW, 4.61.

317   *"The present subject"*   Ibid.

317   *"there were no children"*   CW, 4.62.

317   *"Mrs. Lincoln is a lady"*   Scripps, 81.

318   *"His position on"*   CW, 4.65.

318   *"the act of sending"*   CW, 4.66.

319   *"You can hardly"*   CW, Supp. 1.54.

319   *Having inherited*   CW, Supp. 1.53–54. Donald, *Lincoln Men*, 44–45.

319   *"allow a warm personal"*   CW, Supp. 1.54.

319   *"to see Kentucky"*   CW, Supp. 1.53–54.

319   *"As a friend"*   Donald, *Lincoln Men*, 55.

321   *"closely with them"*   See Carol Gelderman, *All the Presidents' Words: The Bully Pulpit and the Creation of the Virtual Presidency* (New York: Walker, 1997), 11–35.

323   *"My friends"*   CW, 4.190–91.

324   *"in accordance with"*   CW, 4.236.

324   *"I remember all"*   CW, 4.235–36.

325   *"That there are persons"*   CW, 4.266.

325–26 *"with its institutions"*   CW, 4.269.

326   *"you can have no conflict"*   CW, 4.271.

326   *"The mystic chords"*   Ibid.; for a detailed account of the revision, see Douglas Wilson, *Lincoln's Sword: The Presidency and the Power of Words* (New York: Knopf, 2006), 65.

327   *confidence that*   Numbers of contemporary observers, such as Horace Greeley (*Recollections of a Busy Life* [New York: J. B. Ford, 1869]), believed that "Mr. Lincoln entered Washington the victim of a grave delusion. A genial, quiet, essentially peaceful man, trained in the ways of the bar and the stump, he fully believed that there would be no civil war,—no serious effort to consummate Disunion."

328   *expectation of an imperial*   Richard Franklin Bensel, *Yankee Leviathan: The Origins of Central State Authority in America, 1859–1877* (New York: Cambridge, 1990), 61.

328–29 *"political economic foundation"*   Bensel, 57.

331   *"there is much reason"*   CW, 4.437.

332   *"With rebellion thus"*   CW, 4.433.

332   *"This is essentially"*   CW, 4.438.

333   *habeas corpus*   For a full discussion, see Mark E. Neely, Jr., *The Fate of Liberty: Abraham Lincoln and Civil Liberties* (New York: Oxford, 1991).

333   *"The Union must be preserved"*   CW, 5.49.

333   *"the insurrection is"*   CW, 5.51.

334   *"Labor is prior"*   CW, 5.52.

334   *In September 1862*   Wilson, *Lincoln's Sword*, 254–56, argues that 1864 is a more likely date than CW's 1862. The arguments for both dates have plausibility, but the language of the "Meditation" closely parallels that of Lincoln's letter of October 26, 1862, to Eliza Gurney ("He wills it otherwise. . . . He permits it [the war] for some purpose of his own, mysterious and unknown to us"). The year 1862 also connects Lincoln's concern about the ultimate purpose of the war with his moral and practical considerations about emancipation.

334   *"The will of God"*   CW, 4.403–4.

334   *"He could have"*   CW, 5.404.

335   *"light and wisdom"*   CW, 5.478.

335   *"If after endeavoring"*   Ibid.

336   *"May we not justly"*   CW, 6.156.

336   *"we have forgotten God"*   Ibid.

336   *"Committee of colored men"*   CW, 5.370–71.

336   *"do something to help those"*   CW, 5.372.

336   *"there is an unwillingness"*   Ibid.

336   *"It does not strike"*   CW, 5.373.

337   *"I want you to"*   CW, 5.375.

337   *"Take your full time"*   Ibid.

337   *"My paramount object"*   CW, 5.388–89.

338   *"I hope it will not be"*   CW, 5.420.

338   *"Would my word"*   Ibid.

338   *"fifty thousand bayonets"*   CW, 5.423.

338   *"as a practical war measure"*   CW, 5.421.

338   *"No one can tell"*   CW, 5.424.

340   *"In giving freedom"*   CW, 5.537.

340   *Indian tribes*   For a full account, see David A. Nichols, "Lincoln and the Indians," *The Historian's Lincoln: Pseudohistory, Psychohistory, and History*, ed. Gabor S. Borrit and Norman O. Forness (Urbana and Chicago: University of Illinois Press, 1988), 149–69; www.unitednativeamerica.com/issues/lincoln contains a range of views about Lincoln's Indian policy, much of it critical.

341   *"A nation may be"*   CW, 5.527.

341–42 *"That portion of the"*   Ibid.

342   *"So far as I'm"*   see www.dickshovel.com/snell.html.

342   *"killing, indiscriminately"*   CW, 5.525.

343   *"Anxious to not"*   CW, 5. 551.

343   *"I then directed"*   Ibid.

343   *"I have ordered"*   Ibid.

344   *"the hard and cruel"*   CW, 6.152.

345   *"There is a great"*   CW, 6.151.

345   *"if our children"*   CW6.152.

345   *"the President's remarks"*   Ibid.

346   *"In my position"*   CW, 7.17.

346   *"Gen. Lees invasion"*   CW, Supp. 1.194.

347   *"for the sale of"*   CW, 7.515.

347   *"Human-nature will not"*   CW, 8.101.

348   *"This war"*   CW, 7.395.

348   *"The world has never had"*   CW, 7.301.

348   *"The Shepherd drives"*   CW, 7.302.

349   *"I can say nothing"*   CW, 8.237.

350   *"In any future"*   CW, 8.101.

351   *"the unfinished work"*   CW, 7.19.

351   *"of the people"*   Ibid.

352   *"nobly carried on"*   Ibid.

353   *"From every corner"*   Dilworth, 134.

353   *"reasonably satisfactory"*   CW, 8.332.

354   *"both parties deprecated"*   CW, 8.332.

354   *"The Almighty has"*   CW, 8.333; *Matthew*, 18.7.

354   *"If we shall suppose"*   CW, 8.333.

355   *"Fondly do we hope"*   Ibid.

356   *"With malice toward none"*   Ibid.

356   *"in gladness of heart"*   CW, 8.399; Donald, 581.

356   *"re-inauguration"*   CW, 8.400.

Acknowledgments

This book was in preparation over a ten-year period of teaching a course on the literature of the American Civil War to students in the PhD Program in English at the Graduate Center of the City University of New York. These students gave me the benefit of their commitment and the opportunity to think out loud to them and with them. My first reader, Rhoda Weyr, made many helpful contributions. Georges Borchardt, my agent of twenty-five years, cast a wise eye and made thoughtful suggestions in the early stages, as did my estimable friends Charles Molesworth and Lois Wallace. At HarperCollins, I'm indebted to the enthusiasm and the excellent editorial guidance of Tim Duggan, the attention to detail of his assistant Allison Lorentzen, and the copyediting expertise of Jenna Dolan. My thanks to Professor Dan Feller, editor of the Jackson Papers; especially Thomas Michael Coens, editorial associate, for a deeply informed excursus on the vexed question of who wrote the words our early presidents spoke; to Ted Widmer for his thoughts on the same subject; and to Ann Justice, the *Lincoln Herald* business manager, for a timely copy of "Lincoln and Byron, Lovers of Liberty," which I further acknowledge in the endnotes. I'm indebted to Noah J. Kaplan for directing me to a valuable source. Those many estimable Lincoln scholars on whom I rely, who have created an immense biographical, historical, and textual literature on the inexhaustible subject of our sixteenth president, have my respect and appreciation.

INDEX